"With this book, Daniele Ganser has succeeded in conveying historical background knowledge in a compact form, making it easy to read, especially for young people. This is absolutely necessary in view of increasing skepticism toward US policy with uninterrupted transatlantic propaganda in the media."

—Karl-Heinz Peil, *FriedensJournal*

"In his interesting book, Ganser describes in detail the role of the US war machine in enforcing the empire's claims to power."

—Tilo Gräser, *Sputnik*

"Dr. Phil. Daniele Ganser, Swiss historian and peace activist, is one of the outstanding contemporary thinkers who fight against "general memory loss" by profoundly reappraising historical events and making their findings available to the people in a clear and understandable language."

—Afsane Bahar, *Neue Rheinische Zeitung*

"The great thing about Daniele Ganser's books is that they provide solid facts that can be verified at any time, encouraging the reader to draw their own conclusions. In his journey through U.S. history, marked by numerous crimes against humanity, genocides, wars of aggression, and other abysses, the author always appeals to the principle of the human family that unites us all."

—Richard-Heinrich Tarenz, *Wild Magazin*

"Daniele Ganser's *USA: The Ruthless Empire* is interesting and worth reading—because the author does not practice one-dimensional criticism of the USA. He consistently appeals to principles and ideals: UN ban on the use of force, mindfulness and what he calls the human family."

—Erich Gysling, *Infosperber*

"Every war begins with a lie, as Ganser's many examples comprehensively demonstrate. But he also emphasizes that there have always been people guided by ethical values and that in the current peace movement, it is important to maintain these values. In my opinion, this book belongs in every school, university and city library."

—Christiane Borowy on *KenFM*

"A book absolutely worth reading. It opens eyes, creates consternation and shows the only viable way: The path to the future must be a peaceful one!"

—Angelika Gutsche in *Freitag*

USA

THE RUTHLESS EMPIRE

DANIELE GANSER

INTERNATIONAL BESTSELLING AUTHOR

Skyhorse Publishing

I dedicate this book to all the people who reject war, terror, torture, and war propaganda from the bottom of their hearts and who are committed to peace.

Skyhorse Publishing books may be purchased in bulk at special discounts for sales promotion, corporate gifts, fund-raising, or educational purposes. Special editions can also be created to specifications. For details, contact the Special Sales Department, Skyhorse Publishing, 307 West 36th Street, 11th Floor, New York, NY 10018 or info@skyhorsepublishing.com.

Visit our website at www.skyhorsepublishing.com.

10 9 8 7 6 5 4 3 2

Library of Congress Cataloging-in-Publication Data is available on file.

Hardcover ISBN: 978-1-5107-7678-4
Ebook ISBN: 978-1-5107-7683-8

Cover design by David Ter-Avanesyan

Printed in the United States of America

CONTENTS

ACKNOWLEDGMENTS

This book would not have been possible without the research of many other people from whom I was privileged to learn. My first thanks go to US linguist Noam Chomsky, who has been critical of US imperialism for decades and whom I met in the United States. "Don't just rely on conventional accounts of history and political science textbooks—go to the original sources and read the monographs that were written by specialists, memoranda on national security and similar documents," Chomsky advises in his books, and he emphasized it during our personal meeting in his office in Boston. I have followed this advice and profited greatly from it.[1]

I would also like to thank the US journalist William Blum—who unfortunately recently passed away—for his critical work on the CIA's covert operations, and whom I met in Washington and London. My thanks also go to the US Americans John Prados, Richard Gage, and David Ray Griffin, who have critically examined the history of the United States and whom I met in Switzerland and in the States. In Germany, where I have given many lectures on international politics in recent years, I would like to thank the journalists Dirk Müller, Mathias Bröckers, Jürgen Todenhöfer, Rainer Mausfeld, Ken Jebsen, Jens Wernicke and Michael Lüders, because they have never shied away from openly criticizing US imperialism.

In Europe, little is said about US imperialism, even though it has a tremendous influence on international politics. Many know of its existence, but they don't dare to talk about it because they fear personal disadvantages. Even at schools and universities, US imperialism is rarely taught or discussed. Therefore, I wrote this book for young people between the ages of fifteen and twenty-five who want to learn more on the subject of US imperialism. My aim was to write in such a way that anyone without prior knowledge could understand the book. I translated all quoted texts myself. Whenever I cite a quotation or a number, I refer to the source I used in an endnote. This way everyone can verify all the information contained in this book.

Much has been written about the USA. This book is just one perspective among many possible perspectives. Some of the people from whom I learned a great deal, I was never able to meet in person because they had already passed away. These include US Senator Frank Church of Idaho, who published a very important investigation into Central Intelligence Agency (CIA) assassinations. I would also like to thank the Jewish pacifist Murray Polner, who collected and published voices from the US peace movement. Furthermore, I would like to thank US photographer Robert Stinnett, whose research has shed a whole new light on Pearl Harbor and the US entry into World War II. I would also like to thank the courageous and astute US District Attorney Jim Garrison of New Orleans, who investigated the assassination of President John F. Kennedy. Although these authors are no longer with us, their work lives on in their writing.

My thanks also go to my home country, Switzerland, where I was born in 1972 and where I have always been able to live in peace. In Switzerland, I was able to attend excellent schools, where I was inspired by dedicated teachers, and I was privileged to meet many exciting people. Hikes in the beautiful mountains and calm moments next to a sparkling lake gave me strength and inspiration. I would like to thank my wonderful wife Bea, who has always encouraged me to continue along my path to the best of my knowledge and conscience—even when I was lecturing at universities, where I came under pressure for voicing my research results on US imperialism, which is a highly loaded topic. I would like to thank our two children Julia and Noah, because their joy of life shows how wonderful life can be. I would also like to thank my mother Jeannette Ganser, my sister Tea Ganser, and my father Gottfried Ganser—who died in Lugano in 2014—as well as my wife's parents, Hans and Käthy Schwarz. The support of my wonderful family strengthens my peace research profoundly.

A big thank you goes to Dominik and Yvonne Graf for generously supporting my research and whose courage is an inspiration to others. My great thanks also go to my longtime friends Sherpa Hänggi, Tobi Portmann, Marcel Schwendener, Dane Aebischer, Yves Pierre Wirz, Philipp Schweighauser, Laurenz Bolliger, Nick Beglinger, Raymond Schärer, Andreas Zimmermann, Tobi Sutter, Urs Beyeler, and Dani Morf. Peace is very important to all of us and it always forms the basis for exciting discussions. My thanks also go to Alexandre Robaulx de Beaurieux and Dirk Wächter for creating the graphics. I would like to thank my publisher Stephan Meyer for his support in the production and distribution of the book. I thank Orell Füssli Verlag in Zurich, which also published my books *NATO Secret Armies* (2008), *Europe in the Oil Rush* (2012), and *Illegal Wars* (2016), for their many years of good cooperation.

This book was first published in German in April 2020. Thereafter it was translated into French, Italian, and now also into English. I want to thank Stephen Klyne for translating my book into English and Martin Kopatschek for covering the translation costs. My warm thanks also go to Tony Lyons and Hector Carosso from Skyhorse Publishing in New York for publishing *USA: The Ruthless Empire*. The English text is identical to the German original, apart from the chapter on the conflict in Ukraine.

INTRODUCTION

I wrote this book with the intention of strengthening the peace movement. The peace movement includes all the people who reject war and terror and who oppose lies and war propaganda. Peace movements have always existed in countries around the world, including the United States. To prove this point, I frequently quote people of the US peace movement throughout this book. Among them is the African American civil rights activist and pastor Dr. Martin Luther King Jr., who called for nonviolent resistance against the oppression of African Americans and against the illegal war in Vietnam, and women's rights activist Jeannette Rankin of Montana, who as a member of Congress voted against US participation in World War I and World War II, and former National Security Agency (NSA) employee Edward Snowden, who exposed citizen surveillance. Members of the peace movement have always oriented themselves according to their conscience and never just followed public opinion. They publicly rejected war and the lies therein, even when they held a minority opinion. Some members of the peace movement were shot and killed, like Martin Luther King. Others were defamed as "traitors" and "whores," like Jeannette Rankin. Edward Snowden had to leave the US and now lives in Moscow. Their example has inspired other people to take a stand against war, terror, and war propaganda, even when doing so is difficult and takes courage.

The United States is the greatest danger to world peace. But with all criticism of the 300,000 superrich Americans who run the US empire, the peace movement must never be about fostering hatred among nation-states. Many of the 330 million US inhabitants are committed to peace and reject imperialism. They may not hold leading positions in the White House, nor do they dominate Congress, but they are passionately committed to a better and more peaceful world. They are teachers, artists, environmentalists, civil rights activists, yoga teachers, writers, gardeners, and much more. They are hardly known, but everyone in the peace movement has an influence because everything is connected to everything else.

In all of my research I am guided by the following three principles: the UN Prohibition of Violence, mindfulness, and the human family. The UN ban on violence was enacted in 1945 and prohibits the threat or use of violence in international politics. Unfortunately, this ban has been forgotten, and many people have never even heard of it. That is why I often mention it in my books and in lectures, because it is a very important instrument of the peace movement. The principle of mindfulness is also a gem for the peace movement, because humanity has been deceived and confused by war propaganda far too often. However, it needn't be so. When we learn to observe our own thoughts and feelings from a calm distance by practicing mindfulness, we can gain clarity. There is no need to believe everything the media tells us. Mindfulness can help us realize that we are not our thoughts and feelings. We are clear consciousness in which these thoughts and feelings arise and later dissolve, just like clouds in the sky.

The principle of the human family was particularly important to me in writing this book. Unfortunately, throughout history we have repeatedly excluded and killed individual members. We have divided ourselves and devalued each other on the basis of nationality, religion, skin color, gender, and income. During the infamous witch hunts, women were accused of "sorcery" as they were excluded from the human family and burned. During the Indian Wars in North America, Indigenous people were excluded from the human family. They were labeled as "savages," driven out, and killed. In the slave trade, Africans were excluded from the human family. They were labeled as "animals," defamed, and exploited. During the Second World War, Jews were excluded from the human family—they were called "unworthy of life" and were put into concentration camps, where they were gassed. The Vietnamese people were called "termites" by

US soldiers in the Vietnam War, during which they too were excluded from the human family and bombed with napalm. In the course of the so-called "war on terror," Afghans were called "terrorists," excluded from the human family, and killed.

The pattern is clear as it repeats itself: The principle of the human family continues to be violated by excluding and devaluing a particular group of people and then killing them. It is evident that our appearances differ, as do our faiths, nationalities, levels of education, languages, and income levels. In terms of those attributes we are not equal and we never will be, but that does not justify any use of violence. "Our world is definitely facing the problem of various hostilities getting out of control. Humans are specialists in marginalizing others," explains Dutch zoologist Frans de Waal. "Humans demonize people of other nationalities or religions and this, in turn, generates fears and anger. We are quick to call them savages or animals and suddenly it is legitimate to eliminate the savages, because we no longer feel that they deserve sympathy."[1]

In April 2004, the public learned that US soldiers had tortured Iraqis at the Abu Ghraib prison in Iraq. US war propaganda had instilled in American soldiers that Iraqis were bad people, which caused the soldiers to exclude the Iraqis from the human family, which had concrete consequences: US soldier Lynndie England had led a naked Iraqi inmate around the prison at Abu Ghraib. Another Iraqi prisoner was forced to balance on a crate while wearing a black hood and with wires attached to his body. The US soldiers threatened him with fatal electrocution if he were to fall off the crate. "For Europe, these horrific images depicting sex, torture and humiliation were shocking," *Die Welt* commented. The Abu Ghraib scandal was a drastic illustration of what can happen when the people of an entire nation, in this case the Iraqis, are excluded from the human family.[2]

In the face of such violence and brutality, one must not conclude, however, that we humans are incapable of living together peacefully. We very well can, and we do so in millions of different places every day. "Let us first examine our attitude toward peace itself, for too many of us think of it as impossible," President John F. Kennedy declared in one of his speeches. "Too many of us think it is impossible to achieve, but that is a dangerous and defeatist belief. It leads to the conclusion that war is inevitable, that mankind is doomed, that we are in the grip of forces we cannot control." But this is not true, and Kennedy knew it. "Our problems are man-made. Therefore they can be solved by men. The greatness that the human mind can achieve is determined by man himself."[3]

Inspirational figures outside the United States have also shaped the peace movement. In India, lawyer and pacifist Mahatma Gandhi, who is a great role model for me personally, repeatedly emphasized the principle of the human family. "All humanity is one family," Gandhi said. He always used a calm and friendly tone in his protests, free from anger and hatred. Despite their brutal advance, Gandhi did not refer to the Indian police, the Indian government, or the British colonial power as enemies. "I never consider anyone my enemy," Gandhi declared. "All of you are my friends. I want to enlighten and change hearts."[4]

I firmly believe that the peace movement will be stronger in the twenty-first century if it is guided by the principles of the human family, mindfulness, and the UN Prohibition of Violence. Division on the basis of nation, religion, skin color, gender, educational degree, or level of income should be replaced by the insight that all people belong to one and the same human family. You as a reader belong to the human family, no matter where you come from or what your story is. I, the author of this book, also belong to the human family, as do all the people mentioned in this book, victims and perpetrators alike. Together we should learn not to kill each other, because all life is sacred.

CHAPTER 1

THE USA POSES THE GREATEST THREAT TO WORLD PEACE

The United States of America has been the empire since 1945. The term "empire" is used to describe the most influential and powerful country of a given time in terms of economic, political, and military power. The USA prints the US dollar, which is currently the most important world reserve currency. It is a nuclear power, has the highest military expenditures, is home to the largest defense corporations, and boasts the most military bases in foreign countries. The US is a veto power in the UN Security Council and thus can prevent itself from being condemned by the UN Security Council when it illegally bombs other countries and violates the UN ban on violence. Furthermore, the US is in command of NATO, the world's largest military alliance, which currently includes twenty-nine European and North American member states.

Anyone interested in international politics, history, and peace cannot ignore the empire, because the US has had either a direct or an indirect influence on almost every major conflict of the last 100 years and is continuing to shape the wars of the present. An empire is easy to spot—just count the aircraft carriers. The US has eleven nuclear-powered aircraft carriers, more than any other country in the world. The cover of this book features the USS *George Washington*, a symbol for US military supremacy. The newest US aircraft carrier, the USS *Gerald Ford*, was inaugurated by President Donald Trump in 2017. Due to its propulsion by nuclear power, it can stay at sea for decades without ever having to refuel. At $13 billion, the USS *Gerald Ford* is the most expensive warship ever built. By contrast, China currently only has two aircraft carriers, while France, Great Britain, and Russia each have but one.[1]

Empires rise and fall; they do not last. The Roman Empire, the Spanish Empire, the Ottoman Empire, the French Empire, and the British Empire were once great and fearsome. Today however, they no longer exist. The US empire, too, will one day crumble and be replaced by a different power structure. When and how that will happen is currently unknown. When nations spend too much on armaments, "they are likely to overexert themselves," warns British historian Paul Kennedy. "A nation then resembles an old man, trying to do a job that is beyond his strength."[2]

Gallup Surveys 67,000 People in 65 Countries

"Which country poses the greatest threat to world peace today?" The US polling institute Gallup, headquartered in Washington, DC, posed this intriguing question as part of a global survey conducted in 2013. Gallup has been conducting annual global surveys on the state of the world since 1977, but it was not until the new millennium that the US pollsters dared to ask this loaded question, as a result of radio listeners requesting it be posed. The survey polled more than 67,000 people in 65 different countries during September–December 2013, while President Barack Obama was serving his term in office. The question was posed across the globe and the results were very clear.

Of those surveyed, 24 percent—in other words, about a quarter of the world's population—considered the US to be the greatest threat to world peace. The BBC commented that this was "bad news for the US but not entirely surprising." The second most dangerous country, the Muslim nuclear power Pakistan, ranked far behind the US with 8 percent of the votes. China placed third among the most dangerous countries. Merely 5 percent of respondents rated the world's most populous country as the most dangerous. Communist Party–controlled China shared this third place with Israel (5%), North Korea (5%), Afghanistan (5%) and Iran (5%). The countries that followed were also considered major threats to world peace: India (4%), Iraq (4%), Japan (4%), Syria (3%), Russia (2%), Australia (1%), Germany (1%), Palestine (1%), Somalia (1%), South Korea (1%), and the United Kingdom (1%).[3]

The same Gallup poll also wanted to know: "If there were no national borders, which country would you prefer to live in?" With 38 percent, a clear majority of respondents answered that they would choose to live in the same country they currently live in. The majority of people do not want to emigrate, but would rather live close to their respective families. Almost all of them feel attached to the culture, language, landscape, and food of their native country. For those people who do want to emigrate, however, the United States was the most desirable destination country with 9% of respondents' votes, followed by Australia (7%), Canada (7%), Switzerland (6%), France (4%), Germany (4%), the UK (4%), and Italy (3%).

For the US to be perceived as the greatest threat to world peace in 2013 was not an entirely new development. "I think to most Europeans, America currently appears to be the most dangerous country in the world," British historian Arnold Toynbee had said as early as 1971, without having any empirical data from a survey to fall back on. "Considering that America is undoubtedly the most powerful country in the world, there is something very frightening about the transformation of the American image over the past thirty years," Toynbee said, as he was writing while the Vietnam War was ongoing. "It is probably even more frightening for the great majority of the human population who are neither Europeans nor North Americans, but Latin Americans, Asians and Africans," for time and again, he said, the United States has intervened in the domestic affairs of other countries with ruthless violence. Therefore, Toynbee said, the United States is "a nightmare."[4]

After Donald Trump took office in January 2017, the perception of the US did not improve. "Concerns about US power and influence have risen in many countries around the world, while trust in the US president has plummeted," US polling firm Pew found in August 2017. Pew had surveyed people from thirty different countries in North America, South

America, Europe, Africa, Asia, and Australia. This global survey was first conducted in 2013 during the Obama presidency, and then again in 2017 while President Trump held office in the White House. The US was already considered a major threat to the world under President Obama, but after President Trump moved in, distrust in the US increased even further.

In 2017 Pew found that "In 21 of the 30 countries surveyed, the number of people who rate the US as a serious threat to their own country has increased," with people from neighboring countries Mexico and Canada ranking the US as a greater threat than China or Russia. In other NATO countries like Germany, France, the UK, and Holland, participants of the survey in 2017 also rated the US as more dangerous than in 2013. What is more, Pew found that women in Australia, Canada, Japan, France, and the United Kingdom rated the US as a greater danger than men surveyed in those same countries. Similarly, the survey found that people who voted for left-wing parties in the UK, Sweden, South Korea, and Australia considered the US to be a greater danger than people who voted for right-wing parties in the same countries.[5]

Recent research from Germany confirms this critical view of the United States. According to a study conducted by Forsa Gesellschaft für Sozialforschung und Statistische Analysen (Forsa Institute for Social Research and Statistical Analysis) and published in 2018, "79 percent of Germans consider US President Donald Trump to be the greatest threat to world peace. Only 13 percent perceived Russian President Putin to pose a greater danger to the world. Eight percent of respondents found both equally frightening." The US's reputation in Germany has been steadily declining over recent years. "After our loss in World War II, the US went from being viewed as an admirable victor and protective power to being viewed more critically by Germans surprisingly fast," the *Augsburger Allgemeine Zeitung* commented on the Forsa study. According to German study director Manfred Güllner, perception of the US took a major hit after George W. Bush entered the White House in 2001. "By the time of the Iraq war, he was seen as a far more dangerous warmonger than Putin. The Germans had still trusted Bush's predecessor, Bill Clinton."[6]

More recent surveys confirm this perception of the United States. "Germans see the US as the greatest threat to peace, ahead of North Korea,

Turkey and Russia," announced the *Security Report 2019*, which has been conducted annually since 2011. As part of this representative population survey, over 1,200 Germans aged sixteen and over were surveyed by the Center for Strategy and Higher Leadership in Cologne. Almost half of the respondents said they felt that they were living in particularly uncertain times. "The *Security Report 2019* clearly shows: There is one central factor that scares German citizens. It is the USA under Donald Trump's leadership," study director Klaus Schweinsberg stated when commenting on the results.[7]

The survey found that more than 56 percent of Germans see the US as the greatest threat to world peace. In the previous year, 2018, it had been 40 percent. At that time, the majority considered North Korea to be the greatest threat. Study director Schweinsberg described the ascension of the US to the top of the list of greatest threats, and the ousting of North Korea, as a "sad career." Other observers of this development were not entirely surprised. "There have always been Germans that viewed American politics and society critically. US culture is often perceived as superficial and their foreign policy as egotistical," *RTL* commented. "In East Germany, this impression is felt even more strongly than in the West."[8]

Since 1945 the US Has Bombed More Countries than Any Other Nation

Thousands of people in many different countries consider the US to be the greatest threat to world peace by far. Why is this so? The answer is obvious: it is because the US is the empire, and historically, the rise to imperial supremacy has always been based on violence. This belief in violence is reflected in the fact that, contrarily to almost all other Western countries, the death penalty is still carried out in the United States. More importantly, since 1945 no other nation has bombed as many countries as the Americans have. No other country has overthrown governments in as many countries as the US has. Since 1945, no other country has waged as many covert wars as the US and no other nation in the world maintains military bases in so many foreign countries, often despite the disapproval of local citizens. "It has become embarrassing to be American," Paul Craig Roberts commented. He served in Ronald Reagan's administration as Deputy Secretary of the Treasury and became a fierce critic of the White House after leaving politics. "Our country has had four criminal presidents in a row: Clinton, Bush, Obama, and Trump."[9]

US historian Gabriel Kolko, who taught at York University in Toronto, Canada, correctly states that the US "is the country that fought the most wars in the second half of the twentieth century." It is due to this repeated and constant use of force that the US is now classified as the greatest threat to world peace. Historical data reveals that the US has used force, overtly or covertly, against the following countries since 1945. It should be noted at this point, however, that this is not the complete list.

Greece 1946	Cambodia 1969	Sudan 1998
Korea 1950	Laos 1970	Serbia 1999
Iran 1953	Chile 1973	Afghanistan 2001
Guatemala 1954	Nicaragua 1981	Pakistan 2001
Congo 1961	Grenada 1983	Iraq 2003
Cuba 1961	Libya 1986	Libya 2011
Vietnam 1964	Panama 1989	Syria 2014
Indonesia 1965	Kuwait 1991	Ukraine 2014

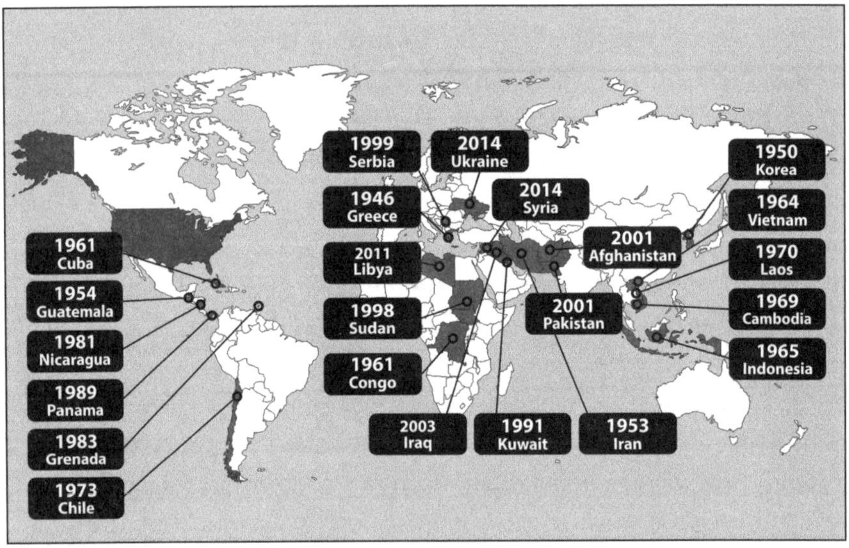

Figure 1. Since 1945, the United States has waged the most wars against other countries.

Former president Jimmy Carter was correct in 2019 when he stated with regret that the United States of America is "the most belligerent nation in the history of the world." Of its 242-year existence as a nation, a mere sixteen years have been spent without war, then ninety-four-year-old Carter observed critically during a church service in Georgia.[10]

Eisenhower Warns Against the Military-Industrial Complex

War is a business. Military expenditures include all expenses incurred when a country maintains armed forces and wages war. This includes the procurement and maintenance of weapons such as aircraft carriers, tanks, and landmines. The defense industry, in turn, profits from these expenditures because it manufactures the products. Military spending also includes expenditures for military research and development. Further included in the military budget are expenditures attributed to the intelligence services to surveil foreign militaries and increasingly also the domestic population. In addition, military spending, of course, also includes expenses for war operations in foreign countries and for training and equipping foreign soldiers in war zones.

A large part of military spending relates to personnel costs, such as wages and pensions for military personnel. At the time of the Vietnam War, all men between the ages of eighteen and twenty-five in the United States were subject to mandatory military service, and registration was compulsory. Many young men protested because they did not want to be deployed to Vietnam for war. To weaken these protests, conscription was suspended in the US in 1973 and a professional army was introduced on a voluntary basis. Much like Ikea employees have a contract with the furniture store, US soldiers today are paid contract workers for the Pentagon. This has greatly reduced the incidence of protests.

Dwight Eisenhower was the general who, during World War II, led the US forces against Adolf Hitler in Europe. He was subsequently elected president and moved into the White House in 1953. As an insider, he knew the military, as well as politics and the defense industry, from firsthand experience and warned against the so-called "military-industrial complex" in his farewell address. Eisenhower meant the tight network between the defense industry, intelligence agencies, Pentagon, lobbies, politics, and the media. The arms industry will always try to influence politicians in order to secure arms contracts and sell their products. Pentagon employees also have a vested interest in war because without war they are out of work.

Unfortunately, Eisenhower's warning was not heard. "Jobs, jobs, jobs," President Donald Trump tweeted after he had signed a massive arms supply deal worth some $350 billion with Saudi Arabia in 2017. After the US had sold F-15 fighter jets to the emirate of Qatar for $12 billion that same year, the Qatari ambassador to the US enthusiastically tweeted that this would create "60,000 new jobs across 42 US states."[11]

In his farewell address on April 17, 1961, Eisenhower warned that the US has "a permanent arms industry of enormous proportions. This combination of a vast military establishment and a massive defense industry represents a new experience in the United States," the outgoing president stressed, warning that the defense industry could gain a dominant influence over policy. "In the bodies of government, we must guard against unauthorized interference, solicited or not, by the military-industrial complex. The potential for catastrophic increases in misplaced power exists today and will continue to pose a problem." Disarmament in mutual respect and trust is "still a valid imperative," the former general said. "Together we must learn how to settle our differences with reason and honest intent, not with weapons."[12]

The warning was correct, but it was ignored. During Eisenhower's presidency, the Pentagon's annual budget amounted to $50 billion. Nonetheless, after Eisenhower's farewell address the Pentagon's budget continued to increase year after year, and ties between the US military and the US defense industry continuously grew stronger as many high-ranking US officers moved into the US defense industry as consultants after their retirement from the armed forces. New wars continued to be waged and demand for new products continued to increase. In 1975, by the end of the Vietnam War in which the US suffered defeat, US military spending had already reached $100 billion per year, double the amount since Eisenhower's warning.

During Ronald Reagan's presidency, military spending exceeded $200 billion per year for the first time. This was even prior to the illegal invasion of the little Caribbean island of Grenada in 1983. Thus, the Pentagon's annual budget had quadrupled since the Eisenhower era. It continued to increase sharply and reached the staggering level of $300 billion by 1986, six times more than during Eisenhower's time in office. President Ronald Reagan fulfilled the arms industry's wildest dreams, thereby strengthening the military-industrial complex. "As a result of America's world power policy and its need for armaments, the Pentagon was considerably upgraded as an economic factor," German political scientist Hartmut Wasser explains. "It is not only an employer in itself, it is also a client and employment guarantor for companies involved in armaments."[13]

US Military Spending Sets World Record

After the fall of the Berlin Wall and the dissolution of the communist Soviet Union, millions of people in the peace movement hoped for a so-called "peace dividend," that is, a reduction in the number of armed forces and a decrease in defense spending. After all, the Pentagon's long-time enemy had now collapsed and a reduction in US military spending from $300 billion to $200 billion per year was at least conceivable, for as President John F. Kennedy had once wisely stated: "Mankind must put an end to war, or war will put an end to mankind."[14]

However, even after the end of the Cold War, the military-industrial complex did not want any budget cuts and the US acted even more aggressively. "In the decade following the fall of the Berlin Wall . . . the US didn't just use its military power to respond to crises," says US historian Andrew Bacevich. "The military has been used to preempt, intimidate . . . and to control, and it did so routinely and persistently. In the age of globalization, the Department of Defense has definitively transformed itself into a ministry of power projection." The Pentagon became a ministry of attack. The goal of the US, Bacevich recognized, consisted of "building a military, political, economic, and cultural empire of global reach."[15]

It is a little-known fact that the Pentagon's accounting practices are sometimes extremely opaque, which suggests corruption. On September 10, 2001, US Secretary of Defense Donald Rumsfeld gave a remarkable speech at the Pentagon, declaring that the bureaucracy in the Department of Defense was too large and that too much money was being wasted. "In this building, money disappears into tasks that are duplicated and into a bloated bureaucracy," Rumsfeld criticized. The Defense Department, he said, has 660,000 civilian employees and 1.4 million active-duty soldiers, plus a million militiamen in the National Guard. Every dollar that disappears into bureaucracy ought to go to the soldiers on the front lines, Rumsfeld complained. Savings of $18 billion a year were theoretically possible, he said, but implementing an austerity program would be difficult. "An institution built with trillions of dollars over the course of several decades cannot be changed on the fly," Rumsfeld cautioned. "Some say it's like turning around a warship; I believe it's even more difficult."[16]

A BBC report on Rumsfeld's speech includes the following startling revelation: "We are unable to account for $2.3 trillion worth of transactions." That is an extremely large sum and should have made headlines around the world. Two-point-three trillion dollars—or $2,300 billion—is several times the Pentagon's annual budget. Presumably, Rumsfeld did not mean that this money had vanished into thin air. According to an internal audit at the Pentagon, many transactions were found not to meet the standards of clean accounting. Rumsfeld complained, "We can't even share information among departments in this building because the information is stored on dozens of different technical systems that are incompatible with each other. We have about 20 percent more infrastructure than we need to support our forces, which costs the taxpayers about three to four billion dollars a year."[17]

The day after Rumsfeld's speech, the US sustained the terrorist attacks of September 11 and all talks about budget cuts were discontinued. What had happened to the $2.3 trillion was never clarified. Rather, military spending was further increased and justified under the "war on terror." In 2001, the year of the terrorist attacks, military spending had amounted to $316 billion. In 2002, it climbed to $345 billion. In 2003, when the US attacked Iraq, the Pentagon budget exceeded $400 billion for the first time. Then in 2005, military spending rose to $478 billion. Every year, several billion dollars were added and the justification was always the war on terror. In 2006, spending was already at $534 billion, and by 2007, the magic mark of $600 billion was reached for the first time. Thus, within six years after 9/11, the Pentagon's budget had doubled. For the military-industrial complex, 9/11 was a fortunate event.[18]

It is interesting to take a closer look at what the US empire spent the grand sum of $600 billion on in 2015. About ten percent of the annual budget, $64 billion, was spent on the so-called "war on terror" in Iraq, Syria, and Afghanistan. An equal amount was invested in research and development. Almost $100 billion was spent on new weapons systems for the Air Force, including thirty-eight new F-35 fighter jets from Lockheed Martin, eighty-six Black Hawk helicopters from Sikorsky, and nine P-8 Poseidon fighter jets from Boeing, which can be used to hunt submarines. Two nuclear-powered *Virginia*-class attack submarines were purchased for $6 billion, as well as new missiles, defense systems, and munitions worth $17 billion. Nearly $6 billion was spent on information and surveillance systems. Over $7 billion was invested in satellites and other space systems. $135 billion was spent on the payment and maintenance of military personnel. As for the remaining sum of $195 billion, the bureaucrats at the Pentagon simply attributed it to operations and maintenance.[19]

The peace movement knows that a lot of good could be done with $600 billion a year. Instead of spending it on war and weapons, the money could be allocated to education and raising awareness of the causes of war, or to the expansion of renewable energies, or to projects to clear plastic out of the oceans, or to alleviate hunger in poorer countries, or to alternative media outlets that expose war lies, or to overcoming fear and trauma, or to mindfulness seminars. All these investments would foster peace and an intact environment, which would be a valuable contribution to maintaining a world fit for grandchildren and future generations. It is a matter of conscience, especially for young people, to see that thousands of people die of hunger every day, even though this issue could be remedied "with just a small part of the resources that are taken up for ever more military expenditure," says former German Chancellor Willy Brandt; he calls this "organized madness."[20]

The money, however, continues to flow in the wrong direction. The same defense companies are awarded contracts over and over again, despite their rarely delivering the weapons systems by the contractual deadlines or at the cost and scope of services promised. President Donald Trump also increased military spending. According to the Stockholm International Peace Research Institute (SIPRI), US military spending amounted to

$649 billion in 2018. The US spent more money on their military than the next eight countries on the top ten list combined. China came in second with $250 billion. Next was Saudi Arabia with $68 billion, followed by India with $67 billion and France with $64 billion. In sixth place was Russia, which spent $61 billion in the same year, just over one-tenth the amount the United States had spent. The UK and Germany followed, each spending $50 billion a year. Currently, the US is pressuring Germany to increase its annual military budget to $80 billion for the coming years, which would place an enormous burden on taxpayers.[21]

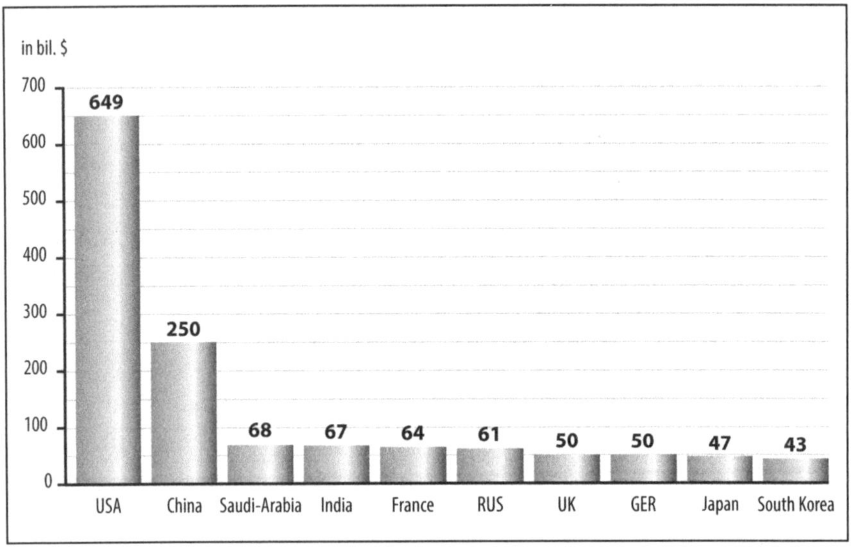

Figure 2. The ten countries with the highest military spending (2018).

There is no turnaround in sight. In 2019 Trump increased the Pentagon's budget to $716 billion for the first time. This equates to nearly $2 billion per day. "Like the sky, the earth and the sea, space has now too become a battleground," Trump declared during the ceremony of signing the budget at a military base in upstate New York. To ensure US space dominance, he said, increasingly high military spending is necessary. The Pentagon and the military-industrial complex were thrilled, and when Trump promised more arms spending at the Pentagon on January 17, 2019, he received thunderous applause. "You're only doing this because I gave you the largest, most comprehensive military budget in our entire history," Trump replied as he thanked the military leaders for their applause. In December 2019, a majority of both Democrats and Republicans in the Senate and in the House of Representatives approved yet another increase in military spending: $738 billion for 2020. Never before in its history has the United States spent more money on war and armaments.

Critics of the military-industrial complex have repeatedly denounced the US's astronomically high arms spending. Republican David Stockman, who represented the state of Michigan in the House of Representatives from 1977 to 1981, was the first to criticize the House of Representatives, calling the military-industrial complex in Washington the "swamp." A reduced military budget of $250 billion a year is enough to defend the United States, Stockman said; there is no need for more. However, the swamp in Washington, which is composed of "arms dealers, intelligence officials, national security bureaucrats, NGOs, think tanks, lobbyists and lawyers," is not interested in saving money, he said. "It is very clear that advocates of the empire don't want this moving train to stop. That's why threats to the American country are always invented and exaggerated. Moreover, vile wars are launched against distant countries in order to secure Washington's global hegemony."[22]

Lockheed Martin Is the Largest Arms Manufacturer in the World

As the US's military spending is by far the highest, it comes as no surprise that the largest defense corporations are headquartered in the United States. US defense contractors benefit from a large domestic market and are represented in every state because members of Congress only vote for new defense programs if their constituency receives orders.

Every year, the Stockholm International Peace Research Institute (SIPRI) publishes a list of the 100 largest arms companies in the world. According to this list, forty-two of them—nearly half—are headquartered in the United States. In 2017, these US defense giants boasted $226 billion in sales, which accounted for 57 percent of all arms sales among the 100 largest defense companies. In total, these 100 largest arms companies recorded nearly $400 billion in revenue from arms sales in 2017. War is a business, and no other country in the world dominates the global arms trade as much as the United

States. "US companies directly benefit from the US Department of Defense's continued demand for weapons," SIPRI expert Aude Fleurant commented.[23]

US defense giant Lockheed Martin, with its 100,000 employees and arms sales worth $45 billion in 2017, is by far the largest arms manufacturer in the world. In second place follows US aircraft manufacturer Boeing, with more than 140,000 employees and $26 billion worth of weapon sales. Raytheon, the US corporation with more than 60,000 employees and arms sales worth $23 billion, ranked third on the list. As has been the case in previous years, the gold, silver, and bronze medals all went to the US in ranking the world's largest arms companies in 2017. BAE Systems of the United Kingdom, which is Europe's largest defense contractor, placed fourth, with their sales totaling $23 billion. In fifth and sixth place among the world's largest defense companies were more US corporations, namely Northrop Grumman and General Dynamics with sales worth $22 billion and $19 billion respectively.[24]

The dominance of US defense companies among the top 100 is overwhelming. By comparison, defense companies from Germany accounted for only 2 percent of the global arms business among the hundred largest corporations in the same year. The largest German arms companies in terms of sales were Rheinmetall (25th), Thyssen-Krupp (53rd), Krauss-Maffei Wegmann (56th), and Hensoldt (74th). In particular, tank manufacturer Krauss-Maffei Wegmann was able to increase its sales. "This figure is mainly due to arms exports to Qatar, in addition to deliveries made to the German armed forces," the *TAZ* commented. RUAG (ranked 95th) was the only Swiss company among the world's 100 largest arms manufacturers. Overall, the USA and European states sold the most weapons. These same states are also the main destination countries for refugees, but this connection is rarely discussed.[25]

The United States Is a Nuclear Power

Probably the most infamous product of the US arms industry is the devastating atomic bomb. On July 16, 1945, the US military detonated an atomic bomb for the first time in human history. It was code-named "Trinity," and this test in New Mexico demonstrated what an incredible destruction an atomic bomb can cause. On August 6, 1945, president and commander in chief Harry Truman ordered the US military's "Little Boy" to be dropped on Hiroshima. Three days later, on August 9, the US dropped the second atomic bomb, "Fat Man," on Nagasaki. Both cities were completely destroyed. In the seconds following the detonation, at least 140,000 people died in Hiroshima and 70,000 in Nagasaki, including many women and children. According to US historian Howard Zinn, another 130,000 residents of the two cities died of radiation sickness within the following five years. The peace movement has always opposed the use of atomic bombs. British philosopher Elizabeth Anscombe, a lecturer in ethics at Oxford University, rightly called Truman a war criminal for dropping two atomic bombs on civilians.[26]

Immediately thereafter, other countries wanted nuclear weapons as well. By 1949, the Soviet Union was able to commence testing of their own atomic bombs. Britain has had atomic bombs since 1952, France since 1960, while China detonated its first atomic bomb in 1964. These five countries are permanent members of the UN Security Council and are the known nuclear powers. They would have preferred to prevent any further proliferation of nuclear weapons and thus created the Treaty on the Non-Proliferation of Nuclear Weapons (NPT), which entered into force in 1970. It prohibits all signing states from building nuclear weapons and has been signed by almost every country in the world. However, India, Israel, and Pakistan never signed the Non-Proliferation Treaty and thus also possess nuclear weapons. So does North Korea, which withdrew from the NPT in 2003 and built nuclear bombs, bringing the total number of nuclear powers to nine nation-states today.[27]

For years, representatives of the peace movement such as the International Physicians for the Prevention of Nuclear War (IPPNW) have been demanding the worldwide abolishment of nuclear weapons, because no one wants an international nuclear war. Article six of the Nuclear Non-Proliferation Treaty requires that all states begin negotiations "in the near future" that will lead to "complete disarmament." This commitment, however, has not been honored, as not a single country has divested itself of its nuclear weapons. There are currently about 14,000 nuclear bombs in the world, most of which are stored in Russia and the USA, which have more than 6,000 nuclear bombs each—an enormous arsenal of destruction. The remaining nuclear powers, France, China, Great Britain, Pakistan, India, Israel, and North Korea, all have inventories of fewer than 300 nuclear bombs.[28]

The United States Has Over 700 Military Bases in Foreign Countries

In addition to possessing a vast amount of nuclear arms, the biggest military budget, and the largest defense contractors, the US empire also has more military bases than any other country. US troops stationed on military bases around the globe can be activated at any time. Civilians are prohibited from entering military bases. I personally tested this a few years ago in Qatar, where I took a cab to a US military base hoping I'd be allowed to visit. Needless to say, I was denied access. Accounting for only the larger military bases with a value greater than $10 million, the US military has over 500 military bases abroad, in addition to more than 4,000 domestic bases, for a total of over 4,500 military bases worldwide, according to the Pentagon's own data.

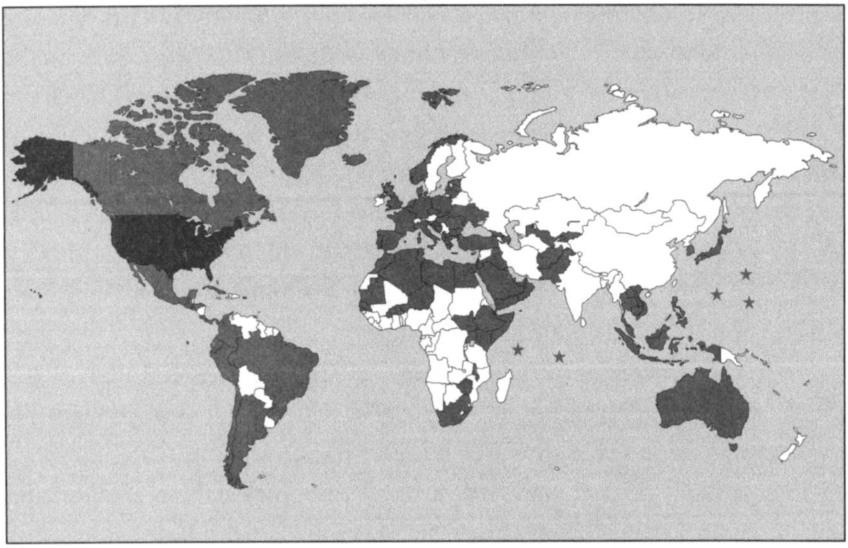

Figure 3. The United States maintains more than 700 military bases in the gray-colored countries.

With 194 US military bases, Germany is the country most heavily covered by American military bases, followed by Japan with 121 and South Korea with 83 respectively. The US also maintains military bases in

Australia, the Bahamas, Bahrain, Belgium, Bulgaria, Cambodia, Canada, Colombia, Costa Rica, Djibouti, Egypt, El Salvador, Greece, Cuba, Honduras, Iceland, Italy, Kenya, Kuwait, Holland, Norway, Oman, Peru, Portugal, Qatar, Romania, Singapore, Spain, Turkey, the United Arab Emirates, the United Kingdom, and other countries.[29]

When studying the locations of US military bases on a world map, it is evident that China, Russia, India, Switzerland, Austria, Iran, and a few other countries do not allow US military bases on their soil. Many other countries, however, are occupied. In 2005, political scientist Chalmers Johnson, who taught at the University of California in San Diego, counted US military bases and concluded that the United States maintained 737 military bases outside the USA. According to Johnson, however, the Pentagon manipulates the data. "If you did an honest count," Johnson explains, "the size of our military empire would probably exceed 1,000 bases abroad. But no one—probably not even the Pentagon—is certain of the exact number." Johnson recognized that these military bases are a clear indication of US military dominance. "There was once a time when you could measure the spread of imperialism by counting colonies. The American version of a colony is the military base," he astutely observed. "By tracking the worldwide distribution of our military bases, one can learn a lot about our ever-growing imperial footprint and the militarization of politics that accompanies it."[30]

Because the US Air Force's bases are spread around the globe, Washington can bomb almost any country in the world while at the same time US warships dominate the oceans. "The United States controls all the oceans. No other power has ever done that," US strategist George Friedman said in Chicago in 2015. "Therefore, we can invade any country in the world and no one can invade us, and it's a beautiful thing."[31]

The United States Has More than 200,000 Troops Stationed Abroad

The United States has more than 200,000 US soldiers stationed at various military bases all over the world. No other nation has sent more of its own soldiers to foreign countries. Surely there would be more peace on earth if every country committed to maintaining a purely defensive army, stationing soldiers only within its own national borders. Currently, the most heavily occupied foreign country is Japan, with 39,600 US soldiers. The second most heavily manned country is Germany, with 34,400 US soldiers. There are 23,300 US troops stationed in South Korea, and there were about 10,100 US troops in Afghanistan in 2018. Over 6,000 US troops were stationed in Iraq, according to figures released by the Pentagon (2018).[32]

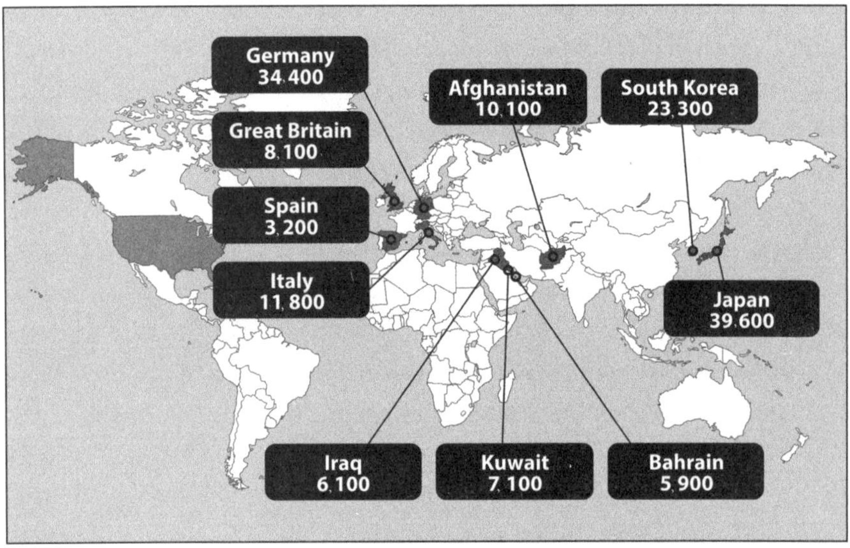

Figure 4. Most US troops are stationed in Japan, Germany, and South Korea (as of 2018).

Various reasons are continuously given to legitimize the maintenance and stationing of troops. During the Cold War, the Pentagon declared that the Soviet Union had to be fought. After the collapse of the Soviet Union, however, the military bases still remained. Next, the Pentagon declared that they needed the military bases to hunt terrorists. "With the war on terror, US imperialism has finally found a doctrine that—unlike the limited geographical front lines of the Cold War—can legitimize a military presence literally anywhere in the world," explains German journalist Knut Mellenthin. "In principle, terrorists can be anywhere and strike anywhere, at any time." In fact and in truth, a military base does not protect against a terrorist attack. None of the 4,000 military bases in the US did anything at all to prevent the terrorist attacks of September 11 in 2001. Talk of fighting terror is war propaganda, and the US military bases serve—as was the case with ancient Rome—to secure US imperial dominance.[33]

The average American is unaware of the fact that the US maintains so many military bases around the world and that so many soldiers are stationed in foreign countries. "Most Americans don't know that the United States dominates the world with its military power," explains Chalmers Johnson, who himself served in the Korean War and later worked as an advisor for the CIA before becoming a fierce critic of the US empire. This ignorance is due to the fact that the US mass media rarely ever mentions the more than 700 military bases and over 200,000 soldiers stationed abroad.[34]

According to Johnson, influential politicians and military officials in Washington see the United States as "a new Rome. The most powerful empire in human history, no longer bound by international law, the interests of allies, or any other restrictions on the use of weapons." The American elites consistently ignore the UN's ban on the use of force in international politics because adhering to it would limit imperial power. There is a preponderance of officers and representatives of the arms industry in high government positions in the US. The glorification of war, power, and the military, combined with propaganda and fake news, will lead to the economic ruin of the country, Johnson predicts, because more and more resources will be put into ever more ambitious military projects.[35]

Occupied Countries Resist

In occupied countries, at least part of the population wants the US to withdraw their troops. Cubans have long demanded the closure of the US military base at Guantanamo, and President Barack Obama had actually promised to at least close the notorious torture prison there, but he did not keep that promise. His successor, President Trump, said he would never give up either the detention center or the US military base in Cuba. According to German historian Manfred Berg, who teaches at the University of Heidelberg, the problems of "imperial overstretch" and the limits of US power are becoming increasingly apparent in the multipolar world of the twenty-first century.[36]

In Japan—the most heavily occupied country by the United States—inhabitants of the island of Okinawa, in particular, continue to resist US troops. "Some residents of the archipelago say that for them, the war has still not ended to this day; they feel that the US continues to occupy their home and that the Japanese central government treats them as second-class citizens," *Die Welt* reports. They complain about the noise of war planes, violent clashes, rapes and murders. Above all, many Japanese feel that the stationing agreement, which protects US soldiers involved in crimes from prosecution by the Japanese justice system, is unjust, and when US soldiers are not held accountable after raping Japanese women, it is very painful for the Japanese. The US, however, does not want to give up its military bases in Japan because from them, it can keep a close eye on the emerging economic power in China.[37]

In Germany, too, some citizens resist US troops and the storage of twenty US nuclear bombs at Büchel Air Base on the border of Belgium and Luxembourg. "The US military does not protect us. Rather, it will contribute to the total destruction of Europe in the event of war," Lieutenant Uwe Schierhorn predicts in the German military magazine *Loyal*. "Wars that contradict the primacy of international law are supported from US bases in Germany." This is unacceptable, Schierhorn said. Germany needs a friendly relationship with Russia and with all the other countries in the world. Therefore, he said, Germany must not participate in Washington's wars of aggression and the US military should be withdrawn.[38]

Albrecht Müller, who served in the chancellor's office under Chancellors Willy Brandt and Helmut Schmidt, also criticizes the American military presence in Germany. Chancellor Angela Merkel is too "closely tied to US policy," Müller said. Therefore, Berlin doesn't demand that Washington order the withdrawal of their troops. "The German government never utters a single word against the use of military bases in Germany for the West's wars, not to mention the lack of criticism of the storage and modernization of nuclear weapons, or the use of Ramstein for drone coordination," Müller observes in the *Nachdenkseiten*. Germany is "at the mercy of American war preparations," he said.[39]

The German ZDF network reports that every year, Germany has to pay $1 billion for US military bases on German soil. This money has to be raised by German taxpayers. Thus, the occupied countries are asked to pay. Currently, the USA is considering whether countries with large US military bases, such as Germany, Italy, and Turkey, "should even be required to pay the salaries of American soldiers and the visits of US aircraft carriers and submarines," ZDF reports. "Special discounts, on the other hand, could be available for countries that align their policies with US policies."[40]

More and more people in Germany are rejecting the paternalism of the United States. Almost half of Germans are now in favor of withdrawing all US soldiers. A poll conducted in 2018 found that support for a withdrawal of US troops in Germany is particularly strong among voters from the Left (Die Linke, 67 percent), the Alternatives (AfD, 55 percent), and the Green Party (Die Grünen, 48 percent). Demonstrations have repeatedly taken place in front of the US military base in Ramstein, where the US operates drone strikes that kill people in Afghanistan and in other countries. I am also an opponent of the US drone war and support the demand for all US soldiers to leave Germany peacefully, as the Russians did. On September 8, 2017, I gave a speech at the "Stop Ramstein Air Base" demonstration at the Erlöserkirche (Church of Redemption) in Kaiserslautern to strengthen the peace movement. Before I spoke, the courageous theologian Eugen Drewermann spoke out and emphatically demanded that Germany should no longer participate in the wars of the US empire in any way. I share this view and am of the opinion that Germany should withdraw from NATO and—remembering its own history—should no longer send troops abroad. Instead, Germany should stand up for international law and peaceful conflict resolution as a neutral country. The German Bundeswehr should be stationed domestically as a purely defensive army.[41]

CHAPTER 2

THE USA IS AN OLIGARCHY

When the world speaks of "America" nowadays, whether in admiration or in fear, the territory of the United States of America is usually what is referred to and not one of the countries in South America, for example Chile or Brazil, though all the people who live there are undoubtedly Americans. For a precise analysis, it is crucial not to speak of "America" in general terms, but specifically of the USA and the 330 million US Americans that live there. Even that is not quite precise enough, for most US Americans have no influence whatsoever on international politics. It is only the superrich, a small group of about 300,000 US Americans, who control US foreign policy and profit from US imperialism. The USA is not a democracy but rather an oligarchy: a country in which the rich rule. Those who ignore the vast gap existing between the rich and the poor in the USA hide the fact that millions of US Americans, too, suffer from consequences of US imperialism because the government invests the money in armaments and war instead of providing a dignified life for the lower class as well.

300,000 Superrich Run the Empire

"Today's inequality is almost unprecedented," Noam Chomsky, one of the most influential intellectuals in the United States, who taught at the Massachusetts Institute of Technology (MIT) in Boston for many years, protested in 2019. For decades, social and economic policy in the United

States has consisted of giving advantages to the rich. This principle has dominated politics and as a result, real power is now concentrated "in a fraction of a percent of the population." These "superrich," as Chomsky calls them, run the empire. "They just get what they want, they basically determine what goes on."[1]

This assessment is consistent with the findings of other US researchers. According to political scientist Jeffrey Winters, who teaches at Northwestern University in Illinois, the superrich use their money to control politics and the media in the United States. Winters further states that the superrich consist of only a tenth of one percent of the US population—about 300,000 people. These superrich either have their own seat in the White House or in Congress, which consists of the Senate and the House of Representatives, or they can call there, arrange for a meeting with the president or congressperson, and put forward their wishes. The poor, by contrast, cannot do so. The superrich can invest their money in politics, the media, and think tanks, which is unthinkable for poor Americans. "It is no longer plausible (if it ever was) to argue that politics in the US is controlled by the people in a democratic way, with each citizen having an equally powerful voice," Winters explains. "Wealth and income play a significant role."[2]

In domestic politics, representatives of the superrich have repeatedly cut taxes or created loopholes for the wealthiest citizens. The superrich do not care if the government accumulates immense debts that it cannot repay, as long as their own wealth is not at risk. During the financial crisis of 2008, when Lehman Brothers went bust, the government intervened on behalf of the superrich, spending billions of dollars to bail out several banks and investors, which in turn greatly drove up national debt. However, as is to be expected in an oligarchy, middle-class homeowners did not receive any help. Middle-class entrepreneurs whose companies go bankrupt cannot expect any help from the state either. Only the superrich can count on the state's help when their investments suffer, because they control the key offices of the state.

In foreign policy, the superrich have secured markets for US products and access to cheap raw materials and labor. When the US empire overthrows the government in a foreign country, it is backed by the interests of the 300,000 superrich and their corporations, as they literally walk over dead bodies to secure their profits. US foreign policy has never been about democracy, freedom, or human rights. War serves the economy and satisfies the greed of the superrich. US governments have worked to secure access to oil, gas, and other raw materials, weaken rivals, and open markets for the products of US corporations. Imperial power serves the moneyed aristocracy. A critique of US imperialism is therefore not directed at the poor people in the US who spend their nights on park benches, but at the superrich.

These connections are well known in the US. "Throughout the twentieth century and into the early twenty-first, the United States has repeatedly used the power of its armed forces and its intelligence agencies to overthrow governments that refused to protect American interests," explains US journalist Stephen Kinzer. "Each time, they disguised their interference under misleading claims, referencing national security and the fight for freedom and democracy. In most cases, however, their actions were based primarily on economic motives—above all, to underpin, promote and defend American business interests around the world and to keep any disturbance away from them."[3]

In his research, US sociologist Peter Phillips, who has taught at Sonoma State University in California, also concludes that the superrich in the United States control the media, the government, and the military. The military alliance NATO, which includes Germany, France, Great Britain, and other European countries, is just a tool to protect the investments of the superrich, Phillips states. War is a business, and selling armaments can yield particularly high returns. Philips explains that the primary goal of the superrich is always to earn a return of 3 to 10 percent or more on their investments, no matter what damage is done to society in the process. The superrich will invest in anything that can generate these targeted returns, including farmland, oil, real estate, information technology, genetic engineering, war industries, and tobacco.[4]

The superrich use the services of banks and investment firms such as BlackRock, Barclays Bank, JPMorgan Chase, and Goldman Sachs to further increase their wealth, and they share the belief that capitalism is good not only for themselves, but also for the development of the entire world.

While the superrich are aware of the consequences of their actions and the undesirable effects like environmental destruction, exploitation, and war, they do not really factor them into their investment decisions, because what counts primarily is the return on the capital invested. "This concentration of wealth has led to a crisis of humanity. Poverty, war, hunger, alienation, media propaganda and environmental destruction have increased to such an extent that the survival of the human species is endangered as a result," warns sociologist Phillips.[5]

More and more people understand that imperial policies are never about values. Rather, they are about power and economic interests. This also applies to the deployment of the German Bundeswehr to Afghanistan. In 2010, the German president at the time, Horst Köhler, dared to say this openly. In an interview on his return flight from a visit to the Bundeswehr in Afghanistan, he said that a country like Germany, "with this foreign trade orientation," must know that "in an emergency, even military deployment is necessary to protect our interests." That statement cost him his office. "He verbalized what other Western politicians think and practice every day," said German journalist Jürgen Todenhöfer. The German president violated the ironclad "hypocrisy commandment," Todenhöfer explains, which has long been the basic consensus of Western civilization: Always think of one's own interests, but never explicitly talk about them. Instead of "interests" and "foreign trade orientation," Köhler simply should have spoken of "values." Then he would have remained the federal president, Todenhöfer believes. "No matter whether Americans or Europeans, they were always concerned with power, markets and money. About their prosperity, their social achievements, their freedom. Never about the freedom of others."[6]

In the US, the superrich recruit well-educated people from the upper middle class to publicly represent and defend their interests in exchange for payment. In modern societies, these actors can be found in the media, foundations, think tanks, law firms, consultancies, and lobbies. The poor, however, cannot invest in politicians, lawyers, journalists, and lobbies. It is not possible for this segment of the population to divert a portion of their income and use it to influence policy. "There is no doubt," comments political scientist Jeffrey Winters, "that the richest US households have enormous wealth with which to influence politics, while most Americans cannot do so." In the USA, politics has become a privilege of the rich.[7]

There Are 100 Million Poor People in the USA

Poor people in the US live in the same nation-state as the 300,000 super-rich, yet they live in a completely different world. Extremely high defense spending has diverted a lot of money that otherwise could have gone to civil projects, where it could be used far more wisely. "The over-indebtedness of the federal budget, the decay of the cities, the collapse of the social system, the high illiteracy rate, the high murder rate, which vastly exceeds any European standards, the many families and semi-families living below the poverty line, and the number of inmates serving time in prisons are reflections of this development," warns Andreas von Bülow, who served as Germany's federal minister for research and technology.[8]

The US has over 2 million prison inmates, more than any other country in the world. The level of concern among the US underclass is high. In most US states, unemployment benefits are no longer paid after six months. Many long-term unemployed people suffer from poverty. To alleviate the plight of the underclass, the US Department of Agriculture distributes food stamps. People of working age between sixteen and sixty are eligible to apply for food stamps if they are trying to find work but their household income is still below the poverty line. This group of people that receive such food stamps is surprisingly large. In 2018, it consisted of 40 million people, or 12 percent of the US population.[9]

The number of people receiving food stamps has grown steadily since the 1960s, even though many people do not even apply for them, be it out of shame or simply because they don't know about the food stamp program. Single households earning less than $1,000 per month are eligible to apply, as are households of four with less than $2,000 monthly income. "No one has to starve here; we're not in Ethiopia," explains Joel Berg, who coordinates soup kitchens in New York. "But the situation is dramatic. Only during the Great Depression of the 1930s were people in this country worse off."[10]

A single person receives a maximum of $190 worth of food stamps each month, wired to a special credit card, which they can use to wait in line at designated stores to redeem the food stamps. "These lines have become a symbol of the new, poorer America," *Die Welt* comments on the social misery. In the food pantries, there are only two choices between products, for example between apple juice or orange juice. Cigarettes and alcohol cannot be bought with food stamps. Hanna Lupien, who serves the poor in New York, says the situation is dramatic. The accusation that many of the needy people are just too lazy to work is not true, Lupien says. "You won't meet any unwilling people here, you'll meet parents who want to feed their children. How many times have I heard the phrase: I haven't eaten in four days because I gave everything to my children."[11]

Poverty in the United States can no longer be overlooked. Nobel laureate Angus Deaton, who taught economics at Princeton University, also criticizes the wide gap between the superrich and the lower class. He demands that the situation of the most vulnerable people in the US be improved. "There are millions of Americans whose suffering due to material poverty and poor health is equal to—or worse than—that of people in Africa or Asia," Deaton laments. Therefore, the US should stop hiding its major poverty problem and help its own underclass before interfering in the politics of other countries.[12]

The gap between rich and poor is also evident in the accumulation of wealth. According to a 2017 Federal Reserve study, 100 million people in the US, which equals to about one-third of the total population, have little to no savings. These people would not be able to pay for emergency costs of $400. For example, they don't have enough money to get their car fixed if it breaks down or to pay for a major repair to their house or apartment. In an emergency, they would have to borrow money from friends, take out a loan, or sell something they own, said the respondents, about half of whom receive food stamps. The Fed study found that one in two of the people in this group were unable to pay the previous month's bills in full, and many said that they had not sought necessary medical care in the past year due to not being able to afford it. The same study found that a quarter of working adults, or 60 million people, have "no pension or savings at all for retirement." As a result, fear of poverty in old age is high among those affected.[13]

There Are 540 Billionaires in the USA

The rich lead a very different life. Globally, there were a total of 18 million dollar-millionaires in 2017. That is less than 0.25 percent of the world's population and roughly equivalent to the population size of the Netherlands. Never before in history have there been so many dollar millionaires. Of these millionaires, most—more than 5 million—live in the USA. Japan follows in second place with 3 million millionaires. Germany and China are each home to one million millionaires. Around 400,000 millionaires live in Switzerland, and another 300,000 millionaires live in India. Some millionaires are greedy, brutal, and ruthless and exploit other people to become even richer. But there are other millionaires who are smart and empathetic, who are committed to making the world a better place. There is hope that at least some of the millionaires will join the peace movement once their material needs are satisfied and they begin to search for meaning in their lives. I know from personal experience that some Swiss millionaires wholeheartedly support the causes of the peace movement. These people are highly educated and completely independent financially. They do not want any more wars and reject war propaganda.[14]

There are major differences within this group of millionaires. The vast majority, about 90 percent of them, have a wealth of between $1 million and $5 million. Individuals with assets of more than $5 million, on the other hand, are rarer, and banks and asset managers refer to them as "high-net-worth-individuals" (HNWI). Those whose wealth exceeds $30 million are very rare. They are referred to as "ultra-high-net-worth-individuals" (UHNWI) in the financial industry. Only a little more than 1 percent of millionaires, about 250,000 people worldwide, belong to the UHNWI group. This number is roughly equivalent to the population of the city of Eindhoven in the Netherlands, or 0.003 percent of the world's adult population. Large wealth managers such as BlackRock, UBS, and Goldman Sachs seek to connect with these ultra-high-net-worth-individuals to manage and grow their wealth, in turn becoming wealthy themselves by charging fees to manage the assets of the UHNWIs. According to the *World Ultra Wealth Report*, most of the UHNWIs lived in the United States in 2017, namely 80,000 people.[15]

Finally, the billionaires sit at the top of the pyramid of the wealthiest people. They have assets of more than $1,000 million. According to the US business magazine *Forbes*, there were about 2,000 billionaires worldwide in 2017. Of them, 540 were US Americans, 250 were Chinese, and 120 were Germans. India had 84 billionaires, Russia had 77, and Switzerland had 32, according to *Forbes*. Hence, there are more billionaires living in the US than in any other country in the world. *Forbes* lists the 400 richest US billionaires every year, including their photo and name. At the time of writing, Amazon CEO Jeff Bezos is in first place with a fortune of over $100 billion, which makes him the richest man in the world. In second place on the *Forbes* list is Microsoft founder Bill Gates. The investor Warren Buffett is in third place, followed by billionaire Mark Zuckerberg, CEO of Facebook, who ranks fourth.[16]

The brothers Charles and David Koch were also in the top ten on the Forbes list with an estimated fortune of $50 billion each. With their network of think tanks, sponsored chairs, and advocacy groups like Americans for Prosperity, they are a well-known example of how billionaires can influence politics. For example, the Kochs provided millions of dollars to support politician Mike Pence, who moved into the White House as vice president under Donald Trump. *Zeit Online* criticized the influence of the two billionaires by stating that an "extremely wealthy clique has seized the state." Former president Donald Trump also claims to be a billionaire. *Forbes* estimated his fortune at over $3 billion and ranked him as the 259th richest US citizen. Trump, in turn, saw this as an insult and claimed that his fortune was more than twice that amount.[17]

The End of the American Dream

While US billionaires are getting richer, the US infrastructure is crumbling, and war veterans are sleeping on park benches. "Anyone who travels to Europe, Japan or even China, immediately notices the decay of the US upon their return, and they often feel as if they are returning to a so-called Third World country," said US American Noam Chomsky. "The infrastructure is crumbling, the health care system is in total despair, the education system is in ruins, nothing works, and all this in a country that has incredible resources." Because wealth is distributed extremely unequally in the US, only the concerns of the superrich are addressed. The lower class and middle class clearly outnumber the superrich, but they feel powerless. They are unable to articulate their predicament and improve it through political reform because their members are much less educated and organized than the superrich. "It takes extremely effective propaganda for people to remain passive in the face of such a reality," Chomsky notes.[18]

Programs that serve the underclass have been cut and laws that make the superrich even richer have been introduced. The superrich weaken all the institutions that combat social, economic, and political inequality, such as public education, health care, welfare, social security, a fair tax system, food stamps, public transportation, and infrastructure. At the same time, the superrich strengthen those institutions that permanently oppress the US population, including domestic security and surveillance systems, militarized police, the Department of Homeland Security, and the military with its network of worldwide military bases. "For the super-rich, nothing has value in itself. Human beings, social institutions, even nature itself, are commodities to be cannibalized for personal gain—to the point of complete exhaustion or collapse," US journalist Chris Hedges says.[19]

Noam Chomsky was born in Philadelphia in 1928 and was able to observe the division of the United States into rich and poor during his lifetime. He said that for a long time, people were inspired by the "American dream," that is, the hope of rising from rags to riches. "Through hard work, even those born into poverty can make it to prosperity," the American dream read. "What is meant by this is that everyone can find a well-paying job, afford a house and a car, and finance their child's education," Chomsky explains. However, there is nothing left of the American dream. Social mobility in the US today is far lower than it is in Europe. Anyone born into a poor family in the US is very likely to remain poor, and can only watch the story of going from rags to riches in movie theaters or on Netflix.[20]

Among the four major ethnic groups in the USA, Black people and Latinos, on average, have a lower level of education and are also more affected by poverty than White people and Asians. That said, even millions of well-educated White US Americans are poor today. "The middle class in America is not doing well. It is now also affecting well-educated White people," the *Neue Zürcher Zeitung* reported in 2016. "Wealth is increasingly concentrated in the hands of a small upper class." Advancement into this upper class is no longer possible for many. Even well-educated people "suddenly find that the American formula, according to which anyone can make it if they just work hard, no longer applies."[21]

In 2011, thousands of protesters marched through Manhattan's financial district in New York as part of the Occupy Wall Street movement, to draw attention to the major grievances that exist. The Occupy movement declared, "We are the 99 percent!" and denounced the overwhelming influence of the richest 1 percent over the 99 percent of the American population and called for greater political control of the banking and financial sectors and a reduction in the influence of business on political decisions. But because the 300,000 superrich control both the economy and politics, nothing has changed. As United States Supreme Court Justice Louis Brandeis once wisely said, "We can have democracy in this country, or we can have great wealth concentrated in the hands of a few, but we cannot have both."[22]

The Superrich Determine Politics

The president is the commander in chief of the US armed forces and therefore formally the most powerful person in the country. The president leads the wars and stands in the media spotlight—and is also a focal point for historians. But behind the president, the superrich pull the strings and determine who is to move into the White House in the first place. The presidential elections, which are held every four years in the US, always bring about much fanfare and a fierce battle between Republicans and Democrats, but they only allow the people to choose their favorite candidate from a small selection of very rich people. Nobody from the middle class—not to mention the lower class—could ever be elected president unless they were backed and supported by the superrich, because they lack the financial resources for election campaigns. US citizens are not consulted on specific issues, such as for example the attack on Iraq in 2003, and their opinions do not matter because the United States is not a direct democracy. Such decisions are made by the president, in consultation with the powerful National Security Council (NSC) and Congress, and always in close coordination with the wishes of the superrich, who control both the White House and Congress.

In 2015, former president Jimmy Carter acknowledged that the superrich hold the strings of power in the United States. "Today, the US is an oligarchy. Political bribery decides who is nominated as a presidential candidate and who is elected president," Carter said resignedly. "And the same is true of state governors, as well as senators and members of Congress." By means of financial contributions, the superrich determine who will be president and who will serve in Congress. In an interview with the famous US television journalist Oprah Winfrey, Carter explained that US presidential candidates must have at least $300 million to spend on their presidential campaign. People from the middle and lower classes can never raise that much money. In addition to the White House, the Senate with its 100 members, and the House of Representatives with its 435 members, are also almost completely in the hands of the superrich. There is no difference between Democrats and Republicans in this regard, Carter said, and no influential third party exists in the United States. "The incumbents, both Democrats and Republicans, see this unrestricted flow of money as a great advantage to themselves. Those who are already in Congress can sell their influence at a premium," Carter explains. "We have now become an oligarchy instead of a democracy," he laments. "And I think that this is the greatest damage to the fundamental ethical and moral standards of the American political system that I have ever seen in my lifetime."[23]

It is very rare to hear such statements in the US media. It is commendable that Oprah Winfrey, who with an estimated fortune of nearly $3 billion is one of the superrich herself, aired Carter's criticism on her own television station. The statement is highly sensitive, but very important nonetheless. As a former president, Carter knows the US political process intimately, and as a retiree who is no longer in office, he can openly express his opinion. The mass media in Europe's German-speaking regions however, ignored Carter's analysis. Leading media outlets such as ARD, ZDF, ORF, SRF, *Spiegel*, *Süddeutsche Zeitung*, and *Neue Zürcher Zeitung* continue to refer to the USA as a democracy and not as an oligarchy, thus obscuring the fact that the 300,000 superrich actually rule the nation.

Large US companies such as defense contractor Lockheed Martin, oil company ExxonMobil, online retailer Amazon, investment bank Goldman Sachs, and asset manager BlackRock employ a large number of lobbyists to enforce the interests of the superrich, which are congruent with the interests of the largest US corporations. By contrast, the weak trade unions and environmental protection associations in the US are almost powerless against them. "Some of the largest corporations employ more than 100 lobbyists, which allows them to be present everywhere and at all times," explains US political scientist Lee Drutman, who teaches at Johns Hopkins University. Corporations declare more than $2.6 billion in lobbying expenditures each year. "For every dollar that unions and public interest groups spend, large corporations and their associations now spend $34."[24]

Every now and then, representatives who refuse to serve only the superrich are elected to the House of Representatives. Alexandria Ocasio-Cortez of New York is among these courageous politicians. In January 2019, at just twenty-nine years old, she became the youngest representative to enter the House of Representatives. "We have a system that is fundamentally broken," Representative Ocasio-Cortez stated during a meeting of the Congressional Committee on Oversight and Reform in Washington. She said that anyone who wants to become president can have their campaign financed by oil and pharmaceutical companies and then, once in office, they adjust the laws to suit the oil and pharmaceutical industries. Therefore, the US is in the hands of the corporations and their owners, the superrich.[25]

In my home country, Switzerland, the superrich from many different countries meet in the snowy mountain village of Davos every year to discuss issues with influential politicians and business leaders at the World Economic Forum. In January 2015, US economist Nouriel Roubini of New York's Stern School of Business told *Bloomberg* that the United States has turned into a plutocracy; it is ruled by the rich. Roubini lamented that the gap between rich and poor is widening in the US. "In a true democracy, the principle should actually be: Every voter has one vote," Roubini said. But the power of the superrich in the US has led to them now holding the reins of power and controlling legislation as they see fit via lobbies and their representatives in Congress. "If you think about it, you come to the conclusion that the US now has a system of legalized corruption," the economist sharply criticized. "Those with a lot of money have greater influence than those with little money. We don't have a real democracy in the US, it's a plutocracy."[26]

US Voters Have Little Influence on Politics

Scientific research confirms this statement by economist Roubini. In April 2014, the BBC referred to a study conducted at Princeton University and reported that the US is now "an oligarchy, not a democracy." "The US is dominated by a rich and powerful elite," the BBC correctly declared. The authors of the Princeton study, professors Martin Gilens and Benjamin Page, had studied the situation in the US very systematically. They had evaluated a period of two decades (1981 to 2002) in which opinions of the US population had been collected and documented by means of public surveys on a total of 1,779 different factual questions. For each of the issues, Gilens and Page were able to indicate whether the majority of the US population was in favor or against it. Additionally, in order to determine class membership of respondents, the researchers only used surveys in which the income of respondents had also been collected. They matched the data with the actual decisions of US politicians and found that the decisions of politicians did not align with the desires of the mass of the population at all, and that the wishes of the lower and middle classes were ignored.[27]

"The desires of the average American appear to have only a very small—almost nonexistent—and statistically insignificant influence on policy," the Princeton University researchers found. As a result, there can be no talk of popular rule. "Our results show that it is not the majority that rules in the US—at least not in the sense that it actually has an influence on political decisions. When a majority of citizens have a different opinion than the economic elite or the organized lobbies, it usually still loses nonetheless." It is the superrich and their lobbies that decide policy in the US. "Our study concludes that the majority of Americans have little influence on the decisions our government makes. Although we Americans are distinguished by many of the features that characterize a democratic system, including regular elections, freedom of speech and assembly, and broad suffrage," Gilens and Page said, "we believe that when politics is dominated by powerful business organizations and a small number of very wealthy Americans, America's claim to be a democracy is in real jeopardy."[28]

As freedom of speech is guaranteed in the United States, critics of the superrich are able to speak out publicly. And they do so, albeit not in the mass media with a wide reach, because they are barred therefrom. American historian Eric Zuesse explicitly regrets that the US has turned into an oligarchy and sharply criticizes this development. "American democracy is but a facade, an empty promise, no matter how often the oligarchs who run our country and control the media claim otherwise," Zuesse commented in *Counterpunch*, a little journal. "In other words, the US is actually very much like Russia and many other obscure 'electoral democracies.' We didn't used to be, but now we are an oligarchy."[29]

Large disparities between rich and poor exist not only in the USA, but in many other countries too, including China. Will the twenty-first century succeed in building a more equitable world? It is at least conceivable, and many people are committed to working toward this goal. As people, we ourselves can shape our coexistence according to our consciousness. "The basic needs of all the people on earth for food, water, shelter and clothing could be satisfied if it were not for the ego's insane, greedy desire for more, which causes such an imbalance in the distribution of resources," explains Eckhart Tolle, a bestselling German author who lives in Canada. According to Tolle, to achieve world peace it is imperative that through mindfulness, people overcome their identification with their own ego and greed.[30]

CHAPTER 3

THE AMERICAN INDIAN WARS

Disclaimer: In historical discourse, it is difficult to avoid using the term "Indians" when referring to First Nations peoples in the United States and Canada. I make every effort to use the respective tribal designations, or terms like "Indigenous peoples" and "Native peoples," which I use interchangeably, but sometimes words like "Indian" or "American Indian" cannot be avoided. As Thomas King states in his book *The Inconvenient Indian: A Curious Account of Native Peoples in America*, "there never has been a good collective noun because there never was a collective to begin with." For all the faults, problems, and ignorance that come with the term "Indian," it still remains the default in most places.

Beginning in the 1500s, Europeans migrated to all parts of the world, conquering and occupying North America, South America, Africa, Australia, New Zealand, India, and the coasts of China by 1900. The primary goal of the Europeans was to trade and realize profits. When the Native people resisted, they were enslaved and killed by the Europeans. Some of the Natives were trafficked and exhibited as attractions in European zoos. The imperial rule of the Europeans over large parts of the world was a brutal system of oppression based on greed for money and raw materials, racism, and missionary zeal.

The Europeans were ignorant and acted very brutally, as they were not willing or able to consider other people as equal members of the human family. The UN ban on violence did not exist at that time, and the Christian commandment "Thou shalt not kill" was disregarded by the imperialists. In North America, the Indigenous population was exterminated. Out of five million Native people who lived in North America before the arrival of the English, only 250,000 were left after the Indian Wars, locked away on reservations. This means that more than four million Natives were killed by war and diseases brought over from Europe. These deaths of over four million Indigenous people are "the first original sin of American society," explains influential US intellectual Noam Chomsky. Even today, this original sin is considered a great shame and it is rarely talked about in the United States.[1]

The feeling of superiority over foreign cultures and the belief in the use of violence were not invented by the US; these ideas stem from European colonialism. Today, fortunately, there are more and more people on both sides of the Atlantic who have an elevated consciousness, practice mindfulness, and are committed to the peace movement. They share the firm conviction that we cannot solve the greatest problems of the twenty-first century by force, and that no culture is superior to any other because all people belong to the human family.

The Great European Powers Divide America among Themselves

When the Italian navigator Christopher Columbus, on behalf of Spain and in competition with Portugal, sought the sea route to legendarily rich India, he sailed across the Atlantic with great privations for almost three long months until he landed his ships on an island in the Bahamas in 1492. At that time, the two continents of North and South America were unknown in Europe. European cartographers of the fifteenth century drew a world map consisting solely of Europe, Asia, and Africa. They knew nothing about the existence of America and Australia. Until the end of his life, Columbus mistakenly believed that he had landed in India. The

European navigators therefore called the various Indigenous peoples of North America Indians. Nowadays, however, these peoples are referred to as Native Americans or Indigenous people.[2]

Italian navigator Amerigo Vespucci, who by order of Portugal explored the east coast of South America in 1501, was the first to correctly suspect that the land discovered was not India but indeed a new continent. Vespucci saw the New World with the eyes of a European and invented names such as "Venezuela," meaning Little Venice, to name the newly discovered territories because the pile dwellings that the Native population had built along the coasts reminded him of the Italian city of Venice. The maps made by Vespucci were very precise, which is why the Europeans named the newfound continent after him and henceforth referred to it as "America."[3]

After Columbus's voyage of discovery, the strong maritime powers Portugal and Spain divided up the world among themselves under the Treaty of Tordesillas in 1494. Without the affected cultures in the foreign countries knowing about it, the Spanish and the Portuguese declared themselves the leading world powers. The Spanish imperialists secured most of the "New World," as they called the Americas: namely most of South and Central America, plus what is now the Caribbean, Mexico, Florida, and Southern California. The Portuguese obtained only Brazil in the Americas. Additionally, outside the New World, they took important ports in Africa, Arabia, and India. In 1498, Portuguese sailor Vasco da Gama was the first European to sail around the southern cape of Africa, crossing the Indian Ocean and reaching the Indian trading city of Calicut. Thus the sea route to India was found, and the Portuguese imperialists founded the trading post of Goa on the west coast of India and conquered Malacca on the strait between the Indian Ocean and the South China Sea.

The colonial powers of Spain and Portugal began the European subjugation of the world. The great European powers of England and France did not push across the Atlantic to the remaining part of the New World—North America—until 1600, because both the Spanish and the Portuguese mistakenly believed that North America was comparatively poor in mineral resources. The Netherlands was another European colonial power. They used force to secure the part of Asia that is now Indonesia. Germany did not become a colonial power until the end of the nineteenth century, when they began to conquer territories in Africa and the Pacific islands. By 1914 the Germans had risen behind Great Britain and France to become the third-largest European colonial power in terms of area, but they were crushed by the other imperial powers during the First World War.

Even at the present day, the languages spoken in the various regions give clear indication of how the Americas was split up; Portugal conquered Brazil, hence Portuguese is spoken there. Throughout the rest of South America, all the way up to Mexico, Spanish is the primary language. France controlled large parts of North America for a while, but later lost and sold many of those territories, which is why French is now only spoken in the Canadian province of Quebec. It was the English settlers who conquered what is now the landmass of the United States and large parts of Canada, which is why English is the dominant language there today. Original languages of the Native peoples, such as the languages of the Sioux or Apaches, have largely died out. Today, almost only European languages are spoken in both North and South America. Old World Europe colonized the New World Americas starting in 1500, while eradicating most of the Indigenous cultures.

1607: The English Establish Jamestown

North America was not uninhabited when the Europeans discovered the new continent. About five million Native peoples lived in what is now the United States and Canada. North American Indians had lived there in various tribes, often nomadic, including the Cherokee, Creek, Iroquois, Apache, Sioux, and Powhatan, for centuries. Before contact with the Europeans, the Natives did not possess firearms, horses, or railroads. Some Native tribes settled in villages and farmed, but most of the Natives were hunters who went after game, especially buffalo. The Indigenous people lived in harmony with nature and had adapted to a vast natural environment. They fished along rivers and in lakes. Many tribes were convinced that nature was inhabited by invisible sacred beings and that land could not be owned or sold. Pollution did not exist in North America at that time.[4]

From coast to coast, North America measures 2,800 miles. Coming from the Atlantic Ocean, the Atlantic coastal plain spreads out first, reaching as far as the Appalachian mountain range. This well-watered area with short but navigable rivers and fertile soil was the first place Europeans settled upon their arrival. Beyond the Appalachian Mountains, to the west, are the vast and flat Great Plains, which extend all the way to the Rocky Mountain range. In the Great Plains lies the Mississippi River, which flows into the Gulf of Mexico and was used by the colonists as a waterway, since there were no roads through the US at that time and travel was very arduous prior to the construction of the railroads. Beyond the Rocky Mountains lies a narrow coastal plain before one reaches the Pacific coast. Nature is beautiful and diverse in North America, as every visitor can see. On my travels, I was particularly impressed by the beauty of Yosemite National Park in California, the wild Pacific Northwest in Washington state, and the turquoise-blue lakes in the region around Banff and Jasper in Canada's province of British Columbia.

Figure 5. 1607: Jamestown—the first permanent English settlement in North America.

The English founded Jamestown in 1607. It was the first permanently inhabited English colony on the East Coast of North America, consisting of only 104 men. These men were English mercenaries and adventurers who reached North America after a long voyage across the Atlantic Ocean and declared the land they entered to be the English colony of Virginia, named after the late, unmarried British Queen Elizabeth I. The English colonists chose a small peninsula in a river, almost 100 kilometers from the coast, to build their fortified base. In honor of their king, who reigned in England at the time, they named it the James River and their settlement Jamestown. The English chose not to build their base right on the coast because they feared being raided by the Spanish, who laid claim to the entire New World. Surrounded by water on three sides and connected to the mainland only by a narrow land bridge, their peninsula could be well defended. In addition to that, the depth of the river allowed ships to reach the secured fort directly from the Atlantic Ocean. Jamestown was the beginning of a development that would eventually lead to the emergence of the US empire. Right from the beginning, this story has been marked by violence and the use of weapons.

For the Native Americans, the arrival of the Europeans was the beginning of the end, the beginning of a great dying. As more and more Englishmen came across the Atlantic in ships and settled on the East Coast, tensions intensified with the Powhatan people, who had lived on the East Coast of North America for centuries. The Powhatan War of 1608 began the long and brutal period of the American Indian Wars. The Powhatan people tried to drive the English out of their land and inflicted heavy losses on the colonists. The English robbed the Natives of grain, burned their homes, and massacred the inhabitants. The Natives laid siege to Jamestown, and the English entrenched themselves in their fort. The siege lasted for several months and many colonials died of undernourishment and disease. In order to survive, the residents of Jamestown were forced to eat horses, dogs, and rats. By May 1610, only sixty settlers were still alive. They decided to leave Jamestown and sail downriver, which prompted the Powhatan people to think that they had won a sure victory. This was to their detriment, however, for they were gravely mistaken.

It wasn't long before other Europeans came across the Atlantic and landed on the East Coast of North America, where they raided the Powhatan villages, burning them to the ground and massacring the inhabitants. From the Natives' point of view, the influx of new settlers from Europe was inexhaustible. In the great Powhatan uprising of 1622, which the English referred to as the "Great Massacre," Powhatan warriors raided

Jamestown and killed 347 of the 1,200 colonists. The English retaliated and by the end of the Powhatan War in 1646, they had almost completely eradicated the Powhatan people. The few survivors were displaced and required to make annual tribute payments to Virginia in the form of furs. For the Powhatan people, contact with the English had ended in disaster.[5]

The Export of Tobacco to London

The inhabitants of Jamestown grew tobacco, which grew excellently in Virginia, in the area surrounding the fort. The dried leaves were of high quality and in 1617, the first shipment of tobacco was exported to England by ship, where it was sold at a profit. Tobacco was in high demand and Virginia became the main supplier to Europe. With the export of tobacco, the British colonialists of Virginia had found a lucrative source of income. However, the colony in Virginia was not independent. The Union Jack, the British flag, flew over Jamestown and Virginia was directly subject to the English king, who appointed a local governor to administer the colony and collect taxes that flowed to London, the center of the British Empire. For weights and distances, the units used in the colony were inches, feet, and miles, which were common in England. A mile is equivalent to 1,609 meters, a foot converts to 30.48 centimeters, and an inch to 2.54 centimeters. To this day, the imperial system of measurement is more popular in the United States, where height is measured not in centimeters but in feet and inches, and velocity is measured in miles per hour, all a reminder that the US was once part of the British Empire.

Some of the Europeans who migrated to North America saw the Catholic Church as their religious and political opponent. Since 1517, when reformer Martin Luther had posted his *Ninety-five Theses* on the door of the All Saints' Church in Wittenberg, Germany, denouncing the Catholic Church's corruption in their sale of indulgences, the division of the reform in Europe led to Catholics and Protestants killing each other in bloody religious wars. The Pope, as head of the Catholic Church, had granted the land that was discovered in the New World to Catholic Spain. However, since the foundation of the Anglican Church in 1534, the British no longer recognized the Pope's supremacy in matters of faith, so his directives on the division of the world were no longer of any significance to them. Some of the Protestants who sailed to North America wanted to create a Protestant empire there that could serve as a counterweight to Spanish Catholicism, which dominated Central and South America. The religious emigrants listened to reformer John Calvin, who had preached that divine grace could be measured by private—and, above all, economic—success. This Protestant ethic gave rise to the spirit of capitalism that still characterizes the United States today. Quite a few religious dissidents from Europe believed that they had found the Promised Land of the Bible in North America. After Virginia, Massachusetts became the second British colony in North America in 1629, with Boston being an important port. The Englishman John Winthrop, who landed in Massachusetts in 1630 with more than 1,000 Puritans and became the governor of the colony, held a sermon to call on his fellow believers to build a "New Jerusalem" in the wilderness, a "city on the hill" from which the sinful world should take a moral example. This sense of mission characterizes the USA to this day.

After the founding of Jamestown in what is now Virginia, thousands of people from England, Scotland, and Ireland emigrated to North America, as well as many Germans, Poles, Swedes, Dutch, and Swiss people. New settlers from Europe were incentivized by receiving about two acres of free farmland, which had been stolen from the Natives. The settlers also brought in viruses and bacteria against which the Natives had not developed any immune defenses, which turned out to be fatal. Smallpox, measles, scarlet fever, and diphtheria wiped out entire villages of Native tribes. After Virginia and Massachusetts, the founding of the colonies of Maryland (1634), Rhode Island (1636), and Connecticut (1636) followed. The colonies of New York, New Jersey, and Delaware had first been developed by the Dutch and the Swedes, but they subsequently came into the possession of the English kingdom. The Dutch established the administrative seat of their own colony of New Netherlands in New Amsterdam on the Atlantic Ocean, but they could not prevail against the British, who conquered New Amsterdam in 1664 and changed the name of the city to New York. With Carolina (1663), New Hampshire (1680), and Pennsylvania (1681), the British expanded their colonial holdings in North America to a total of twelve colonies. Carolina, which was named after King Charles I of England (Latin: Carolus), was divided into North

Carolina and South Carolina in 1729, and in 1732, Georgia was added as the thirteenth colony in the south.

The Thirteen Colonies on the Atlantic

The famous thirteen British colonies are the core of today's United States. All colonies were located on the Atlantic coast and could therefore be reached directly from Europe by ship. The population in the colonies grew rapidly and by 1760 it was already over 2 million people, including 400,000 Black slaves. At that time, no one in London suspected that only a few years later these colonies would break away from the British Empire to establish their own nation. Hardly anyone would have predicted that these small states would eventually expand and conquer the vast region spanning as far as the Pacific coast, eventually forming the United States and rising to become a global empire with military bases in Cuba, Germany, and Japan.

Nowadays, a flight from Frankfurt to New York takes only nine hours. Thanks to aviation, the US is no longer far from Europe. On the airplane, passengers are served a meal with dessert, along with clean water or wine. In addition, guests can choose from a variety of movies to pass the time. But this was not always the case. As late as the eighteenth century, crossing the Atlantic Ocean by sailing vessel to reach the New World could take up to twelve weeks if the wind was not optimal, while even in ideal conditions it took seven weeks at sea.

Not everyone survived the journey. The agony on the ships was great, as a German eyewitness who sailed to Philadelphia in 1750 reported: "Some people are loaded onto the large ships in Rotterdam, others join from Amsterdam. Passengers are packed very close together, like sardines in a can, so to speak . . . During the voyage, misery arises in the ships; stench, steam, horror, vomiting, various sea sicknesses, fever, dysentery, headaches, heat, constipation, ulcers, scurvy, cancer, mouth rot and the like, all of which is caused by old, heavily salted and spiced foods and meats, and from the extreme impurity of the drinking water, due to which many suffer and die in misery. In addition, the lack of food leads to hunger, thirst, frost, heat, dampness, fear, distress, temptation and lamentation, to name just a few of the misfortunes . . . This misery increases to the highest level when having to endure storms that last for three days and three nights, during which everyone believes that the ship will sink with everyone on board."[6]

Many poor emigrants from Europe could not pay for the trip across the Atlantic upfront. The ship captains took them along only on the condition that they work off the costs of the crossing as debtors in the New World. Once in North America, the captain would sell them to their new master, to whom they would become servants or maidservants, usually without pay for a period of four years, after which they would be debt-free.

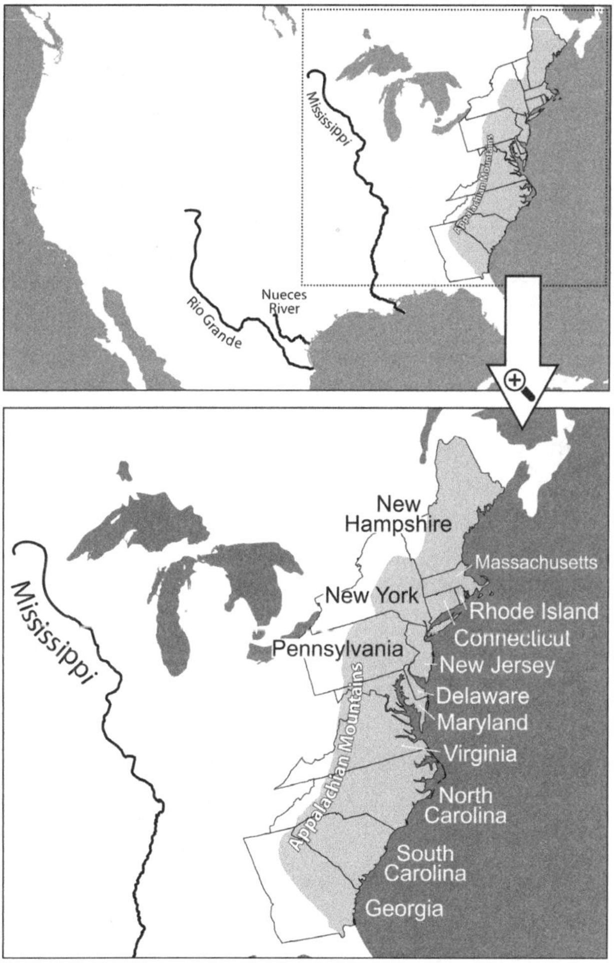

Figure 6. 1732: The thirteen British colonies form the core of what would later become the United States.

Those who survived the harsh and painful crossing of the Atlantic Ocean tried to build their new existence in North America. The European settlers brought with them a variety of farm animals from Europe that had previously been unknown in North America, most notably the horse, but also including goats, sheep, and cattle. The Natives, who lived on the vast and flat prairies, quickly recognized the utility of horses imported from Europe as a means of transportation, which is why the keeping of horses spread among the North American Indians. Conversely, travelers returning to Europe from the New World brought with them plants that had previously been unknown in Europe but then soon enjoyed great popularity, including the potato, tomato, and corn.

1776: The Declaration of Independence

In 1770, Great Britain was one of the leading colonial powers in Europe. The British had valuable trading bases in India, the Caribbean, and North America. The thirteen colonies in North America rebelled, however. The colonists were enraged over the fact that they were only allowed to trade with the British motherland. Furthermore, British King George III had declared that the colonization of North America was over and that it would not extend beyond the Appalachian mountain range. The settlers saw this quite differently: they were grasping for ever more land and wanted to expand westward. They did not like the fact that their colonies were governed by a British governor whom they had not elected. They also felt that it was unfair for them to have to pay taxes to London without being allowed to send a representative to the British House of Commons. Taxation without representation was tyranny, declared those settlers who wanted to separate from London.

When the Crown in England began imposing tariffs on leather, paper, tea, and other products exported from Europe to North America, the inhabitants of the thirteen colonies were very displeased. Although they drank only a little British tea and not much of it was sold throughout the colonies, which meant that tax revenues therefrom were rather low, settlers in the colonies were particularly enraged by the tea tax. To show their dismay, they incited a riot in Boston Harbor in the colony of Massachusetts in 1773, the so-called "Boston Tea Party," during which sixty settlers dressed as Indigenous Americans boarded a British ship and threw 342 crates of the valuable tea overboard, destroying foreign property in doing so. The government in London under King George III reacted sharply to that provocation and sent in troops with orders to end the rebellion in the colonies. What followed was a ban on public gatherings.

Some of the settlers, the Loyalists, wanted to remain a part of the British Empire. But others, the patriots, wanted the exact opposite. The patriots encouraged the rebellion and demanded independence from the British Empire, which in their eyes was unjust and despotic. On April 19, 1775, the first skirmish occurred—the British were now killing each other in North America. After the first day of battles, which occurred near Boston, 368 people had already died, including 273 British soldiers and 95 settlers. In August 1775, the king officially declared the North American colonists rebels. The settlers radicalized, declared a state of war on London, and appointed George Washington, a forty-three-year-old Virginia plantation owner, as commander in chief of their newly created army. Like many other patriots, George Washington had close ties to England. Although he was born in the colony of Virginia, as was his father before him, his great-grandfather was an Englishman from Essex, northeast of London.[7]

The patriots could be called "terrorists" because they were violent, did not shy away from murder, and were pursuing a political objective, namely the withdrawal of British soldiers from the thirteen colonies, but that is not what they are called. The patriots saw themselves fighting for a just cause, resisting the tyrannical British Empire. In US historiography, therefore, they are referred to as "freedom fighters." Even in today's world, it is not so easy to tell the difference between terrorists and freedom fighters, because they all rely on violence and the use of force. The choice of words is ultimately only a question of perspective.

On July 4, 1776, the thirteen British colonies in North America declared their secession from Great Britain and their right to form their own sovereign confederation. The Declaration of Independence, written by Thomas Jefferson, gave birth to the United States. Independence Day is still celebrated every July Fourth as a US national holiday. In the introduction to the Declaration, the founders wisely declared that every person belongs to the human family and that no one should be oppressed: "We hold these truths to be self-evident, that all men are created equal, that they are endowed by their Creator with certain unalienable Rights, that among these are Life, Liberty and the pursuit of Happiness." This formulation was revolutionary and revelatory for that time. The USA was born of noble values. The peace movement today is still guided by the Declaration of Independence and the principle of the human family, the essence of which is that life is sacred.[8]

"According to a popular view of history among many Americans, the history of the United States is a story of the triumph of freedom, progress and democracy," explains Manfred Berg, who teaches history at the University of Heidelberg. But this "glorious tale" does not coincide with the facts. It must be remembered that the very values announced in the Declaration of Independence were not even implemented back then. After all, the settlers in the thirteen colonies had been keeping slaves in those days and by no means were they granted the same rights, not to mention freedom. Furthermore, the Natives were also not considered a part of the human family and the settlers never respected their right to life. Nor did the settlers regard their women as equal to men. In fact, it was not until 1920 that women were granted the right to vote in the United States. Only when it came to the British Empire did the settlers set a different standard and demand that every government protect the freedom of the individual and his or her right to life.[9]

The settlers further proclaimed the right of the people to resist a tyrannical government. If a government, namely the British Empire and King George III, engaged in despotic abuses of power, then the people must overthrow that government, the settlers declared in the Declaration of Independence. "Prudence, indeed, will dictate that Governments long established should not be changed for light and transient causes; and accordingly all experience has shown that mankind are more disposed to suffer, while evils are sufferable, than to right themselves by abolishing the forms to which they are accustomed. But when a long train of abuses and usurpations, pursuing invariably the same Object evinces a design to reduce them under absolute Despotism, it is their right, it is their duty, to throw off such Government, and to provide new Guards for their future security."[10]

Despots who abuse their power must be overthrown by the people. This is the core idea of patriotism. Patriots at that time made a very clear distinction between the people and the government. In this day and age, however, that is no longer the case in the USA. Anyone who speaks out against the government and the president in Washington, denouncing their abuse of power, which representatives of the peace movement have done repeatedly, is defamed and labeled as unpatriotic. This is a twisting of terms, though. The belief that a patriot blindly obeys the government is false and could only be implanted in people's minds through mass media. The redefinition was successful, for anyone who criticizes the so-called "war on terror" nowadays is quickly defamed and criticized for being "unpatriotic."

The Fight against the British Empire

After the adoption of the Declaration of Independence, the USA was not officially independent yet, because the British king did not want to accept the colonies' withdrawal from the British Empire. The settlers rushed to build a regular army and George Washington, the leader of the rebels, led a guerrilla war against the British troops with only 15,000 soldiers. There was no air force at the time and battles were fought mainly on land. The fact that the Royal Navy—the strongest fleet in the world at the time—dominated the Atlantic was of little help for London, because the thirteen colonies were able to grow their own crops and feed themselves. Hence, cutting off supply routes and starving out the enemy, the classic warfare strategy of the British navy, was ineffective against the settlers.

The French watched the rebellion in North America with interest. They wanted the British to be defeated and therefore supplied weapons to the guerrillas in Washington. London, in turn, strengthened its units by recruiting 30,000 mercenaries in Europe, the vast majority of whom were Germans, who were shipped to North America for the war. In addition to that, the British also armed Indigenous people, hoping that would help crush the rebellion. But this did not succeed. France recognized the independence of the thirteen colonies and in 1780 intervened in the War of Independence, siding with the settlers. The tables turned when French soldiers fought against the British alongside George Washington. In the

Treaty of Paris of 1783, the British Empire had to release all thirteen colonies into independence and renounce all territorial claims east of the Mississippi. Only Canada remained under British sovereignty.

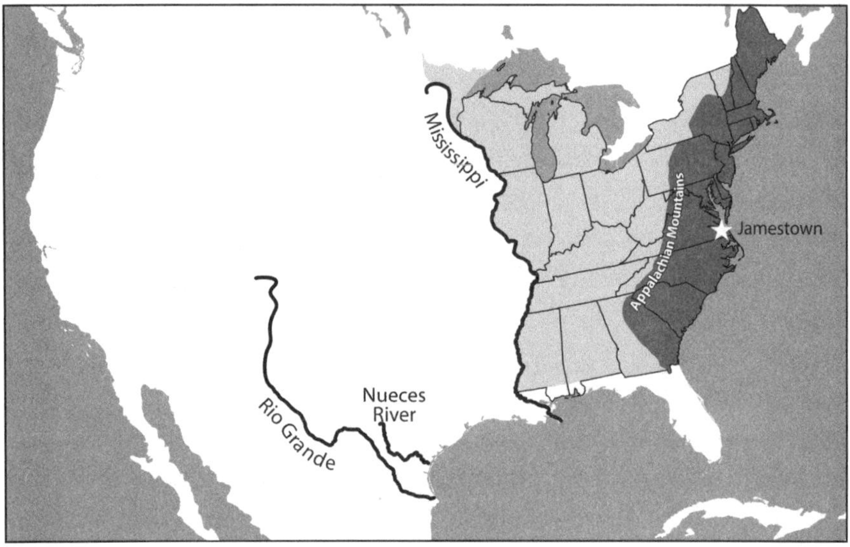

Figure 7. 1783: The United States claims the area east of the Mississippi in the Treaty of Paris.

The Treaty of Paris was a great disgrace to London, but in Paris and Washington it was considered a great triumph. With this treaty, the thirteen colonies also secured the large area between the Appalachian Mountains and the Mississippi River, which enormously increased the national territory of the newly founded United States of America. In return, the US no longer laid claim to any British possessions in the north, which led to the establishment of the national border with Canada. In 1788, under James Madison's leadership, the thirteen colonies adopted a common Constitution and created a legislative branch, consisting of the Senate and the House of Representatives; an executive branch, consisting of a president who would be elected by voters from the individual states; and a judicial branch, consisting of the Supreme Court that acted as the highest legal authority. George Washington, who, thanks to the support of France, had defeated the British, was elected the first president of the United States in 1789.

The settlers' insatiable hunger for more land continued to push the settlement's boundary—the frontier—further westward. The Natives, who resisted the expansion of the settlers, were either killed or driven away. Thus, new states were formed on land that had been stolen from the Indigenous peoples east of the Mississippi River, namely Kentucky (1792), Tennessee (1796), Ohio (1803), Louisiana (1812), Indiana (1816), Mississippi (1817), Illinois (1818), and Alabama (1819), among others. In the north, the US tried to conquer Canada too, but failed because in 1814, during the so-called Second War of Independence, the British burned down the new capital city of Washington and the White House. The US expansion to the west was more successful. In 1803, under Napoleon, France sold its large colony of Louisiana, named after the French Sun King Louis XIV, to the US for the ridiculous price of $15 million. That instantly doubled the US's territory, and the new states of Missouri (1821), Arkansas (1836), Iowa (1846), Minnesota (1858), Kansas (1861), Nebraska (1867), and South Dakota (1889) were created from the vast territory west of the Mississippi. The "Louisiana Purchase" was the largest land deal in history. Again, the Indigenous people who had inhabited the land for generations were displaced by wars.

Why did Napoleon sell such a large area of land for so little money? Because he was preparing for a major war with England in Europe and could not simultaneously maintain a colonial empire in the New World. With his war chest filled to the top, Napoleon intended to take control of all of Europe and then turn his attention back to North America, but he did not succeed. In 1815, English General Wellington and Prussian Field Marshal Blücher defeated Napoleon in the Battle of Waterloo. Today, the name of the city of New Orleans in the state of Louisiana on the Gulf of Mexico is a reminder of the once large colonial possessions of the French in North America. In 1867, the USA acquired Alaska from Russia for another ludicrous price of $7 million, thereby further increasing their territory to a great extent.

To this day, the Statue of Liberty, dedicated in 1886 in the harbor of New York, reminds us of the great influence that France had on the early history of the United States. The statue was crafted by a French artist in Paris, brought across the Atlantic by ships, and reassembled in New York as a gift from the French people. The Statue of Liberty holds a torch in her right hand, a tablet inscribed with the date of the American Declaration of Independence in 1776 in her left hand, and a broken chain symbolizing liberation from British bondage lies at her feet. The thirteen colonies would probably never have gained their independence from Great Britain without the support of France.

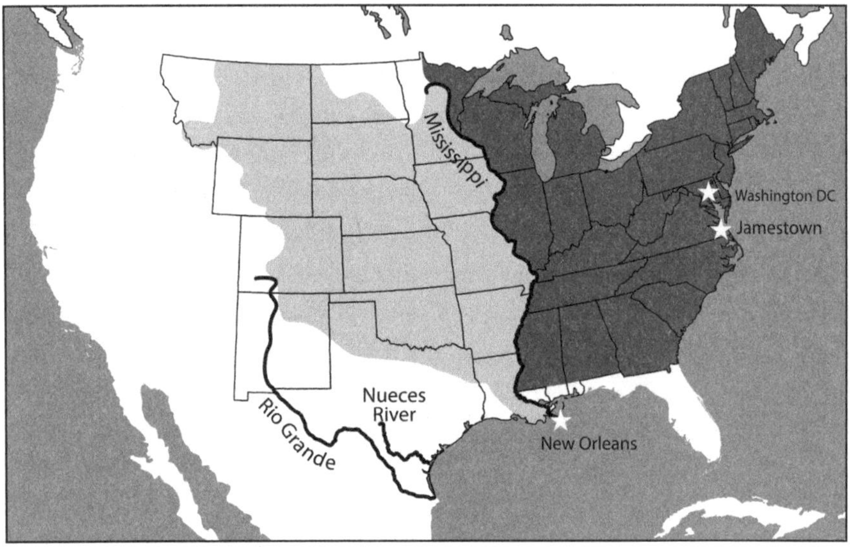

Figure 8. 1803: The United States doubles its area by purchasing the colony of Louisiana (light gray).

1846: The War against Mexico

After the Declaration of Independence and the victory over the British Empire, the leaders of the newly founded USA met in Philadelphia and laid out the Constitutional Convention of 1788, in which the young confederation stated the intent to raise its own army. "No government can exist merely on paper," argued New Jersey State Representative William Paterson. "It always needs a standing army to be able to assert its claim to power." The majority agreed, and shortly thereafter, the US Army was established. No one had any idea at that time that the US Army would devour an extremely large amount of money and attack countless countries on various continents over the course of the following 230 years.[11]

The first sovereign state that the USA attacked was its neighbor Mexico, which had fought for its own independence from Spain in 1821 after the Spaniards, as a colonial power, had exploited the country's gold and silver reserves for 300 years and almost completely wiped out the Indigenous population. The Spanish language and the Catholic faith still characterize Mexico today and are reminders of the Spanish colonial empire. The area of Mexico was significantly larger before the US invasion. The present US states of Texas, California, New Mexico, Arizona, Utah, Nevada, and half of Colorado all belonged to the territory of Mexico and were only conquered by the US during the Mexican-American War.

At first, the US attempted to buy the provinces of Texas and California from Mexico, but Mexico strictly refused any offers. After that, more and more US Americans crossed the border to Mexico and settled in the Mexican province of Texas, until the Mexican government banned the continued immigration of US Americans to Texas in 1830. American settlers, however, ignored the ban and the US government even actively supported the emigration of American settlers to the Mexican province of Texas. US Americans in Texas proudly referred to themselves as "Texans" rather than "Mexicans." They were hostile toward Mexicans and spoke English, not Spanish.

The US continued to expand its sphere of influence. President James Polk of the Democratic Party, who had entered the White House in March of 1845 at the age of forty-nine, deemed it was America's "manifest destiny" for White American settlers to spread across the continent. When the US took up arms in the Mexican province of Texas and declared that Texas should be seceded from Mexico, war broke out. The relatively weak Mexican government tried to put down the revolt in their province of Texas, but the US government in Washington supported the insurgents. As a result, the US succeeded in breaking the province of Texas away from Mexico. Under President Polk, Texas was annexed and integrated into the USA as the twenty-eighth state in December 1845. Mexico was enraged and angered over their loss of territory.

But the USA had not had enough yet. President Polk wanted to conquer the Mexican port cities on the Pacific coast, especially San Francisco, because he saw it as the key to trade with Asia. The US stoked tensions on the border between Texas and Mexico. According to Mexico and common understanding, the border was marked by the Nueces River. President Polk, however, claimed that the border ran further south, along the Rio Grande. Mexico was irritated by President Polk sending US General Zachary Taylor to Texas in January 1846 to cross the Nueces River, and thus the border to Mexico, with an army.

In the disputed border area, General Taylor ordered the US Army to build a fort on the Rio Grande, located about 150 miles south of the generally recognized border. The purpose of this provocation was to incite Mexico to fire the first shot. After months of waiting, the Mexicans, who insisted that the Nueces River was the border between Texas and Mexico, were faced with humiliation and saw their only alternative as a counterattack to drive the United States out of Mexico by force.

"The presence of United States troops on the edge of the disputed territory furthest from the Mexican settlements was not sufficient to provoke hostilities," US officer Ulysses Grant recalled in his memoirs of the outbreak of the war. President Polk therefore urged that an incident be staged. "We were sent to provoke a fight, but it was essential that Mexico should commence it," Grant said. "It was very doubtful whether Congress would declare war; but if Mexico should attack our troops, the Executive could . . . prosecute the contest with vigor."[12]

The US had no right to send its troops into Mexican territory. When the Mexicans attacked the invading US soldiers stationed on the Rio Grande on April 24, 1846, with the intention of driving them out of Mexico, President Polk went before Congress and claimed that Mexico had spilled American blood on American soil. In the House of Representatives, Abraham Lincoln, who was then a representative from Illinois and would later become the sixteenth president of the United States, was not convinced. In a speech given in 1848, Lincoln sharply criticized President Polk, proclaiming that the president must show "that the ground on which the first blood was shed was indeed ours." Lincoln summarized that President Polk was hardly able to do that, and that presumably the president himself was aware that he was in the wrong, for President Polk was a "confused, irritated, and miserably perplexed man."[13]

After the staged incident at the Rio Grande, the US declared war on neighboring Mexico on May 13, 1846. President Polk hypocritically portrayed the United States as a victim in his speech to Congress: "As war exists, and, notwithstanding all our efforts to avoid it, exists by the act of Mexico herself, we are called upon by every consideration of duty and patriotism to vindicate with decision the honor, the rights and the interests of our country." In reality, though, the opposite was true. President Polk had instigated the war by sending US soldiers into Mexican territory. The staged incident on the Rio Grande did not fail to have its intended effect: in the Senate, only 2 senators voted against the war, while 40 supported it, and in the House of Representatives, 190 congressmen voted in favor the war, while only 14 opposed it.[14]

At least a part of the US population disapproved of the attack on Mexico. Already, the US peace movement, small as it was, recognized that the Rio Grande incident had been staged. "Although Texas needed no defense, President James Polk, under the pretext of defending Texas, stationed General Zachary Taylor and his troops beyond the real boundaries of Texas, and even gave them permission to cross the Rio Grande," US civil rights activist William Goodell, who was involved in the movement to abolish slavery and strongly opposed the extension of slavery to newly conquered territories, declared in 1852. "After several unsuccessful attempts to incite the Mexicans to fire the first shot, it was actually our troops who drew first blood, whereupon General Taylor reported to his government that hostilities had commenced. Thereupon President Polk presented a lie to both Congress and the world, claiming that 'Mexico has crossed the border and advanced upon our country. Mexico has spilled American blood on American soil.'" These war lies, Goodell argued, deceived the people as well as Congress.[15]

Other US Americans were also opposed to the Mexican War and voiced their opinions loudly and clearly. Congressman Daniel Webster spoke of a "war of pretexts, in which the true motive is not openly admitted. Instead, false reasoning, evasions, bogus explanations given retrospectively and other methods are used to make the general public believe there is a dispute where in reality there is none." But President Polk was not interested in the peace movement's criticisms and ordered General Taylor to seize the town of Matamoros, which was located south of the Rio Grande on Mexican soil. Upon those orders, the US Navy also attacked the city of San Francisco in the Pacific and captured the Mexican province of California. Mexico had no navy to speak of and thus was powerless against the US Navy. The US also bombarded Mexico City and Vera Cruz. Many women were raped; children and the elderly were killed. US soldiers looted and destroyed the Mexican city of Huamantla and the population was massacred.[16]

"It is a vile and shameful war that we are fighting," Reverend Theodore Parker protested in a public speech in Boston on February 4, 1847. "Young men who should be making hay and serving society are marching in the streets. They are learning how to kill other people. People who have never harmed them—not to mention any of us. They are learning to kill their brothers." This, he said, was not in keeping with the values of Christianity, and the war against Mexico was wrong and mendacious. "A big thug is fighting a little boy here, a weak and sick little boy. And to make matters even worse, the little boy is in the right, and the big boy is in the wrong. But he continues to tell lies, with a straight face, to make it appear that he is right."[17]

By means of extreme force, the US succeeded in defeating Mexico. The war ended with the Treaty of Guadalupe Hidalgo on February 2, 1848, which forced the Mexican government not only to recognize that Texas

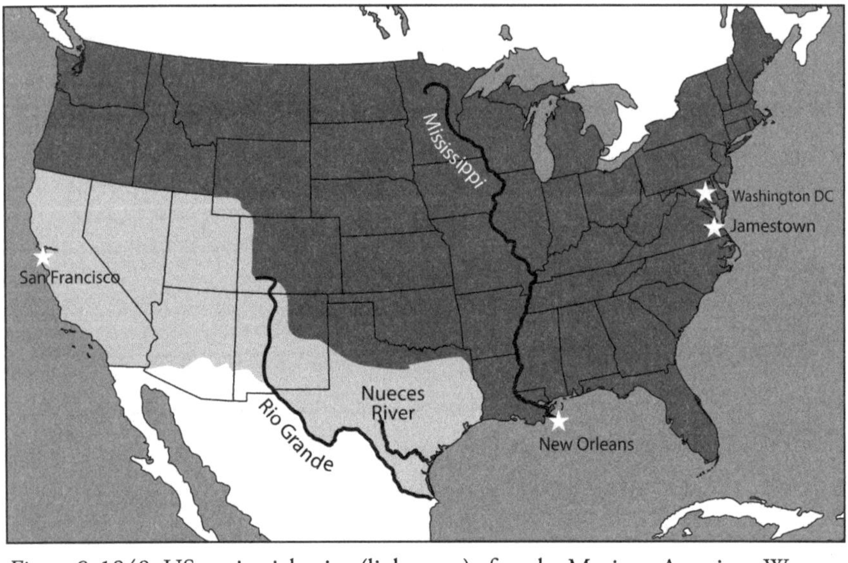

Figure 9. 1848: US territorial gains (light gray) after the Mexican-American War.

now belonged to the United States, but also to cede half of its territory, which included California, to the United States. Mexicans living in this vast area were given the choice of either emigrating to Mexico within a year or becoming US citizens. President Polk had thus massively increased the territory of the USA, but his health had been deteriorating. His secretary of state, James Buchanan, said of President Polk that he had taken on "the appearance of an old man" during his presidency. Polk did not run for reelection after his term ended and died in 1849 at the age of fifty-three. General Zachary Taylor, who had started the war, was hailed as a war hero and elected president to succeed Polk.[18]

The Destruction of the Indigenous Population

Like the British before them, the United States continued the expulsion and destruction of the Indigenous population in the infamous American Indian Wars long after the Declaration of Independence in 1776. The vast regions that the USA had acquired, from France by purchase and from Mexico by war, were of course populated by different Indigenous tribes. As these nations disagreed on how to deal with the US Army and their proceedings, they continued to lose more and more of their habitat.

French historian Alexis de Tocqueville, who traveled to the US in 1826 and was an eyewitness to the expulsion of the Natives, recounts how the colonists broke their word over and over again: "As soon as the European population begins to approach the wilderness inhabited by a Native tribe, the government of the United States usually sends a ceremonial deputation to it; the Whites assemble the Indians on a large plain, and after eating and drinking with them, they explain to them: Beyond those mountains you see on the horizon, on the other side of the lake that borders your territory on the West, you will find vast areas with an abundance of wild animals. Sell us your land here and go over there to live happily ever after. After this speech, they present to the Indians an assortment of weapons, woolen clothes, barrels of brandy, necklaces of glass beads, bracelets of pewter, earrings and mirrors. If they still hesitate at the sight of all these treasures, they are given to understand that they cannot refuse the consent demanded . . . Half convinced, half coerced, the Indians depart and move to the uninhabited areas where the Whites might leave them in peace for hardly ten years. Thus, the Americans acquire whole provinces at laughable prices."[19]

When the Natives did not voluntarily retreat from the White settlers, the US soldiers were ruthless in their conquest. They raided the Native peoples' villages and killed even women and children who were not involved in the fighting. The Indigenous people were not seen as equal members of the human family. They were considered animals and underdeveloped humans. In many places, murdering a Native person was rewarded with a scalping bounty. Scalping is the act of tearing a part of the human scalp, with hair attached, from the skull. The scalps served as evidence of a Native person's death. Native warriors also scalped White people and displayed the scalps as a sign of their courage.

Good Bear Woman, a twenty-nine-year-old Indigenous woman from the Piegan tribe, recalls an engagement of the 2nd US Cavalry under the command of Major Eugene Baker that occurred on January 23, 1870, along the Marias River in Montana: "I saw the soldiers coming over the hill." Piegan Chief Heavy Runner was bewildered, for he had a peaceful relationship with the White people. The US Indian Bureau had even guaranteed him protection in writing. The chief got the letter from his wigwam and brought it to the commander, upon which Cavalry officer Baker read the document and tore it up, recounts Good Bear Woman. "When Heavy Runner turned around, the soldiers shot and killed him." After killing the chief, the US soldiers destroyed the village. "The soldiers chopped down everyone around them . . . and massacred all the men, women and children." Most of the Piegan warriors had left the camp to hunt. Only fifteen of them were in the village; only one even fired back. It was a massacre. Only a few Natives escaped. The woods and the rivers were full of dead bodies. On that day, at least 173 Indigenous people were killed in that village.[20]

The Marias Massacre in Montana was not an isolated incident. There are similar stories from other states. US historian Benjamin Madley, who lectures at the University of California in Los Angeles, can prove that after conquering California in the Mexican War, the US acted ruthlessly against the Indigenous people living there. According to Madley, one must speak of genocide against the Native people in California. Between

1846 and 1873, the number of Natives living in California decreased massively, from about 150,000 to 30,000. The US government, Californian politicians, and US soldiers all actively and deliberately participated in the extermination of the Natives, Madley concludes his findings on the genocide in California.[21]

Today, people in the United States are reluctant to talk about this dark side of history. While in Germany, for example, the crimes of the Third Reich have been processed, the atrocities of the American Indian Wars are suppressed in the USA. "The destruction of Indigenous North America was a key event and must no longer be erased from US history," Swiss historian Aram Mattioli is right to demand. While the United States originally emerged from an anti-colonial revolution, it quickly became a colonial power itself that ruthlessly expanded to the West. Great injustice was also done to the Indigenous tribe of the Cherokee. In Georgia, the White people had promised them their land by treaty. But when gold was found on that land, the treaty was no longer worth anything. President Andrew Jackson acted ruthlessly against the Natives. In 1838 he sent 7,000 US soldiers to force the Cherokee people to move off the land of their ancestors and migrate for more than a thousand miles along the "Trail of Tears" to resettle in Oklahoma. Many died of cold, hunger, and cholera. Those who tried to break out were killed on the spot. "It was a death march. In the end, 4,000 silent graves lined our way," wrote Private Jesse Burnett.[22]

The US film industry has repeatedly depicted the violent clashes between US Americans and Indigenous peoples, but often reverses the roles of good and evil, thus usually portraying the Natives as villains and savages. This despite the fact that the Native people are the original inhabitants of North America, in contrast to the White Europeans, who came and robbed them of their land. Hollywood's imagery, however, is often more powerful than historical research, and constant repetition of such tales has allowed a distorted picture of events to become commonly accepted. In classic Western movies, the cavalry usually comes to the rescue, driving out the evil and brutal Natives and protecting the helpless, innocent, God-believing White settlers. By means of this recontextualization, the USA tries to this day to suppress the crimes that were committed against the Native Americans. Only a few movies show the brutality of the cavalry and the tragedy of the land theft that occurred and arouse the viewer's sympathy for the Indigenous people. One example is *Dances with Wolves*, which is set in 1863, stars US actor Kevin Costner, and features the Sioux tribe.

Historical documents leave no doubt that the immigration of Europeans to North America was a deadly disaster for the Native people. The murdering of the Natives was a serious crime. More than four million North American Indigenous people did not survive the cultural clash with the Europeans. In addition to expulsion and military force, infectious diseases including smallpox, measles, typhoid, diphtheria, and influenza, brought in and spread by the Europeans, wiped out most of the Native population. Furthermore, the near extinction of bison herds during railroad construction robbed the Natives of their livelihood. "A cold wind blew through the plains when the last buffalo fell—the wind of death to my people," Sioux Chief Sitting Bull said, lamenting the promiscuous slaughter of the buffalo by the White man.[23]

1890: The Massacre at Wounded Knee

Sioux Chief Sitting Bull was a contemporary witness who sharply criticized the reckless behavior of the United States. "The love of ownership of property is a disease of the White man," Sitting Bull wisely stated. "These people have created a system of rules, which don't apply to the Rich, but that the Poor mustn't break. They have a religion that the Poor follow, but the Rich do not. They even collect taxes from the Poor to support the Rich and those who rule. They claim that this Mother Earth of ours belongs to them, that it is there for their consumption, and they lock their neighbors away behind fences." The White settlers' greed, he said, was insatiable: "Even if America were twice the size that it is, it still wouldn't be enough for them." With this, Sitting Bull had formulated an early criticism of US imperialism. However, the settlers did not want to hear it. Sitting Bull enjoyed great respect among Native people because of his crushing defeat of General George Custer's troops at the Battle of Little Bighorn in 1876. The US Army classified Sitting Bull as a troublemaker, and in 1890 he was killed during his arrest.[24]

Brutal massacres occurred over and over again. Another one took place at Wounded Knee in South Dakota on December 29, 1890, when the US Army captured Sioux Chief Big Foot and surrounded the 120 men and 230 women who were with Big Foot. The Natives did not resist, and when Colonel James Forsyth ordered the disarmament of the Sioux, they surrendered their rifles while the US Army brought into position its Hotchkiss-type revolver cannons, capable of firing 100 rounds per minute. The commanding US officer was not satisfied with the number of weapons that they had confiscated from the Sioux people and ordered his soldiers to search their tents. They found two more rifles, one of which belonged to a young Sioux man named Black Coyote, who explained that he had paid a lot of money for the rifle and that it was therefore his property. The soldiers grabbed Black Coyote and a shot rang out from his rifle, upon which the soldiers immediately began to fire from the revolver guns they had set up around the camp, literally causing a bloodbath. Unarmed Natives who tried to flee were hunted down and killed. Between 150 and 350 Sioux people died in the hail of bullets, including Chief Big Foot, children, and women with infants in their arms. Colonel Forsyth was not punished after the massacre—instead, he was promoted to major general. The Wounded Knee Massacre ended the American Indian Wars. After that, there were no longer any armed resistances.[25]

Four Million Native Americans Dead

The Australian historian Ben Kiernan, who teaches at Yale University in the United States, correctly states that the war waged against the Native Americans was a "war of extermination." Kiernan estimates that more than five million Indigenous people were living north of the Rio Grande when the first Europeans landed in North America in 1492. He estimates that three centuries later, around the year 1800, only 600,000 Indigenous people remained. More than four million Native Americans had thus not survived the clash with the White settlers from Europe. This immense violence against Native Americans was made possible by widespread racism, Kiernan correctly explains, by which one group of people envisioned a world in which another group of people no longer existed. The murder of the American Indians was only possible because they were not considered part of the human family.[26]

While the Native American population was collapsing, the number of immigrants to the US continued to steadily increase. With the influx of Europeans, the non-Native population in the US grew rapidly from 5 to 75 million people between 1800 and 1900. During that same time, the already decimated Native American population shrank from 600,000 to 250,000 people. From then on and until today, the Indigenous peoples who survived were a minority in their own country. By taking away the Native peoples' hunting grounds and killing the bison, the US government also destroyed the culture of those proud hunters. Surviving Natives were relocated to reservations, where many committed suicide or turned to alcohol.[27]

It is not that there was no violence in North America prior to the Europeans' arrival on their ships. Different Indigenous tribes also fought and killed each other, but not to the point of extermination. The use of violence was far less extreme because there were always wise Native people around who pointed out that we all belong to the human family. Native American medicine men held a worldview that is also the essence of Christian mysticism, Zen, and Sufism. According to this ideology, the divine is understood to be an omnipresent spirit, embodied in all people, animals, plants, and things, from the tiniest atom to the boundless galaxy. The earth is referred to as Gaia and, according to this way of thinking, is a living organism that cannot be bought or owned. Man is not seen as a self-contained entity within the limits of his own skin, but as an energy field that is connected to all of reality. Human beings, therefore, are not separate from the divine. It would never have occurred to the Natives to slaughter all bison, as they only would kill as many animals as they needed for their survival.

Black Elk, the medicine man of the Oglala Sioux, was a representative of the peace movement and described this bond with the human family thus: "The first peace—which is the most important—is that which comes within the souls of people when they realize their relationship, their oneness with the universe and all its powers, and when they realize at the center of the universe dwells the Great Spirit, and that its center is really everywhere, it is within each of us.—This is the real peace, all others are merely reflections of it. The second peace is that which is made between individuals, and the third is that between peoples. But above all, you need to see that there can never be peace between peoples unless the first peace is achieved, which, as I have already said, dwells within the human soul."[28]

CHAPTER 4

THE EXPLOITATION OF SLAVES

If the European settlers that came to North America had been nomadic hunters and gatherers, like most American Indians were, they would not have needed slaves. They were, however, sedentary farmers who worked the land and grew tobacco, sugarcane, cotton, and rice on large plantations. In order to do so, human labor was essential, because at that time, there were no tractors, no combine harvesters, no oil, and no industrialized agriculture. Despite their efforts, Europeans did not succeed in enslaving North American Indians, as they preferred to die in battle, in captivity, or by succumbing to newly introduced diseases. The peoples from Africa, on the other hand, with their dark skin and physical strength, proved to be more resistant. Therefore, the settlers bought Black slaves who had been imported across the Atlantic from Africa.

The Abduction of 12 Million Africans

The Atlantic slave trade was practiced by the European colonial powers of Portugal, Spain, Holland, Denmark, France, and England in order to gain cheap labor for growing raw materials and engaging in large-scale agriculture in their North and South American colonies. The slave trade is an example of how greed and the objective of profit maximization has always led to brutal exploitation. Black slave traders captured Black people from other tribes in West Africa and force marched them in torturous and often deadly treks over hundreds of miles to reach the African coast where they sold them to White Europeans, who then would chain the slaves together, cram them into ships, and bring them to America.

From 1500 to 1850, some 12 million Africans were trafficked across the Atlantic, about one million of whom ended up in the United States. The British, who were the leading slave traders, considered Black people a commodity. When provisions and water supplies were insufficient or when the spread of contagious diseases was feared, some of the human "cargo" was simply thrown overboard in the middle of the Atlantic. The British recognized neither Indigenous Americans nor Black people as members of the human family. This is the only explanation for how quickly White people were willing to kill Black people—or anyone else outside of their race, for that matter.[1]

The United States was not the country with the most slaves. Slavery also existed in the Caribbean and in South America. One example is Jamaican reggae musician Bob Marley, who was born in 1945 to a dark-skinned mother, whose ancestors had been slaves imported from Africa, and a White father, who had served in the British Army. His music, including songs like "Get Up, Stand Up," was closely tied to his African ancestry and contained the message of protesting against oppression. Many slaves were brought to Brazil, where they were put to work to grow sugarcane. Brazil is now the country with the largest population of people of African descent outside of Africa.

The first shipment of twenty African slaves to the colony in Jamestown, Virginia, was by Dutch traders in 1619. The slaves were forced to work in tobacco production without pay. More and more slaves were imported, and by the time the thirteen colonies broke away from Great Britain in 1776, there were already 500,000 slaves working in the United States. While the northern colonies employed fewer slaves, the southern colonies of Virginia, North Carolina, South Carolina, and Georgia built their economic system on the complete exploitation of slaves. Without slave labor, the tobacco plantations of the South would not have been profitable.[2]

US historian Edmund Morgan, who taught at Yale University, has studied slavery intensively and rightly emphasizes that the noble values of the American Declaration of Independence of 1776, including above all the values of freedom and equality, were not implemented with respect to Black people. The entire economic system of the United States was substantially based on racism and the belief that people with white skin were worth more than people with black skin. On this basis of racism, which is contrary to the principle of the human family, exploiting Black people for cheap labor was perfectly legitimate from the plantation owners' point of view. The settlers did not want to acknowledge the blatant contradiction of the values articulated in the Declaration of Independence, a phenomenon that Morgan refers to as the "American paradox."[3]

Because prices for slaves were very low, neither slave traders nor plantation owners had very much concern for their health. The slaves could be abused, raped, sold, or killed, as they belonged to their masters until their death. A quarter of the slaves imported from Africa died in Virginia within the first year of their arrival. If Black slaves resisted any of the injustices or exploitation, the plantation owners would whip or hang them.

In South Carolina and in Georgia, slaves were put to work growing rice, which increased the profits of the plantation owners. Rice farming expanded rapidly and soon there were more Black people in South Carolina than White people. But the work in the rice fields was much harder than on the tobacco plantations, and therefore the mortality rate of the slaves working the rice fields was higher. Time and again there were slave uprisings, but they were always put down with brutal force because the plantation owners regarded slaves as their property, not as equal human beings.

The plantation owners did not necessarily seek enjoyment through sadistic violence; their primary objective was the selfish pursuit of profit without regard for the lives of others. "The origins of slavery on the plantations lie not in a conspiracy to degrade, shame, brutalize, or degrade the social standing of Black people, although all of these things did happen as a result," explains Ira Berlin, a US historian who taught at the University of Maryland. "The gross immorality of slavery cannot hide the real motivation behind American captivity: to use the labor of many to make a few rich and powerful." Greed and profit were the driving principles behind slavery. The noble principle of the Declaration of Independence, "that all men are created equal," was ignored.[4]

In keeping slaves, whose labor they did not pay for, plantation owners became very wealthy and rose to become the most politically influential class in the colonies. To maintain their privileges and facilitate this system of exploitation, plantation owners secured key political positions in the new republic, including the White House. The first president of the United States, George Washington, who held office in the White House from 1789 to 1797, was a racist and a slave owner. He kept meticulous inventory lists with the names of all of his slaves, as he did with the names of his beloved horses. Thomas Jefferson, the author of the American Declaration of Independence, had declared all men free and equal, but owned hundreds of enslaved African Americans who worked at his estate in Virginia while he ruled as president in the White House from 1801 to 1809. The fourth president, James Madison (in the White House from 1809 to 1817), and the fifth president, James Monroe (1817 to 1825), also kept slaves, as did President Andrew Jackson (1829 to 1837) and President John Tyler (1841 to 1845), because they were members of the upper class.

There was nothing the White plantation owners in the United States feared more than slave rebellions. In the Caribbean, Black slaves had risen up against the colonial power of France and founded the free Republic of Haiti in 1804. This news spread to the United States as well. In the summer of 1831, a Black preacher named Nat Turner led one of the most successful uprisings in Virginia. Seventy-five men participated in it. First they murdered their White owners. Then, armed with axes, knives, and hoes, they moved from settlement to settlement, killing nearly sixty White people before being killed by militiamen and a force of White vigilantes. In retaliation to this incident, White people murdered hundreds of slaves and Nat Turner was hanged.[5]

In those days, the general conviction was that White people and Black people could never live together peacefully. While in office, President James Monroe, therefore, considered sending the Black slaves back across the Atlantic and advocated the establishment of a colony in Africa for former slaves. As previously mentioned, Monroe himself was a slave owner from Virginia and was by no means opposed to slavery in principle, but he wanted slaves to at least have the opportunity to emigrate to a state of their own. In 1824, the colony of Liberia was founded and its capital, Monrovia, was named after President Monroe. Most slaves born in the US, however, did not want to emigrate to a foreign country; they wanted to fight for their civil rights in the United States.

Slavery in the USA was first abolished in states where there were only few slaves and where the economic elite did not depend on cheap labor. In 1777, the state of Vermont was the first to ban slavery by law, followed by Massachusetts, New Hampshire, and other northern states, including New York. The African Americans, however, continued to be discriminated against in the North even after slavery was abolished. By no means were they treated as equal members of the human family. African Americans were "creatures of such a low order that they have no rights that a White man is bound to respect," declared the Supreme Court as late as 1858 in a highly controversial ruling. Even where slavery had been abolished, Black people were considered second-class citizens, just like in the apartheid system in South Africa. They were not allowed to vote, appear as witnesses in court, marry outside their race, or live in areas populated by a majority of White folks. Many Black people lived in segregated slums in humiliating poverty. African American children that lived in the North were particularly at risk of being kidnapped, taken to the South, and sold into slavery.[6]

1865: The Civil War and the Abolition of Slavery

In contrast to the northern states, the southern states categorically rejected the abolition of slavery. Plantation owners in Virginia, South Carolina, Georgia, Alabama, Mississippi, and Louisiana had tangible reasons for this, as some 400,000 slaves were working in each of these states by 1860. Rice farming and cotton production, which were based heavily on slave labor, had risen to become capital intensive and profitable industries. When Abraham Lincoln, who was an avowed opponent of slavery, was elected president on November 6, 1860, the United States was deeply divided. The southern slave states seceded from the US and formed their own country, which they called the Confederate States of America. When militias from the southern states attacked the army base at Fort Sumter in April 1861, the Civil War ensued.

In the American Civil War from 1861 to 1865, Northern troops fought against Southern troops. In September 1862, President Lincoln, then commander in chief of the army, granted freedom to all slaves in the rebelling Southern states by decree, thereby weakening the CSA. It was an extremely bloody war, as both sides also attacked the civilian population. For the first time in western war history, land mines, torpedoes, ironclads, and machine guns were used, including the first-ever submarine. The Civil War lasted five years and claimed over 600,000 lives, thus accounting for more US casualties than any other war in which the United States has ever been involved.

Some US citizens protested the Civil War. "War is wrong—wrong yesterday, wrong today, wrong forever," exclaimed author Ezra Heywood in 1863. As a member of the small US peace movement, Heywood advocated for the abolition of slavery and equal rights for women and opposed violence in principle. "Murder is the gravest crime man commits; yet war is murder multiplied by the majority. By what ethic, then, is the man a criminal, and the masses heroes?" asked Heywood, whose faith was rooted in Christianity. "Self-defense is right; but how much of yourself will you save? The self is composed of soul and body; to save your life by sin, you lose your soul; to lose your life for truth, you save your soul. I go for the soul."[7]

Nonetheless, the majority did not listen to the peace movement's message and went to war. US historian Alan Dawley believes that if the Civil War had not eliminated an entire generation of young men, the labor movement would have taken militant action against its employers in the industrialized North and a class conflict would likely have ensued, for there was great tension between the rich upper class and the lower working-class citizens. Among the most hated employers was the capitalist robber baron Jay Gould, a railway magnate who owned a 15,000-mile railroad network. Gould had a very low regard for—and was quite hostile toward—the lower class, declaring: "I can hire one half of the working class to kill the other half."[8]

After the Civil War, the Southern states were readmitted to the United States and the Confederate States of America was dissolved. Abraham Lincoln was reelected president in the final year of the war, and in his inauguration speech for his second term, he stated that he hoped for peace—within the US but also with all other countries in the world. "Let us strive on to finish the work we are in, to bind up the nation's wounds, to care for him who shall have borne the battle and for his widow and his orphan," said Lincoln, "to do all which may achieve and cherish a just and lasting peace among ourselves and with all nations." But President Lincoln did not witness the universal peace he had wished for. On April 14, 1865, as he and his wife attended a theater in Washington, a fanatical Southern sympathizer shot him in the back of the head with a pistol.[9]

After the Civil War ended, the 1865 passage of the Thirteenth Amendment to the Constitution finally abolished slavery throughout the entire territory of the United States forever. The Amendment declared that "Neither slavery nor involuntary servitude, except as a punishment for a crime of which such person shall have been found guilty in due process of law, shall exist within the United States, or in any territory under its jurisdiction." Thus, for the first time in US history, Black men and White men were equal before the law. Women and Native Americans, however, were still not.[10]

The Ku Klux Klan Wants White Supremacy

Even after the abolition of slavery, many former slaves continued to work on the cotton and tobacco fields in the Southern states as tenants. Strict rules on racial segregation were introduced and would apply for another hundred years. Black people had to travel in separate railroad compartments, attend separate schools and hospitals, and use their own public water fountains and toilets. In each case, their facilities were significantly inferior to those of White people. But with their newly introduced right to vote, Black people now had the opportunity to improve their fate. Many African Americans flocked to the polling stations, similar to what occurred in South Africa after apartheid was repealed in 1994. Hiram Revels, an African American from Mississippi, became the first Black senator in 1870 and entered Congress to applause.

Southern White people feared they would lose their influence and formed the Ku Klux Klan shortly after the end of the Civil War. This racist organization attacked Black people before every election and during every single political meeting. As a result, Black people were prevented from exercising their right to vote. In the weeks leading up to the presidential election in 1868, 2,000 Black people were murdered or injured by the Ku Klux Klan in Louisiana. "The message was clear," explains US journalist Eric Hansen: "Don't you dare go vote, you may not return home." In the decades that followed, African Americans rarely succeeded in rising to high political office, as many Black people stopped voting altogether because they feared for their lives. Today, the Ku Klux Klan is widely trivialized as a club of "murderous racists in silly hoods," Hansen explains. "But the Klan had clear political goals and carried them out. That's what made it one of the most successful terrorist groups in the world. It denied democratic participation for a specific segment of the population without destroying democracy as a whole."[11]

The Ku Klux Klan negated the principle of the human family and had no interest in ensuring that democratic rights and equality for all people, regardless of their skin color, were respected in everyday life. In the years from 1920 to 1925, between three and six million Americans joined the racist Ku Klux Klan, which occasionally targeted Jews, Catholics, and other minorities. Most of the victims, however, were African Americans. In Omaha, Nebraska, fourteen-year-old Henry Fonda, who would later become a movie star, watched a lynching from his father's print shop. "It was the most horrible thing I had ever witnessed," Fonda later recalled. "We locked the print shop, went downstairs and drove home without saying a word. My hands were sweaty and there were tears in my eyes. All I could think about was this young black man dangling from the end of a rope."[12]

Dr. Martin Luther King Jr. Strengthens the Civil Rights Movement

It was not until the time of Dr. Martin Luther King Jr., the courageous leader of the African American civil rights movement, and the equality laws of the 1960s that these conditions ended. As an African American, the Baptist pastor categorically rejected the oppression of Black people. Martin Luther King Jr. knew from his own family's experience what he was talking about; his maternal grandfather had been a son of slaves.

Dr. King delivered his famous "I have a dream" speech in Washington, DC, on August 28, 1963. In it, he stressed that the fight for civil rights was important, but neither violence nor hatred should drive that fight. "Let us not seek to satisfy our thirst for freedom by drinking from the cup of bitterness and hatred," King stressed in front of a quarter of a million people, both Black and White. "We must forever conduct our struggle on the high plane of dignity and discipline. We must not allow our creative protest to degenerate into physical violence. Again and again, we must rise to the majestic heights of meeting physical force with soul force."

The people who listened to him were deeply touched. One hundred years before, President Abraham Lincoln had abolished slavery, said King, who deliberately stood in front of the Lincoln Memorial during his speech. Yet "the Negro is still languished in the corners of American society and finds himself an exile in his own land," King charged. The "magnificent words" of the Constitution and the Declaration of Independence, including the promise that all people would be guaranteed the unalienable rights of life, liberty, and the pursuit of happiness, are still not realized for all in the United States, he said. "Let us not wallow in the valley of despair, I say to you today, my friends. And so even though we face the difficulties of today and tomorrow, I still have a dream . . . It is a dream deeply rooted in the American dream. I have a dream that one day this nation will rise up and live out the true meaning of its creed: We hold these truths to be self-evident that all men are created equal." To the applause of the crowd, King spoke about the principle of the human family and exclaimed, "I have a dream that my four little children will one day live in a nation where they will not be judged by the color of their skin but by the content of their character."[13]

Martin Luther King Jr. received the Nobel Peace Prize in 1964 and is the most well-known representative of the peace movement in the United States. "America has become the richest and most powerful nation in the world," King said during a protest against the Vietnam War in Los Angeles in 1967. "But honesty impels me to admit that our power has often made us arrogant. We feel that our money can do anything. We arrogantly feel that we have everything to teach other nations and nothing to learn from them. We often arrogantly feel that we have some divine, messianic mission to police the whole world," he said with justifiable harshness. "Enlarged power means enlarged peril if there is no concomitant growth of the soul . . . Real power consists in using power justly. If we do not use our nation's power responsibly and with restraint, it will behave as Acton's proverb says: 'Power corrupts, and absolute power corrupts absolutely.' Our arrogance can become our undoing." On April 4, 1968, a year after King had delivered this farsighted speech, he was shot and killed in Memphis, Tennessee, allegedly by a crazy lone gunman.[14]

Slavery has been abolished in the United States for more than 150 years. But to this day, racism has still not completely been overcome, neither in the US nor elsewhere. It is still quite easy for demagogues to divide the human family along racial and other objective lines. In addition to the extermination of Native Americans, the exploitation of African Americans is the second original sin of the USA. African Americans have never received any reparations for centuries of exploitation.

"The attribution of 'racial characteristics' with consequent exclusion of one group from another neither began with nor ended with Black people," explains Toni Morrison, an African American Nobel laureate in literature. "Cultural characteristics, physical features, religion and other belief systems have always been, and indeed continue to be, the focus when developing strategies for achieving domination and power." During both the American Indian Wars and slavery, racism prevailed among the White population in the United States, who excluded red-skinned people and black-skinned people from the human family. This resulted in a lot of suffering.[15]

CHAPTER 5

NORTH AMERICA IS NOT ENOUGH

After its Declaration of Independence in 1776, the young nation of the USA had conquered the entire area between Canada to the north and Mexico to the south in just a hundred years, driving out or killing the Indigenous people living there and taking large areas from Mexico. But this was not enough for the USA, and rich entrepreneurs and politicians sought to conquer even more territories. Their eyes fell on the archipelago of Hawai'i in the Pacific, the islands of Cuba and Puerto Rico in the Caribbean, and the archipelago of the Philippines off the coast of China. In 1823, with the so-called Monroe Doctrine, the US had forbidden Europeans to intervene in either North or South American affairs, while promising not to do so in Europe either. When the US realized that the European colonial power Spain, which then ruled Cuba and the Philippines, was showing weaknesses, Washington decided to oust the Spanish. "American factories produce more than the American people can make use of, American soil produces more than they can consume," declared Senator Albert Beveridge of Indiana in 1897. "Destiny has predetermined our policy. The commerce of the world must and will be ours."[1]

1898: The Explosion of the USS *Maine*

In 1895, when an uprising broke out among the local population in Cuba against the colonial power of Spain, which had exploited the country for centuries, the United States added fuel to the tensions by supplying the Cuban rebels with weapons. The White House wanted war, so the public was antagonized by war propaganda. Journalists William Hearst of the *New York Journal* and Joseph Pulitzer of the *New York World* led the smear campaign. Hearst sent cartoonist Frederic Remington to Havana. "Nothing to report. All quiet. There is no war here. Would like to return home," Remington telegraphed from Cuba, to which Hearst replied, "Please stay. Supply the pictures, I'll supply the war."[2]

The *New York Journal* and the *New York World* then told their readers invented and exaggerated stories about Spanish atrocities against the Cuban population to alarm the US population: "Blood in the streets, blood in the fields, blood on the doorsteps, blood, blood, blood! . . . Is there none so wise, so brave, to help this country infested with bloodlust?" the warmongers wrote. Hearst knew that in war propaganda, it is not crucial whether something is true or not. What matters is that it is constantly repeated and communicated to the population through many media outlets.[3]

The United States now needed only one dramatic incident, and it came promptly. On January 25, 1898, despite Spanish protests, the American warship USS *Maine* entered Havana Harbor and dropped anchor. To avoid being branded an aggressor, the US commander forbade his crew to go ashore and set foot on Cuban soil. Not everyone in the US thought it was a good idea to send a warship to Cuba, given the tense situation. Senator Mark Hanna, a Republican from Ohio, observed that sending the USS *Maine* to Havana was "like lighting a match in an oil well for fun."[4]

On the tropically hot night of February 15, 1898, with the thermometer reading over 100 degrees Fahrenheit, the USS *Maine* exploded at its anchorage in Havana, killing 266 US citizens, including 238 sailors and 28 marines. This was a shock to the US American population, causing anger and grief. Without any evidence to back his claim, the warmonger Hearst immediately blamed Spain for the attack, and on February 20, 1898, he published a drawing depicting the destroyed ship in the *New York Journal* under the headline "What the *USS Maine* Looks Like, Destroyed in Havana Harbor by Spanish Treachery." This was a complete lie, for Spain had nothing to do with the USS *Maine*'s explosion. Hearst, however, did not care about that. He knew that the human psyche is very receptive to explanations—especially in the days following a catastrophe—and stores them as true facts without further examination, so long as they sound plausible and are repeated often enough. Together with Joseph Pulitzer, Hearst developed the catchy battle cry "Remember the *Maine*—to hell with Spain." This chant was easy to remember because it rhymed, even by people who could not read a single word.[5]

In the month after the explosion, after newspapers had already blamed Spain, a team of experts from the US Navy found that a terrorist attack, in which a mine detonated under the ship, had been the cause of the explosion. The Spanish insisted they were innocent and did everything they could to avoid a war with the United States. A Spanish group of experts, who had not been allowed to inspect the ship on board, believed that the USS *Maine* had exploded from inside. A close examination of the destroyed ship would have revealed whether the blast holes were pointing outward or not and thus would clarify whether the explosion had occurred inside or outside the ship. In order to clarify this important question, the Spanish suggested that an impartial group of experts should investigate the cause of the explosion. But the US refused, saying it did not want an independent investigation.

At that time, newspapers were the most important medium for spreading war propaganda, as smartphones, the internet, and television did not exist yet. Most journalists could not afford to have their own opinion. They had to follow the paper's narrative (i.e., the political-ideological orientation of the newspaper owners), as US journalist John Swinton, writing for the *New York Tribune*, had explained a few years prior to the *Maine* explosion in a remarkably frank speech in New York on April 12, 1883: "There is no such a thing in America as an independent press, unless it is out in country towns. You are all slaves. You know it, and I know it. There is not one of you who dares to express an honest opinion. If you expressed it, you would know beforehand that it would never appear in print." Swinton was a member of the labor movement and made his speech to other journalists who were relatively poor like himself, not to the rich owners of the paper. "The man who would be so foolish as to write honest opinions would be out on the street hunting for another job. The business of a New York journalist is to distort the truth, to lie outright, to pervert, to vilify, to fawn at the feet of Mammon, and to sell his country and his race for his daily bread, or for what is about the same—his salary. You know this, and I know it; and what foolery to be toasting an 'Independent Press'! We are the tools and vassals of rich men behind the scenes. We are jumping-jacks. They pull the string and we dance. Our time, our talents, our lives, our possibilities, are all the property of other men. We are intellectual prostitutes."[6]

1898: The Conquest of Cuba and Puerto Rico

The fact that the newspapers had enraged the population and Congress through war propaganda was entirely in accordance with the Republican president William McKinley, who served in the White House from 1897 to 1901. Under the US Constitution, only Congress may declare war; on April 11, 1898, McKinley made a dramatic speech, asking Congress for permission to go to war against Spain. On April 19, the Senate and the House of Representatives jointly passed a resolution calling on Spain to withdraw from Cuba and authorizing President McKinley to use any military means necessary to secure Cuba's independence from Spain. As a result, Spain declared war on the United States on April 24, 1898. Warmonger William Hearst of the *New York Journal* self-satisfyingly asked, "How do you like the *Journal*'s war?"[7]

President McKinley certainly did not want to surrender Cuba to the Cuban rebels who were fighting for their independence from colonial Spain. Rather, he sought to replace Spain's domination in Cuba and on the Caribbean island of Puerto Rico with US domination. The "inalienable rights" set forth in the Declaration of Independence, including the right to life, liberty, and the pursuit of happiness, did not apply to the islanders' struggle for freedom. It was the first war fought by the United States outside of North America. President McKinley stated that it was "to the advantage of the American military to have the Army and Navy prove themselves in a real engagement."[8]

Beginning April 22, 1898, US warships blocked all Cuban ports, thus cutting off the Spanish from their supply routes. In June 1898, US troops landed in Cuba and fought the Spanish. In the naval battle of Santiago de Cuba on July 3, the Spanish lost their entire Atlantic fleet. Without supplies, the Spanish were lost on the Cuban island and they were defeated by the US Army. On July 25, US soldiers also landed on the island of Puerto Rico, which had been controlled by the Spanish. The US achieved a quick victory; after only three months and 550 casualties on the American side, the Spanish-American War was over. On December 10, 1898, Spain and the US signed a peace treaty in Paris, according to which Cuba and Puerto Rico formally became independent from Spain and fell under the sphere of influence of the United States. The old colonial power of Spain was humiliated and the mood in Madrid was downcast. Meanwhile in Washington, spirits were high and Secretary of State John Hay spoke of a "brilliant little war."[9]

After their liberation from the colonial power of Spain, the rebels in Cuba failed to take control of Cuban politics and the economy. After the Spanish left Cuba, US investors cooperated with a few individuals from Cuba's upper class to take control of the sugar plantations, mines, telephone network, and energy production. The US United Fruit Company secured 800,000 hectares of land for sugarcane cultivation. On March 2, 1901, Congress passed the so-called Platt Amendment, making Cuba a "protectorate" of the United States. The United States did not want to speak of a colony, even though this was exactly what it was. The Cubans were forced to give the US a piece of land on the southeast part of the island, where the US Navy built the infamous Guantanamo Bay Naval Base, which still exists today—against the will of the Cuban government.

The Jones-Shafroth Act of 1917 declared the island of Puerto Rico a "territory" of the United States, and it has remained so to this day. Once again, the USA did not want to speak of a colony. All Puerto Ricans were granted US citizenship and the dollar was introduced as the national currency. Contrary to US states like Alaska or Hawai'i, however, Puerto Rico is not a state and Puerto Ricans therefore have no voting rights in US presidential elections. In the House of Representatives in Washington, Puerto Rico is represented by one delegate, but that delegate does not have the right to vote. "Most people in this country, even the educated ones, know very little or nothing at all about our overseas possessions," said a US report from World War II. "In fact, most do not even know that we have such overseas possessions. They believe that only foreigners like the British have an 'empire'. Therefore, Americans are sometimes surprised to hear that we too, have an empire."[10]

After having already defeated the British, the United States beat its second major European power in Spain. But not all US Americans were pleased with this development. "Spain was the first, and for a long time the greatest imperial power in modern history," sociologist William Sumner, who taught at Yale University, explained after the short Spanish-American War. The US, he said, has always resisted imperial domination and championed freedom and self-determination. But the year 1898 was "a great turning point" in the history of the United States, Sumner correctly recognized, because it now became obvious that the US was also committed to expansion and imperialism and was invading foreign islands that were clearly not part of US territory.[11]

Sumner cautioned that in conquering Cuba, the US had adopted the same negative qualities of the Spanish imperialists. "We have beaten Spain in a military conflict, but we are submitting to be conquered by her in the field of ideas and policies," he warned. Anyone who studies the colonial histories of England, Spain, and France, he said, recognizes that these countries were "hated all over the globe." The United States would now make the same mistakes by occupying other countries and telling the people there how to live. "We assume that what we like and practice, and what we think better, must come as a welcome blessing to Spanish-Americans (i.e., Cubans) and Filipinos. This is grossly and obviously untrue. They hate our ways. They are hostile to our ideas. Our religion, language, institutions, and manners offend them. They like their own ways, and if we appear amongst them as rulers, there will be social discord in all the great departments of social interest." It was a shame, he said, that the United States had jettisoned the principles of equality and liberty set forth in the Declaration of Independence that had once guided it in its struggle against the British Empire.[12]

It was not until 1911, long after the US war against Spain that took place in Cuba and Puerto Rico had ended, that the USS *Maine* was raised and closely examined. The respected American industrialist Edward Atkinson concluded that the *Maine* had indeed been destroyed from within—as the Spanish had suspected—by a combination of gas and electricity. Spain had had nothing to do with the sinking of the *Maine* whatsoever. Just like the incident by the Rio Grande that had triggered the war with Mexico in 1846, the war against Spain in 1898 began with a lie.[13]

In 1976, an official investigation conducted by Admiral Hyman Rickover of the US Navy confirmed that the blast holes pointed outward and that the explosion had thus occurred inside the USS *Maine*. The only thing that remained unclear was what had caused the explosion inside the ship. At that time, ships were running on coal; according to Admiral Rickover, an undetected smoldering fire in the coal bunker might have triggered the disaster. The burning coal may have heated the steel bulkhead to the adjacent ammunition bunker to such an extent that the black powder stored therein was ignited and caused the shells that were also deposited there to explode.[14]

Admiral Rickover thus assumed an unfortunate accident inside the ship, which coincidentally occurred just as tensions between the US and Spain were at their highest point and war was imminent. That said, it is also conceivable that the fire in the coal bunker of the *Maine* was deliberately ignited with the intent of causing an explosion, for the warmongers in the USA knew that with the murder of 266 of their own sailors, the US population could be brought into revolt. It is impossible to prove such a thesis, though, and for many it is unthinkable that a government would kill its own soldiers to start a war. But anyone who has studied international politics for long enough knows never to rule out such criminal behavior on the part of top politicians and military leaders.

Historical sources that are available today prove that in 1962, US General Lyman Lemnitzer proposed a top secret plan called Operation Northwoods in Washington. This plan involved blowing up a US ship off the coast of Cuba to stage a war. "We could blow up a US ship in Guantanamo Bay and blame Cuba, and the casualty lists in the US newspapers would cause a useful wave of national indignation," said General Lemnitzer, chairman of the Joint Chiefs of Staff and thus the highest-ranking officer in the Pentagon. President John F. Kennedy, however, did not support this secret plan and therefore it was not carried out. Nonetheless, Operation Northwoods shows that a warmonger is always convinced that violence and lies are permitted in order to achieve victory. The principle of the human family, according to which all life is sacred, is completely foreign to a warmonger.[15]

1893: The Coup d'État in Hawai'i

The island paradise of Hawai'i is known for its white sandy beaches, emerald green seas, and coconut palms. It is located about 2,400 miles from the mainland of the USA. Washington, however, was focused not on the beautiful nature of Hawai'i, but on its strategic location. At the time, China was an interesting market for America, and Hawai'i was conveniently located on the shipping route between the US West Coast and China. Halfway across the Pacific Ocean, Hawai'i was a place for American merchant ships to stop off en route to their destination in Asia. Beginning in 1830, after missionaries and whalers had landed on the archipelago, US investors began to grow sugarcane in Hawai'i. The US and Hawai'i agreed to import Hawai'ian products duty-free, upon which the export of sugar to the US increased markedly.

For the Indigenous people of Hawai'i, the arrival of White people was a disaster because of the diseases they introduced. The Native population shrank from about 400,000 Hawai'ians before the arrival of White people to just under 60,000 by 1870. Many Hawai'ians lost their land and had to work on plantations owned by White masters. Among other immigrants who worked on the plantations for next to nothing were Chinese, Japanese, and Portuguese people. Queen Lili'uokalani, who ruled Hawai'i, watched this development with concern and tried to balance the interests of the Natives and the immigrants. "Liliuokalani is a symbolic figure for many Hawaiians. She was the first reigning queen, she fought for independence and the preservation of Hawaiian culture. She campaigned for more freedoms for girls and women, and she wrote more than 200 songs," reports the *Frankfurter Allgemeine Zeitung*. Lili'uokalani was the most popular monarch among Hawai'ians. In spite of her popularity among the people, she was overthrown by the United States.[16]

The US citizens living in Hawai'i, many of whom were wealthy sugarcane plantation owners, lobbied for the queen to be overthrown. With the support of US diplomat John Stevens, the US American plantation owners called upon the US military for help and on January 17, 1893, the coup occurred. The warship USS *Boston* landed in Honolulu and a small detachment of 162 US Marines marched through the city with their rifles and cannons. Queen Lili'uokalani, who watched the invaders, could have confronted the US soldiers with far more armed Hawai'ians, but refrained from a confrontation to avoid bloodshed. The queen knew that a violent incident would have provided an excuse for Washington to send even more soldiers.

The quiet conquest of Hawai'i did not go unnoticed. President Grover Cleveland of the Democratic Party, who had taken office after the coup d'état on March 4, 1893, condemned the coup in Hawai'i in his State of the Union address to both houses of Congress on December 18, 1893. The overthrow, he said, was wrong and a disgrace to the national honor of the United States. "The lawful Government of Hawai'i was overthrown without the drawing of a sword or the firing of a shot," President Cleveland said. "By an act of war, committed with the participation of a diplomatic representative of the United States and without the authority of Congress, the government of a feeble but friendly and confiding people has been overthrown." President Cleveland, who had been the governor of New York before moving into the White House, fired diplomat John Stevens, who had been involved in the coup. "A substantial wrong has thus been done," President Cleveland said, "which a due regard for our national character as well as the rights of the injured people requires we should endeavor to repair."[17]

But restoring the monarchy in Hawai'i was not what the men who had carried out the coup wanted. They declared Hawai'i a republic, and without having a democratic election, lawyer Sanford Dole became its first and only president. The coup plotters adopted a new constitution under which only a few of the Natives and none of the Asians were allowed to vote or hold office. In addition, anyone who wanted to vote had to take an oath, under which they agreed not to support the restoration of the monarchy. Supporters of the queen tried to save Hawai'i's independence and reinstate Queen Lili'uokalani, but their attempt to do so failed. The queen was arrested on January 16, 1895, tried for treason—by none other than the coup plotters themselves—and imprisoned at Iolani Palace in Honolulu.

James Dole, the cousin of coup leader Sanford Dole, founded the Hawaiian Pineapple Company in 1901. The company grew pineapples in Hawai'i, printed the name "Dole" on all pineapple cans and pineapple juice boxes in red letters, and exported them to the United States for high profits with much success. The Dole company still exists to this day and is one of the largest suppliers of bananas and pineapples that are grown and canned on plantations throughout Latin America, Thailand, the Philippines, and Hawai'i. There have been repeated accusations of the company exploiting plantation workers and using dangerous plant poisons.[18]

President Cleveland, who did not seek another term, was succeeded by Republican William McKinley on March 4, 1897. President McKinley was an imperialist, and after declaring war on colonial Spain, in addition to fighting in Cuba and Puerto Rico, the United States also fought in the Philippines, which is located on the other side of the Pacific. Therefore, Hawai'i became crucial as an American military base. "We need Hawaii, just as much as we needed California, and even more," McKinley exclaimed. "That is our manifest destiny." The president asserted with conviction that the United States had a divine mandate to expand in order to demonstrate the way of life of a free and godly society to the rest of the world.[19]

At the suggestion of President McKinley, Hawai'i was annexed by a joint declaration of the Senate and the House of Representatives on July 7, 1898. Thus, with the stroke of a pen, without a shot being fired, the US took over the island kingdom as a colony. The Hawai'ian flag over Queen Lili'uokalani's residence was lowered and the Star-Spangled Banner was raised. Coup leader Sanford Dole was appointed the first governor of the colony of Hawai'i, which was now formally a territory of the United States. The Hawai'ian language, hula, was replaced by English. The imperialist McKinley had thus supported the coup, while his predecessor, President Grover Cleveland, had still rejected it.

As was previously the case in Cuba, the US Navy established a military base in Hawai'i. Located on the island of Oahu, Pearl Harbor served as an important base in the ongoing war against the Philippines. During World War II, Pearl Harbor would rise to become the most famous US military base in the world after the Japanese attacked it, which deeply shocked the US population and led to the US entering into the war. It was not until 1959, after World War II, that Hawai'i was incorporated into the United States as the fiftieth state. The injustice done to the Kingdom of Hawai'i by the coup d'état and the annexation of the archipelago remained a taboo subject for a long time. It was not until November 23, 1993, that President Bill Clinton signed the Apology Resolution in which Congress offered "an apology to Native Hawaiians on behalf of the United States for the overthrow of the Kingdom of Hawaii" and "the deprivation of the rights of Native Hawaiians to self-determination."[20]

1898: The Conquest of the Philippines

Simultaneously with the wars in Cuba and Puerto Rico, the United States also attacked the weakened colonial power of Spain in the Philippine archipelago. It should be quite obvious that this war was not a case of US defense or a claim to territory near the border. Manila, the capital of the Philippines, is over 8,000 miles away from Washington. But for imperialist President William McKinley, no distance was too great. He sent Admiral George Dewey into battle, who within six hours succeeded in wiping out the entire Spanish Pacific fleet in the Bay of Manila on May 1, 1898, losing only a single sailor in the process. A US anti-imperialist thus aptly commented: "Dewey took Manila at the loss of one man and all our principles."[21]

The Philippine rebels, much like the Cuban rebels, mistakenly took the US as an ally at first, only later realizing that the US had no interest in freeing the territories occupied by Spain. The Treaty of Paris sealed the defeat of Spain on December 10, 1898, and neither the rebels from Cuba nor the rebels from the Philippines were allowed to participate in the peace negotiations, making it clear that neither their freedom nor their opinions had never been a concern. Spain had to cede Cuba and the Philippines to the United States, along with the island of Puerto Rico in the Caribbean and the island of Guam in the Pacific, both of which were former Spanish colonies. For the loss of territory, Spain received $20 million from the

US. Guam is still a US colony today. The inhabitants of Guam are second-class citizens and are not allowed to vote in US presidential elections; their delegate to the House of Representatives has no voting rights. The US military has taken possession of the island of Guam and operates the Andersen US Air Force Base without regard for the Indigenous people or the environment.[22]

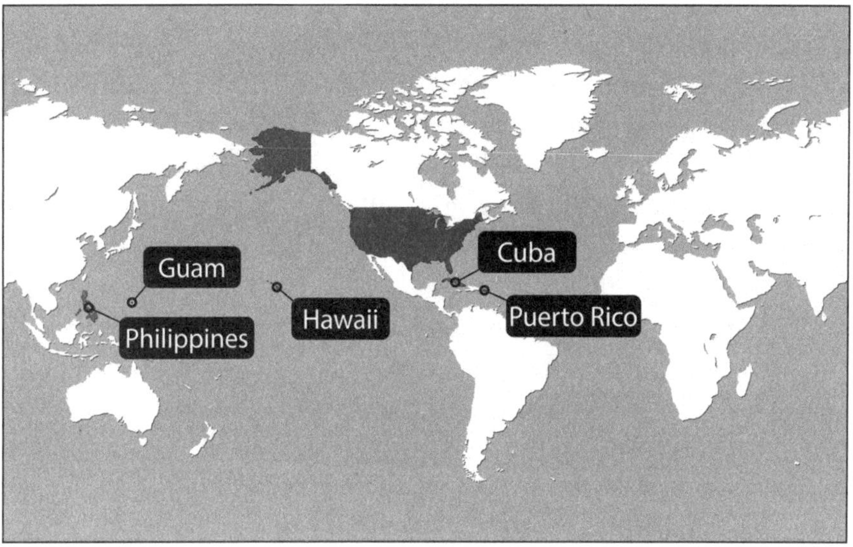

Figure 10. 1898: Hawai'i, Cuba, Puerto Rico, Guam, and the Philippines are conquered by the USA.

On July 15, 1898, while the wars with Cuba and the Philippines were ongoing, the American Anti-Imperialist League was founded in Boston, with US author Mark Twain among its members. They sharply criticized the war against the Philippines. "Nine months ago . . . Not one American in 500 could have told you what or where the Philippines were," protested Henry Van Dyke, a member of the Anti-Imperialist League. "How can we just abandon the principles our fathers fought and died for?" The peace activists recalled that the Declaration of Independence emphasized that governments derive "their just powers from the consent of the governed," but that this very principle was now being violated by the US in Cuba, Puerto Rico, Guam, and the Philippines. "When imperialism comes in at the door, democracy flies out at the window," Van Dyke warned. "An imperialistic democracy is an impossible hybrid; we might as well speak of an atheistic religion, or a white blackness."[23]

Despite its protests, the peace movement had no influence on the course of the war. Economic interests were stronger and US investors had no interest in giving up their Philippine colony. American corporations established pineapple plantations and other large monocultures on the island of Mindanao. The Filipinos, however, refused to submit. In February 1899, under their leader Emilio Aguinaldo, they rebelled, upon which President McKinley ordered the US Army to put down the rebellion and convert the Filipinos to Christianity. "Life, liberty, and the pursuit of happiness" did not apply to the Filipinos; White US Americans believed that Filipinos were inferior human beings. William Taft, Governor General of the Philippines, referred to the insurgents as "our little brown brothers."[24]

More than 70,000 US troops landed in the Philippines and ruthlessly targeted the Native population, viewing them not as members of the human family but as either underdeveloped humans or just simply as dogs. "Every one of us wanted to kill niggers," one US soldier wrote home. "Shooting people is worlds better than hunting rabbits." The extremely brutal Philippine-American War lasted from 1899 to 1902 and ended with the suppression of the Philippine independence movement. More than 20,000 Filipino rebels and 4,000 US troops were killed. In addition, 200,000 Filipino civilians also lost their lives, many of them to cholera.[25]

Newspaper readers in the United States learned very little about the atrocities committed by the US Army in the Philippines. In November 1901, the *Philadelphia Ledger* reported on the war this way: "The present war is no bloodless, opera bouffe engagement; our men have been relentless, have killed to exterminate men, women, children, prisoners and captives, active insurgents and suspected people from lads often up, the idea prevailing that the Filipino as such was little better than a dog . . . Our soldiers have pumped salt water into men to 'make them talk', and have taken prisoners people who held up their hands and peacefully surrendered, and an hour later, without an atom of evidence to show that they were even insurrectos, stood them on a bridge and shot them down one by one, to drop into the water below and float down, as examples to those who found their bullet-loaded corpses."[26]

William Jennings Bryan, who represented Nebraska in the House of Representatives and later served as secretary of state under President Woodrow Wilson, strongly opposed the brutal conquest of the Philippines. "If we have an imperial policy we must have a great standing army," Bryan declared. Before the war with Spain, the US had an army of only 25,000 soldiers, but President McKinley had increased the US Army to 100,000 soldiers. "The spirit which will justify the forcible annexation of the Philippine Islands will justify the seizure of other islands and the domination of other people," Bryan aptly predicted. "With wars of conquest we can expect a certain, if not rapid, growth of our military establishment." But this would fundamentally change the character of the United States. "Those who would have this nation enter upon a career of empire must consider not only the effect of imperialism on the Filipinos but they must also calculate its effects upon our own nation. We cannot repudiate the principle of self-government in the Philippines without weakening that principle here," Bryan wisely warned, but his warning was ignored.[27]

With the conquest of Cuba, Puerto Rico, the Philippines, Guam, and Hawai'i, the US became a colonial power. On September 6, 1901, at the height of his popularity, President McKinley was shot by an anarchist who cited US atrocities in the Philippines as the reason for the assassination attempt. The president succumbed to his injuries a few days later, and the assassin was executed by electric chair. As for the imperial course of the United States, it was not altered by the presidential assassination. With the ascension of Vice President Theodore Roosevelt to the presidency, an even more radical imperialist took the helm and continued McKinley's expansionist policies. "We will do our part in the mission of our God-protected race in civilizing the earth," said Republican Senator Albert Beveridge of Indiana. "Where will we find the buyers of our products? The Philippines gives us a base at the gateway to the East."[28]

Major General Smedley Butler's Warning

Among the US soldiers who were sent to the Philippines was Smedley Butler. He had already left school at the age of seventeen to join the marines. Private Butler first fought in Cuba, and was later sent to the Philippines as an officer in 1899 at the age of eighteen. In his first combat assignment there, he led 300 US soldiers to vanquish the rebels. He later fought for the US in China, Mexico, Haiti, and other countries, and he was awarded the Medal of Honor—the highest and most prestigious military decoration that may be awarded by the US government—twice during his military career. With the rank of major general, Butler retired from the marines in 1931.[29]

In 1935, after his retirement, Butler published a remarkable book in which he openly declared that war is "a racket" (i.e., organized crime) and that US wars have always served US economic interests and the superrich. Major General Butler was an insider, he was a whistleblower, and even though his analysis is more than eighty years old, nothing has changed to this day. "War is nothing but a dirty business," Butler warned. "A racket is best described, I believe, as something that is not what it seems to the majority of the people. Only a small 'inside' group knows what it is about. It is conducted for the benefit of the very few, at the expense of the very many. Out of war a few people make huge fortunes." Butler knew that investors in the US always want to make profits and that greed drives them. "The trouble with America is that when the dollar only earns 6 percent over here, then it gets restless and goes overseas to get 100 percent. Then the flag follows the dollar and the soldiers follow the flag."[30]

Wars are fought to protect investments and to realize the highest possible returns. Wars are fought to satisfy the greed of a small group. The soldiers themselves often pay for war with their lives or their mental health, as many soldiers are traumatized after killing others. "I wouldn't go to war again as I have done to protect some lousy investment of the bankers," Butler explained as a retired officer. "There isn't a trick in the racketeering bag that the military gang is blind to. It has its 'finger men' to point out enemies, its 'muscle men' to destroy enemies, its 'brain men' to plan war preparations, and a 'Big Boss'; Super-Nationalistic-Capitalism. It may seem odd for me, a military man, to adopt such a comparison. Truthfulness compels me to. I spent thirty three years and four months in active military service as a member of this country's most agile military force, the Marine Corps. I served in all commissioned ranks from Second Lieutenant to Major General. And during that period, I spent most of my time being a high class muscle man for Big Business, for Wall Street and for the Bankers. In short, I was a racketeer, a gangster for capitalism. I suspected I was just part of a racket at the time. Now I am sure of it."

Not every soldier in the world is convinced that he is serving the moneyed aristocracy. Many officers are fooled by fine and noble words like nation, freedom, or democracy. They rarely stop to consider who has a stake in the war they are fighting. Such was the case with Smedley Butler. "Like all the members of the military profession, I never had a thought of my own until I left the service," Butler recalls. "My mental faculties remained in suspended animation while I obeyed the orders of higher-ups. This is typical with everyone in the military service." Not only the principal, (i.e., the moneyed aristocracy afflicted with greed), but also the soldiers and officers must be without conscience and consciousness in their actions. For as soon as they discover their conscience, wake up and develop compassion for foreign people and cultures, and recognize them as members of the human family, they are lost to structures that demand blind obedience and the killing of fellow human beings.

In Europe, justified criticism of the United States' wars are sometimes dismissed by using a catchword like "anti-Americanism." This term, however, is imprecise and should be avoided, because America is a double continent that consists of North America and South America. When the US wages war against Nicaragua, it is a conflict within America. The term "anti-Americanism" cannot capture such a conflict because both the USA and Nicaragua belong to the Americas. US officers like General Butler knew that US imperialism raged ruthlessly in Latin America. "I helped purify Nicaragua for the international banking house of Brown Brothers in 1909–1912," Butler recalls. "I brought light to the Dominican Republic for American sugar interests in 1916. In China I helped to see to it that Standard Oil went its way unmolested. During those years, I had, as the boys in the back room would say, a swell racket. Looking back on it, I feel that I could have given Al Capone a few hints. The best he could do was to operate his racket in three districts. I operated on three continents."[31]

To put an end to the wars, Smedley Butler provided some recommendations and proposed that a law be passed, stipulating that the US Navy may only operate within 200 miles of the US coastline and must serve exclusively to defend the country. Additionally, he proposed that prior to any war, a vote should be held in the United States. According to this clever proposal, neither the president, nor the senators and representatives, nor the elderly and often already infirm chairmen of the banks, nor the owners of the large armament companies, nor the journalists, all of whom never go to war themselves, should be allowed to participate in that vote. "Only those who would be called upon to risk their lives for their country should have the privilege of voting to determine whether the nation should go to war," Butler insisted, plausibly predicting that if followed, his recommendations would quickly put an end to the wars.

Needless to say, his wise and prudent proposal was not implemented.[32]

CHAPTER 6

THE USA AND WORLD WAR I

If war is a racket, that is to say organized crime, as Smedley Butler aptly put it, then World War I is among the greatest crimes of the twentieth century. The United States repeatedly waged war against major European powers and defeated them. The United States never fought against all the European powers simultaneously, they always fought against individual nations while allying with other combatants. In the eighteenth century, the United States, supported by France, defeated the great European power of Great Britain on the North American mainland. Then they allied with the rebels in Cuba and the Philippines to defeat colonial power of Spain.

In World War I, the United States landed US troops on European soil for the first time. Had the British, the Germans, the Austrians, the Russians, the French, and the Turks fought against the US together, it would have been impossible for the US to win in Europe. But the Europeans had been at odds with each other for centuries, killing one another, thereby weakening each other among themselves. The US was well aware of the historical tensions in Europe and they won the First World War alongside Great Britain, France, and Russia, the so-called Triple Entente, over the European superpowers of Germany, Austria-Hungary, and Turkey, the so-called Central Powers of World War I.

1914: The Beginning of the First World War

The Great War, as World War I was referred to at the time, between the Triple Entente and the Central Powers lasted from 1914 to 1918 and cost the lives of about 20 million people. Together with the Second World War, the First World War is one of the greatest disasters in history, because it brought unspeakable suffering to so many people. Only a small group, the so-called "merchants of death," as they were fittingly called in the United States, made money from the war. The unifying idea of the human family was disregarded by all the powers involved during the Great War. Forty nations participated in the war. People were turned against each other along national borders, whereupon young men in different national uniforms shot each other. For the first time in the history of warfare, tanks and poisonous gas were used. The First World War was a cruel slaughter.

Historians continue to argue to this day about which country is to blame for the complicated outbreak of the Great War and about what set it off in the first place. The First World War was triggered by a political assassination: on June 28, 1914, the Austrian heir to the throne, Archduke Franz Ferdinand, and his wife were assassinated by a Serb of Bosnia and Herzegovina. The assassination took place in Sarajevo, the capital of the crown land of Bosnia and Herzegovina, which was then part of Austria-Hungary. The public was shocked and the so-called July Crisis ensued, which ultimately led to the war. Germany, under Emperor Frederick William II, immediately backed Austria-Hungary, which put pressure on Serbia and demanded Austrian participation in the investigation of the assassination. But the Serbian government, which was supported by Great Britain and encouraged by Russia's promise of military support in case of an armed conflict, refused to let Austria partake in the investigation. A month after the assassination, on July 28, 1914, Austria-Hungary declared war on Serbia. Russia, which had assured Serbia of its support, then assured itself of France's loyalty to the alliance and that France could count on the alliance of Great Britain, because since 1907, the three nations of Great Britain, France, and Russia had been allied in the Triple Entente. Thus, shortly after the assassination in Sarajevo, Serbia, Russia, France, and Great Britain on one side faced off against Austria-Hungary and Germany on the other side.

If Serbia had assured Austria-Hungary of full cooperation in the investigation of the murder of the Archduke and his wife, or if Austria-Hungary had exerted less pressure on Serbia, it might not have come to war. Furthermore, without the active involvement of Russia, the Triple Entente probably would not have been activated. Be that as it may, Russia, France, and Great Britain mobilized their troops. This was a shock for Berlin, which wanted to avoid war on two fronts at all costs. Therefore, on July 31, 1914, Germany issued an ultimatum to both Russia and France, demanding neutrality from France in the event of a German-Russian conflict and a halt to Russia's mobilization. But when Moscow did not respond, Germany declared war on Russia on August 1, 1914. And because France, which was backed by Great Britain, also refused to declare neutrality, Germany declared war on France on August 3, 1914. If France had remained neutral, the heavy battles between Germany and France that resulted in the loss of so many lives would probably never have occurred. Germany hoped for the neutrality of Great Britain. However, when German troops attacked France from the Northeast and violated the neutrality of Belgium on August 3, 1914, Great Britain declared war on Germany on August 4, 1914. Initially, the Ottoman Empire tried to stay out of the conflict by remaining neutral, but in November 1914, Great Britain, France, and Russia declared war on Turkey. This meant that all the major European powers were at war and Europe was in flames.

In his book *Germany's Aims in the First World War*, published in 1961, German historian Fritz Fischer, who taught at the University of Hamburg, argued that Germany was solely to blame for the outbreak of the First World War. Fischer believed that Berlin had urged Vienna to declare war on Serbia right away. "As Germany willed and coveted the Austro-Serbian war and, in her confidence in her military superiority, deliberately faced the risk of a conflict with Russia and France, her leaders must bear a substantial share of the historical responsibility for the outbreak of general war in 1914," Fischer wrote. "This responsibility is not diminished by the fact that at the last moment Germany tried to arrest the march of destiny, for her efforts to influence Vienna were due exclusively to the threat of British intervention and, even so, they were half-hearted, belated and immediately revoked."[1]

I do not share Fischer's assessment. In my view, the claim that Germany was solely to blame for the outbreak of the First World War was a lie that Great Britain, the United States, and France pushed through at Versailles, in order to weaken Germany in the long term and to eliminate it from the ongoing imperial race for overseas colonies. The July Crisis of 1914 cannot be attributed to just one country as the sole culprit. Certainly Germany is partly to blame for World War I, but no more so than the other countries involved, which also sought confrontation.

Based on his research published in 2012, Australian historian Christopher Clark, a professor at the University of Cambridge in England, has also concluded that there is no sole culpability on the part of Germany. Clark's book examines the July Crisis of 1914 and the complicated and opaque subsequent outbreak of the war in detail. "There is no smoking gun in this story; or, rather, there is one in the hands of every major character. Viewed in this light, the outbreak of war was a tragedy, not a crime." Clark believes that the European states, "the protagonists of 1914," were "sleepwalkers" that stumbled into World War I.[2]

Britons Gerry Docherty and Jim Macgregor came to yet a different conclusion in their investigation that was published in 2013, in which they stated that according to their view, Great Britain was responsible for the First World War. The British had sought to defeat Germany in military combat long before the start of the Great War. In 1891, at the suggestion of determined British imperialist Cecil Rhodes, influential British and US officials decided to strive for and permanently secure worldwide dominance of the two Anglo-Saxon powers and to oust the German colonies from Africa. Rhodes, a racist who had come into great wealth by means of dealing in the diamond business, saw the British as the "first race of the world" and thought nothing of the principle of the human family. The Anglo-Saxons viewed the growing economic strength of Germany with great unease. A secret elite of very wealthy and influential men in London and Washington then decided to lure Germany into war with the objective of weakening it permanently, by arranging the murder in Sarajevo. This plan was successfully implemented, but kept secret from historical research.

Whether Docherty and Macgregor's view of World War I is correct, I do not know, but it is interesting, and therefore it should be discussed.

According to my personal experience, however, this view of World War I is taught neither in schools nor at universities in Germany, Austria, or Switzerland. "The truth of how it all began and how it was unnecessarily and deliberately prolonged beyond 1915 has been successfully covered up for a century," Docherty and Macgregor write. "A carefully falsified history was created to conceal the fact that Britain, not Germany, was responsible for the war." Long before the Sarajevo murder, the course had been set by the British for war, he said. After the end of the war, "Britain, France, and the United States laid the blame squarely on Germany and took steps to remove, conceal or falsify documents and reports to justify such a verdict."[3]

The Merchants of Death Profit from the War

President Woodrow Wilson of the Democratic Party, who ruled in the White House from 1913 to 1921, watched the carnage in Europe from a safe distance and declared that he would not deploy US soldiers to intervene in the European war because the vast majority of the US population professed isolationism and strongly opposed interfering in World War I. Of the nearly 100 million people living in the United States at the time, more than a third had either been born in Europe or had parents that had been born there. The cultural ties between the US and Europe were strong and remain so today.

This does not mean, however, that the US maintained a neutral position throughout the First World War. Economically, the US clearly sided with Great Britain and France and supported the Triple Entente with loans, food, weapons, and chemical products. US exports increased threefold during the Great War. The US loans to the Triple Entente, totaling more than $4 billion, were strategically most important. In addition, US arms industry exports, including weapons and munitions, were highly lucrative. "Economically, the war was a blessing for America," the *Handelsblatt* wrote in 2014, a hundred years after the outbreak of the Great War. The trade in war supplies "turned the country into a world power. No other nation profited as much from the conflict."[4]

Indeed, victory in World War I was of utmost importance for the rise of the United States as a world power. "While Europeans were beating each other to death and ruining each other for comparatively insignificant patches of land, a nation that—by European standards—had no army at all rose to become a world power that outflanked all the other nations through peaceful trade," says German historian Jörg Friedrich, describing the role of the United States at the time. Without the steady stream of weapons and munitions from the US, Britain, France, and Russia would probably have been defeated by 1915, Friedrich believes. "After a quarter of a year, the United States was the material backbone for the Triple Entente, while the demand for war supplies was the economic backbone of the United States. Certainly the USA could have existed without the European war, albeit not as what they became as a result of it, but the war would hardly have continued without the United States. It would have collapsed by necessity. The United States formed the key power long before a single soldier had landed in Europe."[5]

The powers of the Triple Entente did not have sufficient funds to pay for the many war materials they imported from the United States. Therefore, influential US banks extended loans in the millions, thus keeping the war going in Europe. Initially, the US government had refused to allow American banks to lend to nations at war, arguing that this would undermine US neutrality. In September 1915, however, President Wilson suddenly had a change of heart and gave US banks a free pass to do as they pleased. That same month, J. P. Morgan issued a $500 million loan to Great Britain and France. More million-dollar loans from Wall Street to Great Britain and France would follow, and by 1917, the British War Office had borrowed $2.5 billion from J. P. Morgan and other US banks. After the war had ended, in 1919, Great Britain alone owed US banks the sum of $4.7 billion, which was staggering for that time. US banks had granted only $27 million in loans to Germany during the same period.[6]

The peace movement in the US was critical of these war deals and aptly described the individuals and companies involved as "merchants of death." Sixteen years after the end of World War I, in 1934, US Congress formed an investigative committee under the chairmanship of Senator Gerald Nye of North Dakota to shed more light on the reasons for the US's entry into the war in 1917, and the profits of the merchants of death. Senator Nye was a staunch opponent of US war operations in foreign countries. "When this Senate inquiry is completed, we shall know that war and preparation for war is not a matter of national honor and national defense, but a matter of profit for the few," Senator Nye wisely recognized.[7]

Since its merger with Chase Manhattan Bank in 2000, JPMorgan Chase has become the largest bank in the United States, measured by its total assets, and the third-largest company listed on a stock exchange in the world. Today, JPMorgan Chase is one of the biggest banks in the world. How this bank came to power and influence has largely been forgotten. The Nye Committee's investigation confirmed that the bank of J. P. Morgan, which is based in New York, played a central role in the financing of World War I. Among the 200 witnesses questioned by Senator Nye were US banker John Pierpont Morgan Jr. as well as US American arms dealer Pierre du Pont, both of whom were merchants of death. J. P. Morgan handled all US munitions sales to Great Britain during the First World War. In addition to that, J. P. Morgan headed the syndicate of US banks that supported the Triple Entente with billions of dollars in loans. According to the testimony of an employee of the US firearms manufacturer Colt, given to the investigating committee chaired by Senator Nye, the sale of arms during the war "brought out the ugliest side of human nature; including lies, deceit, hypocrisy, greed, and bribery, all of which played a central role in the transactions."[8]

The merchants of death were openly discussed in the United States at the time. "Let's examine the case of our friends, the du Ponts, who produce gunpowder," Major General Smedley Butler calculated after the war. How did their company fare during the war? Prior to the Great War, from 1910 to 1914, du Pont had made $6 million in profits per year, he said. "That wasn't much, but it was enough for the du Ponts to get by," Butler commented dryly. During the war, though, du Pont's annual profit rose to a staggering $58 million, he said. "Almost ten times as much as in a normal year," Butler explained. "Profits had increased by 950 percent!" That is why business owners, who weren't fighting in the trenches themselves, were interested in the war. US steel producer Bethlehem Steel also profited from World War I. Prior to the war, from 1910 to 1914, when the corporation was producing steel to build bridges and railroad tracks, its annual profits were $6 million. But then the company switched to producing war products and made a profit of $49 million every year during World War I, Major General Smedley Butler explained. Bank profits were also huge, but they were not publicly reported. In normal times, he said, a company in the US might reap 6, 10, or even 12 percent in profits. "But war-time profits—ah! That is another matter—twenty, sixty, one hundred, three hundred, and even eighteen hundred percent—the sky's the limit," Butler observed of the merchants of death.[9]

Because US banks such as J. P. Morgan had lent the British over $4 billion to finance their arms purchases, the US power elite certainly did not want Germany to be the victor of the Great War. Should the Germans have been victorious, the loans to the Triple Entente would have been a terrible investment. For the banks in the USA, repayment of these loans plus interest was crucial. Victory over Germany, however, was by no means a certainty. "In early March of 1917, upsetting reports were pouring into the Oval Office in Washington: Mutiny in the French army! In addition to that, the collapse of Russia was gradually becoming apparent, and Germany, with its submarines, seemed to be gaining control of the high seas. A German victory, which would have resulted in the total loss of the war bonds issued to the Triple Entente, had to be prevented by all means necessary, because a collapse of the J. P. Morgan empire would have meant an implosion of Wall Street," explains German historian Wolfgang Effenberger, who, in cooperation with Willy Wimmer, has published a comprehensive study on the First World War. It was not until the United States entered the war that the tables turned in favor of France and Great Britain, thereby securing their ability to repay the loans to the merchants of death.[10]

The Federal Reserve Act of 1913

President Woodrow Wilson was a loyal servant of the US banks throughout his presidency. In April 1913, prior to the outbreak of World War I, he sponsored a secret bill for a central banking law that greatly increased the power of banks in the United States. He did this at the urging of his advisor Edward Mandell House and influential US bankers such as J. P. Morgan and Paul Warburg. Largely unnoticed by the American public, this important bill was passed by the House of Representatives as the

Federal Reserve Act on December 22, 1913. The following day, the Senate also approved it. With Wilson's signature on December 23, the controversial Federal Reserve Act went into effect the day before Christmas Eve 1913. For the banks, it was a great triumph, but the US public took no notice of it.

It was no coincidence that the Federal Reserve Act was passed in a great hurry, right before Christmas, when most congressmen and the majority of the population had turned their attention to Christmas and the holidays with their families. In fact, not everyone voted on this extremely important bill, because some of the representatives and senators had already gone home for Christmas. The Federal Reserve Act gave US banks the power to create money privately. With this law, US Congress relinquished the prerogative to print money and entrusted this task to the US banks that had joined together in the Federal Reserve System (the Federal Reserve, or just the Fed) and had spent vast amounts of lobbyist funds for this law. This was nothing less than a revolution in US financial history.

To this day, the Federal Reserve Act allows the Fed to create money and lend it to the US government at interest. "When necessary, the Federal Reserve prints dollar bills like the company Hakle prints toilet paper," Walter Wittmann, who taught economics at the University of Fribourg, once commented dryly in Switzerland. In being able to raise or lower interest rates, the Fed controls the course of the economy. This enormous privilege of the Fed has been criticized over and over because the member banks of the Federal Reserve System and their owners are private companies that have gained enormous power through this privilege of being able to create money, thus controlling the money supply. Among the strongest critics of the Federal Reserve System and of Wall Street in the United States is Republican Ron Paul, who served as a representative for Texas in the US House of Representatives from 1976 to 2013. "We have to abolish the monopoly power of the Federal Reserve, because this power is not legitimate," he insisted, but he was unable to win a majority for this cause in Congress.[11]

1915: The Sinking of the *Lusitania*

During World War I, the German fleet was inferior to the British fleet. The British had naval bases all around the world and ran on oil, while the

German ships were powered by coal. Germany had only two bases at Kiel and Wilhelmshaven, plus a single overseas base at Kiautschou in northeast China. Even before the outbreak of the Great War, the British had carefully been planning the blockade of German ports. Once the war began in August 1914, the British navy immediately established its blockades, which thrust Germany into a famine that continued until June 1919, resulting in 700,000 deaths. With the blockade, Winston Churchill, the British First Lord of the Admiralty, sought the "economic strangulation" of Germany. It took Germany nearly six months to react, and they did so in February 1915 with the deployment of German submarines, which sank the British ships in an attempt to break the blockade.[12]

At the beginning of World War I, there were no tensions between Germany and the United States. However, the British wanted to draw the United States into the war against Germany. On May 7, 1915, a German submarine sank the British passenger ship *Lusitania* off the south coast of Ireland by firing a torpedo at it, killing 1,198 people, including 128 US citizens. This caused tensions between the United States and Germany to become serious for the first time. The *Lusitania*, one of the fastest Atlantic steamers, operated between Liverpool and New York, making the crossing in just four days.

What hardly anyone knew at the time was that the British used the passenger ship to secretly bring war supplies from the US to Great Britain. The explosive cargo was disguised as "hunting ammo." President Woodrow Wilson was informed of this fact by his Secret Service immediately after the sinking of the *Lusitania*. According to the cargo list, there were 1,248 boxes of 7.5-centimeter grenades, 4,927 boxes of rifle cartridges, and 2,000 boxes of small arms ammunition on the ship. But "Wilson was determined to cover up the truth," *Der Spiegel* reports. The loading list disappeared into a secret archive and "the transcripts of the testimonies of the surviving sailors and passengers were removed."[13]

Because the British wanted to bring Germany to its knees by setting up their naval blockades, the German government declared all waters around Great Britain a war zone in February 1915, where any enemy ship would be destroyed by German submarines without warning. Secretary of State William Jennings Bryan believed that US citizens should principally stay out of the war zone, because otherwise they would risk being killed. Germany had a right, Bryan said, to prevent war munitions from being supplied to its enemies. Four days before the fiasco, Bryan had advised President Wilson that the *Lusitania* was a disguised munitions carrier. Bryan asked the president to warn the US population, but Wilson refused.[14]

One of the warmongers in the United States was Texas-born US diplomat Edward Mandell House, who had supported Woodrow Wilson's presidential candidacy while he was still governor of New Jersey. House became President Wilson's closest confidant and foreign policy advisor, although he never held the office of secretary of state. House traveled to the capital cities of Europe during World War I and conferred with the decision makers. Before the incident with the *Lusitania*, the British foreign secretary asked House, "What will America do if the Germans sink a passenger ship carrying American tourists?" to which House replied, "That would get us into the war."[15]

But House was wrong. The US did not immediately enter the war after the sinking of the *Lusitania*, even though that had been the intention of Great Britain. British journalist Nicholas Tomalin, who produced a documentary on the subject for the BBC and ARD, argues that the *Lusitania* was deliberately steered in front of the torpedo tubes of German submarines by the British Admiralty under Winston Churchill in order to provoke the enemy into action and to get the United States involved in the war on the side of London. Gerd Schultze-Rhonhof, a major general in the German armed forces, also believed that the sinking of the *Lusitania* was "obviously a move by the First Lord of the British Admiralty to win over the American people to join England in the war."[16]

The German embassy in Washington was aware of the danger that the sinking of transatlantic steamers could draw the United States into the European war on the side of Great Britain. On April 23, 1915, the embassy therefore issued a warning in US newspaper ads, advising against the boarding of all transatlantic steamers: "Notice! Travelers intending to embark on the Atlantic voyage are reminded that a state of war exists between Germany and her allies and Great Britain and her allies; that the zone of war includes the waters adjacent to the British Isles; that, in accordance with formal notice given by the Imperial German Government, vessels flying the flag of Great Britain or of any of her allies are liable to their destruction in those waters and that travelers sailing in the war zone on ships of Great Britain or her allies do so at their own risk."[17]

President Wilson's closest advisor, House, correctly recognized that with the sinking of the *Lusitania*, hatred for Germany had increased and that the US's entry into the war was drawing nearer. On May 30, 1915, House noted in his diary: "I have decided that war with Germany is inevitable." In public, President Wilson continued to emphasize that the United States was neutral and would not send soldiers onto European soil. This won him voter support. In the US election campaign, Democrats campaigned for Wilson using the slogan "He has kept us out of war!" The people mistakenly saw President Wilson as a guarantee for peace. Thus, on November 7, 1916, Wilson secured his reelection and a second term in the White House.[18]

1917: The USA's Entry into the First World War

After his reelection, however, President Wilson immediately sought to enter the war so as to protect the investments of US banks. In order to change the minds and hearts of the isolationist American population and of Congress and win them over to the idea of sending US soldiers to mainland Europe for the first time, the president needed a sensational event. Once again, it was the British who played a key role. On January 19, 1917, a telegram arrived at the German embassy in Washington, which was then forwarded to the German embassy in Mexico. In it, German state secretary Arthur Zimmermann, the head of the Foreign Office, instructed the German ambassador to Mexico to form an alliance between Germany and Mexico in case the United States were to abandon its neutrality and intervene in the First World War. If that were to become a reality, the government of Mexico was promised support from Germany for the recovery of parts of the territory lost to the United States in 1848, when Mexico had to cede California, Nevada, Arizona, New Mexico, and Utah to the United States in the Treaty of Guadalupe Hidalgo. The Zimmermann telegram was top secret, encrypted, and intended only for internal communication among German diplomats.

However, it was intercepted and decrypted by British naval intelligence and passed on to President Wilson.

To stir up hatred toward Germany, President Wilson had the intercepted telegram published. On March 1, the Zimmermann telegram appeared in the *New York Times*. The US public was appalled. The American newspapers claimed that Germany had formed an alliance with Mexico and would try to seize the US states bordering Mexico. This, however, was not true; Germany had not yet entered into an alliance with Mexico. The telegram only asked the German ambassador in Mexico to consider such an alliance if the US abandoned its policy of neutrality and declared war on Germany. This information, however, was deliberately withheld from the US American newspaper readers.

The publication of the Zimmermann telegram and the simultaneous sinking of US American merchant ships by German submarines created a shift in public opinion that President Wilson immediately took advantage of. The president appeared in front of Congress on April 2, 1917 with the request that members of Congress declare war on Germany: "I advise that the Congress declare the recent course of the Imperial German Government to be in fact nothing less than war against the Government and people of the United States," Wilson declared in his speech. The president asserted that he was not seeking war, but that it was being forced upon the USA by Germany. "We enter this war only where we are clearly forced into it because there are no other means of defending our rights . . . It is a fearful thing to lead this great peaceful people into war . . . But the right is more precious than peace," Wilson said.[19]

While the majority of both the Senate and the House of Representatives agreed with President Wilson, there was opposition as well. In the House of Representatives, fifty congressmen voted against the war, including Jeannette Rankin of Montana, who was the first woman to be elected to Congress in US history. Six senators opposed the war too, including Republican Bob LaFollette of Wisconsin, who wisely called for an immediate referendum on peace or war, and he confidently predicted the people of the United States would oppose the war against Germany by a margin of 10 to 1. He had received 15,000 letters and telegrams from 44 different US states, LaFollette told the Senate, more than 90 percent of which did not want involvement in the war in Europe. The US media then defamed Senator LaFollette, labeling him an "agent of the German Kaiser." The referendum he demanded was not held, since people in the USA are never allowed to vote on the commencement of a war.[20]

On April 6, 1917, the United States declared war on Germany, and in December, they declared war on Austria-Hungary. In the same year, the military draft was introduced in the US for all men between the ages of eighteen and thirty. In July 1917, 14,000 US troops landed in France. This was the first time in its history that the US had deployed soldiers onto European soil. By the end of the war, it would amount to two million US soldiers. The French Parliament was delighted by the US entry into the war alongside the Entente and praised the decision as "the greatest act since the abolition of slavery." British prime minister Lloyd George also praised the US decision to go to war against Germany, saying that Germany was the "bloodiest enemy that has ever threatened liberty."[21]

The British and the US Americans knew exactly how to use war propaganda to direct the thoughts and emotions of their own population, and to stir up hatred against the enemy. British newspapers portrayed the Germans, Austrians, and Turks as violent brutes and thus excluded them from the human family. For example, on August 27, 1914, The *Times* of London quoted an eyewitness who claimed to have seen "German soldiers chop off the arms of a baby that was clinging to its mother's skirt." Five days later, the *Times* claimed: "They cut off the little boys' hands so that France should have no more soldiers."[22]

US War Propaganda against Germany

Germany was also systematically defamed in the United States. On April 14, 1917, just eight days after entering the Great War, President Wilson approved an annual budget of $5 million for the Committee on Public Information (CPI), which was responsible for US propaganda during World War I. Under the direction of journalist George Creel, the CPI funded hundreds of thousands of public speakers to make short speeches, along with writers, cartoonists, and journalists, who were all drumming up support for the war. German soldiers were drawn with horns protruding from their Satanic heads and defamed as "brutal and blood-thirsty beasts and vandals." The brutal CPI posters shocked the public, among which were depictions of a helpless mother from whose arms German soldiers were grabbing hold of a baby. The German emperor was portrayed as a criminal, and the Prussian pickelhaube (a spiked helmet) became the mark of the barbaric and dangerous German. Another CPI poster portrayed Germany as a savage gorilla with huge fangs and a pickelhaube, kidnapping a defenseless young virgin, accompanied by the call to "Destroy this mad brute!" and an invitation to enlist in the US military.[23]

Moving images were used in propaganda for the first time during World War I and they were even more popular among the public than caricatures. The CPI and the emerging Hollywood industry worked in close cooperation. Movies like *The Kaiser, the Beast of Berlin* played in US theaters millions of times. Another movie called *To Hell with the Kaiser* was so popular that in Massachusetts, the police had to stop people without tickets from storming the theater. Intense propaganda and constant repetition kept the population on course for war. US journalists who opposed the war were defamed. "Should a journalist report on the war critically, the CPI's response was not long in coming. He would be publicly smeared, accused of having poor character and labeled a traitor to the fatherland," reports German journalist Andreas Elter.[24]

Hatred toward Germany increased in the United States. German was canceled as a subject in schools, and institutes of German studies were closed at universities. German books were removed from public libraries or could no longer be borrowed. The hamburger was renamed the "liberty steak" and sauerkraut became "liberty cabbage." The anti-German witch hunt put massive pressure on Germans living in the US and on Americans with German roots. "German-born citizens were often tarred and feathered and chained up in public parks, where they had to shout 'To hell with the Kaiser' and kiss the US American flag," reports German historian Rolf Steininger, who taught at the University of Innsbruck. Even lynchings occurred during these tense times. In Illinois, the German-born Robert Prager was hanged as an alleged spy; the perpetrators were acquitted.[25]

With the passage of the Espionage Act on June 15, 1917, all pacifist speeches that could have counterbalanced propaganda were criminalized. The Espionage Act made it a "crime" to "convey information with the intent to interfere with the operation or success of the armed forces of the United States," that is to say, it was forbidden to make speeches that undermined the will to war. Therefore, the Espionage Act targeted not only spies, but also pacifists, and for that reason it is among the most repressive laws in US history. Any expression that can "cause insubordination, disloyalty, mutiny, or refusal of duty, in the military or naval forces of the United States . . . shall be punished by a fine of not more than $10,000 or imprisonment for not more than twenty years, or both." This was massive intimidation of the opponents of the war. The law was a significant restriction on freedom of speech and expression, and was in direct violation of the First Amendment of the US Constitution, which states: "Congress shall make no law . . . abridging the freedom of speech, or of the press."[26]

Not everyone abided by the new law, though. On June 16, 1918, the courageous US socialist Eugene Debs delivered a speech against World War I in Canton, Ohio, in which he said: "Wars throughout history have been waged for conquest and plunder." Debs went on to state that "The master class has always declared the wars; the subject class has always fought the battles." War is not in the interest of the working class, Debs told his audience. "The master class has had all to gain and nothing to lose, while the subject class has had nothing to gain and all to lose—especially their lives." Why then, he said, are the people who fight the wars not allowed to vote on whether a war shall be declared? "If war is right, let it be declared by the people. You—who have your lives to lose, you certainly above all others have the right to decide the momentous issue of war or peace," Debs exclaimed to applause, demanding a referendum, which did not occur.[27]

The US government was infuriated. Debs was indicted under the repressive Espionage Act and was ordered to appear before a judge. More than a hundred years later, whistleblowers Edward Snowden and Julian Assange were also charged under the Espionage Act, which severely restricts free speech. "Your Honor, years ago I recognized my kinship with all living beings, and I made up my mind that I was not one bit better than the meanest on earth," Debs, who represented himself in court, said in his defense. "I said then, and I say now, that while there is a lower class,

I am in it, and while there is a criminal element I am of it, and while there is a soul in prison, I am not free." The judge was not convinced. Debs, a peace activist, was sentenced to ten years in prison and began serving his sentence in the federal penitentiary in Atlanta, Georgia, in April 1919. He was released early in December 1921 after President Warren Harding pardoned him for the remainder of his prison term.[28]

In February 1917, when Russia was immersed in the Communist revolution and as the Eastern Front fell out against Germany, the Germans increased the pressure on Great Britain with their 145 submarines, successfully sinking British ships in the process of breaking the naval blockades. At the time, British Admiral John Jellicoe, commander of the Grand Fleet, told his US counterpart Admiral William Sims: "We cannot possibly keep fighting if the losses continue to be so high. The Germans will win the war if we can't put a stop to these losses—and we need to do so soon." It was not until the US entered the war that the tables turned. Industry in the US supported the Entente and the US began building ships faster than German submarines could sink them.[29]

The US entry into World War I was decisive. The US was victorious alongside the British and the French in the fight against Germany and Austria. Of the two million US soldiers who landed in France, over 116,000 fell. European casualties were even greater, surpassing those of all previous wars. Germany counted two million fallen soldiers, and Austria-Hungary lamented more than one million dead soldiers. All in all, nearly ten million soldiers and between eight and ten million civilians died in Europe, the latter often from disease or starvation, bringing the total death toll of World War I to nearly 20 million people.[30]

Reparations and the Treaty of Versailles of 1919

With the victory in World War I, the United States rose to become the new dominant power in the world. The merchants of death who had made obscene profits from the war were not convicted; nothing could be proven. World War I ended with the signing of the Treaty of Versailles in France on June 28, 1919. The famous War Guilt Clause placed the sole blame for the outbreak of the war on Germany, even though this was not true. Germany was compelled to pay some $33 billion in war reparations to the Entente.

Thomas Lamont, a top employee of the US bank J. P. Morgan, personally took part in the negotiations in Versailles and ensured that the German reparations payable to Great Britain and France would enable them to repay the gigantic sums they had borrowed from the merchants of death in the United States during the war. Germany also had to surrender all of its colonies and ten percent of its national territory, which meant that millions of German citizens suddenly found themselves outside the borders of their shrunken country.[31]

Germany felt that the draconian terms of the Treaty of Versailles were unjust, but could do nothing about it in the face of total military defeat. Without US intervention in World War I, "there would have been no Treaty of Versailles, no National Socialism (i.e., Nazism), no Hitler as Reich Chancellor, no World War II," Gerd Schultze-Rhonhof, a major general in the German armed forces, believes. When the German government refused to pay the high reparations, French troops occupied Düsseldorf and Duisburg on March 8, 1921. Whereupon Germany resumed paying the reparations, which flowed back to the United States via Paris and London. As Germany began to default on their reparations payments, French and Belgian troops occupied the Ruhr area again in 1923. A new payment schedule then allowed Germany to avoid a total collapse, as the shaky international financial architecture rested on German war reparations. President Wilson, however—one of the central players in World War I—had nothing more to do with the settlement of reparations. During a speech on September 19, 1921, he suffered a severe stroke and was paralyzed on one side of his body for the rest of his life.[32]

"Versailles became the great trauma of the Germans," explains German historian Eberhard Kolb, who taught at the University of Cologne. Both left-wing and right-wing parties rejected "peace by dictation," as they called it. "On no issue were the divided parties and political camps so united as in their condemnation of the peace treaty, with Article 231—the War Guilt Clause in particular stirring the minds and being rejected almost unanimously," Kolb said. Reparations payments were hated in Germany and strengthened the rise of Adolf Hitler's National Socialist German Workers' Party (NSDAP). When Hitler and the Nazis came to power, they refused the repayment of foreign debt.[33]

It was only after Germany was once again defeated by the USA in the Second World War that Berlin resumed paying reparations. In 2010, Germany paid "the last installment of its war debt," *Die Zeit* reported. On German Unity Day, the last €200 million was transferred. This marked the end of all reparations payments. The burden placed on the German Reich by the Treaty of Versailles was a "favoring factor for Hitler's seizure of power," *Die Zeit* explained to its readers. Historian Eberhard Kolb adds: "Those were enormous sums of money and contributions in kind that Germany made as 'reparations.'"[34]

CHAPTER 7

THE USA AND WORLD WAR II

With the Second World War, the United States of America, under President Franklin D. Roosevelt, finally rose to become the greatest power on earth. World War II, which began in 1939, is the greatest man-made catastrophe in the history of mankind. It ended in 1945 with the detonation of two nuclear bombs over the Japanese cities of Hiroshima and Nagasaki and was characterized by a high degree of brutality and ruthlessness. In the end, some 60 million people lost their lives, the majority of whom were civilians, as well as an undetermined number of seriously injured and traumatized casualties. Never before, and never since, has a war claimed so many victims. With 27 million people dead, 14 million of them civilians, the Soviet Union suffered the greatest losses. Germany counted more than six million dead, including one million civilians. The war was also a disaster for Poland, which lamented six million deaths, including more than five million dead civilians. Japan lost about four million people, including nearly two million civilians. The US counted 400,000 dead soldiers but virtually no dead civilians because the war was not fought in North America. World War II strengthened the peace movement and the postwar generation in their firm conviction that conflicts must be resolved without violence whenever possible, and that no one should be excluded from the human family.[1]

1933: The Reichstag Fire

How had the National Socialist German Workers' Party (NSDAP) succeeded in so skillfully diverting the population of poets and thinkers onto the path of their own demise? With lies and propaganda. The Reichstag fire played a decisive role in the Nazis' seizure of power. Four weeks after Adolf Hitler was appointed Reich Chancellor, on the night of February 27, 1933, there was a fire in the Reichstag, the seat of the German parliament in Berlin. Hitler reacted hysterically, crying out that the fire was a communist act and thus the beginning of a communist uprising. But this was a lie. There is every indication today that the Reichstag fire was a covert Nazi false flag operation. The Sturmabteilung (SA)—which literally translates to "Storm detachment"—was the Nazi Party's paramilitary wing and probably responsible for carrying out the attack. Reichstag president Hermann Göring, who resided in the Reichstag President's Palace, near the Reichstag, and Joseph Goebbels, Hitler's minister of propaganda, most likely had the fire lit by SA members and then blamed the crime on Marinus van der Lubbe, a mentally impaired communist from Holland. The SA members escaped through an underground tunnel connecting the Reichstag building and the President's Palace.[2]

After the fire, Reich Chancellor Hitler had communist workers, social democratic workers, intellectuals, and politicians persecuted and arrested. Left-wing newspapers were closed down. The right to free speech, the right of freedom of press, and the right to assembly were abolished. Why did the masses in Germany deliberately turn a blind eye as more and more neighbors just disappeared overnight? Because many gave in to Nazi propaganda. The same slogans were repeated over and over again, dividing the human family. Joseph Goebbels believed that "the people are usually much more primitive than we imagine. The essence of propaganda is therefore simplicity and constant repetition."[3]

Van der Lubbe was sentenced to death and executed, despite the fact that he was almost certainly innocent. "The theory that Marinus van der Lubbe set fire to the Reichstag all by himself is absolutely unarguable," said US historian Benjamin Hett, adding that the "evidence to the contrary is overwhelming." A single person could not possibly have set so many fires, he said. What is more, items used to set fires in the Reichstag were found that van der Lubbe did not even use—such as an incendiary torch that police discovered in the plenary hall. "The most likely version is that a small group of SA men, probably led by fire expert Hans Georg Gewehr of the SA, prepared and ignited the fire in the plenary hall without van der Lubbe knowing anything about it," explains Hett, who has investigated the Reichstag fire in detail. The Dutchman van der Lubbe had merely been a pawn.[4]

The Principle of the Human Family Is Betrayed

Reich Chancellor Adolf Hitler and all the leading Nazis declared the Germans to be the "Germanic master race." All others were labeled "subhumans" and excluded from the human family. Any empathy with the enemy was forbidden. "One principle must absolutely apply to the SS man: honestly, decently, faithfully and comradely we must be to members of our own blood and to no one else," insisted Heinrich Himmler, head of the Schutzstaffel (SS)—which translates to Protection Squadron—on October 4, 1943, at the SS Group Leaders' Day in Posen, Poland. "How the Russians are doing, how the Czechs are doing, is totally indifferent to me," Himmler said. "Whether the other nations live in prosperity or whether they die of hunger, that interests me only insofar as we need them as slaves for our own culture, otherwise it does not interest me. Whether or not 10,000 Russian women die of exhaustion during the digging of an anti-tank ditch interests me only insofar as the anti-tank ditch for Germany is completed." A deep and wide anti-tank ditch is dug for the purpose of preventing enemy tanks from advancing. "I wish that the SS face the problem of all foreign, non-Germanic peoples with this attitude, especially the Russians."[5]

Every division of the human family and devaluation of a select group erases compassion. The Nazis divided the human family into "good Germans" and "worthless subhumans." This racism was inhuman and deadly. The Jews were excluded from the human family by the Nazis and six million of them were killed in concentration camps. Additionally, thousands of mentally and physically disabled people were murdered by the Nazis. The splitting of the human family and the devaluing of a particular group is always the same. In North America, during the American

Indian Wars and the slave trade, the US had devalued Indigenous people as "barbaric savages" and Black people as "animals," thus excluding them from the human family. In World War II, the USA defamed the Japanese as "yellow apes" and dropped atomic bombs on them. However, the claim that certain races or ethnic groups are inherently superior or inferior to others is false. History shows that whenever the principle of the human family has been betrayed, great suffering has ensued.

The USA Supplies Adolf Hitler with Oil

Often the story of World War II is told in a way that portrays the US as an uninvolved spectator on the sidelines until the incident at Pearl Harbor, by which the Japanese dragged the US into the war against its will. But this is not true. The US had already influenced the war behind the scenes before it officially entered it by supplying Reich Chancellor Adolf Hitler with crude oil. This was decisive, for the Second World War was characterized by a high degree of mobility on land, at sea, and in the air. This mobility, as all the warring parties knew, could only be guaranteed by the influx of energy, primarily from oil. However, Germany and Italy did not have any significant sources of oil of their own and were therefore dependent on imports.

Italy, under Prime Minister Benito Mussolini, pursued an aggressive foreign policy and attacked Ethiopia on October 3, 1935. Nonetheless, Italy's oil tap was not turned off. The League of Nations, a collective peace-keeping system created after World War I, condemned Italy as an aggressor and imposed sanctions, but the cutoff of oil supply to Italy, which British Foreign Secretary Anthony Eden had demanded, was explicitly excluded from the sanctions. "If the League of Nations had followed Eden's advice and extended the economic sanctions to oil in the Ethiopia dispute," Mussolini later told Hitler, "I would have had to withdraw from Ethiopia within a week. That would have been an incredible disaster for me."[6]

Germany was also left high and dry. Adolf Hitler knew that the small oil wells on German soil yielded too little for a war of attack. In the so-called "Reich Drilling Program," Hitler had oil drilled throughout Germany, but only with very modest success. The Nazis therefore tried to produce crude oil from German coal, which was abundantly available in their own land. The chemical company IG Farben, headquartered in Frankfurt am Main, was the leading producer of substitute petroleum from coal. They had several production plants including one in Leuna, which is why the synthetic fuel from coal was known as "Leuna-Benzin." However, the conversion process was costly: approximately five tons of coal were required to produce one ton of gasoline. "The question of how high the production costs are for these raw materials is irrelevant," Adolf Hitler declared. German fuel had to become "a reality, even if sacrifices are necessary to achieve it."[7]

But on the eve of the Second World War, despite Leuna-Benzin and the Reich drilling program, Germany was far from being able to meet its fuel needs from domestically produced crude oil and refined coal. A country's crude oil consumption is measured in barrels, each of which contains 159 liters. Of the 100,000 barrels of oil per day that Germany needed in 1938, only 2,000 were produced synthetically from coal, while another 10,000 barrels could be obtained from Germany's own few oil sources. With these 12,000 barrels, Hitler was able to cover only twelve percent of his oil needs and was heavily dependent on imports of 88,000 barrels per day from abroad.[8]

US journalist Russell Freeburg, who served as a soldier in World War II and later wrote for the *Chicago Tribune*, and Robert Goralski, who also served as a US soldier in World War II and later worked as a journalist for *NBC News*, collaboratively investigated the oil trade during World War II. At the time, the USA was the world's largest producer of crude oil. At the beginning of the war, the US produced 3.5 million barrels per day, which was 60 percent of the world's total production. By 1945, the US had been able to increase its oil production to 4.7 million barrels per day. Those who fought with the USA in World War II had enough oil and won. Those who fought against the USA did not have enough oil and lost.[9]

Freeburg and Goralski proved that the USA was Adolf Hitler's most important oil supplier. Shortly before the war broke out, Germany had been acquiring 25,000 barrels of oil per day from the USA, as well as 10,000 barrels each from Romania and Mexico, plus some smaller quantities from Venezuela, Russia, Iran, and Peru. Hitler could not be certain that the USA, under President Franklin D. Roosevelt, would continue to supply

Germany with oil even after showing military aggression. A first stress test for German oil imports came on March 7, 1936, when Hitler occupied the demilitarized Rhineland. With this aggression, Hitler violated the Treaty of Locarno, in which France, Belgium, and Germany had agreed not to alter the western border drawn in the Treaty of Versailles—which Germany considered unjust—by force. Russia promptly stopped supplying oil to Germany after the occupation of the Rhineland. However, since the USA, Venezuela, and Romania continued to provide oil, Germany's supply remained secure.[10]

The next test came in the summer of 1936, when Hitler and Mussolini supported the military coup of fascist General Francisco Franco in Spain. Franco's Spanish coup plotters had overthrown Spain's democratically elected republican government in February 1936, but their aerial warfare capabilities were rather basic, so they asked Germany and Italy for help. Thus, in July 1936, the Germans and Italians started sending transport aircraft to Spain. As the Spanish Republicans, who were supported by the Soviet Union and volunteer socialist fighters from various other European countries, became more successful and had cornered General Franco and the coup plotters, Hitler dispatched the Condor Legion on October 30, 1936. Petroleum-powered German warplanes, including fighter jets and bombers, directly intervened in the Spanish Civil War, and the bombing of the Basque town of Guernica on April 26, 1937, became infamous. The massacre was captured in a painting by the famous Spanish painter Pablo Picasso as a symbol of the horrors of war. Operation Condor was top secret. The German pilots entered Spain as vacationers and operated in uniforms that did not give any indication of their origin. In Germany, the existence of the Condor Legion was denied until the outbreak of World War II. The support from Germany's air force is considered important for General Franco's victory in the Spanish Civil War. Nonetheless, the USA continued to supply Adolf Hitler with oil.[11]

Henry Ford Supplies the Wehrmacht with Military Vehicles

Not all influential people in the USA were hostile toward Adolf Hitler. American car manufacturer Henry Ford, who—like Hitler—was a steadfast anti-Semite, admired the Nazis. In August 1938, on his seventy-fifth birthday, he was therefore awarded the Grand Cross of the Order of the German Eagle, which is Nazi Germany's highest award for foreigners. Hitler had a portrait of Henry Ford hanging in his office. Ford supplied both sides during World War II. The Ford Motor Company was the third-largest supplier of armaments to the US Army. At the same time, Ford's factories also supplied masses of military vehicles to the German Wehrmacht (armed forces). "If the German industrialists who were tried at Nuremberg were guilty of crimes against humanity, so were their partners in the Ford family," explains British historian Antony Sutton. "But the Ford story was covered up by Washington, like everything else involving the Wall Street financial elite."[12]

Under Hitler, Germany was responsible for the outbreak of World War II, historical research has proven this beyond doubt. That said, the USA and Great Britain were not just uninvolved spectators. According to German philosopher Edgar Dahl, President Roosevelt had deliberately stoked tensions between Germany and Poland, which contributed to the outbreak of World War II. US-born political scientist Guido Preparata, who teaches at Kwantlen Polytechnic University in Vancouver, Canada, also believes that the British and the US Americans had an interest in the outbreak of World War II. "The victorious powers deliberately conjured Hitler in order to eliminate Germany as a potential threat to the geopolitical interests of the Anglo-American confederation once and for all," says Preparata, whose research findings are barely discussed in Germany. Hitler's "military aggressiveness" and "racist hostility toward Russians and Slavs" led Germany to its downfall. "It was an immeasurable triumph for the Anglo-Americans," Preparata said.[13]

Even after Germany's attack on Poland on September 1, 1939, and the subsequent commencement of World War II, Roosevelt surprisingly did not stop supplying Adolf Hitler with oil. After taking Poland, the Germans, who continued to be supplied with oil from the USA, landed in Norway in April 1940 and soon took control of the entire country. Denmark was also occupied by the Wehrmacht. In the spring and summer of 1940, Belgium, Holland, Luxembourg, and France all fell. Only Great Britain could not be defeated by Germany in the Battle of Britain, an air battle in the fall of 1940, whereupon Hitler postponed his planned invasion of the island. In 1941, Yugoslavia and Greece also fell. Within an astonishingly short period of time, Germany had occupied almost all of Europe with blitzkriegs (lightning warfare). The basis for Hitler's operations was oil, almost all of which Germany had to import.

1940: The Reelection of President Roosevelt

England was on the brink of defeat, threatened by the landing of German troops and suffering from the blows of German submarines, when in September 1940 President Franklin D. Roosevelt delivered fifty US warships to Great Britain. But arms supplies were not enough to guarantee the security of Britain. In the summer of 1941, the highest-ranking officer in the US Army, Chief of Staff General George Marshall, wrote to President Roosevelt: "Great Britain has reached the limits of her usable manpower. We must supplement her forces . . . Germany cannot be defeated solely by supplying arms to friendly nations or by air and naval operations. It will require strong land forces." Marshall called for US entry into the war alongside England and for US soldiers on European soil.[14]

President Roosevelt shared this opinion. The US population, by contrast, as well as Congress was strictly against it. President Roosevelt knew, though, that if the United States were to become involved in a war with Japan, it would probably trigger a domino effect that would lead to war with Germany, because Japan, Germany, and Italy had pledged mutual support in the Tripartite Pact on September 27, 1940. "In the first place, Roosevelt wanted to go to war against Germany," explains US journalist George Morgenstern of the *Chicago Tribune*, the leading isolationist newspaper in the United States of its time. "But when Hitler would not give him an excuse to declare war, he turned to the Pacific and Japan to enter the war in Europe through the back door. The Tripartite Pact would then ensure that he would ultimately get into war with all three partners if he started it with one."[15]

The public regarded President Roosevelt as a friend of the little man and a representative of peace, but this impression was erroneous. British historian Antony Sutton revealed that Roosevelt's rise was made possible by the superrich. According to Sutton, the wealthy du Pont and Rockefeller families had supported Roosevelt in the 1932 election campaign, which got him into the White House in 1933. Sutton's research concludes that nearly 80 percent of the money that Roosevelt required for his political campaign came from Wall Street. Roosevelt himself was well aware of his dependence on the superrich and also knew that they had been controlling politics from behind the scenes since President Andrew Jackson (1767–1845)—the seventh president of the United States—had held office. "The real truth of the matter is, as you and I know, that a financial element in the large centers has owned the government of the US since the days of Andrew Jackson," President Roosevelt wrote in a confidential letter to US diplomat Edward Mandell House in 1933. Of course, this statement was not made public.[16]

While the Second World War was raging in Europe and in Asia, President Roosevelt was reelected on November 5, 1940. Since he had already served two four-year terms since 1933, it was unclear whether he would run again. Never before had a president served more than two terms—after World War II this was even explicitly forbidden. In addition, the president suffered from polio; he was largely paralyzed from the waist down and therefore used a wheelchair. Many US Americans mistakenly believed that Roosevelt was the right man to keep the country out of the war. This was because Roosevelt had always told the people that he would not lead the US into war. On October 30, 1940, shortly before Election Day, Roosevelt gave a speech in Boston in which he promised: "I have said this before, but I shall say it again and again and again: Your boys are not going to be sent into any foreign wars." The people believed him and elected the Democrat to a third term with 54 percent of the vote. However, Roosevelt had deceived the people, as he was definitely not a man of peace.[17]

1941: The USA Halts Oil Deliveries to Japan

On Wikipedia, both the German and the English articles about the attack on Pearl Harbor state that this "surprise military strike" was completely unexpected for the USA. But this is not true. Not only did President Roosevelt and his closest associates know about the imminent attack, they had deliberately provoked it by halting all oil deliveries to Japan. This was indeed a conspiracy, that is to say, a collusion among two or more people. There have always been conspiracies throughout history. But on Wikipedia, in the entry on Pearl Harbor, this real conspiracy is dismissed as a "conspiracy theory" that is supposedly "rejected by the majority of historians for lack of serious evidence." Of course, historians have differing views on Pearl Harbor. Some of them, including Manfred Berg, who teaches at the University of Heidelberg, do indeed classify this event as a surprise attack. Others, however, do not. There has never been a poll among historians in all the countries around the world, nor has there been one in just the German- or English-speaking world, that would show what the majority thinks about Pearl Harbor. Wikipedia's assertion is without foundation. The *Neue Zürcher Zeitung* also misleads its readers: "The attack was a total surprise and caught the US Americans unprepared," it claims. But this is not correct. Only the US American people and the Congress were surprised. The president and the conspirators were not. As a matter of fact, President Roosevelt and his closest advisors had done everything to provoke Japan into firing the first shot at the USA.[18]

An incredible amount of effort is being put into deceiving the masses about the events concerning Pearl Harbor. The feature film *Pearl Harbor*, which was produced for $130 million and starred Ben Affleck and Kate Beckinsale, was released in the United States in 2001, and millions of people have seen it. The movie portrays the Japanese attack as a complete surprise. Readers of the newspaper *Rubikon* are better informed. "President Roosevelt knew of Japan's impending attack on Pearl Harbor, but concealed his knowledge from those affected," reads an article published in 2018. The *Rubikon* article goes on stating that "Roosevelt then used the outrage over the slaughter to tune a reluctant US population to supporting US participation in World War II."[19]

The facts clearly show that Roosevelt intentionally escalated tensions with Japan immediately after his reelection. The US Office of Naval Intelligence (ONI) knew the weaknesses of the Japanese. On October 7, 1940, ONI employee Arthur McCollum had presented a step-by-step plan, known as the "Eight Action Memo," on how to provoke Japan into attacking the United States. Roosevelt wanted Japan to commit the first overt act of war because the US population and Congress needed to be shocked in order to convince them of the need for war against Japan and Germany.[20]

The provocation plan in the McCollum memo, which was proposed by the ONI, suggested sending a "division of long range heavy cruisers" to Japan. Roosevelt followed the plan and in March and July 1941, he sent naval task forces across the Pacific into Japanese territorial waters, which was a clear violation of international law, with the objective of provoking the Japanese. The US warships, which did not fire any shots, suddenly and repeatedly appeared in the strait between the Japanese islands of Kyushu and Shikoku, the main operational area of the Imperial Japanese Navy. The provocations, however, were not enough to induce Japan to take aggressive action against the United States. The Japanese contented themselves with diplomatic protest and complained about the unauthorized intrusion of US warships into Japanese territorial waters.[21]

Another suggestion in the provocation plan was to "Keep the main strength of the US fleet now in the Pacific, in the vicinity of the Hawaiian Islands." The US's Pacific Fleet should be withdrawn from its bases on the US West Coast and moved far out into the Pacific, closer to Japan. Roosevelt implemented this proposal as well. Admiral James Richardson, the commander of the Pacific Fleet, thought this was a mistake and tried to change the president's mind. The admiral criticized the lack of dry docks and low ammunition and fuel supplies in Hawai'i. In addition, he said, troop morale declined when men were continually separated from their families. It would be much wiser to leave the fleet on the West Coast. President Roosevelt, however, insisted that the Pacific Fleet be moved to Hawai'i. Admiral Richardson gained the impression that Roosevelt was "fully determined to take the United States to war."[22]

The Hawai'ian archipelago is located far out in the Pacific Ocean. Honolulu, the capital of Hawai'i, is about 2,400 miles—or a five-hour flight—from San Francisco. From Tokyo to Hawai'i, it is about 4,000 miles, or an eight-hour flight. When Admiral Richardson was instructed to issue a press release stating that he himself had asked to have the fleet stationed in Hawai'i, he refused. "That would make a perfect fool of me," Richardson said. As a result, on February 1, 1941, President Roosevelt stripped him of the command of the Pacific Fleet and gave it to Admiral

Husband Kimmel. The latter was very pleased with the promotion and the four silver stars that shone on his white uniform. Discharged Admiral Richardson, on the other hand, was very disappointed. "The president packed my sea bag for me," he commented dryly.[23]

The US naval intelligence provocation plan also proposed cutting Japan off from any oil supply. In doing so, the US hit the Japanese at their weakest point, for Japan, like Germany and Italy, had little to no crude oil of its own. For the aggressive war that the Japanese were waging in Asia, they were 100 percent dependent on oil imports. Eighty percent of these came from the United States, the most important oil exporter at the time. The other 20 percent came from the Dutch colony of the Dutch East Indies—now Indonesia.[24]

The Japanese also imported raw materials from Manchuria—which today belongs to China and Russia—and built the South Manchurian Railway in the early twentieth century to bring the raw materials to Korea and ship them to Japan from there. In the so-called Mukden Incident, which happened on September 18, 1931, Japanese officers blew up their own railroad in Manchuria and blamed the act on China. This false flag operation was a devious stratagem of war. It served to sell the Japanese public on expanding their military into mainland China. Japanese troops then occupied Manchuria and proclaimed the Japanese colonial empire of Manchukuo. When the League of Nations protested, Japan withdrew from the League. At first, the Chinese failed to coordinate a resistance because their country was in the midst of the Chinese Civil War. But then China armed itself to drive the Japanese out of Manchuria again, upon which, on July 7, 1937, the Second Sino-Japanese War began.[25]

Despite the war of aggression that Japan had been waging against China since 1937, the USA had continued to supply oil to Tokyo and they had also supported Chiang Kai-shek in the Chinese Civil War. But then, in October 1940, the Dutch, under pressure from the US, halted all oil deliveries to the Japanese. Immediately, a Japanese delegation traveled to Indonesia. The furious Japanese accused the Dutch of being mere puppets of Washington and demanded assurances of further oil supplies. But the Dutch refused and ensured that Japan would no longer receive any oil from Indonesia.[26]

Soon thereafter, the US also reduced its oil exports to Japan, causing the Japanese to panic. In May 1941, all oil shipments from the US East Coast to Japan were banned, while shipments from the West Coast and the Gulf of Mexico were still permitted. But then, on July 25, 1941, a little more than four months before the incident in Pearl Harbor, Roosevelt completely shut down oil exports to Japan. From that point on, no one from the United States was permitted to supply crude oil to the Japanese. "There will never again be such an opportune time as at this moment, to cut off oil supplies to Japan," commented Harold Ickes, who managed the nation's energy reserves and was thus Roosevelt's coordinator for affairs related to oil.[27]

For Japan, the discontinued oil supply was a catastrophe. In August 1941, two Japanese oil tankers were anchored in the port of Los Angeles, empty and still waiting for oil that had been contractually promised but was never delivered. It wasn't until November that the two Japanese tankers weighed anchor and headed back across the Pacific without any cargo. "If there is no oil supply, battleships and other warships are nothing but scarecrows," protested a Japanese admiral. He was absolutely right, and so the stage for war was set. US missionary Stanley Jones, who acted as an unofficial mediator between the Japanese and the White House, saw through Roosevelt's unscrupulous game. "I am not sure that the highest officials in the executive branch of our government really wanted peace," Jones said. "The attitude of some of our officials seemed to be: through this oil embargo, we have got Japan by the throat and we are going to strangle it."[28]

In addition to the oil embargo, J. P. Morgan and other US banks froze all Japanese assets in the United States in July 1941. Furthermore, the US also imposed an embargo on the supply of iron and steel. "We cut off their access to their money, their fuel and their trade," explained Joseph Rocheforts, a US naval intelligence officer with ONI. "We tightened the screws more and more. They saw no other means than war to get out of this stranglehold." As an ONI radio intelligence officer, Rocheforts was acutely aware of the Japanese response, and after the Japanese raid on Pearl Harbor and the deaths of 2,403 US citizens, he commented: "It was a pretty cheap price to pay for the unanimity of the nation."[29]

The British, under Prime Minister Winston Churchill, welcomed the rising tensions between Washington and Tokyo. Churchill had repeatedly asked Roosevelt to defend British colonial possessions in Singapore against Japan. Churchill desperately wanted Washington's entry into the war against Germany because it was the only way to save the British Empire, at least in part. "Britain was obviously trying to drag us into the European war, as Mr. Churchill later publicly admitted," Stanley Jones correctly recognized.[30]

The Japanese prime minister, Prince Konoe Fumimaro, was greatly concerned by the discontinuation of American oil supplies and the threat of confrontation with the United States. He therefore immediately requested a summit meeting with President Roosevelt, but Roosevelt refused. The Japanese Army leaders were desperate. "At present, oil is the weak point of our national strength and fighting power," senior military officials told the Japanese emperor on September 6, 1941. "More and more time is passing and our ability to wage war is fading away; the Empire will soon become militarily powerless." Foreign Minister Teijiro Tojoda believed Japan was being encircled with an ever-tightening chain "forged under the leadership and participation of England and the United States. These two countries are behaving like a cunning dragon that is pretending to be asleep."[31]

After the Japanese Prime Minister Prince Konoe had failed with his peace initiative, the Konoe cabinet resigned on October 16, 1941, whereupon General Hideki Tojo and the radical military took over the government of Japan. General Tojo declared that there was only one solution left for Japan: the conquest of the Dutch East Indies in order to gain direct access to the local oil resources. Because Germany had occupied the colonial power of Holland in Europe, Japan believed that the Dutch colony, which was barely guarded, would be easy prey. However, the Japanese knew that the US would not just simply abandon Indonesia and the other colonial empires in Asia that were controlled by white men to the Japanese, especially not the Philippines, which was a US colony. Tokyo believed that the only thing that could stop the Japanese conquest program was the US Pacific Fleet and therefore decided to attack it before the Japanese ships ran out of oil.

The USA Surveils Japanese Radio Traffic

ONI had succeeded in intercepting and decrypting both the diplomatic and the military communications of the Japanese without the Japanese taking notice of it, as US journalist Robert Stinnett proves in his detailed study on Pearl Harbor. Japan was surrounded by US radio listening stations that were distributed throughout the Pacific. These radio reconnaissance stations were located in the Philippines, on the islands of Guam, Midway, Wake, and Hawai'i, and on the West Coast of North America in San Diego, San Francisco, and Alaska. This comprehensive surveillance system was supplemented by frequent exchanges with the British reconnaissance stations in Singapore, Hong Kong, and Vancouver Island in British Columbia, and the Dutch radio listening station in Batavia.[32]

The intercepted data was extremely valuable and was referred to as "Magic" within Naval Intelligence. Only the president and his closest advisors had access to the Magic information. The transcripts of the radio interceptions were placed in a leather briefcase at the Naval Office in Washington, which an ONI officer delivered to President Roosevelt at the White House every day. The president monitored the Japanese and shared the information only with his closest aides. "We know what they know, but they don't know that we know it," clarified Chief of Staff General George Marshall accurately.[33]

Only about thirty-five men and one woman in Washington had access to the Magic data. Only these conspirators knew about the imminent Japanese attack on the US in Pearl Harbor, but they did not share their knowledge with the US population or with Congress. They were all convinced that US entry into the war was right and important. In addition to Roosevelt, this tight circle of power included his cabinet, which consisted of men that he had selected himself: Secretary of War Henry Stimson, Secretary of the Navy Frank Knox, Secretary of State Cordell Hull, Chief of Staff George Marshall, Director of ONI Theodore Wilkinson and his closest aides, Chief of Military Intelligence General Sherman Miles, and the only woman, Agnes Meyer Driscoll, the highest-ranking civilian cryptanalyst of the US Navy in Washington.[34]

It was not until after the war that it was confirmed that the Japanese secret code had been cracked "many months before Pearl Harbor," and that the men in Washington who had access to the intercepted messages were "almost as well informed about Japan's plans and intentions as if they had sat on the war council in Tokyo," says US journalist George Morgenstern. To keep its secret concealed for as long as possible, the US Navy made all listening radio operators and cryptanalysts who had been involved in skimming and analyzing Japanese communications swear to secrecy. Any member of the navy who divulged anything about the successful work of US radio reconnaissance would be punished by imprisonment and loss of pension. This threat worked, as most of those involved took their secret to the grave.[35]

1941: The Japanese Attack on Pearl Harbor

In 1941, Japan had a powerful naval force with ten aircraft carriers, while the US naval force was still much weaker with only seven aircraft carriers. Two of their carriers, the USS *Lexington* and the USS *Enterprise*, were stationed at Pearl Harbor and were under the command of Admiral Kimmel. His superior, Admiral Harold Stark, who had access to the invaluable Magic data as the US Navy's chief of operations in Washington, wanted to protect these two aircraft carriers and ordered Admiral Kimmel to use them to transport fighter jets to the islands of Wake and Midway. The *Enterprise* departed Pearl Harbor on November 28, 1941, escorted by eleven of the newest warships in the Pacific Fleet. The *Lexington* departed Pearl Harbor on December 5, 1941, escorted by eight modern warships. After that, there were no more aircraft carriers left at Pearl Harbor, only old warships that were left over from World War I.[36]

On November 25, 1941, Isoroku Yamamoto, the commander in chief of the Imperial Japanese Navy, ordered his ships to leave the ports of Japan, sail across the North Pacific, and attack the American fleet in Hawai'i. The ONI succeeded in intercepting and decoding Yamamoto's encrypted order, which instructed the Japanese fleet to "advance into Hawaiian waters under the strictest secrecy of its movements and full vigilance against submarines and aircraft, and there attack the main force of the US fleet in Hawaii immediately after the commencement of hostilities and deal it a fatal blow."[37]

On December 7, 1941, Japan attacked the Philippines and occupied the US colony. On the same day, the Japanese also attacked Pearl Harbor with a huge fleet that consisted of six aircraft carriers and an escort of battleships, cruisers, and destroyers. The twenty-seven Japanese warships were accompanied by a fuel convoy consisting of seven tankers and thirty submarines. Just off the coast of Hawai'i, 351 Japanese military aircraft took off from the Japanese aircraft carriers and bombed the US naval base. Because the American warships were all moored to the shore in close vicinity to each other and most of the US aircraft were on the ground, they were an easy target. The Japanese killed 2,403 US Americans, destroyed 164 aircraft, and sank eighteen older US American ships.

Before the attack on Pearl Harbor, a clear majority of the US population had opposed going to war. But the Japanese attack completely changed the mood and generated anger and grief among the US population, since no other country had ever bombed the US before. No sooner had news of the Japanese attack made the rounds than young Americans volunteered at Army recruiting offices to defend their country en masse. The public was shocked, Congress was enraged, and the newspapers drummed up support for the war. "When the first news came that Japan had attacked us, my first emotion was one of relief," Secretary of War Henry Stimson, who had access to the Magic data, noted in his diary. "The indecision was over, and the crisis had come in a way that would unite all our people." Stimson, like President Roosevelt, wanted to go to war. The attack was a surprise to neither of them.[38]

The US Congress Declares War on Japan and Germany

The day after the Japanese attack, Roosevelt was furious in his address to Congress. Their approval was important because Article 1, Section 8 of the US Constitution states that "Congress shall have the right to declare war," which means that only Congress has the power to declare war, not Roosevelt himself. He could have spoken about the Japanese invasion of the Philippine colony and its occupation by Japan, since that was also ongoing, but he did not. Mentioning the Phillipines would have reminded people that the United States had also invaded foreign countries and held them as colonies. Instead, the president focused his speech on Hawai'i and declared that the date of December 7, 1941, would live on as "a day of infamy." Congress was convinced and both houses overwhelmingly passed the declaration of war on Japan. In the Senate, with its 100 members, there was no dissenting vote. In the House of Representatives, with its 435 seats, 388 of those present voted in favor of the war, while 41 abstained. Only women's rights and peace activist Jeannette Rankin, a Montana Republican, voted against the war. Supported by the House majority, President Roosevelt signed the declaration of war against Japan on December 8, 1941. Three days later, on December 11, Germany and Italy declared war on the United States. This immediate decision by Hitler was surprising, because according to the Tripartite Pact, there would have been an obligation to provide military support only in the event of a US attack on Japan.[39]

Congresswoman Rankin had already opposed the war against Germany in 1917. Even after Pearl Harbor, she refused to vote in favor of war, stating: "While I believed, with the other members of the House, that the stories which had come over the radio were probably true, still I believed that such a momentous vote—one which would mean peace or war for our country—should be based on more authentic evidence than the radio reports now at hand." Of course, she said, it is right and important to defend the United States. "But taking our army and navy across thousands of miles of ocean to fight and die certainly cannot come under the heading of protecting our shores . . . It is my belief that all the facts . . . should be given to the Congress and the American people." Yet that is exactly what did not happen. Congress was kept in the dark about the fact that the US government had intercepted and decrypted Japanese radio transmissions. Had this been known to Rankin and other congressmen, the vote would probably have been different.[40]

After her courageous vote, Jeannette Rankin was defamed and ridiculed on the radio and in the newspapers. Some called her a "whore," others referred to her as an "aide to Hitler" or an "old hag" as well as a "disgrace to the nation" and a "traitor." But friends came to her apartment and supported her during this difficult time. "I have nothing left but my integrity," Rankin told them. Some sent her letters, saying they admired her courage. "Probably a hundred men in Congress wanted to do what she did. But none had the courage to do it," the *Kansas Gazette* wrote. Her supporters knew that Jeannette Rankin's commitment was always to peace, civil rights, and the principle of the human family. In India, she had met with famous peace activist Mahatma Gandhi. But voting against the war ended her political career in the United States. Before Christmas 1942, when her term ended, she addressed Congress one more time, arguing that Roosevelt had deliberately left Japan no alternative but to attack the United States and that he had economically strangled Tokyo by blocking their oil supply. Roosevelt had wanted war, but Congress had always been against it until Pearl Harbor caused a complete change of heart and Roosevelt received his declaration of war. "What luck that man has!" remarked Jeannette Rankin, adding, "Was it luck?"[41]

Admiral Kimmel and Lieutenant General Short are Dismissed

President Roosevelt chose Admiral Husband Kimmel, commander in chief of the Pacific Fleet stationed in Hawai'i, and Lieutenant General Walter Short, commander of US Army forces stationed in Hawai'i, as scapegoats. After the attack, the president quickly ordered an investigation under Judge Owen Roberts, and ten days later, Kimmel and Short were found guilty of "dereliction of duty" and thus held mainly responsible for the defeat. Roosevelt relieved both of their commands and retired them, which was a humiliation.

It was not until later that Admiral Kimmel realized his own superiors in the Naval Office in Washington had deliberately concealed relevant information about the impending Japanese attack on Hawai'i. "It had something of a deliberate deception about it," Admiral Kimmel told the congressional committee investigating Pearl Harbor after the war. "I had asked for all the vital information. I had been assured that I would have it. I appeared to be receiving it. My current assessment of the situation was built on that basis. Yet, in fact, the most vital information from the intercepted Japanese messages was withheld from me." Secretary of the Navy Frank Knox had access to the Magic data, but did not share it with Admiral Kimmel. "This failure not only deprived me of essential facts," Admiral Kimmel said, "it misled me."[42]

Lieutenant General Short also realized, to his dismay, that his superiors in Washington had deliberately not relayed the very important information to him. The War Department under Chief of Staff General George Marshall in Washington knew that Japanese spies in Hawai'i had been reconnoitering the location of the US American warships. Marshall, who had access to the Magic data, should have informed Short, but he did not do so. "[The War Department] should certainly have let me know that the Japanese were getting reports of the exact location of the ships in Pearl Harbor," Short protested. The intercepted Japanese documents were "analyzed critically, really a bombing plan for Pearl Harbor," Short said. "The War Department was aware of the fact that I did not have this information, and it had already decided that I should not get it."[43]

Roosevelt's conspirators had not shared the Magic data with top US officers in Hawai'i, much less with US soldiers. "All this information was denied to General Short and me," Admiral Kimmel protested. "Had we been furnished this information as little as two or three hours before the attack, which was easily feasible and possible, much could have been done." The admiral explained that he would have sent the fleet into the open sea. Instead, it lay in the confined harbor at the mercy of Japanese bombers, torpedo planes, and submarines. Lieutenant General Short stated that with two hours' warning, he would have been able to get most of his planes in the air to intercept the attacking Japanese. But as it was, most of the planes were destroyed on the ground before they could even take off. "I cannot understand now—I have never understood, I may never understand—why I was deprived of the information available in the Navy Department in Washington," Admiral Kimmel stated disappointedly.[44]

It was only after their deaths that the US Senate rehabilitated the two commanders, passing a resolution on May 25, 1999, in which it was finally admitted that important information available in Washington had been withheld from Kimmel and Short. "Information gleaned from intercepted and decoded Japanese radio transmissions in late 1941 were not passed on to commanders in Hawai'i," the *New York Times* summarized, without mentioning that the entire history of the United States' entry into the Second World War must therefore be rewritten. Senator William Roth, Republican of Delaware, expressed regret that the two US officers had been deprived of important information "which had been available in Washington."[45]

The Ongoing Debate Over Pearl Harbor

To this day, many US Americans, as well as many Europeans, are unaware of the fact that Roosevelt was not surprised by the Japanese attack on Pearl Harbor and that he had even provoked it by imposing the oil embargo. "As a veteran of the Pacific War, I felt a sense of outrage as I uncovered secrets that had been hidden from Americans for more than fifty years," explained Robert Stinnett, who had himself served in the US Navy during World War II and later worked as a journalist for the *Oakland Tribune* in California after the war. After many long years of research, Stinnett published his detailed study on Pearl Harbor in 2000. In it, he convincingly documents that the devastating attack on the naval base in Pearl Harbor "was not a surprise to President Franklin Delano Roosevelt and many of his top military and policy advisors."[46]

George Morgenstern, associate editor of the *Chicago Tribune*, had come to the same conclusion as early as 1947, after evaluating the investigation of Pearl Harbor by the congressional committee that met from November 1945 to May 1946 and interviewed many relevant witnesses. Morgenstern said that for years after Pearl Harbor, "the story was carefully cultivated that the Japanese attack was a treacherous surprise, launched when there was no remotest reason for expecting it." The American people did not know that US Naval Intelligence had decrypted Japanese communications and had been relaying them to President Roosevelt daily. For many people, it is completely unthinkable for their government to have its own citizens killed by a political opponent in order to set the country up for war. But in the case of the Japanese attack on the Pacific Naval Station Pearl Harbor, that is exactly what happened. According to George Morgenstern, "They reckoned with cold detachment the risk of manipulating a delegated enemy into firing the first shot, and they forced 3,000 unsuspecting men at Pearl Harbor to accept that risk."[47]

Whenever there is a conspiracy—and that is the case with Pearl Harbor because Roosevelt and his closest associates deliberately withheld the Magic data—it is expected that, over the years, an insider will break their silence. And that is indeed what happened. Among the few people who were briefed before the Japanese attack was Don Smith, the director of war services for the Red Cross in Washington. Don Smith died in

1990 at age ninety-eight. In 1995, his daughter Helen Hamman stated that Roosevelt had secretly informed her father of the coming Japanese attack. "Shortly before the attack in 1941 President Roosevelt called Smith to the White House for a meeting concerning a top secret matter," Smith's daughter recalled. "At this meeting the President advised my father that his intelligence staff had informed him of a pending attack on Pearl Harbor, by the Japanese. He anticipated many casualties and much loss, he instructed my father to send workers and supplies to a holding area at a port of entry (P.O.E.) on the West Coast where they would await further orders to ship out, no destination was to be revealed. He left no doubt in my father's mind that none of the Naval and Military officials in Hawaii were to be informed and he was not to advise the Red Cross officers who were already stationed in the area. When he protested to the President, President Roosevelt told him that the American people would never agree to enter the war in Europe unless they were attacked within their own borders." Her father had obeyed the president's order and remained silent for a very long time, even though he thought the whole thing was morally wrong. It wasn't until the 1970s that he told his story to his children, "and it bothered him a great deal," his daughter said.[48]

The USA Drops Nuclear Bombs over Japan

Immediately after the attack on Pearl Harbor, war propaganda ensued, dividing the human family and stirring up hatred. The US soldiers called the Japanese "yellow monkeys," "half-men," and "rats." And the Japanese, for their part, raged against the US Americans, calling them "decadent devils." Due to this division and one-sided, biased reporting, all empathy was lost. US citizens with Japanese roots became victims of numerous assaults. In the states along the West Coast, where most US Americans of Japanese descent resided, the US government even resorted to relocation: beginning in March 1942, more than 100,000 US Americans with Japanese ancestry were moved from the West Coast to the interior, where they were confined to shanty towns far away from larger villages and guarded by the US military. It was not until the 1980s that Congress acknowledged that the internment of Japanese Americans was wrong and that at the time, racial prejudice, wartime hysteria, and failure of political leadership had done grave injustice to the internees.[49]

Japan was devastatingly hit by the USA in World War II. More than a million Japanese fell victim to the brutal aerial war that the United States waged against Japan under General Curtis LeMay. The US dropped napalm on Tokyo and other cities. Many Japanese civilians died in the flames. "The largest one-day act of terrorism in human history was March 9 and 10, 1945, when we burned Tokyo and killed between 80,000 and 120,000 people in one night," explains US peace activist Daniel Ellsberg, who has consistently spoken out boldly against the US's illegal wars. The dropping of atomic bombs on Hiroshima and Nagasaki were the second and third-largest terrorist attacks. In war, it is forbidden to kill civilians; it is a war crime. Soldiers are only allowed to shoot at other soldiers. But that distinction was ignored in the carnage of World War II on every battleground. "Curtis LeMay said that we all would have been tried as war criminals if we had lost the war. I think he was right," Robert McNamara, who served in the US Air Force during World War II and later rose to become US secretary of defense, said remorsefully. "He acted like a war criminal—just like I did."[50]

US journalists on the front lines did not criticize the burning of civilians because they did not consider themselves critical observers of the US military; they saw themselves as partners. "We were all part of the war effort. We came to terms with it. Not only that, we even consented to it," said US writer and later Nobel laureate John Steinbeck, who worked as a war correspondent during World War II. "That's not to say that the correspondents were liars, but we only ever covered parts of the whole story, and we firmly believed that this was the thing we had to do." Canadian war journalist Charles Lynch, who accompanied US troops in Europe, was even more self-critical: "What we wrote was absolute crap. We were a propaganda arm of our governments. At the start the censors enforced that, but by the end we were our own censors. We were cheerleaders." During World War II, there was no fundamental criticism of the narrative of Pearl Harbor, or of the war in general, as would later emerge during the Vietnam War.[51]

President Roosevelt's health suffered greatly from the stress of warfare. He had chronically high blood pressure, was frequently tired, and appeared greatly aged. At the end of his life, he felt a sharp pain in the back of his head and on April 12, 1945, he died of a cerebral hemorrhage at the age of sixty-three. When a US president dies in office, the vice president immediately comes into power. The ruthless new president, Harry Truman, like Roosevelt a Democrat, ordered the nuclear bombs to be dropped on the Japanese cities of Hiroshima and Nagasaki in August 1945. It was the first, and so far the only, time in human history that atom bombs killed thousands of civilians within seconds. President Truman later stated that the use of the atom bombs was necessary. But that was not true. "It is my opinion that the use of this barbarous weapon at Hiroshima and Nagasaki was of no material assistance in our war against Japan," Admiral William Leahy declared after the war. "The Japanese were already defeated and ready to surrender because of the effective sea blockade and the successful bombing with conventional weapons." After the war, the US established military bases on occupied Japanese islands that have remained in operation to this day, even though many Japanese oppose it.[52]

When a nuclear bomb detonates, it generates extremely high heat, which immediately destroys the human body. More than 140,000 people died in Hiroshima after the explosion, and another 70,000 in Nagasaki. President Truman is a war criminal because never before in human history had a single person killed so many other people so quickly. The survivors suffered great agony. Setsuko Thurlow was a thirteen-year-old girl when she survived the explosion of the atom bomb in Hiroshima. "When I speak about my experience of the atomic bombing of Hiroshima, often the first thing that comes to mind is an image of my four-year-old nephew Eiji—transformed into a charred, blackened and swollen child who kept asking in a faint voice for water, until he died in agony." Thurlow, a peace activist, has since campaigned for the global abolition of nuclear bombs, for which she and her fellow campaigners from the International Campaign to Abolish Nuclear Weapons were awarded the Nobel Peace Prize in 2017.[53]

The USA Does Not Open the Second Front until 1944

In terms of casualties, the battle between Germany and Russia claimed the most lives in World War II. After occupying Europe, the German

Wehrmacht had attacked the Soviet Union with three million soldiers on June 22, 1941, before the Japanese attack on Pearl Harbor, as part of Operation Barbarossa, reaching the outskirts of Moscow in late autumn. Adolf Hitler declared that Germany must conquer "living space in the East." Elites in the US and Great Britain were very pleased that Hitler was taking action against the Communists in Russia. "If we see that Germany is winning the war we ought to help Russia and if Russia is winning we ought to help Germany," Senator and future president Harry Truman of Missouri wrote in the *New York Times* on June 24, 1941, immediately after Operation Barbarossa had begun. "And that way let them kill as many as possible, although I certainly don't want Hitler to win in the end."[54]

German and Soviet soldiers fought fierce battles on the Eastern Front. After the US's entry into the war, the Soviet Union under General Secretary Josef Stalin repeatedly demanded that President Roosevelt and Prime Minister Churchill coordinate a landing in Western Europe and establish a second front in France, in order to force Adolf Hitler to withdraw parts of his forces from the Eastern Front, which would relieve the Soviet Union. In May 1942, Soviet Foreign Minister Vyacheslav Molotov traveled to Washington and London and personally delivered the Soviets' urgent requests. Roosevelt and Churchill assured him of the establishment of the Second Front, which would come to be known as the Western Front. Molotov stressed that it was important to establish this second front in France as soon as possible, because then Hitler could be defeated as early as 1942. Roosevelt assured him that "the American Government hopes for and is striving to establish the Second Front in 1942," but Churchill was against it. Thus, the entire year of 1942 passed without the promised Second Front being established.[55]

In July 1942, however, the British, under Lieutenant General Bernard Montgomery, were able to stop the German advance across North Africa, which was led by Field Marshal Erwin Rommel, at the border between Libya and Egypt by cutting off all fuel supplies. Rommel's tanks stood still after the British had sunk German fuel ships in the Mediterranean. "In targeting our fuel supply," Rommel said, "the British struck the part of our mechanism on which the functioning of everything else depended." Without crude oil, Germany was defeated in North Africa. "The bravest man is of no use without a cannon, the best cannon is of no use without plenty of ammunition, and the cannon and ammunition are of little use in a war of movement if they cannot be moved by vehicles with enough gasoline." To his wife, Rommel wrote: "Gasoline shortage! It is enough to make one cry."[56]

Roosevelt and Churchill could have stopped the supply of oil to the Eastern Front by bombing the German oil infrastructure, too, but they did not do so. Roosevelt also knew that Stalin felt betrayed because the British and the United States had failed to fulfill their promise to establish the Second Front in France in 1942. "The fact that the Soviet Union is bearing the brunt of the fighting and losses during the year 1942 is well understood by the United States," Roosevelt wrote to Stalin on August 19, 1942, "and I may state that we greatly admire the magnificent resistance which your country has exhibited. We are coming as quickly and as strongly to your assistance as we possibly can and I hope that you will believe me when I tell you this."[57]

The Soviet Union could not understand why Great Britain and the US did not establish the Second Front in France, because by doing so, the Second World War could have ended much sooner. "Today, as in the past, I see the main task in the quickest possible establishment of the Second Front in France," Stalin stressed on March 16, 1943, adding that a landing in Sicily or North Africa would not be a substitute because only a second front in France would force Hitler to withdraw a significant part of his troops from the Eastern Front. Stalin said that he hoped for the establishment of the Second Front in France by 1943 at the latest, but that the vague statements of the Western powers filled him "with grave concern."[58]

The year of 1943, however, also passed and the United States and Great Britain still had not opened a second front in France. Soviet soldiers perceived this as a serious breach of loyalty and realized that they had to either defeat the Germans by themselves or meet their own deaths. The battles were extremely brutal. Soviet diplomat Valentin Falin, who served as the Soviet Union's ambassador to Germany in the 1970s, explains that 10 million Third Reich soldiers and officers were either killed, wounded, or captured on the Eastern Front, which accounted for three-quarters of the Germans' entire losses. Thus, Falin makes it clear on which battlegrounds the Second World War was decided. It was the Soviet Union under Stalin that defeated Adolf Hitler, not the United States, which only intervened once Hitler was in retreat.[59]

If the US had opened a second front in France in 1942 or 1943, and if it had also turned off Hitler's oil tap completely, as it had done to Japan in 1941, World War II would have ended much sooner. But the US American company Standard Oil, founded by John D. Rockefeller, continued to supply Germany through its Spanish channels, even as the Germans attacked the Soviet Union. While the Germans only received a little oil from the United States, it was still enough to keep a part of its Wehrmacht mobile. According to Valentin Falin, in 1944 Germany was still receiving a daily average of 12,000 barrels of gasoline and other petroleum products from the US, delivered via Spain. Thus the reality is, Falin sums up, that throughout almost the entire war, about one-seventh to one-tenth of all German submarines, aircraft, and tanks that were used against the USSR, and later also against the USA, was powered by fuel that "came from Western pumps."[60]

The turning point came in February 1943, when the German soldiers surrendered at Stalingrad. From then on, Moscow launched their counteroffensive and Soviet soldiers pushed the Germans back. Both Churchill and Roosevelt realized that the Soviets could possibly occupy all of Germany by themselves, in which case Germany would then have entirely come under the control of Moscow. But Churchill and Roosevelt definitely did not want that to happen. Therefore, on June 6, 1944, as part of Operation Overlord, they finally opened the Second Front and landed in Normandy, France. At the same time, the British and the US Americans deployed their bombers in an effort to eliminate Germany's synthetic oil production. This was a devastating blow to the Third Reich and Germany was unable to counter this superior force. On April 30, 1945, Adolf Hitler ultimately committed suicide in the Führerbunker in Berlin. Germany then surrendered unconditionally on May 8, 1945, upon which it was, like Austria, occupied by troops from the victorious Allied powers of the United States, Great Britain, the Soviet Union, and France.

The four victorious powers assumed sovereignty over the German Reich and divided its territory into occupation zones. The former capital, Berlin, at that point located in the middle of the Soviet zone, was also divided into four sectors in which the supreme commanders of the four occupying powers established their headquarters.

Increasing tensions between the United States and the Soviet Union led to the division of Germany. From 1949 onward, Germany was split into two parts, where the West became the Federal Republic of Germany and was under the influence of Washington, and the East became the German Democratic Republic and was under the influence of Moscow. Only after the fall of the Berlin Wall and the end of the Cold War was this division overcome. Germany reunified in 1990.

With their defeat in World War II, Germany, Italy, and Japan left the circle of the great military powers. The Second World War also weakened the Western European states of France, the Netherlands, and Great Britain, so much so that they had to give up their colonial empires in the decades following the end of the war.

The United States, on the other hand, rose to become the most powerful nation in the world and has been the empire since 1945. After the surrender of Japan on September 2, 1945, US American troops occupied the main Japanese islands and established large military bases there. The USA also established large military bases in Germany and Italy, which still exist today, despite the fact that some of the population is opposed to it.

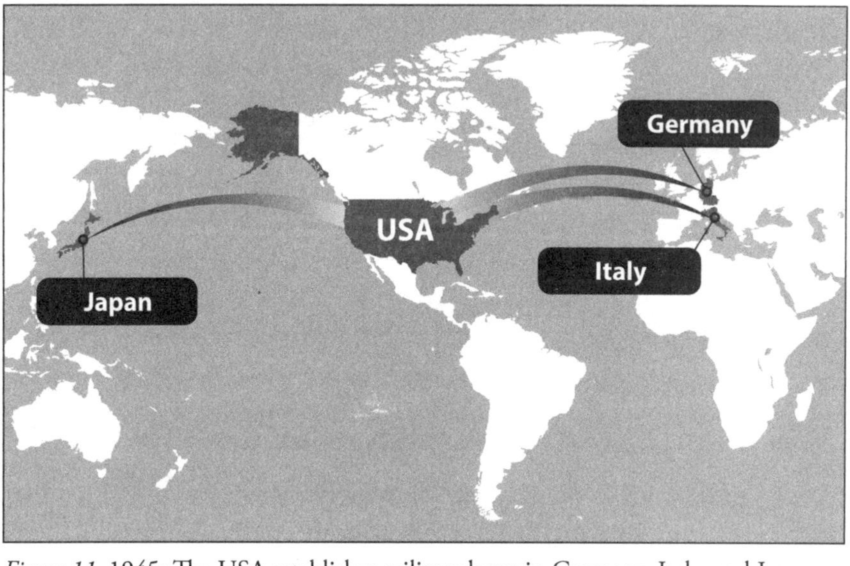

Figure 11. 1945: The USA establishes military bases in Germany, Italy, and Japan.

CHAPTER 8

COVERT WARFARE

After the Second World War, the UN ban on the use of force, which explicitly prohibits wars, was adopted. Since then, wars are permitted only in self-defense or with an explicit mandate from the UN Security Council and thus the consent of veto powers Russia, China, France, Great Britain, and the United States. However, the United States, as well as other nations, has not always abided by the UN's ban on the use of force. To hide its wars from the public, the United States relied on covert warfare. This includes acts of war against sovereign states in which the aggressor does not openly appear. For example, a foreign government is overthrown by US intelligence agencies or US Special Forces that cooperate with locally recruited mercenaries, without a declaration of war passed by Congress. At the same time, the US president and his senior officials that are in charge of covert operations publicly deny any involvement. This has created the culture of lies that now characterizes Washington. "In American politics today, the ability to lie convincingly has come to be considered an almost prima facie qualification for holding high office," US historian Eric Alterman aptly explains.[1]

1947: The USA Establishes the National Security Council

The most important political, legal, and moral outcome of World War II was not the surrender of Germany, Italy, or Japan but the founding of the United Nations at the San Francisco Conference on June 26, 1945, and the ban on the use of force that was adopted. For the first time in human history, war was prohibited as a means of international policy, with the exception of self-defense or with a mandate from the Security Council. Article 2(4) in the UN Charter clearly declares the prohibition of force: "All members shall refrain in their international relations from the threat or use of force against the territorial integrity or political independence of any state, or in any other manner inconsistent with the purposes of the United Nations." The UN ban on the use of force forms the core of international law today. Even though it has often been violated, it is one of the most important principles of the peace movement, next to the principles of the human family and mindfulness. Shortly after the San Francisco Conference, on December 10, 1948, the UN General Assembly adopted the Universal Declaration of Human Rights, which is based on the principle of the human family. Article 1 states: "All human beings are born free and equal in dignity and rights. They are endowed with reason and conscience and should act towards one another in a spirit of brotherhood."

President Harry Truman and his successor Dwight Eisenhower never thought of respecting the ban on the use of force. With its victory in World War II, the US had achieved global imperial supremacy, which it now wanted to secure and expand. "We have about 50 percent of the world's wealth, but only 6.3 percent of its population . . . we cannot fail to be the object of envy and resentment," US historian George Kennan declared in a sober analysis in 1948. "Our real task in the coming period is to devise a pattern of relationships which will permit us to maintain this position of disparity," he advised. "To do so, we will have to dispense with all sentimentality and daydreamings . . . We should cease to talk about vague and . . . unreal objectives such as human rights, the raising of the living standards, and democratization . . . We are going to have to deal in straight power concepts. The less we are then hampered by idealistic slogans, the better."[2]

On July 26, 1947, Congress passed the far-reaching National Security Act, which took US foreign policy to a whole other level and continues to shape it to this day. The War Department was renamed the Department of Defense, merged with the Department of the Navy, and housed in the newly built Pentagon in Arlington, Virginia, on the border of Washington.

The same law also created the CIA, the powerful US foreign intelligence agency, and gave it broad powers to conduct covert warfare. The CIA was given the mandate to "perform such other functions and duties related to intelligence affecting the national security as the President or the Director of National Intelligence may direct." This vague formulation gave the appearance of a solid legal basis while avoiding explicitly violating the US Constitution and the UN ban on violence. Clark Clifford, legal advisor to the White House, explained that covert warfare was not mentioned by name because we felt it would "harm our national interests to publicize the fact that we are engaged in such actions."[3]

The act also created the powerful National Security Council, the NSC, which is chaired by the president. The NSC generally meets in the Situation Room, located in the windowless basement of the White House. It is where the top officials of the executive branch are united. The NSC has repeatedly defied the ban on violence. The NSC's meeting minutes are kept secret; they are not made public. In addition to the president, the vice president, secretary of state, and secretary of defense attend NSC meetings, and as required, the CIA director, national security advisor, chief of staff, and other senior officials. The NSC shapes US foreign policy. "The council is the highest level of the policy establishment," explains US historian John Prados. Council members hold "the keys of power" and command the US Army and all US intelligence agencies.[4]

1948: The CIA Manipulates the Elections in Italy

With the creation of the CIA, the president had a new tool with which he could exert covert influence in any country of the world without the public knowing about it. "The CIA conducts covert operations on behalf of the president," Ralph McGehee said, explaining the main function of the new intelligence agency. McGehee, who served in the CIA for twenty-five years, emphasized that "most of the personnel, most of the money, and most of the energy" within the CIA was devoted to covert operations, not to gathering intelligence.[5]

Italy had the misfortune of being the first country ever to be attacked by the CIA in an undeclared secret war. The NSC commissioned the CIA to prevent Italian leftists from winning the first national election in Italy after World War II on April 16, 1948. President Harry Truman was very concerned because the Italian Communist Party, the PCI, and the Italian Socialist Party, the PSI—both of which had fought against fascist dictator Benito Mussolini and therefore enjoyed high prestige—had formed an electoral alliance for the Italian elections, the Fronte Democratico Popolare (FDP). Observers expected the FDP to win a majority in the Italian parliament, since it had already been victorious in local elections.

To prevent this from happening, the CIA created a new party and named it the Christian Democratic Party (Democrazia Cristiana Italiana, DCI), which was riddled with confederates, monarchists, and World War II fascists. The CIA pumped $10 million into the DCI while slinging fictitious mud at the Communists and Socialists. The CIA was successful. The DCI won 48 percent of the vote and 307 seats in the Italian parliament and was allowed to form the government, while the leftist FDP unexpectedly won only 13 percent of the vote and, as the loser, had to settle for only 200 seats in parliament. Thus the CIA had successfully excluded the Communists from the Italian government. The US Army expanded its military bases in occupied Italy, and under the DCI government, Italy joined the newly created military alliance NATO as a founding member on April 4, 1949.[6]

President Truman was delighted with the success in Italy. To expand the CIA's power and reach, the National Security Council passed Directive NSC 10/2 on June 18, 1948, which authorized the CIA to conduct covert operations worldwide. The NSC entrusted the CIA with "propaganda, economic warfare, preventive direct action, including sabotage, anti-sabotage, demolition and evacuation measures." In addition to that, the new law gave the CIA the mandate to arm syndicates in foreign countries, which remains the classic covert warfare operation to this day. The CIA was responsible for "subversion against hostile states, including assistance to underground resistance movements, guerrillas and refugee liberation groups," the new law decreed. All of these covert, top secret operations, NSC 10/2 emphasized, had to be "planned and executed that any US Government responsibility for them is not evident to unauthorized persons and that if uncovered the US Government can plausibly disclaim any responsibility for them."[7]

1953: The CIA Overthrows the Government in Iran

These texts were not just dry theory—they were actually implemented. In August 1953, by order of the NSC, the CIA and the British foreign intelligence service MI6 overthrew the democratically elected Iranian prime minister Mohammad Mossadegh. The prime minister had nationalized Iranian oil, which enraged the British, who viewed Iranian oil as their colonial possession. Mossadegh mistakenly believed that the United States was his ally in the fight against the British because the United States, too, had once freed itself from the British Empire. "We share with you a love of liberty," Mossadegh affirmed to Truman in Washington. "We have been less fortunate than you in wrestling our prized freedom from that country which in 1776 had to yield it to you."[8]

President Truman had not wanted an illegal coup in Tehran. But when President Dwight Eisenhower moved into the White House on January 20, 1953, things changed. The new president gave Allen Dulles, the ruthless head of the CIA, orders to overthrow the Iranian prime minister. Dulles authorized $1 million to be used for any action that would bring it about. The evening news in 1953 just reported on the unrest that had led to the government overthrow in Iran. The involvement of the CIA and of MI6 remained concealed from television viewers and newspaper readers. At CIA headquarters, however, they were better informed and delighted at hearing the news. "It was a day that should never have ended," as per the CIA. "For it was so full with excitement, fulfillment and jubilation that it is doubtful whether this will ever be possible again."

The overthrow of the Iranian government was a clear violation of the UN ban on violence and a tragedy for Iran. "The things we did were covert," Eisenhower later noted in his diary. "If they were made public, we would not only have been embarrassed . . . but our chances of doing anything similar in the future would almost entirely have vanished into thin air."[9]

1954: The CIA Overthrows the Government in Guatemala

In Guatemala, Jacobo Arbenz became president in January 1951 after winning a large majority in a democratic election. Arbenz, the son of a Swiss immigrant, was convinced that the lower class was being exploited in many countries around the world. In Guatemala, a rich upper class owned large estates, controlled the most powerful companies, and skimmed off huge profits for themselves, while the poor people owned no land and had to work for next to nothing, barely enough to feed the family or buy medicine in case of illness. Arbenz therefore carried out a land reform. He distributed large areas of land, much of it uncultivated, to some 100,000 landless peasants. This made him the archenemy of the large landowners and the powerful American United Fruit Company, which owned a lot of land in Guatemala. Arbenz offered the United Fruit Company only $525,000 as compensation for the land, the exact same amount that the company had declared as the value of the land for tax purposes. Today, the United Fruit Company is called Chiquita and is one of the largest banana producers in the world.

The CIA was not amused by Arbenz's land reform. CIA director Allen Dulles was a shareholder in the United Fruit Company and his brother, Secretary of State John Foster Dulles, also owned a large stake in the company. The Dulles brothers' New York law firm, Sullivan & Cromwell, was legal counsel to the United Fruit Company. This meant that the exact same men who sat on the NSC in Washington were also shareholders of the United Fruit Company. Thus, the NSC mandated the CIA to overthrow President Arbenz. General Robert Cutler, who was the chairman of the NSC and signed off on the covert operations, simultaneously sat on the board of directors of the United Fruit Company.[10]

The US's illegal war against Guatemala, which was a clear violation of the UN's ban on violence, began on June 18, 1954. Gangs that had been armed by the CIA invaded Guatemala from neighboring country Honduras, while planes bombed various ports, military installations, a school, the international airport, and numerous towns. On June 27, 1954, President Arbenz was forced to flee. Castillo Armas, the rebel leader who was paid by the CIA, declared himself the new president of Guatemala on September 1, 1954. Armas stopped the land reform, expropriations that had already taken place were declared invalid, and the United Fruit Company got all the land back. In addition to that, the new government banned the banana workers' union, and particularly active unionists were murdered. The Chiquita coup was successful, but was kept secret from the US population.[11]

1961: The CIA Assassinates Prime Minister Lumumba in Congo

The CIA operated on every continent and also influenced politics in the Democratic Republic of the Congo. Belgian King Leopold II declared the African country, about the size of western Europe, to be his private property in 1885. The capital was then named Leopoldville; later it was renamed Kinshasa, which remains its name to this day. Belgian, British, and US companies mined copper, cobalt, diamonds, gold, tin, manganese, and zinc in Congo, and exploited the land while brutally oppressing the local population. After World War II, however, resistance began to rise in Congo. "Our goal is the liberation of the Congo from the colonial regime, the absolute emancipation of the country," declared Patrice Lumumba, a missionary student who led the country to independence.[12]

After Congo gained independence from Belgium, the charismatic Lumumba became the first freely elected prime minister of the young African republic on June 30, 1960. During the celebration of independence, Belgium's King Baudouin praised colonial rule. Lumumba, though, disagreed and criticized the years of exploitation. "We have known grueling labor and had to do it for wages that did not allow us to stave off hunger, to clothe ourselves, or to live in decent conditions, or to raise our children as loved beings," Prime Minister Lumumba said. "We have known ridicule, insults, beatings dealt out incessantly morning, noon and night because we were Negroes . . . We will not forget the massacres in which so many perished, nor the cells in which those were thrown . . . who did not want to submit to a regime of oppression and exploitation."[13]

The United States and Belgium were worried and considered Prime Minister Lumumba a danger, not least because he also wanted to nationalize mining companies that operated in the Congo. To deprive the prime minister of control over the mineral resources, Washington and Brussels encouraged the secession of the resource-rich provinces of Katanga and Karzai by supporting the separatist forces there. President Eisenhower decided that Lumumba had to be overthrown. At an August meeting of the NSC in 1960, Eisenhower authorized his unscrupulous CIA director, Allen Dulles, to "eliminate" Lumumba. This was a blatant violation of the UN's ban on violence. Robert Johnson, who took minutes at the

NSC meeting, later recalled the shock that went through the room when President Eisenhower gave the assassination order. "There was a stunned silence for about fifteen seconds and the meeting continued." Johnson said that nothing about this lethal order was ambiguous. "I was surprised that I would ever hear a president say anything like that in my presence or the presence of a group of people. I was startled."[14]

Allen Dulles instructed Lawrence Devlin, the head of the CIA station in Congo, to initiate and coordinate the assassination of Lumumba together with the Belgians. On September 14, 1960, the army under Colonel Joseph Mobutu took power in a coup coordinated by the United States and Belgium. Prime Minister Lumumba was arrested by Mobutu's troops, tortured, and delivered to his archenemies, the secessionists in Katanga, where he was shot on January 17, 1961. To cover up the evidence, Lumumba's body was dissolved in battery acid. After the brutal murder of the courageous prime minister, the United States put Joseph Mobutu in place as the new president of the Democratic Republic of the Congo. Mobutu was a brutal dictator and ruled the country under the name "Zaire" for more than thirty years, guaranteeing European and American corporations advantageous conditions in the extraction of raw materials while hiding his money in bank accounts in Switzerland.[15]

1961: The Assassination of Trujillo in the Dominican Republic

Nowadays, the Dominican Republic in the Caribbean, with its white sand beaches, is a popular vacation destination for sun-seeking tourists from all over the world. But for three decades, the island's inhabitants suffered under dictator Rafael Trujillo, who came to power in a 1930 coup d'état that was supported by the United States. Trujillo ruled the country like a Chicago gangster boss for thirty-one years, murdering his opponents to stay in power. Nevertheless, Trujillo enjoyed support from the US because he staged himself as a defender against communism. President Franklin Roosevelt even received the tyrant in the White House. Roosevelt's Secretary of State Cordell Hull said, "He's a son of a bitch, but he's our son of a bitch!"[16]

But when Fidel Castro took power on the neighboring island of Cuba in 1959 and overthrew US-backed dictator Fulgencio Batista, Washington decided that Trujillo was no longer the right man to lead the Dominican Republic. On the evening of May 30, 1961, with support from the CIA, Dominican rebels gunned down Trujillo in his Chevrolet in San Cristobal. According to the investigation conducted by the US Senate, his killers were trained and armed by the CIA. Senators said, however, that it was not clear whether President Trujillo was killed with the weapons the CIA had supplied to the rebels. In 1962, the Dominican people elected writer Juan Bosch to be president. President Bosch strengthened the country through social reforms, but was overthrown by the CIA just seven months later because he sought greater independence from the United States.[17]

Quite often, the CIA is referred to as an "intelligence service," but that is misleading, for the impression that is then created in the media consumer's mind is that the CIA is primarily concerned with collecting and evaluating "news," and that the CIA does the same thing as journalists at a newspaper agency or students in a history seminar, which is a lot of reading and a lot of writing.

But that is false. Of course, the CIA does collect information about foreign governments and individuals and makes it available to the various branches of the US government. Far more important than the Analysis Division, however, is the CIA's division for covert operations, the Special Activities Center. This division has actively intervened in international politics repeatedly, organizing the overthrow of Mossadegh in Iran in 1953, the overthrow of Arbenz in Guatemala in 1954, and the assassinations of Lumumba in the Congo and Trujillo in the Dominican Republic in 1961.

Because the CIA carried out assassinations to achieve political objectives, the US foreign intelligence service is not fundamentally different from a terrorist organization such as the IRA or the RAF, which also used violence to achieve political goals. Noam Chomsky therefore refers to the United States as "the leading terrorist state." This statement is true and well founded. In November 1975, the US Senate published an explosive 350-page report and exposed the CIA's assassination efforts. At the time, it was a scandalous sensation. The report was written by an investigative commission of eleven senators chaired by the courageous Democratic

Senator Frank Church of Idaho. It was the most thorough and honest investigation into assassinations that the Senate had ever done. CIA agents subsequently traveled to Idaho and prevented Senator Frank Church from being reelected in 1980.[18]

"We believe that the public is entitled to know what instrumentalities of their Government have done," the Church Commission stated in its assassination report. "The Committee believes the truth about the assassination allegations should be told because democracy depends upon a well-informed electorate."

In the report, the senators expressed their "distaste for what we have seen," but that they still had faith in the USA. "The story is sad, but this country has the strength to hear the story and learn from it," the senators believed. "We must remain a people who confront our mistakes and resolve not to repeat them. If we do not, we will decline; but, if we do, our future will be worthy of the best of our past."[19]

1963: The Assassination of President Diem in Vietnam

The CIA's assassinations, the senators found, spanned the globe. In Vietnam, the US had divided the country after the defeat of colonial power France and secured the rule of corrupt President Ngo Dinh Diem in South Vietnam. But then the CIA changed tactics and supported a coup that overthrew Diem. Supporting coups is, of course, illegal. The Church Commission believed, however, that the killing of President Diem during the coup d'état on November 1, 1963, was probably a spontaneous action by the coup plotters. At least there is no evidence that the US purposefully planned Diem's murder, the senators said; the main objective of the action was the coup, not the murder.[20]

The Pentagon Papers also confirm that the US overthrew Diem. "For the military coup d'état against Ngo Dinh Diem, the US must accept its full share of responsibility," assert the Pentagon Papers, which used to be top secret. "Beginning in August of 1963, we variously authorized, sanctioned and encouraged the coup efforts of the Vietnamese generals and offered our full support for a successor government . . . We maintained clandestine contact with them throughout the planning and execution of the coup."

In addition to Ngo Dinh Diem, his brother Nhu was also killed during the coup d'état. "Whoever has the Americans as allies does not need enemies." Madame Nhu, his widow, sarcastically commented on her husband's death.[21]

1970: The Assassination of General Schneider in Chile

In Chile, Salvador Allende, a doctor and socialist, received the most votes during the presidential election on September 4, 1970. This did not please the US empire, so when Commander in Chief René Schneider of the Chilean army resisted US urges to stage a military coup, the CIA organized a commando unit that kidnapped and shot him on October 22, 1970. General Schneider succumbed to his injuries three days later. He was loyal to the Chilean constitution and acted as a shield for President Salvador Allende. The Church Commission revealed that the CIA had organized General Schneider's kidnapping and supplied weapons to the terrorists. However, there was no evidence that the United States sought the assassination of General Schneider or expected him to die after the CIA commando kidnapping, the US senators said.[22]

President Richard Nixon considered President Allende to be a danger. "Washington has always regarded democratic socialism as a greater threat than totalitarian communism," explains Canadian journalist Naomi Klein. Allende's example inspired many people in Latin America. Therefore, the CIA promoted the mistaken belief within Chile's military that Allende and his faithfuls were Russian spies. "In truth, the military itself was the real enemy, because it was willing to turn its weapons against the population it had sworn to protect," Klein said. After three years of sabotage and destabilization activities, Schneider's successor, General Augusto Pinochet, carried out the CIA coup on September 11, 1973, overthrowing President Allende. Of course, this coup was also illegal and a violation of both the Chilean constitution and the UN ban on violence.[23]

General Pinochet attacked the presidential palace La Moneda in the center of Santiago, Chile, with bombers and tanks, setting fire to parts of the building. Salvador Allende was in the building with his loyal adherents and chose to commit suicide to spare himself humiliation and torture at the hands of the coup plotters. Pinochet seized power and secretly had

Allende buried in the seaside resort of Vina del Mar. Dictator Pinochet was extremely brutal against the population and imprisoned 8,000 leftist dissidents and supporters of Allende. Many were tortured. Some were thrown from airplanes into the Pacific Ocean. Others were taken to bridges, shot, and thrown into the river. President Gerald Ford, who moved into the White House after Nixon resigned in 1974, declared that what the US was doing was "in the best interests of Chile, and certainly in our best interests." It was not until Chile returned to democracy in 1990 that Allende's remains were transferred to the capital, Santiago. "Allende is the most famous of at least 3,000 victims during the Pinochet dictatorship," commented *Die Zeit*. The CIA's coup d'état in Chile was a crime against humanity.[24]

1967: Che Guevara Is Shot in Bolivia

After the United States had conquered Cuba in 1898, local dictators, backed by Washington, ruled the island as an informal colony of the US, securing favorable terms for US American corporations and the military base at Guantanamo for the US Navy. But then, in 1959, Cuban Fidel Castro and Argentine doctor Ernesto "Che" Guevara worked together to overthrow US-backed dictator Fulgencio Batista, who had been plundering the island for years. This greatly angered Washington and so the two revolutionaries, Fidel Castro and Che Guevara, were targeted by the CIA.

In the 1960s, Guevara was the world's most prominent critic of the United States. As a twenty-five-year-old doctor, Guevara had witnessed the CIA's overthrow of Arbenz in Guatemala up close. He believed in revolutionary violence as a means of international politics and called for the "annihilation of imperialism by eliminating its most powerful base: the imperialist rule of the United States of North America." After the Cuban Revolution, Guevara served as Cuba's minister of industry, but he left the island in 1965 to organize a revolution in Bolivia.[25]

As commander in chief, President Lyndon Johnson ordered the US military and intelligence services to kill Che Guevara. In June 1967, the US sent sixteen men of the US Special Forces Green Berets to Bolivia as instructors. They formed the 2nd Ranger Battalion with selected Bolivian soldiers and together they captured Guevara. After a brief interrogation, the thirty-nine-year-old revolutionary was shot dead. On October 11, 1967, President Lyndon Johnson's national security advisor, Walt Rostow, informed him of the top secret operation: "CIA tells us that the latest information is that Guevara was taken alive. After a short interrogation to establish his identity, General Ovando—Chief of the Bolivian armed forces—ordered him shot." The CIA cut off Guevara's hands from his lifeless body and sent them to Washington to verify the revolutionary's identity.[26]

1961: The CIA's Assassination Attempts on Fidel Castro

The CIA attempted to assassinate Cuban president Fidel Castro several times, but without success. Senior CIA official Richard Bissell, who taught at the elite Yale University, joined the CIA in 1954. Richard Bissell was a stern thinker. As CIA Director Allen Dulles's right-hand man, Bissell was in charge of covert operations. It was Bissell who, at the beginning of 1961, had given CIA employee William Harvey the task of setting up an assassination division in the CIA, which internally ran under the inconspicuous name of "Executive Action." According to Dulles, the rude and potbellied Harvey had a "cop mentality" that could be put to good use in the assassination field. During internal CIA meetings, Harvey would excite his superiors by pulling out one of his many pistols, spinning the cylinder, and checking the ammunition as if he were about to fire.[27]

The CIA knew that Fidel Castro enjoyed smoking. The Church Commission revealed that in February 1961, the CIA had given an assassin cigars that had been infused with a potent poison that was supposed to be lethal upon contact with the mouth. However, the attack was unsuccessful. The CIA also asked the Mafia to kill Fidel Castro. In September 1960, at the CIA's request, former Federal Bureau of Investigation (FBI) agent and private investigator Robert Maheu met with John Rosselli in Beverly Hills. Rosselli was a gangster in the Mafia's Las Vegas milieu, and Maheu offered him $150,000 to assassinate Castro. When Rosselli signaled interest, he obtained poison vials and weapons from William Harvey to pass on to hitmen that the Mafia hired in Cuba. For many people today, it is still very hard to believe that the CIA was plotting assassinations with the Mafia like a terrorist organization, but the Church Commission has proven it to be true.[28]

With Rosselli's help, the CIA established contacts with mafiosi Salvatore Giancana and Santos Trafficante. The ruthless CIA did not care that Giancana was on the list of the ten most wanted criminals in the United States. The Mafia rejected the CIA's proposal to just simply gun down President Castro in a mobster attack. Giancana suggested slipping poison pills into Castro's drinks. Rosselli gave the poison pills, which had been provided by the CIA and successfully tested on monkeys, to an assassin in Cuba in 1961, along with several thousand dollars. This assassination attempt also failed. A year later, the US provided poison pills, explosives, detonators, rifles, pistols, radios and marine radars to hired assassins. These assassination plans did not lead to President Castro's death, either.[29]

The Cubans were not unaware of the CIA's many assassination attempts on their president. On October 10, 1961, Cuba informed the UN that the United States was plotting to assassinate Castro and his brother Raul. Cuba stated that this was an unconscionable violation of the UN's ban on violence. The US ambassador to the UN, Adlai Stevenson, stated that this "repugnant accusation" was completely "ridiculous" and that the United States, "despite the little affection it had for Fidel Castro and his followers, rejected assassination as a means of achieving its political goals." This was not true, but it is unclear whether Ambassador Stevenson knew about the CIA's assassinations, which at the time were top secret.[30]

Fidel Castro was an avid diver. In early 1963, the CIA planned to place an exotic shell that would explode on contact in an area where Castro often went diving. However, the plan was deemed unfeasible and was therefore abandoned. Later, the CIA prepared a diving suit that they laced with a drug that would produce a chronic skin disease and a breathing apparatus poisoned with tubercle bacilli to be given to Castro as a gift. However, Castro received normal scuba diving equipment from another source, and the deadly CIA gift never left the lab.[31]

When mobster John Rosselli was called to testify before senators on the subject of assassinations, he openly stated that he had known all along that the assassination attempts on Fidel Castro had been funded by the CIA. Shortly thereafter, John Rosselli's remains, which were chopped up and cut into pieces, were found floating in an oil barrel in Dumfoundling

Bay in Florida. The US Department of Justice claimed it was an organized crime murder, and the CIA concurred.[32]

CIA Director Allen Dulles Directs the Killers

As it is Congress's job to oversee the executive branch of the US government, the senators, led by Frank Church, wanted to find out who in the White House and in the CIA had given the orders for the many assassinations. At the lowest level in the CIA, William Harvey was responsible for these "executive actions." Above him, the deputy director of plans, Richard Bissell, and his successor, Richard Helms, had authorized the assassination attempts on Fidel Castro. This the senators could establish beyond doubt. Within the CIA, the deputy director of plans is responsible for covert operations. The senators were also able to prove that CIA director Allen Dulles had coordinated the assassination attempts as a gray eminence, like a Mafia godfather behind the scenes. Dulles had died by the time of the investigation, so the senators could not question him directly. Richard Bissell, on the other hand, was still alive and confirmed before the Church Commission that Dulles had been aware of and had authorized the assassination attempts on Fidel Castro. Dulles had also been informed about the cooperation with the Mafia. He had never actually approved it in writing, "only with a nod," according to Bissell.[33]

By contrast, Dulles's successor, John McCone, who was appointed by President Kennedy, told the senators that he had not known about all of these assassinations. He claimed that he had not discussed them with Dulles, and that he had never authorized any assassinations. The high-ranking CIA employees who were involved in the assassinations, Richard Helms and Richard Bissell, confirmed that after Dulles was dismissed, they did not inform his successor McCone about the assassinations, even though these top secret operations continued.[34]

The CIA is an instrument of the US government and, like the Pentagon, reports to the president. However, no president of the United States ever signed a written assassination order on Che Guevara, Lumumba, or Castro, so as to be able to credibly deny such illegal operations if they were ever to be discovered. Because the subject was too sensitive, much of it was only agreed on verbally. According to Richard Bissell, even the word "assassination" was avoided. The presidents were kept in the loop by using vague and cryptic expressions like "make Castro disappear," "remove Castro," or "take Castro out."

"It is difficult to tell at what level the assassinations were known and authorized," the senators fretted. The method of credible denial protected both high-ranking officials and presidents from prosecution and other negative consequences by never communicating with their subordinates about particularly sensitive and illegal operations in writing, but always orally. When Senator Church wanted to know why CIA employees had talked about this issue "in riddles to one another," Richard Bissell replied, "I think there was reluctance to spread even on an oral record some aspects of this operation."[35]

The senators were able to clearly demonstrate that Allen Dulles was the gray eminence directing the assassinations while President Eisenhower kept as much distance as possible from these operations. The goal had been for the president to be able to credibly claim that he knew nothing about the operations in case they were to become known, Bissell explained. He himself did not inform President Eisenhower about the assassination operations. Bissell claimed that he was under the impression that Dulles had informed President Eisenhower in a "circumlocutious" or "oblique" way, but he did not know that for sure, it was only his "personal opinion."[36]

Did President Kennedy know about the assassination attempts on Fidel Castro? Ted Sorensen, Kennedy's chief advisor, told the US Senate Select Committee that Kennedy never allowed assassination attempts on Castro; "such a thing was foreign to his character," Sorensen said. Kennedy had resented the fact that Allen Dulles often did not give him explicit information on specific operations, Sorensen added. Defense Secretary Robert McNamara and Secretary of State Dean Rusk also said that Kennedy had not known about the assassination attempts on Castro. Only Bissell, the CIA operative responsible for the assassinations, disagreed, stating he believed that Dulles had informed Kennedy about the assassinations in a covert manner. He said that while he had no evidence of this, it was his "personal opinion." Kennedy could not contradict this personal opinion because he had already been assassinated at the time of the Church investigation.[37]

It must be assumed today that the idea of carrying out targeted assassinations originated within the CIA, presumably with Dulles, who directed the assassinations of Prime Minister Lumumba in the Congo and Fidel Castro in Cuba. However, the senators could not conclusively determine whether Eisenhower or Kennedy had authorized the assassination attempts on Castro. "It is also possible that there might have been a successful 'plausible denial' in which Presidential authorization was issued but is now obscured," the senators said. The Church Commission held, however, that the presidents ultimately bore the responsibility even if they had not been informed. "Whether or not the respective Presidents knew of or authorized the plots, as chief executive officer of the United States, each must bear the ultimate responsibility for the activities of his subordinates." Political responsibility for the assassinations did not lie with the CIA, but with the White House and the NSC, which is headed by the president.[38]

Allen Dulles lied and killed repeatedly throughout his career. The longtime chief of counterintelligence in the CIA, James Jesus Angleton, confirmed to reporters two years before his death in 1985 that Dulles was one of the CIA's "grand masters" and that the CIA's leading men all had a dysfunctional relationship with the truth. "Fundamentally, the founding fathers of US intelligence were liars. The better you lied and the more you betrayed, the more likely you would be promoted." Angleton revealed. "These people attracted and promoted each other. Outside of their duplicity, the only thing they had in common was a desire for absolute power." The CIA literally walked over dead bodies to achieve this and had no interest in the principle of the human family or the UN's ban on violence. "You know, the CIA got tens of thousands of brave people killed," Angleton observes, which makes the CIA almost indistinguishable from a terrorist organization. "Allen Dulles, Richard Helms, Carmel Offie and Frank Wisner were the grand masters," Angleton says. "If you were in a room with them you were in a room full of people that you had to believe would deservedly end up in hell."[39]

1961: The CIA's Illegal Attack on Cuba

The CIA did not limit itself to assassination attempts in an effort to get rid of Fidel Castro; it also waged a secret war against Cuba. In March 1960, when the Cuban Revolution was a year old, President Eisenhower agreed to a recommendation by Allen Dulles and ordered the recruitment, equipping, training, and financing of armed units from Cuban exile circles in Florida to overthrow Castro. Dulles promised that the overthrow of Fidel Castro would go as smoothly as the 1953 coup d'état in Iran. The CIA recruited Cuban exiles in Florida and trained them in Guatemala as part of "Operation Zapata." The money, weapons, and trainers came from the United States. In August 1960, President Eisenhower approved a budget of $13 million for the illegal war against Cuba.[40]

When Cuban intelligence learned of the planned invasion through its informers in Florida, Cuban foreign minister Raul Roa addressed the UN General Assembly in November 1960. There he reminded the audience of the UN's ban on violence, which clearly prohibits all UN member states from threatening or using any kind of force in their international relations. Roa asked the World Peace Organization to investigate whether the US was indeed preparing to invade Cuba. But US ambassador James Jeremiah Wadsworth flatly rejected Roa's speculations, calling them "monstrous distortions and absolute falsehoods."[41]

After John F. Kennedy entered the White House as the new president in January 1961, replacing President Eisenhower, he was briefed by the CIA's Allen Dulles and Richard Bissell on the planned invasion of Cuba. President Kennedy, as commander in chief, had the power to call off the invasion of Cuba, but he did not. The young and charismatic president also used the instrument of deception toward the public. On April 11, 1961, four days before the illegal attack, Kennedy was asked at a press conference about Cuba. He replied that he would not, "under any circumstances, trigger an intervention by armed forces of the United States in Cuba." Later, one commentator called this "an exquisite feat of deceptiveness," because in fact it was not US soldiers, but exiled Cubans trained by the CIA, who carried out the invasion from Guatemala and Nicaragua.[42]

The illegal CIA attack began with the bombing of Cuba on April 15, 1961. B-26 bombers flown by CIA pilots took off from Nicaragua and destroyed part of the Cuban air force. The CIA had obtained the B-26 bombers from the US Air Force and painted the Cuban flag underneath the wings and "FAR" (Fuerzas Armadas Revolucionarias), the acronym for the Cuban Armed Forces, on the tail so that it could portray the whole operation to the public as an "internal Cuban revolt." President Castro, who had expected the invasion, was prepared for it. When the bombs fell, he is reported to have said: "This is the aggression." The bombing was followed by the invasion with ground troops on April 17, 1961. When the CIA-trained Cuban exiles landed on the Bay of Pigs beach, they were taken under fire by Cuban T-33 fighter planes, and the transport ship carrying the invaders' munitions for the next ten days was sunk. This left the invading forces without any supplies. Thus, the CIA's covert war against Cuba had failed.[43]

1961: Kennedy Fires CIA Director Allen Dulles

As commander in chief, Kennedy would have had the option of using the US military and waging an open war against Cuba. Kennedy had US aircraft carriers in close proximity to the island, but he decided against it. He accepted the defeat and, as announced at the aforementioned press conference, forbade the Pentagon to intervene with US soldiers. "I was assured by every son of a bitch I checked with—all the military experts and the CIA—that the plan would succeed," Kennedy protested angrily after the fiasco. But that was a mistake; the plan was not successful. From that day on, a fierce dispute erupted between the White House and the CIA. The president's anger had direct consequences for the powerful CIA director, Allen Dulles, who had led the CIA for eight years. Kennedy fired Dulles, along with Richard Bissell, the chief planner of the Bay of Pigs invasion. Thus, the people responsible for assassinations were suddenly out of a job.[44]

Allen Dulles felt severely humiliated by the dismissal and considered the much younger Kennedy a security risk to both the CIA and US imperial interests. Dulles was ruthless. He had had people assassinated several times before and had a network of killers at his disposal. Now he decided that Kennedy had to be taken out. Although it cannot be proven, there is much to suggest that Allen Dulles ordered the assassination of President John F. Kennedy and then tried to cover it up, as will be seen in the following chapter.

CHAPTER 9

THE ASSASSINATION OF PRESIDENT KENNEDY

President John F. Kennedy, who moved into the White House in January 1961, wanted to break new ground in US foreign policy. He refused to support the CIA with Pentagon troops during the Bay of Pigs invasion when it became clear that the coup attempt against Fidel Castro would fail. Furthermore, during the Cuban Missile Crisis of 1962, which brought the world to the brink of nuclear war, Kennedy refused to follow the advice of his senior generals who had proposed an invasion of the island, opting instead for a naval blockade. Kennedy then negotiated with Nikita Khrushchev, the premier of the communist Soviet Union, and promised him to refrain from any further attacks on Cuba. Khrushchev, in return, withdrew Soviet nuclear weapons from Cuba. The president also ordered his military to remove American nuclear weapons from Turkey. Kennedy distrusted the CIA and wanted to withdraw US intelligence from South Vietnam as well.

Some people in the CIA and at the Pentagon hated Kennedy and came to the conclusion that the charismatic young president was a danger to US imperial supremacy and thus had to be eliminated. Allen Dulles, the old and deceitful former CIA director whom Kennedy fired after the Bay of Pigs fiasco, was a mortal enemy of the president. Although it cannot be proven, evidence suggests that the unscrupulous Dulles organized

Kennedy's assassination and then, as an influential member of the Warren Commission that investigated the murder, covered his tracks, and focused public attention on Lee Harvey Oswald, framing him for the murder. Due to Oswald then also being shot and never being able to defend himself, a figurative fog spread over the whole affair, which prevented any clear view. This could only be to Allen Dulles's satisfaction. He died in 1969 at the age of seventy-five without ever being questioned about his role in the presidential assassination in front of a judge.

November 22, 1963: Crime Scene, Dallas

In November 1963, President John F. Kennedy and his wife Jackie flew to Texas for a campaign trip. This particular state was not an easy place for Kennedy. In hardly any other state was the president less welcome. There had even been death threats against the president, calling him a communist and a traitor to his country. On November 22, 1963, President Kennedy drove through the city of Dallas in the presidential limousine with an open top. The reception in Texas was unexpectedly friendly, with people on the roadsides enthusiastically cheering for the president and his attractive wife. At Dealey Plaza, an open park area that forms the western boundary of downtown Dallas, the motorcade on Elm Street suddenly came under fire at 12:30 p.m. The president was shot. One of the shots hit the president in the head. The driver of the presidential limousine raced to the nearby Parkland Hospital, but all help came too late for the president. At 1:00 p.m. local time, Kennedy was pronounced dead by the attending physicians.

The Secret Service, actually responsible for the security of the president, had done a poor job of protecting him that day. The windows and roofs of the buildings along the route had not been secured. The Secret Service had also decided to not use the protective dome of the presidential limousine. In addition to that, the route through Dallas on the day of the attack had been changed at short notice. The motorcade had to make a sharp turn at Dealey Plaza and reduce its speed to just under ten miles per hour, which deprived the young president of any protection, and he thus became an easy target for his assassins.

A careful autopsy should have been conducted on President Kennedy's body at Parkland Hospital. His wounds should have been examined in detail, in order to determine how often and from which directions he had been shot, but that did not happen. "The body of the President was forcibly taken away from the authorities of Texas, who would have been responsible for the autopsy," surgeon Charles Crenshaw later protested. He had tried in vain to save the life of the fatally wounded Kennedy at Parkland Hospital. Despite the fierce opposition of Dr. Earl Rose, chief of forensic pathology at Parkland, Secret Service agents took the body at gunpoint at 2:00 p.m. that same day. "If Dr. Rose hadn't stepped aside, I'm sure these criminals would have shot him," Crenshaw said, recalling the abduction. "They would have killed me and anyone else who got in their way." The Secret Service took the body to Air Force One, the president's plane, by ambulance. Then they flew the body to Andrews Air Force Base near Washington, where the body was loaded into another ambulance at 5:00 p.m. It was driven to the Naval Hospital in Bethesda, Maryland, where an autopsy began at 7:00 p.m. At Bethesda, high-ranking military officials, the very circles that saw Kennedy as a danger to imperial foreign policy, were in command of, and directed, the autopsy. These military officials manipulated the autopsy report. "Had the postmortem been done in Parkland, more questions would have arisen, and the autopsy photographs would have documented a different story, one that would have taken the investigation in a different direction," said Crenshaw.[1]

Vice President Lyndon Johnson was on the plane too. He was sworn in as the new president of the United States while still in flight. In a coup d'état that lasted only six seconds, Johnson had ascended to the top of the executive branch without a popular election. The power elite knew that imperial policies were much more implementable with Johnson, and he did not disappoint the power elite. President Johnson escalated tensions with Vietnam and sent more than two million US troops to Southeast Asia. After Kennedy's assassination, the US sank into shock and mourning. Kennedy only lived to be forty-six, leaving behind a young wife and two young children. In Europe, too, people mourned the unscrupulous murder of the young, handsome, and charismatic president. In Berlin, acting mayor and later German Chancellor Willy Brandt said, "A flame has gone out for all the people who hope for peace, justice and a better life. The world has become much poorer this evening."[2]

The Fairy Tale of the Mad Lone Perpetrator Lee Harvey Oswald

Like the events of Pearl Harbor and 9/11, the assassination of President Kennedy is one of the key occurrences in American history. Countless books have been published on the subject. That President Kennedy was assassinated is undisputed. That he was not strangled, poisoned, or stabbed, but shot, is also beyond doubt. What is disputed in historical research, however, is the question of whether Kennedy fell victim to a conspiracy involving several gunmen or whether a crazed lone gunman shot the president. This is the first question that every researcher must answer when dealing with the President Kennedy's assassination. If he was shot by a crazed lone perpetrator, then it was not a conspiracy, for a single individual cannot conspire with himself. If two or more shooters shot Kennedy on behalf of third parties, then it was a conspiracy because the shooters and principals had to conspire in secret beforehand.

Just half an hour after Kennedy's death, a young man named Lee Harvey Oswald was arrested in a movie theater in the neighborhood of Oak Cliff in Dallas. He was alleged to have shot the president from the fifth floor of the Texas School Book Depository, located at Dealey Plaza, after which he went to the movie theater. Oswald, who was only twenty-four years old and had been working at the depository for a month, vehemently denied the crime, stating that he had not shot anyone and that he was just a "patsy." At Dallas police headquarters, Oswald was questioned under chaotic circumstances. Although such interrogations are routinely recorded even for lesser felonies, the Dallas police interrogated the alleged assassin of the president for twelve hours without running a tape or having a stenographer present. This was not just sloppiness, it was the deliberate covering up of the defendant's statements.[3]

During a trial, the accused has the right to defend himself with the help of his lawyers. But young Oswald was never tried because Jack Ruby, a Dallas bar owner who maintained close ties to the Mafia and intelligence agencies, shot Oswald two days after the assassination, November 24, 1963, in the basement of the Dallas police station as he was being transferred to the county jail. This happened in front of live television cameras and the nation was shocked once again. Now not only President Kennedy was dead, but the man whom the police and the media had presented as the president's killer, without a trial, was dead too. Jack Ruby was found guilty of murder and sentenced to death. He died in prison on January 3, 1967, due to cancer.

Today, if you look up the article on Lee Harvey Oswald in Wikipedia, you will read that Oswald was "the assassin of President Kennedy." As many journalists, pupils, and students copy information from Wikipedia, many newspapers and theses still claim that Oswald, a crazed lone perpetrator, shot Kennedy. Many indications suggest, however, that the story of the crazy lone perpetrator is nothing but a fairy tale.

The most obvious and substantial evidence that exonerated Oswald was the nitrate test he took on the evening of the assassination. A nitrate test can detect gunshot residue on the hands and clothes after a firearm has been used. Such tests are important because they are based on the laws of science. For example, if a breathalyzer test indicates zero blood alcohol content, police may not arrest a motorist for drunk driving. The nitrate test result showed that Oswald had not fired a gun in the previous twenty-four hours. Therefore, Oswald could not be the killer. Nevertheless, the Dallas Police Department presented Oswald as the suspected murderer to the media, which immediately resulted in a premature snap judgment. At the same time, the important information involving the negative nitrate test was kept secret from the media for ten months until it was finally released as part of the Warren Commission report.[4]

Another weighty piece of evidence that Oswald was not Kennedy's killer emerged immediately after the assassination. Witnesses in Dallas stated that at the time of the crime, Oswald was not in the place from where President Kennedy was shot. The superintendent of the depository, Roy Truly, and Patrol Officer Marrion Baker both ran into the School Book Depository building immediately after the shooting, where they found Oswald in the cafeteria on the first-floor, drinking a Coke he had gotten from the vending machine. Only ninety seconds had passed since the first shot was fired, and Oswald appeared calm and composed. Nevertheless, investigators later claimed that this nimble Oswald had shot the president from the sixth floor of the School Book Depository building moments before, then raced down four floors, grabbed a drink from the vending machine, and calmly greeted

Superintendent Truly and Police Officer Baker, all in just ninety seconds. After that, he supposedly went to the movies, where he was arrested. This is not believable. Oswald was most likely not in the location from which the shooting occurred at the time of the crime.[5]

Moreover, Oswald's fingerprints could not be found on the Mannlicher-Carcano rifle with which he allegedly shot the president. This cheap, second-rate Italian rifle is not suitable for a presidential assassination. When three National Rifle Association marksmen were called upon to shoot the twenty-three-year-old rifle with an awkward reloading mechanism at a dummy from a similar distance, all three of them failed. Only one of the three champion shooters was able to fire three shots within the allotted time of six seconds. None of the master shooters hit the enlarged head or neck of the target mannequin even once. But this is exactly what Oswald is said to have succeeded in doing twice. It is not feasible that Oswald accomplished a feat that master marksmen could not duplicate.[6]

The School Book Depository was located behind the president when the shots were fired, but more than fifty witnesses had reported shots fired from a grassy knoll in front of the president on the edge of Dealey Plaza. Abraham Zapruder, an amateur videographer and bystander who had happened to be filming the presidential visit to Texas at the time of the assassination, was able to prove with his film that these witnesses were not all mistaken. Zapruder's film shows Kennedy's head being violently thrown back to the left by the fatal shot. This means that someone must also have shot the president from the front. That could not have been Oswald, because he was behind the president in the School Book Depository, drinking a Coke.

The nitrate test had shown that Oswald had not shot a firearm. Witnesses on the scene had confirmed that Oswald had not been on the sixth floor at the time of the shooting. Good marksmen had not been capable of hitting a dummy at a similar distance with the Mannlicher-Carcano rifle. And according to the Zapruder film and various witnesses, Kennedy had been fired upon not only from the School Book Depository but also from the front, from the grassy knoll, whereupon the president died in the crossfire. This circumstantial evidence suggests that the story of

Oswald being a crazed lone assassin is not credible and that the president was the victim of a conspiracy.

1964: The Warren Commission Report

After the assassination, the Dallas Police Department and the FBI took over the case. The powerful sixty-eight-year-old FBI chief, J. Edgar Hoover, a close confidant of President Lyndon Johnson, immediately and emphatically advocated the theory of the mad lone gunman. Already on November 24, 1963, a few hours after Oswald had been shot, Hoover declared: "The thing I am concerned about . . . is having something issued so we can convince the public that Oswald is the real assassin." The FBI followed this premise, thus shaping the historiography of the Kennedy assassination. For the domestic intelligence agency, Kennedy's assassination is both the most important and the most explosive case in its entire history. Isn't it strange that the FBI did not pursue all leads, but immediately settled on the story of the crazed lone gunman?[7]

After the murder, Congress should have convened a commission of inquiry, because it is the responsibility of the legislature to control the executive branch. But Lyndon Johnson, who had risen to the presidency as a result of the murder, beat Congress to the punch and on November 29, 1963, he founded the President's Commission on the Assassination of President Kennedy, a.k.a. the Warren Commission—named after its chairman, Earl Warren, who was then a justice of the US Supreme Court in Washington. By selecting the seven members of the Warren Commission himself, President Johnson was able to control the narrative of history. The most important member of the Warren Commission was former CIA director Allen Dulles, Kennedy's mortal enemy. Furthermore, Congressman and later President Gerald Ford, who *Newsweek* described as "the CIA's best friend in Congress," also sat on the commission. The Warren Commission ignored the numerous and credible witnesses who had heard shots being fired from the grassy knoll. It also ignored the Zapruder film that showed Kennedy being hit from the front.

In its final report, released in September 1964, the Warren Commission claimed, as did the FBI, that Oswald was the sole perpetrator and that he shot Kennedy from behind. There had been no conspiracy of multiple perpetrators. Oswald had fired three shots from the Texas School Book Depository with the Italian military rifle. The first shot had missed, the second had caused Kennedy's neck wound and all the injuries to Texas governor John Connally, who was sitting in front of Kennedy, and the third had been the fatal headshot. The president had thus been struck down with two hits. "There is no credible evidence whatsoever that Kennedy was shot from the front," the Warren Commission claimed in its 880-page report. "The shots that killed Kennedy were fired by Lee Harvey Oswald."[8]

But the many gunshot wounds to Kennedy and Governor Connally did not fit the two-shot story presented by the Warren Commission. According to their report, Oswald's second shot had caused Kennedy and Connally a total of seven entry and exit wounds, with the bullet changing its trajectory several times. In Kennedy research, this second bullet is therefore referred to as the "magic bullet." It allegedly entered the president's back at a downward angle, because the School Book Depository was behind the presidential limousine. It then moved upward and left Kennedy's body from the front of his neck. Then it pierced Connally's torso, then his wrist, and then it lodged into Connally's thigh. Later, the magic bullet reappeared on the stretcher in the hallway of Parkland Hospital and miraculously matched the empty shell casings found in the building of the School Book Depository.

The *New York Times*, the *Washington Post*, and *Newsweek* all praised the adventurous Warren Commission report as a "masterpiece" upon its release. But it was not. Rather, the report had very serious flaws, and one in particular that almost no one knew about at the time. The Warren Commission report did not disclose the important fact that there was an assassination division within the CIA that had carried out the assassination of Prime Minister Lumumba in the Congo just two years earlier. The report also did not reveal that the CIA had made several unsuccessful assassination attempts on Fidel Castro. No one in the public at the time knew that the CIA was engaged in assassinations around the world, and no one suspected that former CIA director Allen Dulles, who had directed the assassinations of Lumumba and Castro, was manipulating the Warren Commission's work. "None of the testimony and none of the documents the Warren Commission considered mentioned the CIA assassinations," the Church Commission noted when it published its assassination report in 1975.[9]

For a long time, the Warren Commission shaped the official historiography of the assassination of President Kennedy. But when it became public in the 1970s that the CIA had been involved in assassinations, in September 1976 the House of Representatives voted 280–65 for a new investigation. The House Select Committee on Assassinations, composed of fourteen members, presented an alternative narrative in 1979, also stating that Oswald had fired on the president, but adding that there was likely another, unknown gunman. The committee felt obligated to commend the work of the Warren Commission and asserted that they believed, as the Warren Commission did, that Lee Harvey Oswald fired three shots at the president from the fifth floor of the School Book Depository. Unlike the Warren Commission, however, the investigating committee saw "a high probability" that two men had shot Kennedy. This marked the first time that the official historiography parted from the story of a crazed lone gunman. "The Committee believes, on the basis of the evidence available to it, that President John F. Kennedy was probably assassinated as a result of a conspiracy. The Committee is unable to identify the other gunman or the extent of the conspiracy," read the report's findings.[10]

1967: Jim Garrison Reopens the Case

One of the first to question the story outlined in the Warren Report was Jim Garrison, a courageous and astute New Orleans district attorney. He ordered all twenty-six volumes of the Warren Commission and carefully read through every one of them. He did not just read the final report—he read every testimony that the various witnesses had given. The report did not convince him. The evidence against Oswald was weak because he had not confessed to the crime and he had not been seen on the sixth floor of the depository at the time of the crime. The nitrate test showed that Oswald had not fired any guns that day. Most importantly, it was absolutely unacceptable to ignore all the credible witnesses who said they heard shots being fired from the grassy knoll in front. At the beginning of the investigation, Garrison later wrote, he had only suspected that intelligence services had somehow been involved in the assassination, but he did not know which service or services. As time passed and more leads emerged, however, the evidence pointed increasingly toward the CIA.[11]

In 1967, in New Orleans, Garrison opened the first criminal investigation into the president's assassination. The Garrison trial was the first—and to date has remained the only—court case on the Kennedy assassination. Garrison dismissed the story of the mad lone gunman for lack of plausibility and stated that an honest consideration of all the testimony clearly proved that Kennedy was the victim of a conspiracy. "I am quite certain that Lee Harvey Oswald did not fire a single shot on November 22, 1963," Garrison stated. The negative nitrate test, Oswald's poor performance as a marksman in the navy, his less than aggressive character, and the poor quality of the Mannlicher-Carcano rifle were all pieces of evidence that all but confirmed that he did not kill anyone, said Garrison, adding that Oswald had been framed.[12]

For over five years, the Zapruder assassination footage had been concealed from the public. The FBI had given a copy of the film to the Warren Commission, which suppressed the explosive footage. It was not until District Attorney Garrison obtained a court order that the Zapruder film was shown to the public for the first time. It was in a packed courtroom in New Orleans. John Nichols, associate professor of pathology at the University of Kansas, had studied the Zapruder film closely. As an expert witness in the courtroom, he stated that after having looked at the slides, photographs, and Zapruder's film, he concluded that "they show a shot coming from the front." In addition, he said, Kennedy was also shot from behind. This meant that multiple gunmen must have fired at the president from different locations, which is why the story of the crazed lone gunman was no longer credible.[13]

Surgeon Charles Crenshaw, who saw Kennedy's body, also believes that the president was shot from the front, twice: once in the neck and once in the right side of his head, which is why the entire right side of Kennedy's brain was ripped away. Kennedy's wounds came from bullets "fired at him from the front, not from behind as the public has been led to believe," Crenshaw explained, calling the Warren Commission's magic-bullet theory ridiculous. Crenshaw, a medical doctor, was pressured into keeping quiet for many years, which he did out of fear. "I reasoned that anyone who would go so far as to eliminate the President of the United States would surely not hesitate to kill a doctor," he later said, explaining his behavior. The other doctors were also silent. "We all cared too much about our medical careers," Crenshaw said. It was not until 1992 that he made his knowledge public. In his book he declared that he considered the Warren Commission report "a fairy tale" and "a downright insult to the intelligence of the American people." The US population suppresses the truth because it is too painful, he said. "People within our government assassinated the president of the United States," Crenshaw said. "It was a coup d'état."[14]

Director Oliver Stone, a three-time Oscar winner who is known primarily for political films, retold the criminal investigation of District Attorney Garrison in his film *JFK*, which was released in 1991. In the movie, Kevin Costner plays Garrison. Oliver Stone also shows the Zapruder film, which had since become world famous. "I tried with my film . . . to reopen the already closed files on the assassination," Oliver Stone explained. *JFK* claimed that there was a conspiracy all the way up in government circles, that "members of the CIA and the FBI" were in on it. "They were all in the service of the military-industrial complex, which President Eisenhower warned us about," Oliver Stone said. Kennedy was assassinated, he said, because he did not want the war against Vietnam and Cuba and was about to drastically change the direction of American foreign policy.[15]

Jim Garrison shared this view. "What happened at Dealey Plaza in Dallas on November 22, 1963, was a coup d'état. I believe that it was instigated and planned long in advance by fanatical anti-communists in the United States intelligence community. It was carried out, most likely without official approval, by individuals in the CIA's covert operations apparatus and other collaborators outside the government. It was covered up by individuals of like mind in the FBI, Secret Service, Dallas police, and military. Its purpose was to stop Kennedy from seeking détente with the Soviet Union and Cuba and ending the Cold War."[16]

The CIA Claims That There Was No Conspiracy

The CIA watched Jim Garrison's work closely and with concern. It bugged his office, and CIA employees who posed as volunteers infiltrated his task force, copying all relevant documents and passing them on to the CIA. Richard Helms was the deputy director of planning for covert operations at the CIA at the time of the Kennedy assassination, and in that capacity, succeeding Richard Bissell, he was also in charge of assassinations. Helms, who was promoted to director of the CIA in 1966, knew all of the CIA's illegal covert operations and did not want Jim Garrison to shed light on them. Victor Marchetti, a senior staff member at CIA headquarters, attended Helms's morning situation meetings and testified that Garrison and his investigations were regularly discussed there.

"Disinformation is a large part of its [the CIA's] covert action responsibility, and the American people are the primary target audience of its lies," revealed Ralph McGehee, who worked at the CIA for twenty-five years. Even after Kennedy's assassination, the CIA tried to direct public opinion. Garrison's thesis, which concluded that several gunmen had assassinated the president and that he was therefore the victim of a conspiracy, greatly troubled the CIA and its director. In January 1967, as criticism of the Warren Report and its findings blaming a confused lone gunman grew louder, Richard Helms ordered that a secret three-page memorandum be sent to all CIA stations around the world, recommending that all theories differing from the Warren Report be dismissed as silly conspiracy theories. The CIA memorandum, titled "Defending Against Criticism of the Warren Report," was classified at the time. Today it is officially declassified and anyone can read it.[17]

The memorandum said that according to one poll, 46 percent of the US public believed that Oswald did not act alone. "This trend in public opinion is of concern to the US government and to our organization," the memorandum lamented. It said the CIA must ensure that criticism of the Warren Commission did not spread abroad, and therefore must emphasize with "all contacts with friendly elites," especially politicians and publishers, that "the Warren Commission conducted as thorough an investigation as was humanly possible and that the critics' allegations are without any serious basis." All conspiracy theories concerning the Kennedy assassination were to be rejected on the following grounds: The conspiracy theories were spread by communists. The conspiracy theorists had made up their minds before the facts had been established. The conspiracy theorists were pursuing political or financial interests. The conspiracy theorists' research was inaccurate. A large conspiracy could never be kept secret for long. The deaths of key witnesses were due to natural causes.[18]

After the terrorist attacks of September 11, 2001, the terms "conspiracy theory" and "conspiracy theorist" were used again to ridicule critical questions about 9/11, just as they had been after the murder in Dallas. Few knew that the CIA had already called for combating conspiracy theories as early as 1967. "This directive, with relevant instructions for action and argumentation, laid the foundation for the reinterpretation of the originally neutral term 'conspiracy theory' into a vocabulary with negative connotations, triggering unease and fear, which has functioned as an instrument of discipline and control in public discourse ever since," explains German journalist Mathias Bröckers. "No one can deny that there are real conspiracies," but according to the CIA brief, "legitimate questions about official pronouncements are declared thought crimes from which public consciousness must be protected."[19]

This loaded term "conspiracy theory" is still in use today and it characterizes the portrayal of the Kennedy assassination in Wikipedia. The Warren Report is presented as "conclusive," even though it is not. At the same time, any criticism of the Warren Report is treated under the heading of "conspiracy theories," which immediately triggers unease and dismissal in the minds of less informed readers. In the spirit of the CIA, Wikipedia claims that the critics of the lone-gunman theory have presented a multitude of circumstantial evidence and arguments why Oswald could not be the perpetrator, or at least not the sole perpetrator. But they have failed to agree on a coherent counter thesis that would answer the open questions more conclusively than the Warren Report.[20]

The Revenge of CIA Director Allen Dulles

US journalist David Talbot, who has repeatedly attracted attention with well-researched books, supports the thesis that former CIA director Allen Dulles had the president assassinated. "Allen Dulles was one of the most cunning masters of covert power America has ever produced," Talbot explains. Under him, the CIA "evolved into an effective assassination machine." Any national leader who he saw as a problem for American interests, Dulles considered "fair game." His wife, Clover Dulles, had a nickname for her cold, ambitious husband: "The Shark." But Allen Dulles never spoke to her about his secret assassination operations. In a diary she left to her children, Clover Dulles noted, "My husband doesn't converse with me, not that he doesn't talk to me about his business, but that he doesn't talk about anything."[21]

During World War II, Allen Dulles had been stationed in Bern, working for the Office of Strategic Services, the US foreign intelligence agency and precursor to the CIA. From Switzerland, he kept an overview of the European theater of war. He also maintained close relationships with high-ranking Nazis, including SS General Karl Wolff, for whom he interceded at the end of the war to ensure that he was allowed to appear at the Nuremberg trials as a witness rather than as a defendant and thus received only a minor sentence. In 1945, back in the United States, Dulles became president of the influential Council on Foreign Relations (CFR), which includes several thousand people from the top echelons of US society. It is considered a network of the rich and influential. During his time as president of the CFR, Dulles wrote a study that led to the creation of the CIA in 1947. Then he joined the CIA as director of covert operations in 1950, which made covert military operations the CIA's primary function. In 1953, newly inaugurated President Dwight Eisenhower promoted Dulles to CIA director. Dulles was cold and calculating, and he liked to think of himself as a chess master. He also supported assassinations if they served his purpose. Talbot reports that Dulles had been the master of sinister deeds that empires crave, and was capable of "great personal cruelty."[22]

When Jim Garrison suspected CIA involvement in Kennedy's assassination, he wanted to subpoena the retired Allen Dulles. It had come to the attention of the district attorney that during the nine years Dulles had headed the CIA, General Charles Cabell had been his deputy and in that capacity had led the Bay of Pigs invasion. When it had failed, General Cabell had called the president and asked him to give takeoff clearance to US fighter jets standing by on aircraft carriers off the coast of Cuba. But Kennedy had forbidden the use of the military and, after the Bay of Pigs disaster, had fired not only Allen Dulles but also General Cabell. After that, it was no secret in Washington that both Dulles and Cabell hated the young president.

General Cabell's brother, Earle Cabell, was the mayor of Dallas. Garrison found it reasonable to assume that it had been at the mayor's request that President Kennedy's motorcade was diverted onto Elm Street in Dallas on such short notice. This had forced the president's limousine to make a sharp turn and reduce its speed to just under ten miles per hour, making the president an easy target for his assassins. Did the Warren Commission not notice this? Why had Mayor Cabell not been questioned? Garrison wanted to question Allen Dulles about this and sent a subpoena to Washington. But it was intercepted, and shortly thereafter, District Attorney Garrison received a short letter from the United States Attorney General in Washington, informing him that he declined to serve Mr. Dulles the subpoena, Garrison recalled.[23]

Even though Allen Dulles enjoyed the protection of influential people, he and the CIA were not without controversy in Washington in the 1960s. After the Bay of Pigs invasion, former President Truman confided to writer Merle Miller that he regretted creating the CIA. "I think it was a mistake," Truman said. "If I had known what was going to happen, I never would have done it." Under President Eisenhower and Allen Dulles, he said, the CIA was out of control. The unscrupulous men in the CIA "have become a government of their own, and of course quite secret. They are accountable to no one," Truman said anxiously. "In a democratic society, that is a very dangerous thing."[24]

After his dismissal, Allen Dulles harbored a great hatred for the young President Kennedy. Dulles would not step down and "turned his Georgetown home into an anti-Kennedy government in exile," David Talbot reports. In that home, he hosted Kennedy's opponents. In the weeks leading up to Kennedy's assassination, Talbot says, the frequency of meetings at Dulles's home increased. Dulles was not present at the crime scene in Dallas. He was at a secret CIA facility in northern Virginia known as "the farm." Talbot is convinced that the former CIA director was centrally involved in the presidential assassination and used the same team against Kennedy that he had assembled to kill foreign statesmen. Talbot cannot produce concrete evidence, such as a letter from Allen Dulles to a CIA employee ordering Kennedy's assassination, because such a letter probably does not exist. If Allen Dulles ordered the presidential assassination, he was far too clever to do so in writing.[25]

More than fifty years after the assassination, all of the secret files on the Kennedy assassination had been scheduled to be released in 2017, after the embargo period had expired. However, the CIA vetoed the request and not all files were released. "The US foreign intelligence agency CIA had advised the government to keep some of the papers under lock and key," the *Neue Zürcher Zeitung* reported. President Donald Trump concurred with the CIA's suggestion, which was also supported by the FBI. As a result, important files on the assassination of President Kennedy are still under lock and key today, which prevents a full investigation into this unscrupulous crime.[26]

CHAPTER 10

THE VIETNAM WAR

US involvement in what would later become the Vietnam War began on September 2, 1945, when Japan signed its surrender on the battleship USS *Missouri* in Tokyo Bay and World War II ended. On that very same day, Ho Chi Minh, the president of the Democratic Republic of Vietnam, signed the Declaration of Independence of Vietnam in Hanoi. First the Vietnamese fought against the colonial power France in the Indochina War from 1946 to 1954, then they fought against the US empire in the Vietnam War from 1964 to 1975, defeating both of their opponents. Today, the Communist Party (CPV) rules Vietnam. The Vietnamese population does not have a choice of voting between different parties.

1954: France Loses Its Indochina Colony

The Vietnamese Declaration of Independence began with the same words as the US Declaration of Independence: "All men are created equal. They are endowed by their Creator with certain inalienable rights, among them are Life, Liberty, and the Pursuit of Happiness." During World War II, the US had been supporting Ho Chi Minh and his fighters for the independence of Vietnam, or Viet Minh, with shiploads of weapons to weaken Japan. In doing so, the US relied on the principle of "the enemy of my enemy is my friend." Ho Chi Minh believed that the US was promoting democracy worldwide, stating: "A people who have courageously opposed French domination for more than eighty years, a people who have fought side by side with the Allies against the Fascists during these last years—such a people must be free and independent."[1]

However, the French had no interest in granting independence to their colony of Indochina. Since 1887, the current territory of Vietnam, Laos, and Cambodia had belonged to the French colonial empire, which had been exploiting it from Paris, over 6,000 miles away. The French tire factory Michelin owned and maintained rubber plantations in Indochina. Anyone who rebelled against French rule was arrested, deported to a prison on an island off the coast, and tortured. In Saigon, the colonialists built magnificent villas. But the French did not see themselves as oppressors. "The superior races," asserted French prime minister Jules Ferry in the late nineteenth century, "have the duty to civilize the inferior races."[2]

According to Colonel Fletcher Prouty, who served in the US Air Force during World War II, the United States provided arms support to both the Vietnamese independence movement and the French colonial power. After the surrender of Tokyo, large stocks of US armaments were still stored on the Japanese island of Okinawa. Instead of being shipped back to the US, they were forwarded to Korea and Indochina, where wars would soon break out. "We don't have a precise answer to the question of why we provided US weapons to Ho Chi Minh in 1945 and then a few years later provided $3 billion worth of weapons to his enemies, the French," Prouty stated pensively. "At the end of World War II, all that was certain was that there had to be a war in Indochina."[3]

In November 1946, French warships bombarded Haiphong, killing 6,000 Vietnamese. France believed it could win a quick victory. But soon the French forces were in trouble and asked the US for help. The US supplied tanks, rifles, and ammunition. According to the formerly secret Pentagon Papers, the US also bore 78 percent of the French's war costs. However, due to the fact that the US was supplying Vietnamese insurgents with weapons at the same time, Paris was not able to win. Communist China also supported the Viet Minh. Colonel Prouty believed that US weapons, particularly heavy artillery, helped the Viet Minh defeat the French at Dien Bien Phu on May 8, 1954, which forced the French to withdraw. The actions of the USA in Vietnam are reminiscent of the arms supplies to the Cuban rebels, which had contributed decisively to the defeat of the European colonial power Spain in Cuba in 1898. The Vietnamese lamented 300,000 deaths in the War of Independence, and France lost 100,000 soldiers.[4]

Vietnam Is Split into Two Parts

At the Indochina Conference in Geneva in 1954, the defeat of the French, and with it the end of the First Indochina War, was announced. France vacated Indochina, which led to Laos and Cambodia also becoming independent states. This would have been a fitting opportunity to also let Vietnam, under Ho Chi Minh, become independent. The United States, however, had other plans. The country was split at the seventeenth parallel and disintegrated into a communist North Vietnam, ruled by President Ho Chi Minh and with Hanoi as its capital, and a military dictatorship in South Vietnam, with Saigon as its capital. The victorious Viet Minh retreated to the North. In South Vietnam, the US installed as president Ngo Dinh Diem, a Catholic who had previously been living in exile in New Jersey. Everyone was promised that free elections would be held throughout the country in 1956, after which Vietnam would be reunified.

However, President Diem did not keep this promise. He knew that he would have lost to Ho Chi Minh in free elections. He could afford this word-breaking behavior only because the US backed Diem and his artificially created state of South Vietnam. The Vietnam War was not necessary; there were many alternatives. "The obvious alternative was to allow Ho and his Communist-dominated Viet Minh to take over the whole of Vietnam," explained the US ambassador to Japan, Edwin Reischauer. "This would have happened early if the United States had made quite clear in 1945 that it did not approve of the revival of colonialism in Asia and would give it no support. It would still have happened if we had not given massive aid to the French war effort after 1949. It would have happened if we had been willing in 1954 to support the Geneva agreements and had not tried to build up a permanent regime under Diem in South Vietnam."[5]

But Washington did not want to let Vietnam become independent and sent General Edward Lansdale, a covert warfare specialist, to South Vietnam. General Lansdale headed the CIA's office in Saigon and fueled tensions by having terrorist attacks carried out against the Viet Minh in North Vietnam. CIA-hired agents blew up post offices in North Vietnam, poured sugar into the tanks of Ho Chi Minh's military trucks, rendered fuel supplies unusable, distributed anti–Viet Minh leaflets, and printed counterfeit money that they circulated in North Vietnam. CIA director Allen Dulles and other warmongers in Washington desired an increase in tensions.[6]

Officially, the United States was not involved in any combat operations. When the CIA station in Saigon requested large combat helicopters from the US Army in 1960, the secret shipment first had to be approved by the National Security Council in Washington. Then the helicopters were "cleaned" so that they could not be identified as coming from the US Marine Corps. They bore no insignia and no serial numbers. South Vietnamese gunners then fired from the gunships at people whom the CIA had labeled "bandits," "communists," and "Viet Cong" in efforts to exclude them from the human family. These were often hungry refugees from the North who, after the chaotic withdrawal of the French, had been drifting through South Vietnam in search of food and stealing it from the villages. This marked the beginning of direct US involvement in combat in Vietnam. The helicopters were flown and maintained by American "advisors," (i.e., CIA employees). These were former marines who were familiar with the helicopters. "They had left the service, only to get a higher salary and a guarantee that they could return directly to their old units without the loss of promotion rights," Prouty said, explaining the hide-and-seek game.[7]

The CIA was supported by the US Army's Special Forces, the Green Berets. These Special Forces were the first US soldiers to secretly arrive in South Vietnam in May 1961. They helped build an army in the newly created state of South Vietnam. The Green Berets trained the South Vietnamese, but did not participate in combat operations themselves. Thus, the US operated behind the scenes in Vietnam. At the time, the US population did not know that the United States was involved in military operations in Vietnam.[8]

After Kennedy took office in January 1961, the situation changed. Kennedy distrusted the CIA after the fiasco in Cuba and was worried

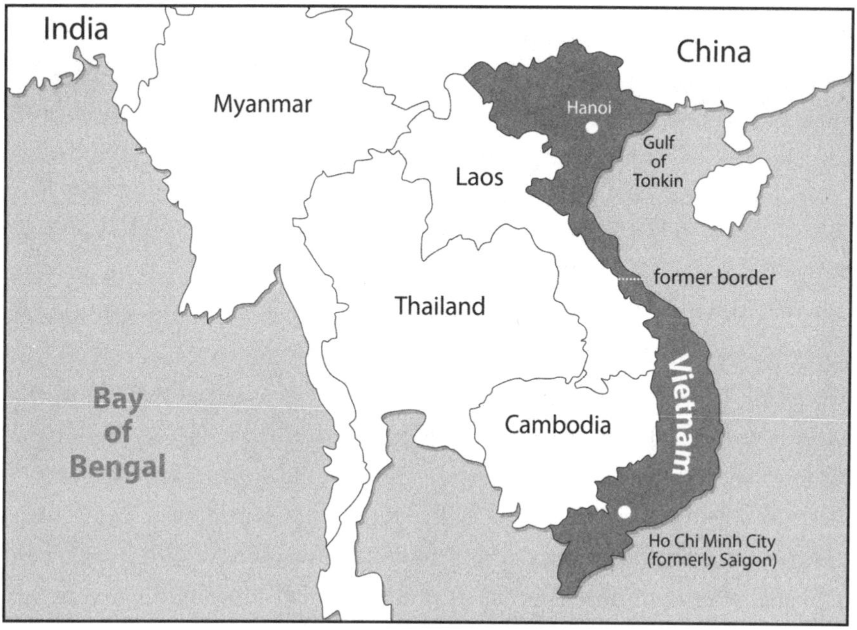

Figure 12. The United States attacks Vietnam in 1964.

about the increasing tensions in South Vietnam and the suppression of the Buddhist majority. The corrupt Catholic President Diem had filled all key state positions with Catholics and was ruthlessly cracking down on Buddhists. In the summer of 1963, Vietnamese Buddhist monk Thich Quang Duc set himself on fire at a busy intersection in Saigon, where he burned as a human torch to protest the oppression of Buddhists. "Human beings burn surprisingly quickly," reported US journalist David Halberstam, who was an eyewitness. "Behind me I could hear the sobbing of the Vietnamese, who were now gathering. I was too shocked to cry, too confused to take notes or ask questions, too bewildered even to think." Buddhist monks like Thich Quang Duc are not afraid of death and practice mindfulness so as not to cause suffering. It is their belief that consciousness cannot be extinguished even if the body decays. "As he burned he never moved a muscle, never uttered a sound, his outward composure in sharp contrast to the wailing people around him," Halberstam said.[9]

According to the Pentagon Papers, in 1963 there were still 16,000 US American "advisors" in Vietnam. President Kennedy wanted to withdraw them gradually. Secretary of Defense Robert McNamara "directed that a comprehensive long range program be developed for building up SVN [South Vietnamese] military capability and for phasing out the US role." President Kennedy, the Pentagon Papers confirm, made "a real attempt to extricate the US from direct military involvement."[10]

In his memoirs, McNamara confirms that on October 2, 1963, less than two months before his assassination, Kennedy had told the NSC in the basement of the White House that he wanted all "advisors" back from South Vietnam by the end of 1965. On October 11, 1963, Kennedy signed National Security Action Memorandum 263, ordering the withdrawal of 1,000 US advisors from Vietnam by the end of 1963 and the withdrawal of all Americans by 1965. "If Kennedy had lived, all the insanity we've seen in Vietnam since 1964 would never have happened," Fletcher Prouty explained regretfully. Kennedy's withdrawal plans were clear and definite, but at the very time that he wanted to withdraw, chaos in South Vietnam grew. Corrupt President Diem, who never had much popular support, was assassinated by his generals, who were supported by the CIA, during a military coup in Saigon on November 1, 1963. This left South Vietnam leaderless. That same month, on November 22, President Kennedy was shot in Dallas. With that, the withdrawal plan also died.[11]

1964: The Lie about the Gulf of Tonkin Incident

After the double murders in Saigon and Dallas, Kennedy's vice president Lyndon Johnson took over the administration and declared he would not give up Vietnam. Johnson stopped the withdrawal and escalated the war. He sent 4,000 additional military advisors to South Vietnam and directed the CIA to work with the South Vietnamese to expand covert military operations against North Vietnam. Special Forces carried out acts of sabotage against bridges, railroads, and port facilities in North Vietnam, kidnapped North Vietnamese, and bombed villages near the border.[12]

Under a top secret CIA program, called Operational Plan 34A (OPLAN 34A), high-speed patrol boats were delivered to South Vietnam. These boats were used to destroy North Vietnamese military installations, such as weapons caches and radar installations from the coast, under cover of night. These attacks on North Vietnamese infrastructure were directed by the CIA and carried out by the South Vietnamese. Although these actions had been sanctioned by the NSC, they were illegal and completely unknown to the US public. Only a few US senators saw through the intrigue and called for an end to the CIA's provocations. "This is a fight which is not our fight into which we should not have gotten in the first place," Democratic senator Ernest Gruening of Alaska declared on March 10, 1964. "The time to get out is now before the further loss of American lives. Let us get out of Vietnam on as good terms as possible—but let us get out."[13]

President Johnson and the CIA, however, did not want to get out at all. In fact, they were looking for a pretext that would spiral the US into open warfare. "Johnson was pathological in his ability to lie," explains US historian Peter Kuznick, who teaches contemporary history at the American University in Washington. To get Congress excited about the Vietnam War, President Johnson twisted the facts and claimed that North Vietnam had attacked a US warship in the Gulf of Tonkin, even though this was not true. In reality, the opposite was true. The CIA had attacked North Vietnam under OPLAN 34A. Moreover, in an effort to provoke North Vietnam, Johnson, as commander in chief, had sent the USS *Maddox* warship into the Gulf of Tonkin, east of the North Vietnamese port city of Haiphong. North Vietnam assumed that the *Maddox* was supporting the attacks by the patrol boats.[14]

On August 4, 1964, in a speech broadcast late at night on US television, President Johnson lied that North Vietnam had attacked the *Maddox*. "As President and Commander in Chief, it is my duty to the American people to report that renewed hostile actions against United States ships on the high seas in the Gulf of Tonkin have today required me to order the military forces of the United States to take action in reply," Johnson said. "The initial attack on the destroyer *Maddox*, on August 2nd, was repeated today by a number of hostile vessels . . . This new act of aggression, aimed directly at our own forces, again brings home to all of us in the United States the importance of the struggle for peace and security in southeast Asia . . . Firmness in the right is indispensable today for peace." As early as August 5, 1964, on the orders of President Johnson, the US Air Force dropped bombs on North Vietnam. Thus the Vietnam War had officially begun.[15]

The US press adopted President Johnson's war lies and portrayed the US as an innocent victim of Vietnam that had to respond to an insidious and evil attack. "Our Destroyers Attacked Second Time. American Planes Retaliate with Hit on North Vietnam," read the headline in the *Washington Post* on August 5, 1964. The *New York Times* also drummed up support for the war, reporting on its front page that same day, "President Johnson has ordered retaliatory action against gunboats and supporting facilities in North Vietnam after renewed attacks against American destroyers in Gulf of Tonkin."

The US attack on North Vietnam was illegal and a clear violation of the UN ban on violence. But at the meeting of the UN Security Council in New York on August 5, 1964, events were misrepresented. The British stated that the US had been attacked by North Vietnam and therefore they had a right to self-defense under Article 51 of the UN Charter. "[Due] to the repeated nature of these attacks and their mounting scale, the United States Government has a right, in accordance with the principle of self-defense . . . to take action directed to prevent the recurrence of such attacks on its ships," the British UN ambassador said. "Preventive action in accordance with that aim . . . is fully consistent with Article 51 of the Charter."[16]

The synchronized press, together with the White House, influenced not only the public, but also Congress. As early as August 7, 1964, Congress passed the Gulf of Tonkin Resolution, authorizing President Johnson to "take all necessary measures to repel any armed attack against the forces of the United States and to prevent further aggression." The House of Representatives blindly followed the president's presentation and adopted the resolution by a vote of 416–0 after only forty minutes of debate. In the Senate, eighty-eight senators voted yes. Only two senators, Democrat Wayne Morse of Oregon and Democrat Ernest Gruening of Alaska, voted no. The Gulf of Tonkin incident was "the inevitable and foreseeable concomitant and consequence of US unilateral military aggressive policy in southeast Asia," Senator Gruening stated. If the Johnson administration had "been waging peace with the same energy and fervor with which we have been waging war," it would agree with him that all soldiers should be withdrawn from Vietnam, Gruening said in his astute speech.[17]

Senator Morse also opposed the Vietnam War. "I believe that history will record that we have made a great mistake in subverting and circumventing the Constitution of the United States," he warned anxiously. "I believe that within the next century, future generations will look with dismay and great disappointment upon a Congress which is now about to make such a historic mistake." Senator Morse was right. But the efforts of the two senators who were committed to peace and opposed the Vietnam War were not supported. Both failed to win reelection in 1968.[18]

The parallels to the illegal attack on Iraq in 2003, and the lie regarding weapons of mass destruction (WMD) presented by President George W. Bush, are obvious. "As was later the case before the military campaign in Iraq, in 1964 Congress also gave an American president general power of attorney to go to war on the basis of a lie," charged Swiss journalist Martin Kilian in the *Tages-Anzeiger*. Congress was easily fooled. "I don't normally assume that a president lies to you," Democratic Senator William Fulbright of Arkansas later said, justifying his approval of the Gulf of Tonkin Resolution.[19]

President Johnson's lie was that he had claimed that North Vietnam had started it. But that was not true. The CIA had started it by repeatedly attacking North Vietnam with high-speed patrol boats, including the attacks on August 2, 1964. North Vietnam retaliated by sending three speedboats of their own into the Gulf of Tonkin, a stretch off the coast of North Vietnam, to intercept the attacks. When the North Vietnamese speedboats came closer than six miles to the USS *Maddox*, the latter opened fire. One of the North Vietnamese speedboats was hit by the *Maddox* and four Vietnamese crewmen were killed. The North Vietnamese did fire torpedoes, but they were not able to hit the *Maddox*. The American warship was neither hit nor damaged in the skirmish on August 2, and no US soldiers were killed.[20]

Captain John Herrick of the *Maddox* wanted to leave the area after the skirmish, but his superiors at the Pentagon ordered him to return to the Gulf of Tonkin. "The vessel's primary purpose was to act as a seagoing provocateur—to poke its sharp gray bow and the American flag as close to the belly of North Vietnam as possible, in effect shoving its 5-inch cannons up the nose of the Communist navy," US journalist James Bamford said, explaining President Johnson's tactics. "The *Maddox*'s mission was made even more provocative by being timed to coincide with commando raids, creating the impression that the *Maddox* was directing those missions and possibly even lobbing firepower in their support."[21]

On August 4, Secretary of Defense Robert McNamara reported to President Johnson that the *Maddox* had again been fired upon by torpedoes. This was a lie. It was a "torpedo attack that never happened," *Spiegel* later declared. The National Security Agency, which is responsible for worldwide surveillance and decryption of electronic communications, declassified more than 140 formerly top secret documents on the Gulf of Tonkin incident in December 2005, including a study by NSA historian Robert Hanyok. This study confirms what other historians had long suspected: there was no attack on US ships in the Gulf of Tonkin on August 4, 1964. "The overwhelming body of reports, if used, would have told the story that no attack occurred," Hanyok concludes.[22]

The skirmish on August 2 was provoked by the CIA, and the alleged attack on the *Maddox* on August 4 was a pure fabrication. Gene Poteat, the CIA's senior radar analyst at the time, correctly recognized that Johnson wanted war and that he had staged the incident. "It's pretty clear that they had made up their minds on how they were going to proceed, the president and McNamara. They wanted war. I was stunned when I read the paper the next morning and the air strikes had begun," Poteat later recalled. "I believed there was nothing wrong with getting the facts before you start. It would have been easy to determine whether it was a credible attack or not, and fairly quick."[23]

Some senators recognized, at least in retrospect, that President Johnson had lied to them in 1964. "The country and this committee were dragged, under false pretenses, into a conflict that has cost thousands of lives and that has done massive damage to our country's moral standing in the world," Senator Albert Gore Sr. said in 1968. Indeed, the Gulf of Tonkin incident was an unconscionable war lie. When Robert McNamara was asked in 1999 whether or not the "attack" on the *Maddox* had occurred on August 4, 1964, he candidly admitted to the *Guardian*, "I think it is now clear it did not occur."[24]

The USA Uses Napalm on Babies and Buddhists

As commander in chief, President Johnson waged a merciless war against Vietnam. Between 1964 and 1975, the US dropped three times as many bombs on the small country as it had dropped over all theaters of war combined during the entire Second World War. In addition to conventional bombs, the US also used napalm bombs. Napalm is a viscous, sticky mass made from gasoline. It sticks tenaciously to people while it burns and horribly scorches their skin. US chemist Louis Fieser of Harvard University had invented napalm in 1942. The US Air Force had already gained initial experience with napalm during World War II, when they dropped napalm bombs on Berlin in March 1944 and when they used more than 16,000 tons of napalm in the bombing of Japan in 1945. Large cities such as Tokyo, Kawasaki, and Osaka burned like tinder because the Japanese had relied on lightweight construction, using wood and paper to build their cities in an effort to protect themselves against recurring earthquakes.[25]

The houses in the Vietnamese villages were also made of combustible material like palm fronds, which burned quickly and easily. The US dropped 388,000 tons of napalm over Vietnam. Aerial bombers dropped the incendiary bombs over the Vietnamese villages from low altitudes. Small US warships sailed the rivers of Vietnam and used napalm flamethrowers with a range of 500 feet to wipe out villages located along the rivers. "Anyone who survives a napalm attack is apt to be dreadfully burned," the *New York Times* reported, "and, without first rate medical care, is condemned to a lingering, painful death or, at best, permanent disfigurement."[26]

In 1972, as a nine-year-old Vietnamese girl, Kim Phuc ran from her napalm-ravaged village with severe injuries. Vietnamese photographer Nick Ut's black-and-white image of Kim, naked and screaming, went around the world as the "Napalm Girl" and became the most famous image of the Vietnam War. She had torn off her burning clothes and survived the napalm attack, even though a third of her body, including her entire back, neck, and left arm, was burned. It took several skin transplants to ensure her survival. Despite her ongoing pain, Kim Phuc has chosen not to hate, but to forgive the United States. She always emphasizes that we all belong to the human family. For this, she was honored with the

2019 Dresden Peace Prize. "I got burned so much, but my face and my hands are still beautiful," she said later. "I learned to count my blessings," meaning not to pay attention to what is negative, but to think of what is positive. "Love is more powerful than any weapon," she emphasized, thus encouraging many people.[27]

Louis Fieser, the inventor of napalm, and the company Dow Chemical, which produced it, were sharply criticized by the US peace movement during the Vietnam War. Scientists and arms manufacturers, they said, were complicit in the great suffering made possible by their inventions and products. "It is not my business to deal with the political or moral issues," Fieser said, disavowing any responsibility. "I couldn't foresee that this stuff was going to be used against babies and Buddhists. The person who makes a rifle . . . he isn't responsible if it is used to shoot the president."[28]

1970: The Peace Movement and the Kent State Massacre

On March 8, 1965, after intensive bombing, the first US combat troops landed on Da Nang Beach in South Vietnam. For the first time since the Korean War, US combat troops officially and visibly reentered Asian territory. By the end of 1967, President Johnson had increased troop strength in Vietnam to 500,000 US troops. In total, the United States would send 2,500,000 US troops to Vietnam over the course of the war. Today, the US has a professional army. But at that time, military service was mandatory in the US for males eighteen and older. This was another reason why many young men protested against the Vietnam War. Only influential politicians were able to protect their sons during Vietnam, by stationing them at posts within the USA, away from any danger.

Many young men believed the president and were convinced of the validity of the Vietnam War. "When the government said that the communists were taking over Vietnam and if we didn't stop them there we would have to stop them eventually in San Diego, I took that at face value," recalls US soldier William Ehrhart. According to information disseminated by the mass media, "Communists from North Vietnam, backed by the Russians and Chinese, were waging a brutal war of conquest against the free republic of South Vietnam," Ehrhart said. "I had no reason at that time to distrust my government, my teachers, or the *New York Times*," said the veteran, who enlisted in the US Marines at only seventeen after graduating from high school, the legally required schooling, and was soon thereafter sent to Vietnam, where he served for thirteen months.[29]

One of the important principles of the peace movement today is that one must never blindly trust the US president and the mass media. It wasn't until Vietnam that Private William Ehrhart saw through all the propaganda. "The US population was told that we were in Vietnam to repel a foreign attack. But I found out that we were the aggressors, we were the foreigners, and the people we were supposed to be defending hated us because we were poisoning their forests with chemical defoliants and burning their fields with napalm," said Ehrhart, who became a peace activist after the war and warned students in the US not to go to war. "I repeatedly participated in the destruction of individual homes and entire villages. I was there when civilians in Vietnam were brutally interrogated and unarmed men, women and children were killed, their livestock and all their crops were also wiped out." When all of Vietnam fell to the communists after the war, he said, it became apparent that the so-called domino theory, according to which communism would spread across the entire world after a victory in Vietnam, was not true. The Communists' victory in Vietnam "was reported on the evening news and had little more influence than a severe fire in Cleveland," Ehrhart recognized.[30]

Those who saw through the war lies protested the war. Many had no interest in defending a corrupt regime in South Vietnam and fighting the guerrillas of the National Front for the Liberation of South Vietnam, a.k.a. the Viet Cong. The "hippies" wanted to defeat the war with the power of love. They were also called "flower children" because they wore colorful clothes and flowers were their symbol of nonviolence. In 1965, 20,000 demonstrators surrounded the White House. The Vietnam War dominated the discussion in the USA like no other topic. World boxing champion Muhammad Ali also refused military service, declaring: "My conscience won't let me go shoot my brother . . . They never called me nigger, they never lynched me . . . How can I shoot them poor people?" Students distributed leaflets that read, "Moral is to oppose the immoral war in Vietnam and to paralyze the war machine. Immoral is to obey the orders of an immoral state." In public places, the hippies criticized

President Lyndon B. Johnson (LBJ), chanting, "Hey, hey, LBJ, how many boys did you kill today?"[31]

Led by Dr. Martin Luther King Jr., more than 300,000 people turned out for a protest march in New York in April 1967. It was the largest anti-war demonstration in the history of the United States up to that time. In October 1967, opponents of the war organized sit-ins to block access roads to the Pentagon, the command center of the Vietnam War. That same month, violent riots broke out at the University of Wisconsin as police beat down war opponents and used tear gas on them. This, in turn, mobilized even more students. On May 4, 1970, during a demonstration at Kent State University in Ohio, two male and two female students were shot and killed by the US National Guard, while others were seriously injured. "The National Guard troops were stunned too," recalled student Chrissie Hynde. "We looked at them and they looked at us. They were just kids, nineteen years old, like us. But in uniform. Like our boys in Vietnam."[32]

The Kent State Massacre shook the United States. More than four million students and 350,000 university staff and faculty members took to the streets nationwide. Many universities suspended classes. "While we destroy Vietnam," noted US journalist Izzy Stone, "the war destroys our country." As a result of the Vietnam War, a war-critical public movement was forming that had previously never existed. Not during the American Indian Wars, nor the war against Mexico, nor the wars against Cuba and the Philippines, nor even during the two world wars. By the end of 1970, more than half of US Americans opposed the Vietnam War.[33]

The Vietnam War was the first war to be televised. Fighter jets were often shown taking off into the setting sun. This was entirely in the Pentagon's interest, because it made the war look good. The footage was broadcast in color, directly to the viewer sitting in the armchair in front of the TV. People had never seen anything like it before. From time to time, critical reports were broadcast on television that showed the suffering of the Vietnamese people. One such report was done by Canadian journalist Morley Safer and aired on CBS on August 5, 1965. Safer accompanied US Marines as they entered the village of Cam Ne in South Vietnam and showed how the residents were forced to abandon their palm frond–covered huts, after which the marines burned down the village. It was the first somber report on the conditions in Vietnam. The US public, however, would not believe what they saw with their own eyes. Safer was defamed, labeled a communist, and CBS was accused of lying. President Johnson was not amused either and called CBS president Frank Stanton the morning after the broadcast: "Frank," said an authoritative voice, "are you trying to kick my ass?" "Who is this?" the sleepy Stanton replied. "Frank, it's me, your president. Yesterday your people took a shit on the American flag."[34]

1965: The USA Overthrows President Sukarno in Indonesia

While the war raged in Vietnam, Indonesia took a clearly anti-imperialist course, much to the annoyance of the United States. After a bloody fight for liberation, led by Achmad Sukarno, the country had freed itself from the Dutch colonial power in 1949, upon which Sukarno was elected the first president of Indonesia. In 1955, President Sukarno founded the Non-Aligned Movement in the Indonesian city of Bandung, together with well-known politicians from Asia and Africa, such as Jawaharlal Nehru from India and Gamal Abd el Nasser from Egypt. This movement called itself the "Third World," rejected both imperialism and racism, and wanted to progress on an independent path between capitalism and communism. This did not please Washington, and the CIA immediately classified President Sukarno as a communist.

On September 30, 1965, the previously unknown "September 30 Movement" attempted a poorly planned coup in Indonesia, during which six generals of the Indonesian military were killed. The coup attempt was blamed on the Indonesian Communist Party, which was the third most powerful communist party in the world with more than three million members. The coup failed and its exact background remained obscure. Presumably the NSC, aided by the CIA, had "provoked a fight between the left and the right, assuming that the right would ultimately win in an armed confrontation," explains Canadian historian Geoffrey Robinson, who teaches at the University of California.[35]

On the orders of General Mohamed Suharto, the army then performed a counter-coup, and over a period of six months engaged in a merciless hunt for real and alleged communists, members of the unpopular Chinese minority and supporters of President Sukarno. More than 500,000 people were killed in one of the largest mass murders since the end of World War II. President Sukarno was gradually ousted, and on March 11, 1966, General Mohamed Suharto, who was supported by the USA, took over the reins of government and declared himself the new president a year later. As Indonesia's new strongman and a loyal follower of Washington, President Suharto opened his country to Western investors and ruled as dictator until 1998.

Indonesia is struggling to come to terms with the 1965 massacre, and none of the perpetrators have had to answer for their actions in court yet. This is partly because the US had supported Suharto's seizure of power from the background, which is completely unknown to the population in the USA. The CIA had compiled lists of more than 5,000 "communists" and distributed them to the Indonesian military. "I know we had a lot more information than the Indonesians themselves," explained Marshall Green, US ambassador to the Indonesian capital of Jakarta at the time of the coup. The Indonesian military hunted down and killed those who were on the lists, along with their entire families and many more who were not on any list. Once dead, their names were checked off on the list. "No one cared, as long as they were communists, that they were being butchered," explained Howard Federspiel, the expert on Indonesia at the US State Department's Bureau of Intelligence and Research. The label "communist" was enough to exclude thousands of Indonesians from the human family. As late as 1990, Robert Martens, who worked at the US embassy in Jakarta, still thought it was right that the United States had supported the coup with these death lists. "It really was a big help to the army," Martens explained. "They probably killed a lot of people, and I probably have a lot of blood on my hands, but that's not all bad. There's a time when you have to strike hard at a decisive moment."[36]

The My Lai Massacre Is Uncovered

When President Johnson declared that he would not be running for reelection in 1968, the charismatic Robert Kennedy, John F. Kennedy's younger brother, inspired the imagination of war opponents and decided to run for president. "I've got to find out who killed my brother," Robert Kennedy said. He believed that his brother had been the victim of a conspiracy and he suspected the CIA to be the breeding ground, as it was also fomenting tensions in Vietnam and Indonesia. But Robert Kennedy was never able to prove this thesis because he did not make it to the White House. On June 6, 1968, during the election campaign, he was shot in Los Angeles and buried at the National Cemetery in Arlington, just like his brother had been before him.[37]

Richard Nixon of the Republican Party was elected president on November 5, 1968. Nixon, a paranoid character who hated Communists, Jews, and Black people, had promised his constituents that he would end the Vietnam War within six months. Once he moved into the White House in January 1969, however, Nixon and his security advisor and later secretary of state, Henry Kissinger, escalated the war. Born in Germany, the Jewish Heinz Kissinger had fled to the United States with his family to escape the Nazis before World War II. As national security advisor, Kissinger played a dominant role on the NSC and called for ruthless action against the Vietnamese. "I refuse to believe that a little fourth-rate power like North Vietnam doesn't have a breaking point," Kissinger said.[38]

US soldiers killed many civilians in Vietnam. This is illegal and a war crime. In November 1969, Seymour Hersh, a critical US journalist, reported on a massacre that US troops had carried out in the village of My Lai in South Vietnam on March 16, 1968. Under the command of Officer William Calley, US soldiers had raided the village. Infants, pregnant women, and the elderly were raped, scalped, and hacked into pieces. In the end, 504 dead civilians lay on the ground, including 173 children and 76 babies. Similar crimes had occurred in many other villages, too. When Officer Calley later was questioned about the massacre in court, he would not or could not see that he had committed a war crime in My Lai and that he had betrayed the principle of the human family. "I didn't kill a person that day in My Lai, it wasn't me as a person that did it," the traumatized Calley stated, adding that he did it for his country, the United States of America, and that he and his comrades were not there to kill human beings, they were there to kill an ideology: "to destroy communism."[39]

Despite the US's use of extreme force, it lost the war in Vietnam. After many years of fighting, the Vietnamese gained their independence and unified the divided country. More than three million Vietnamese people died in the war, including two million civilians. The USA mourned 58,000 dead soldiers, more than in any other war since 1945. Many US veterans were severely traumatized, as they had seen very little of the world before they were sent to Vietnam. "500,000 of us attempted to take our own lives," explained veteran William Ehrhart. Fifty-five thousand were successful in their tragic suicide attempts or died of drug overdoses or in deliberate car crashes. This means that almost as many veterans died by suicide in the USA as had died on the battlefields in Vietnam, which is why the total count of US American deaths caused by the Vietnam War amounts to over 100,000 US soldiers. But Washington never even thought about renouncing violence from then on.[40]

President Nixon brought the last American combat troops back to the United States in March 1973. But that did not mean that the war was over. The US continued to fly air strikes against North Vietnam and supplied money and weapons to South Vietnam in an effort to put it in a position to fight North Vietnam and the Viet Cong on its own. The war dragged on for two more years until the South Vietnamese army collapsed and North Vietnamese troops captured Saigon in April 1975. Nixon was never punished for his illegal wars because he was not fundamentally different from other US presidents in that regard. "I think, legally speaking, there's a very solid case for impeaching every American president since the Second World War," said Noam Chomsky, an active member of the US peace movement. "They've all been either outright war criminals or involved in serious war crimes."[41]

The Secret War against Cambodia and Laos

Against the advice of Secretary of Defense Melvin Laird and Secretary of State William Rogers, President Nixon gave the order to bomb the neutral country of Cambodia, adjacent to Vietnam, in March 1969. This was a clear violation of the UN ban on violence. Nixon, however, did not care. He also stepped up the bombing campaign against South Vietnam. "We are going to raze this goddamn country to the ground," Nixon declared, close to insanity. "Now we haven't got a damn thing left to lose."[42]

Nixon also attacked another neutral neighbor of Vietnam, Laos, in yet another UN violation. The CIA built an army of children in Laos and sent them to fight the Vietnamese. "Most of the soldiers were children, young boys, 14, 15, 16 years old," revealed US journalist Douglas Valentine, who has closely studied the CIA's illegal operations in Southeast Asia. The CIA sent "thousands and thousands of these young boys to their deaths trying to stop the Viet Cong from coming down the Ho Chi Minh Trail through Laos. They just used this mountain tribe as expendable cannon fodder," Valentine said. "And they do this sort of thing all over the world all the time." But these secret CIA wars are never reported in the US media, because the CIA successfully prevents it. "So, mere civilians in the United States really never know what's going on," Valentine lamented in 2019.[43]

President Nixon hid the illegal attack on Cambodia from Congress. The US Air Force pretended to have bombed targets in Vietnam and falsified flight data. Only the president and a small group of conspirators in the military knew which targets were bombed in Cambodia. During situation briefings in South Vietnam, a US unit was briefed on alleged military targets in South Vietnam. Then, in a second situation briefing with only officers who were in on the conspiracy, the names of the alleged South Vietnamese targets were assigned to real targets in Cambodia.[44]

It was not until April 30, 1970, that Nixon announced to the public that he was also bombing Cambodia. "USA, get out of Cambodia," opponents of the war immediately demanded. Some members of Congress also felt betrayed and declared that they had never agreed to the bombing of Cambodia. The people of Cambodia paid a high price for the US's ruthless attack on their country. More than 150,000 civilians died as a result of the bombs that B-52 military aircraft dropped on their country. "This drove the villagers into the arms of the Khmer Rouge," commented *Geo* magazine. This was because the air strikes mainly hit the farmers, which is why Nixon's hail of bombs provided "the decisive reason for the rise of the Khmer Rouge." The CIA knew that Nixon's illegal war strengthened the Khmer Rouge, the Cambodian communist party. "They are using damage caused by B-52 strikes as the main theme in their propaganda," the CIA reported on May 2, 1973. "This approach has resulted in the successful recruitment of young men. Residents say the propaganda campaign has been effective with refugees in areas that have been subject to B-52 strikes."[45]

The dropping of US bombs on Cambodia did not end until Congress cut the necessary funding in August 1973. However, the nightmare in Cambodia did not end there, as the Khmer Rouge did not just simply vanish into thin air. In fact, they overthrew the government in the capital Phnom Penh in April 1975 and established a communist dictatorship. Under dictator Pol Pot and his reign of terror, the principle of the human family was brutally betrayed between 1975 and 1979. Approximately two million people, one-fifth of the country's population, were exterminated by the communist Khmer Rouge in planned barbarism. The Khmer Rouge hated the Vietnamese and invaded Vietnam repeatedly. Approximately 30,000 civilians in South Vietnam were killed in the process. The Vietnamese army reacted to these border violations by invading Cambodia on December 25, 1978, in an effort to liberate the country. Within two weeks, Khmer Rouge rule collapsed, Pol Pot was overthrown, and the nightmare ended. The defeated Khmer Rouge fled across the border to Thailand, where they settled in the jungle.[46]

The Brits and the USA Arm the Khmer Rouge in Thailand

It is a little-known fact in Europe and the United States that after the humiliating defeat at the hands of Vietnam, Washington secretly began to support Pol Pot and his brutal Khmer Rouge in the jungles of Thailand. Why were they training communists who had previously carried out genocide? Because the CIA hated victorious Vietnam and acted according to the principle that "the enemy of my enemy is my friend." The cynical operation was a "policy of hate," explains US historian Jack Colhoun.[47]

"The US had been secretly funding Pol Pot in exile since January 1980," the courageous Australian journalist John Pilger also confirms. "The extent of this support—$85 million from 1980 to 1986—was revealed in correspondence to a member of the Senate Foreign Relations Committee." The US supported the Khmer Rouge with uniforms, money, and satellite imagery; weapons were supplied from China because China also hated the communist government in Vietnam. In Thailand, on the border with Cambodia, the CIA set up several training camps for the Khmer Rouge. In November 1980, Ray Cline, deputy director of the CIA, visited these camps.[48]

The Khmer Rouge were not only trained by the CIA and US Special Forces such as the Green Berets. From 1983, British special forces, the Special Air Service (SAS), who had been sent to Cambodia on a secret mission by British prime minister Margaret Thatcher directly after the Falklands War in 1982, also trained the Khmer Rouge. This top secret operation was unknown to the public in the UK and in the USA. When the Iran-Contra scandal broke, the US Special Forces withdrew in 1986 because President Ronald Reagan could not afford another scandal. After that, the British continued the operation by themselves. When John Pilger made this public, 16,000 people wrote letters of protest to Prime Minister Thatcher, who denied everything. In a reply to opposition leader Neil Kinnock of the Labour Party, she declared: "I confirm that there is no British government involvement of any kind in training, equipping or co-operating with the Khmer Rouge or those allied to them." But this was a lie. When John Major replaced Margaret Thatcher as prime minister, his government was forced to admit in 1991 that the SAS had indeed trained the Khmer Rouge. "We liked the British," one Khmer Rouge fighter told John Pilger. "They were very good at teaching us to set booby traps. Unsuspecting people, like children in paddy fields, were the main victims."[49]

John Pilger was able to speak with elite SAS soldiers who had served in Thailand. "We trained the Khmer Rouge in a lot of technical stuff—a lot about mines," a British SAS soldier confirmed to him. "We used mines that came originally from Royal Ordnance in Britain, which we got by way of Egypt with marking changed . . . We even gave them psychological training. At first, they wanted to go into the villages and just chop people up. We told them how to go easy." British peace activist Rae McGrath, who is involved in mine disarmament and removal around the world, criticized the SAS for teaching the Khmer Rouge the use of "improvised explosive devices, booby traps and the manufacture and use of time-delay devices." McGrath recognized that "the SAS training was a criminally irresponsible and cynical policy."[50]

Coming to terms with the crimes of the Khmer Rouge in Cambodia is proving difficult. The brutal dictator Pol Pot died in 1998 without having been arrested or punished for his crimes. After his death, the Khmer Rouge Tribunal was established in Phnom Penh. Two high-ranking and brutal Khmer Rouge leaders, Ta Mok, the number two behind Pol Pot, and Kaing Guek Eav, who had run the torture center in Phnom Penh, were arrested. But Benson Samay, Ta Mok's lawyer, demanded that the US and Britain also be indicted for their roles in the violent excesses in Cambodia. "All the foreigners involved have to be called to court, and there will be no exceptions," exclaimed Samay. "Madeleine Albright, Margaret Thatcher, Henry Kissinger, Jimmy Carter, Ronald Reagan and George Bush . . . we are going to invite them to tell the world why they supported the Khmer Rouge."[51]

However, this never came to pass. The trial of Ta Mok kept being postponed until he eventually died in prison in 2006 without being tried. Only Kaing Guek Eav, who is known as Duch, confessed to his crimes. In 2010 he was found guilty of participating in the killing of at least 14,000 people in prison S-21 and was sentenced to life in prison. The verdict was historic because it was the first guilty verdict against a leading member of the communist dictatorship, more than thirty years after the Khmer Rouge's reign of terror. The responsible politicians from the USA and Great Britain, who had crushed Cambodia with their hail of bombs and then trained the Khmer Rouge in Thailand, never sat in the dock.[52]

CHAPTER 11

THE IRAN-CONTRA AFFAIR

In the fall of 1986, the so-called Iran-Contra affair became publicly known. The scandal allowed a rare glimpse behind the scenes of US power politics. President Ronald Reagan's administration had funneled proceeds from secret arms deals with Iran to brutal guerrillas in Nicaragua, the so-called contras, aiding them in the overthrow of the Nicaraguan government. This was explosive for several reasons. First, the secret war that the contras were waging against the Nicaraguan government with the help of the CIA violated the UN ban on violence and was thus illegal under international law. Second, Congress had explicitly prohibited the CIA from using the funds appropriated for the contras to overthrow the government. Therefore, the covert operation also violated US law. Third, Iran had been a political enemy of the United States since the Islamic Revolution in 1979, and arms sales to Iran violated the strict economic embargo imposed by Congress. But none of this mattered to the CIA, which helped the contras smuggle tons of cocaine into the US so that they could finance their illegal war, which was another serious offense. The Iran-Contra affair showed, as *Die Zeit* in Germany summed it up at the time, that under President Reagan, the White House "conducted foreign policy contrary to reason and against the law."[1]

1981: The USA's Secret War against Nicaragua

When actor Ronald Reagan was elected president of the United States on November 4, 1980, and moved into the White House the following January, he appointed his campaign manager Bill Casey as the new CIA director. Casey was a shady character. A Wall Street swashbuckler, he had made his fortune selling tax loopholes. "His talent lay in bending rules to the breaking point," reports US journalist Tim Weiner of the *New York Times*. Much like former president Richard Nixon, Casey took the view that "if it's secret, it's legal." The new CIA director maintained a close relationship with President Reagan and also sought him out privately to make important decisions. "All Casey needed was a few minutes with the president, a wink and a nod, and he was off," Weiner said.[2]

Bill Casey, like many of his predecessors, was fascinated by covert warfare. He set his sights on Nicaragua, where the Somoza clan had ruled with dictatorial force since 1934. For decades, the Somozas had done everything they could to show their unreserved support for the United States. In international organizations such as the UN and the Organization of American States, the Somoza clan always voted with the US and also supported the illegal US coup d'état in Guatemala in 1954, as well as the illegal US invasion of the Bay of Pigs in Cuba in 1961. Dictator Somoza had even offered to send Nicaraguan troops to Vietnam, but Washington declined. In return, for many years the US ensured the survival of the brutal Somoza regime, which was its closest confidant in Central America.[3]

When the Sandinistas overthrew the corrupt dictator Anastasio Somoza in 1979, he fled to Miami. Washington took no pleasure in the change of power in Nicaragua. The Sandinistas implemented social reforms in their country to improve the situation of the lower class. Many poor Nicaraguan peasants gained access to education for the first time and learned to read and write. In addition, the leftist Sandinistas maintained close relations with Cuba and countries in the Warsaw Pact. CIA director Casey came to the conclusion that the Sandinistas were communists and therefore had to be overthrown.

Nicaragua is bordered by Honduras to the north and Costa Rica to the south. The Sandinistas' opponents (i.e., the National Guard of the ousted dictator Somoza), had retreated across the northern border into neighboring Honduras after the revolution. These men formed the core of the contras. In consultation with Bill Casey, on December 1, 1981, President Reagan gave the CIA a mandate to conduct "paramilitary operations against Nicaragua." Months earlier, the CIA had already made contact with the contras in Honduras. Now the CIA began to train them in secret and to supply them with weapons and money. The secret war against Nicaragua, which began with this decision by President Reagan that would turn out to be fatal for the people of Nicaragua, remained completely unknown to the US population at first. Casey had convinced President Reagan that if the right-wing contras took Nicaragua by storm and overthrew the Sandinistas in the capital city of Managua, it would be no big deal.[4]

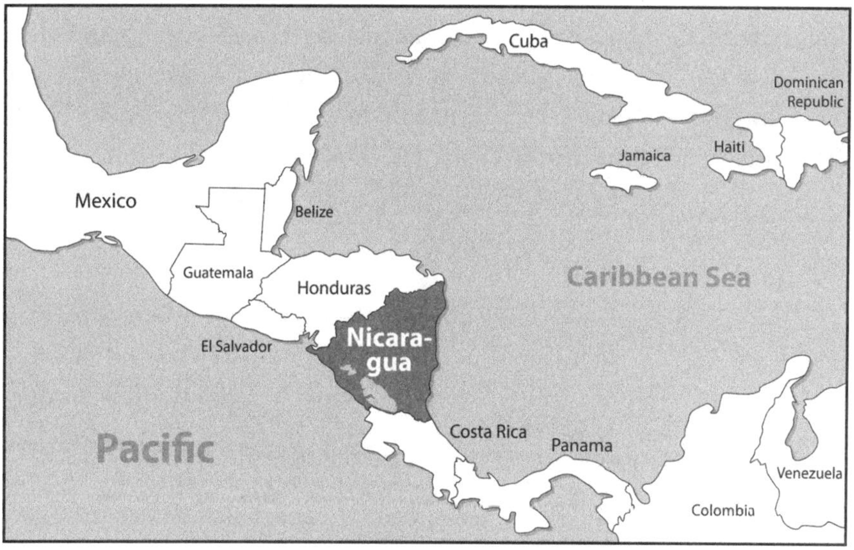

Figure 13. The secret war of the USA against Nicaragua was illegal.

The USA's secret war against Nicaragua was illegal. "Armed attack (armed aggression) is the most serious and dangerous form of aggression," the UN General Assembly declared in 1974, recalling the UN's ban on violence of 1945. The UN defines as an act of aggression, and thus as a crime of aggression, "the invasion or attack by the armed forces of a State of the territory of another State" as well as "bombardment by the armed forces of a State against the territory of another State," and also "the blockade of the ports or coasts of a State by the armed forces of another State." Washington did not violate these particular principles, at least not at the beginning of the secret war, because the United States was not using US forces. Instead, the CIA was fighting a secret war and arming the contras to fight it. However, that in itself was illegal too, because the UN ban on violence also explicitly prohibits secret wars: "the sending by or on behalf of a State of armed bands, groups, irregulars or mercenaries, which carry out acts of armed force against another State," as the UN General Assembly states.[5]

The unscrupulous Casey, however, was concerned neither with international law, nor with US law, as would later become apparent. In Honduras, north of Nicaragua, the US began building airfields, military bases, and radar installations for the contras. The contras blew up bridges between Honduras and Nicaragua, set fire to houses, and shot local security forces. Like the Khmer Rouge, the contras were very brutal and showed no respect for the principle of the human family. To break Sandinista morale, the contras raped and tortured Sandinista women. The contras, a US investigative report noted, were responsible for "reckless attacks on civilian targets, kidnappings, rapes, murders, mutilations, and other forms of violence."[6]

President Reagan and CIA director Casey watched these atrocities from a safe distance, holding their protective hand over these brutal bandits and asserting that the contras were "freedom fighters." The contras attacked Nicaragua from Honduras and then retreated back across the border. Within the CIA, Duane Clarridge, the chief of the Latin America division, was in charge of the secret war in Nicaragua. The contras laid mines, stole livestock, burned crops, and carried out terrorist attacks on Nicaraguan civilians in an effort to destabilize the country and bring about an overthrow of the Sandinista government. Interrogation of former contra leaders, as well as other witnesses, revealed that the contras "tortured, dismembered, beheaded, or gouged out the eyes of unarmed civilians, including women and children."[7]

Officially, the United States had not declared war on Nicaragua. But the CIA's secret war was indeed real and brutal. Contra leaders were flown to the US and trained by American special forces and CIA experts in

Florida and in California. In its manuals, the CIA explicitly advised the contras to use force against civilians. US pilots flew operations against Nicaraguan troops and supply flights for the contras. The CIA bugged Sandinista offices so the US could observe how Nicaragua and the government in Managua responded to contras attacks. "The surveillance operation for Nicaragua is even greater than the one for the Soviet Union. We can hear a toilet flush in Managua," boasted one CIA analyst.[8]

Congress Prohibits a Coup d'État in Nicaragua

The CIA's secret war against Nicaragua did not go unnoticed by Congress. Members of Congress, however, reacted in a confusing way. On the one hand, Congress approved several million dollars in "aid" to the contras, while at the same time forbidding the CIA from using these funds to overthrow the Sandinistas in Nicaragua. Congressman Edward Boland of Massachusetts, who as chairman of the Intelligence Committee was better informed about the CIA's covert operations than his fellow congresspeople, introduced a bill to that effect, which was passed as the Boland Amendment by the House of Representatives on December 8, 1982, and signed by President Reagan that same month. Reagan, who had a history in the film industry and was accustomed to playing various roles, declared with a straight face that the United States was not out to overthrow the regime in Nicaragua. "That was the first time the well-loved president lied to Congress to protect the CIA's covert operations," commented journalist Tim Weiner, "but not the last."[9]

Bill Casey also did not think it necessary to abide by the restrictions imposed by Congress. As director, Casey had a budget of $3 billion a year to spend on the CIA. His goal was to use the contras to overthrow the Sandinistas, even though Congress had explicitly forbidden it.

The CIA worked closely with John Negroponte, the US ambassador to Honduras, and the Pentagon's Special Forces to train the contras. They also trained the contras in Costa Rica, which borders Nicaragua to the south. Many of the Special Forces were veterans of the Vietnam War. They possessed comic books that had been used to teach Vietnamese peasants how to take control of a village by killing the mayor, the police chief, and militia members. The CIA translated this "manual for murderers" into

Spanish and distributed the booklets to the contras. The brutality that had already struck the Vietnamese now struck the majority of the poor peasants in Nicaragua.[10]

In May 1983, President Reagan admitted for the first time that his administration was supporting the "freedom fighters" in Nicaragua. In an attempt to fully ruin Nicaragua's already severely weakened economy, Casey had the Nicaraguan port of Corinto, which lies on the Pacific Ocean, mined in April 1984. In addition to that, the CIA blew up oil storage facilities and pipelines in Nicaragua. These were obviously illegal acts of war, which the CIA had carried out without informing Congress beforehand. Even members of Congress who had otherwise supported aggressive US foreign policy reacted angrily because they realized that the CIA was not complying with the laws passed by Congress. On October 12, 1984, Congress strengthened the Boland Amendment and strictly prohibited any further funding of the contras by the CIA or the Pentagon. The law "clearly ends US support for the war in Nicaragua," Congressman Boland believed.[11]

The UN also condemned the CIA's war against Nicaragua as a serious breach of the law. On June 27, 1986, the International Court of Justice (ICJ), the principal judicial organ of the UN in The Hague, condemned the US for their actions. "The Court rejects the justification of collective self-defense maintained by the United States and finds that the US has unlawfully interfered in the internal affairs of another state by supporting the contras," the judges stated. By bombing Nicaraguan ports and mining Nicaraguan waters, the US violated the prohibition of the use of force against another state, they said. The Court declared that "the United States is obliged to put an immediate end to all such unlawful actions . . . And to pay reparations to Nicaragua."

CIA director Bill Casey and President Reagan chose to ignore the ruling.[12]

The NSC Opens a Secret Bank Account in Switzerland

The tightening of the Boland Amendment should have ended the CIA's secret war against Nicaragua. But Reagan and Casey would not back down and sought new ways to continue military aid to the contras in secret. Casey decided to keep the CIA at arm's length. Instead, he made use of the NSC's infrastructure. He gave NSC staffer Oliver North, a veteran of the Vietnam War, the assignment of finding new sources of funds for the contras. "This was a dangerous misuse of the NSC staff," Congress later complained, since only the CIA was allowed to conduct covert warfare.[13]

Oliver North approached various countries, asking for donations to support the contras. He managed to raise more than $40 million, including $32 million from Saudi Arabia and $2 million from Taiwan. Private individuals donated another $2 million and were allowed to take a photo with President Reagan in return. While this was going on, Langhorne Motley, a senior official in the US State Department, assured Congress that the Reagan administration "would not solicit or encourage any third country" to give funds to the contras.

Again, this was not a reflection of the truth. Congress was deceived and later protested that it was not acceptable for US covert operations to be funded by foreign countries without the knowledge of Congress; this was "dangerous and improper" because it created dependence on the sponsors.[14]

CIA director Casey and Oliver North chose retired US General Richard Secord to handle the money transactions in a way that kept them secret. General Secord, who, like North, was a veteran of the Vietnam War and a specialist in covert operations, opened a secret bank account in Switzerland, so that Congress could no longer monitor the flow of funds. Together with his confidant Albert Hakim, Secord set up a covert system he called "the Company."

The Company had its own planes, landing fields, ships, and staff to support the contras. Hakim and Secord did not work for free; they diverted more than $4 million to themselves, as Congress would later find. By outsourcing the secret war in Nicaragua to private individuals who also personally enriched themselves, the Reagan administration "violated fundamental principles of the US Constitution," an investigation by the US House of Representatives correctly stated.[15]

The CIA and the Cocaine Trade

The new money for the contras came not only from the donations collected by Oliver North, but also from the drug trade. Colombian cocaine can be sold in the US for great profit. In 1988, courageous US journalist Leslie Cockburn, who investigated the war in Nicaragua intensively, revealed that the contras were directly involved in cocaine trafficking in Central America, and that the CIA was supporting them in their operations. Senator John Kerry of Massachusetts, who later served as secretary of state during the Obama administration, also shed light on this issue. "It seems as though stopping drug trafficking in the United States has been a secondary US foreign policy objective," Senator Kerry protested at the time. That goal, he said, is repeatedly sacrificed for other objectives, "such as changing the government of Nicaragua, supporting the government of Panama, using drug-running organizations as intelligence assets, and protecting military and intelligence sources from possible compromise through involvement in drug trafficking." But he said it made no sense at all for the US government to spend millions of dollars fighting drugs while secretly engaging in drug trafficking itself. "This is insane," Senator Kerry said.[16]

On April 13, 1989, a Senate committee chaired by Senator Kerry issued a 144-page report on drugs and the contras, concluding that the CIA-backed contras had trafficked cocaine intensively. "There was substantial evidence of drug smuggling through the war zones on the part of individual contras, contra suppliers, contra pilots, mercenaries who worked with the contras, and contra supporters throughout the region," the final report said. President Reagan's administration, however, did nothing about it; on the contrary. "US officials involved in Central America failed to address the drug issue for fear of jeopardizing the war efforts against Nicaragua," the senators found. The CIA was well informed about the drug trade and was pleased to have found in it a source of funding for the contras. "Senior US policy makers were not immune to the idea that drug money was a perfect solution to the contras' funding problems," the report stated.[17]

As president, Reagan presided over the secret meetings of the NSC. Attendees included CIA director Bill Casey, Vice President George H. W. Bush, Secretary of Defense Caspar Weinberger, and Secretary of State George Schultz. NSC staffer Oliver North only played a minor role in this round. He reported to National Security Advisor Robert McFarlane and, beginning in 1985, to McFarlane's successor, Admiral John Poindexter.

"Never, ever" did he do anything during his five years on the Security Council that had not been secured beforehand by his superiors, North affirmed. "My military training inculcated in me a strong belief in the chain of command," he said. His superiors, he said, came to him and said, "Take care of it." These insiders also knew that the United States was secretly selling weapons to Iran and using the profits to fund the contras.[18]

Saddam Hussein Invades Iran and Uses Poisonous Gas

In 1979, as the Sandinistas overthrew dictator Somoza in Nicaragua, Saddam Hussein took power as president in Iraq. The CIA had supported his rise to power, knowing very well that Saddam Hussein was brutal. Shortly after seizing power, Hussein publicly defamed members of his Ba'ath Party, upon which they were taken away and murdered. Hussein had received the death lists from the CIA, which was helping him secure his power. James Critchfield, the CIA station chief in Baghdad at the time, acknowledged that the CIA basically "created Saddam Hussein."[19]

When fundamentalist Ayatollah Khomeini took power in neighboring Iran in 1979 and overthrew pro-Western Shah Mohammad Reza Pahlavi, Saddam Hussein decided to attack Iran and drive Khomeini out of Tehran. On September 22, 1980, the Iraqi army attacked Iran on a 600-kilometer front in the First Gulf War. It was an illegal war of aggression without a UN mandate. Saddam Hussein was therefore a war criminal, because the UN ban on violence prohibits wars of aggression. Dictator Hussein hoped to achieve a quick victory, but he did not succeed. The war dragged on until 1988 and claimed more than 400,000 lives. Former US secretary of state Henry Kissinger knew of the deep hatred between Hussein and Khomeini. "I hope they both kill each other," Kissinger declared cynically. "It's too bad they both can't lose."[20]

The First Gulf War was fought with great brutality. The principle of the human family was disregarded. Hussein launched air strikes against the Iranian capital city, Tehran, and the USA supported him. Under director Bill Casey, the CIA supplied Hussein with military intelligence technology and war-relevant information obtained from US spy satellites. To weaken Iran, "we did indeed tilt toward Iraq," confirmed Philip Wilcox, the US State Department's liaison to the CIA. "We provided Iraq with intelligence, took Baghdad off the list of state sponsors of terrorism . . ." The US used the brutal dictator to expand its influence in the oil-rich region. "Many began to view Iraq optimistically as a potential factor for stability, and Saddam Hussein as a man with whom we could work," Wilcox explained of the strange alliance between Washington and Baghdad.[21]

With the help of Western companies, Hussein was able to produce chemical weapons, including mustard gas and sarin. To avert defeat by Iran, Hussein did not shy away from war crimes and used chemical weapons against his neighboring country. Documented poison gas attacks by Saddam Hussein on Iranians took place in 1983 and 1984, and victims of the poison gas attacks were shown to the international press in Tehran. Some poisoned Iranians were flown to Switzerland, Austria, Sweden, and Germany for treatment. After that, the Europeans also knew about the violations in the Gulf, but US policy was not criticized.

German journalist Udo Ulfkotte discovered that some of the poison gas that Hussein used had come from Germany, and that the US had supported the use of poison gas. "I was working as a journalist for the *Frankfurter Allgemeine Zeitung*. In early July 1988, I was on the front lines of the war between Iraq and Iran," Ulfkotte recalls. "That's when I became an eyewitness to how, under American supervision, the Iraqis gassed the Iranians with German poison gas—mustard gas." Ulfkotte was outraged. The poison gas had come directly from Germany, declared as pesticides. Ulfkotte was eager to report on this in the German media, but ran into a wall of silence. "I thought this was going to be a huge story, worldwide," Ulfkotte recalled in an interview with German journalist Ken Jebsen. "But at the Sheraton Hotel in Baghdad, the Americans, the Iraqis and the Germans celebrated the gassing! I flew back to Frankfurt, but even the *FAZ* would only print one tiny little story on it. I was even forbidden to pass on my gruesome photos to the magazine *Stern*, or I would be fired." In the German mass media, Saddam Hussein's crimes were covered up so as not to snub the USA.[22]

The USA Sells Weapons to Iran Despite Embargo

In Nicaragua, the contras were financed not only by donations from wealthy individuals and by profits generated from the cocaine trade, but also by top secret US weapons sales to Iran. This sale was triggered by an event that no one in Washington had anticipated. On June 14, 1985, the terrorist Organization of the Oppressed on Earth, with ties to Lebanese Hezbollah, hijacked US Trans World Airlines Flight 847 with 153 passengers on board. The terrorists brought the plane into Lebanon and landed it in Beirut, where women and children were released. When the hijackers realized that US Navy diver Robert Stethem was among the passengers, they killed him and dumped his body on the runway.

Washington was alarmed and consulted with Israel's prime minister Shimon Peres. The government of Israel proposed that the US sell missiles to Iran to effect the surrender of US hostages held in Lebanon, the congressional report found. Iranian arms dealer Manucher Ghorbanifar assured CIA director Casey that Iran was very interested in US weapons to defend against Saddam Hussein's attacks. Arms deals with Iran would free the hostages, the arms dealer explained, because Iran had influence over Hezbollah.[23]

Officially, however, at that time there was a strict embargo imposed on Iran—by the USA. No one was allowed to deliver weapons to Iran, not even drills or baby food. Nevertheless, on August 3, 1985, President Reagan gave the CIA permission to conduct a secret arms deal with Iran. Former CIA director George H. W. Bush, who served as vice president under Reagan, also supported the secret arms deal. Later, after the Iran-Contra affair, he would rise to the presidency himself. In September 1985, the US sent weapons to Iran through Israel for the first time. The first shipment included 504 American TOW anti-tank missiles. The CIA obtained the anti-tank missiles from the Pentagon at the bargain price of $3,500 each and sold them to the Iranians at the extortionate price of $10,000 each. The profits from the arms trade flowed into the Swiss bank account, which was managed by Richard Secord, and from there to the contras in Nicaragua. Iran asserted its influence over Hezbollah, and a US hostage was released. Iran then demanded HAWK surface-to-air missiles. The NSC supported the secret deal, and in November 1985, a small plane delivered a shipment of HAWK air defense missiles marked with Hebrew lettering from Tel Aviv to Tehran.[24]

By engaging in this secret operation, members of the NSC violated two laws that had been enacted by Congress. First, it was forbidden to support the contras with money. And second, it was forbidden to sell weapons to Iran because the country was under a US embargo. Robert McFarlane, who served in the NSC as Reagan's national security advisor from 1983 to 1985 and who drove the covert operation, did not care. "There is no place in government for lawbreakers," Congress later protested when the secret operation was exposed. "The president is responsible for this policy" because, as commander in chief, he also wages US covert wars, Congress correctly recognized. They warningly quoted Supreme Court Justice Louis Brandeis, who had once said, "Crime is contagious. If the government becomes a law-breaker, it breeds contempt for the law: it invites every man to become a law unto himself, it invites anarchy."[25]

The Iran-Contra Affair Shakes Public Trust

History teaches that secret operations do not remain secret forever, and so it was in this case. US drug trafficker Barry Seal and his pilots flew with their little transport plane from Arkansas to Colombia. After loading cocaine from the Medellin cartel, his pilots would stop to refuel in Honduras and then fly back to the US with the cocaine, where they would drop it with parachutes for the drug traffickers to pick up in their trucks and then sell to addicts on the streets of New Orleans, Miami, and New York. Barry Seal's pilots made several flights a week. Per flight, they were able to transport 200 to 500 kilograms of cocaine into the US, which was worth about $13 million on the street. The CIA knew about this drug ring and in 1982 it convinced Seal to add an element to his flights, which was to fly weapons from Arkansas to the contras in Honduras. In return, the CIA protected Seal from the US Drug Enforcement Administration (DEA), which was fighting the drug trade, and equipped his planes with high-tech gear.[26]

This cooperation was interesting for both parties. However, on October 5, 1986, a Seal transport plane, which was to deliver five tons of weapons and ammunition to the contras, was shot down by the Sandinistas in Nicaragua. CIA employee Eugene Hasenfus, the only survivor, was arrested and confessed in front of running cameras that the US was supporting the contras with weapons and that he had successfully dropped weapons and ammunition for the contras several times before. In Washington, efforts were made to limit the damage. President Reagan asserted to the media that the White House had nothing to do with Hasenfus and the arms shipments to the contras. But that was not the truth.

On November 3, 1986, the Lebanese newspaper *Al-Shiraa* publicized the fact that the United States had sold arms to Iran in order to free hostages. President Reagan, on the advice of CIA director Casey, again denied everything. On November 10, he declared on television, "Our government has a firm policy not to capitulate to terrorist demands. That 'concessions' policy remains in force, in spite of the wildly speculative and false stories about arms for hostages and alleged ransom payments. We did not—repeat—did not trade weapons or anything else for hostages—nor will we." With this, the US president had lied to the entire population.[27]

The Reagan administration was under a lot of pressure because all the high-ranking members of the NSC were directly involved in both scandals. Attorney General Edwin Meese, who was in on the covert operations, presented a pawn. On November 29, 1986, he directed the public's interest to NSC employee Oliver North, who had previously been completely unknown to the public. This took more powerful men like President Reagan and Vice President Bush out of the line of fire. The attorney general explained that there was indeed a link between the illegal aid to the contras in Nicaragua and the Iranian-American arms-for-hostages scandal, since funds from arms deals between Israel and Iran had flowed to the contras. The only person within the US government who knew exactly about this, Meese claimed, was Oliver North of the White House NSC staff. From that moment on, Oliver North was the center of media attention.

The Conspirators Are Not Sentenced to Jail

The US Congress established a commission, chaired by Lee Hamilton of Indiana, which held hearings from May to August 1987 that were broadcast on US television and shook the nation. Oliver North had to testify before the committee and admitted that he had been involved in the covert operations, but stressed that he had no regrets. "I must confess to you that I thought using the Ayatollah's money to support the Nicaraguan resistance was a right idea . . . I advocated that, and we did it," North said. CIA director Casey had praised the approach as the "ultimate covert operation." Congress would have liked to have heard the CIA director as well, but he collapsed in his office on the seventh floor of the CIA headquarters. Doctors diagnosed a malignant brain tumor, and Bill Casey died on May 6, 1987.[28]

President Reagan addressed the nation on March 4, 1987, attempting to clarify his earlier lies in a strange televised address. "A few months ago I told the American people that I did not trade arms for hostages. My heart and my best intentions still tell me that is true, but the facts and evidence tell me it is not. As the Tower board reported, what began as a strategic opening to Iran deteriorated in its implementation into trading arms for hostages." With that, the president publicly admitted that he had lied. However, this did not lead to a criminal conviction or his resignation. Reagan never went to prison and died in Los Angeles in 2004.[29]

The contras never succeeded in overthrowing the Sandinistas in Nicaragua. The population voted the latter out of office in 1990, upon which they had to relinquish power. In the United States, however, the secret war against Nicaragua almost brought down the government. National Security Advisor Admiral John Poindexter, who had coordinated Iran-Contra trade at the NSC, was indicted for participating in a criminal conspiracy. Poindexter was accused of lying to Congress, deceiving the government, and destroying evidence. All of this he had done. Thus, on April 7, 1990, a court found him guilty on all charges and sentenced him to six months in prison. But then a year later, another court overturned that verdict and all charges were dropped.

A criminal case was also brought against Oliver North in April 1988. The court found North guilty of illegally supplying arms to Iran and using the profits from these transactions to support the contras. North admitted to all of it. He also admitted to lying to authorities and destroying incriminating emails that had been exchanged within the Reagan administration. The court sentenced him to three years in prison and a $150,000 fine for participating in a conspiracy. But due to a procedural error, this sentence was also overturned by another court. Oliver North also remained a free man and did not have to go to prison.

Lawrence Walsh, the courageous independent investigator and prosecutor during the Iran-Contra affair, also indicted Defense Secretary Caspar Weinberger for being directly involved in the illegal arms deal with Iran and the illegal war in Nicaragua, and for lying to Congress about both. However, on December 24, 1992, shortly before President Bush was succeeded in the White House by President Bill Clinton, Bush pardoned his colleague Weinberger and other senior officials involved in the Iran-Contra affair. "The Iran-Contra cover-up, which has continued for more than six years, has now been completed," Special Investigator Walsh resignedly said, noting that none of the perpetrators went to prison. "It demonstrates that powerful people with powerful allies can commit serious crimes in high office, deliberately abusing the public trust without consequences," he stated with regret.[30]

1991: The Nayirah Testimony and the War against Kuwait

It is astonishing that on November 8, 1988, the US population elected the Republican George H. W. Bush as its new president, even though he had been directly involved in the brutal US war against Nicaragua as vice president and had also supported the illegal sale of weapons to Iran. Full of self-confidence, former CIA director George H. W. Bush moved into the White House on January 20, 1989.

Iraqi president Saddam Hussein believed that newly elected President Bush would support further Iraqi expansion, since the US had already endorsed the attack on Iran in 1980. On August 2, 1990, Hussein attacked the neighboring country of Kuwait with 100,000 soldiers and conquered the small country within a very short period of time. This war was illegal because the UN ban on the use of force explicitly forbids wars of aggression. Before his campaign, Hussein called the American ambassador in Baghdad, April Glaspie, to the government palace on July 25, 1990, and informed her of his planned war of aggression, because he wanted to be sure of Washington's support or neutrality. At the time, Ambassador Glaspie replied, "I have a direct instruction from the President [Bush] to seek better relations with Iraq," only to add, "We have no opinion on your Arab-Arab conflicts like your border dispute with Kuwait," adding that the US hoped that Hussein could resolve the problem by whatever means he thought were appropriate.[31]

Through this statement by Ambassador Glaspie, the cunning Bush lured the brutal Hussein into a trap. The US pretended that it was, once again, giving Saddam Hussein free range, but as it would turn out, that was not the case. Ramsey Clark, who served as US attorney general under President Johnson, believed that President Bush deliberately fomented the border conflict between Iraq and Kuwait. "The US government used the Kuwaiti royal family to provoke an Iraqi invasion," Clark said. The goal of George H. W. Bush's intrigue, he said, was "to provoke an Iraqi invasion that would justify a massive assault on Iraq to establish US dominion in the Gulf."[32]

In public, President Bush expressed outrage at Iraq's invasion of Kuwait. At the UN, the United States protested Iraq's violation of the UN's ban on violence. President Bush declared that it was not acceptable for one country to invade another, even though he himself had invaded Panama on December 20, 1989, without a UN mandate and therefore illegally. Then he overthrew Manuel Noriega during "Operation Just Cause." Dictator Noriega had been on the CIA's payroll for at least ten years, had met with CIA director Bill Casey in Washington in 1983, had supported arms deliveries to the contras via Panama, and had trafficked in cocaine. It was only when the Iran-Contra affair blew up that the corrupt Noriega lost his protection and President Bush ousted him. "It was the seventh time the United States had invaded Panama since it had kidnapped the province from Colombia in 1903 to build the canal," commented US journalist William Blum.[33]

The public in the US hardly criticized the invasion of Panama, but was opposed to a move on Iraq, which was located much further away, in the Middle East. To overcome this public opposition, President Bush and the Kuwaiti royal family worked together to spread war propaganda, consulting the American public relations firm Hill & Knowlton for support. To shock the public, Hill & Knowlton developed the "Nayirah Testimony," which demonized Iraqis and depicted them as barbarians. On October 10, 1990, a fifteen-year-old girl, introduced as Nayirah, was in tears when she told the US Congressional Human Rights Caucus that she had worked in a hospital in Kuwait during the invasion and that she had watched Iraqi soldiers take babies out of their incubators and throw them on the ground, where they were left to die. It was all a lie; Nayirah had never worked in the hospital in Kuwait. But President Bush seized on this shocking story and repeated it on television, claiming that 312 newborn babies had died in this way. It was not until after the war that the incubator story turned out to be a lie and that Nayirah's real name was Nijirah al-Sabah. In fact, she was the daughter of the Kuwaiti ambassador to the United States. George H. W. Bush had, yet again, successfully deceived the public.[34]

On January 17, 1991, the United States began massive airstrikes on Kuwait and Iraq as part of Operation Desert Storm. Under the command of US General Norman Schwarzkopf, an international force of 960,000 soldiers, of which the United States provided three-quarters, drove the Iraqis out of Kuwait. Black smoke from burning oil wells darkened the sky. CNN portrayed the war as a technical spectacle and as a display of fireworks, while brutal images were censored. The reality was quite different. Iraqi soldiers lying in trenches were buried alive by armored American bulldozers pushing sand into the trenches. According to Reuters, 85,000 Iraqis were killed in this Second Gulf War, despite its only lasting three months. It was a slaughter. The force led by President Bush lost only 313 soldiers, including 266 from the US, 44 British, two French, and one Italian. Japan and Germany did not send any troops but financed part of the war costs. On April 3, 1991, President Bush declared Kuwait liberated and the short war over. Shortly thereafter, the United States opened its first permanent military base in the Persian Gulf and stationed tanks, aircraft, and other military materiel in Kuwait.[35]

CHAPTER 12

THE SEPTEMBER 11 ATTACKS

With more than eight million inhabitants, New York is the largest city in the United States, ahead of Los Angeles and Chicago. The terrorist attacks of September 11, 2001, a.k.a. 9/11, shook not only everyone in this famous city, but the entire world. Along with the assassination of President John F. Kennedy and the Japanese attack on Pearl Harbor, it is among the key events in the history of the United States. All three events deeply frightened and shocked the US population, and in each case, the president took his country to war immediately thereafter.

In 1941, President Roosevelt used the shock of Pearl Harbor to lead the US population into war against Germany and Japan. At the time, the US population did not know that President Roosevelt and his closest confidants had been informed about the coming Japanese attack.

After the assassination of President Kennedy, President Johnson went off to fight the Vietnam War. Again, at the time, the US population did not know that the alleged attack on the USS *Maddox* in the Gulf of Tonkin on August 4, 1964, had never occurred and was a pure fabrication. They also did not know that President Kennedy wanted to withdraw all US advisors from Vietnam in an effort to end the conflict in Southeast Asia.

After 9/11, President George W. Bush, who had taken office just eight months earlier, in January 2001, declared the so-called "war on terror" and attacked Afghanistan in 2001, and then Iraq in 2003. President Bush claimed that Iraq had something to do with the 9/11 terrorist attacks and that he had weapons of mass destruction, neither of which was true.

A New Pearl Harbor

To date, 9/11 has been the largest terrorist attack in history, leaving about 3,000 people dead. It is still not entirely clear what exactly happened at the time. Three different versions of the story are still circulating; everyone has to make up their own mind on which of the three versions they believe to be true. The first version of the story, the official narrative of President Bush, states that the attacks were carried out by Arab Muslims from the al-Qaeda terrorist network and that the US government was taken completely by surprise (the "surprise" story). The second story states that the attacks were carried out by radical Muslims, but that President Bush's administration, as was the case with Pearl Harbor in 1941, knew of the impending attacks and deliberately allowed them to happen in order to shock the US population (the "let it happen on purpose" story). The third story states that 9/11 was a false flag attack organized by criminals within the US intelligence community, who blew up the Twin Towers and the Pentagon and blamed the crime on Muslims in order to wage war in the Middle East (the "make it happen on purpose" story). This chapter will lay out some of the many unanswered questions about 9/11, including the failure of the US Air Force, the trading of put options, and the collapse of WTC7 (World Trade Center Building 7). Hopefully, historical research in the future will be able to fully illuminate the events that occurred on 9/11 and find the entire truth.

In September 2000, a year before the terrorist attacks, the neoconservative think tank known as Project for the New American Century wrote a strategy paper titled "Rebuilding America's Defenses." In it, the authors called for the USA to expand its imperial power following the collapse of the Soviet Union. "This report proceeds from the belief that America should seek to preserve and extend its position of global leadership by maintaining the preeminence of US military forces," the authors proclaimed. It was necessary to massively increase US military spending and buy state-of-the-art weapons, they said, because the US military needed to be able to fight multiple wars in different countries at the same time. "The process of transformation . . . is likely to be a long one, absent some catastrophic and catalyzing event—like a new Pearl Harbor," the authors concluded.[1]

The readers of the study had no idea that exactly one year after the publication of this paper, something like a new Pearl Harbor would actually take place, namely an attack on the US mainland resulting in many casualties. On Tuesday, September 11, 2001, at 8:46 a.m., a hijacked passenger plane, American Airlines flight 11, crashed into the North Tower of the World Trade Center (WTC) in New York. Fifteen minutes later, United Airlines flight 175 flew into the South Tower of the WTC. While the Twin Towers were still burning, word arrived that another passenger plane, American Airlines flight 77, had hit the Pentagon in Washington at 9:37 a.m. Shortly before 10:00 a.m., the South Tower, WTC2, collapsed. Huge clouds of dust billowed through the streets of New York, while firefighters, other first responders, and residents ran for their lives. Shortly after 10:00 a.m. a fourth passenger plane, United Airlines flight 93, crashed near Shanksville, Pennsylvania. At 10:28 a.m. the North Tower, WTC1, also collapsed. Most people watched the terrorist attacks live on television and they were shocked. The collapse of the Twin Towers was shown over and over again. Later in the afternoon, at 5:20 p.m., WTC7 also collapsed, even though it had not been hit by a plane. According to US journalist Bob Woodward, President George W. Bush noted in his diary that evening: "The Pearl Harbor of the 21st Century took place today."[2]

2004: The Failed Kean and Hamilton Investigation

After the attacks, active members of Congress should have conducted a critical investigation, similar to the one that Senator Frank Church had led in the 1970s, which examined the CIA's assassinations. But that was not what happened. Instead, President George W. Bush and Vice President Dick Cheney selected ten people who were no longer in Congress and put this hand-picked group in charge of the investigation. At first, they wanted to appoint former secretary of state Henry Kissinger to lead the investigation, but when the victims' families protested this, the White

House had to drop that plan. As a result, in December 2002, President Bush appointed former New Jersey governor Thomas Kean as head of the investigative commission. Lee Hamilton, who had served in the House of Representatives for the state of Indiana until 1999, was appointed as deputy head. Kean and Hamilton, along with historian Philip Zelikow, wrote the official narrative of the 9/11 terrorist attacks and submitted their 567-page final report on July 22, 2004. In it, they confirmed the "surprise" story presented earlier by President Bush, according to which the Saudi Osama bin Laden had planned the terrorist attacks in Afghanistan and then nineteen Muslim terrorists from the al-Qaeda network had carried them out. The report concluded that the attacks took the US by complete surprise.[3]

But how had Kean, Hamilton, and Zelikow arrived at this conclusion? How could they prove the culpability of Afghanistan or Osama bin Laden? During the war against Afghanistan, which began immediately after the terrorist attacks, October 7, 2001, US military personnel had detained various Muslims and flown them to the US military base at Guantanamo Bay in Cuba, where they were tortured. The CIA was responsible for the tortures at Guantanamo. Their methods included sleep deprivation and waterboarding, which involves causing the torture victim to experience the sensation of drowning. The CIA provided more than 100 interrogation reports stemming from Guantanamo Bay to Kean, Hamilton, and Zelikow, who were not themselves involved in the act of torturing, but they based their report on it. More than a quarter of all footnotes in their final report refer to "intelligence reports." The US's principal witness, Pakistani Khalid Sheikh Mohammed, was also tortured. It is a well-known fact, however, that torture does not serve to establish the truth. Torture victims later stated that they only testified so that they would not continue to be tortured. The cover of the Kean-Hamilton book should have indicated that the official 9/11 report was based on torture. Historian Philip Zelikow later attempted to justify this highly questionable procedure by stating that the "CIA and the administration refused to give us direct access to the detainees." Be that as it may, such an approach involving torture is not admissible in historical research. Any torturer can write a book and claim anything in it, noting that his torture victims confirmed it. Because the report by Kean, Hamilton, and Zelikow is based on torture, it cannot be trusted.[4]

Moreover, the report failed to account for the correct number of skyscrapers that collapsed in New York: the collapse of WTC7, which was not even hit by an airplane, is completely missing. This is a gross failure. The official historiography of Kean, Hamilton, and Zelikow on 9/11 can therefore not be taken seriously. "The Commission avoids another embarrassing problem—explaining how WTC7 could have collapsed, also at virtually free-fall speed—by simply not mentioning the collapse of this building," protested theologian David Ray Griffin, who has researched 9/11 extensively.[5]

The fact that Kean, Hamilton, and Zelikow were not conducting an honest investigation also became apparent to some more aware members of the investigative commission. Commission member Max Cleland, who had lost both legs and an arm in the Vietnam War and later served as a senator from Georgia, was the first to see through the cover-up. The White House, he said, had continually obstructed the investigation, claiming 9/11 had something to do with Iraq. "They had a plan to go to war [with Iraq], and when 9/11 happened that's what they did; they went to war," explained Cleland. The president determined which documents the commission would even be allowed to examine, and Kean, Hamilton, and Zelikow bowed to that dictate. "This is ridiculous," Cleland correctly recognized, but he was largely ignored by the media. He said that the Warren Commission investigation of the Kennedy assassination had already failed, and now the same thing was happening with 9/11. "It should be a national scandal," Cleland protested. In December 2003, he resigned from the commission headed by Kean and Hamilton because he did not want to be part of the cover-up.[6]

In 2006 Lee Hamilton admitted to CBC News that he didn't think for a minute that they had gotten it all right. He said that they only wrote a first draft of the whole story. The pressure on the investigative commission had been so great that it would be really "amazing if we got everything right," Hamilton acknowledged, without specifically addressing the thorny issue of torturing witnesses or apologizing for the commission simply ignoring the collapse of WTC7 altogether. Hamilton had already chaired the investigation of the Iran-Contra affair, and at that time had prevented the CIA's cocaine trafficking from being exposed. Together with Kean, he published another book in which he admitted that their investigation was "doomed to fail" because they were denied access to important documents and people. Essentially this all means that today there exists no credible official US investigation into the terrorist attacks of September 11, 2001.[7]

Total Failure of US Air Defense

In the late 1980s, Catherine Austin Fitts served in the Department of Housing and Urban Development under the administration of George H. W. Bush. She has never believed President George W. Bush's official narrative of 9/11. Fitts recalls that already back in the 1980s, there had been a general distrust of the government in Washington, especially among African Americans. She noticed that in the month following 9/11, African Americans "viewed the attacks differently" than White people. Fitts recalls that White people firmly believed that the USA had been "attacked." African Americans, however, felt that the whole story did not seem to add up. Over time, Fitts explained in 2018, distrust grew among White people as well, and they "realized something was wrong."[8]

Fitts found it particularly astonishing that US fighter jets had not intercepted the four much slower passenger planes after it was determined that they had been hijacked by terrorists. Therefore, Fitts already knew on the day of the attacks that this was a "false flag operation," because as someone who knew the security protocols of the Federal Aviation Administration (FAA), she knew immediately that such an attack could not be carried out without "help from the inside." George W. Bush's administration, she said, had deceived the US population. Fitts further stated that the masses were manipulated by the images that were constantly repeated on TV. People did not even wonder why the US air defenses had failed. Fitts said that while she does not own a television set herself, she noticed that the people who did have a TV and watched it all the time were "much more likely to believe the official narrative."[9]

If air traffic controllers lose contact with a passenger aircraft or if an airliner goes off its scheduled path, the military is usually informed immediately, upon which it scrambles fighter jets that make contact with the passenger plane. Why did this not happen on September 11, 2001? After the terrorist attacks of 9/11, it turned out that the US Air Force was conducting various exercises on September 11, 2001. As part of these exercises, the military also simulated aircraft hijackings and air strikes on the United States. This caused confusion among the military personnel involved, as well as among civilian personnel in the FAA. Richard Clark, who was in charge of counterterrorism at the National Security Council in the White House, remembers calling Chief of Staff Richard Myers during the attacks to inquire about their air defense, in response to which Myers informed him of the ongoing exercises and replied, "Not a pretty picture, Dick. We are in the middle of Vigilant Warrior, a NORAD exercise."[10]

Why were the air defenses not working that day? That question remains unanswered to this day. The North American Aerospace Defense Command (NORAD) is responsible for air defense in the USA and is divided into different sectors. The hijackings and the terrorist attacks took place in the Northeast Sector (NEADS) of NORAD. The FAA called NEADS at 8:37 a.m. to request assistance, explaining, "We have a problem. We have a hijacked aircraft headed towards New York. We need someone to scramble some F-16s or something up there to help us out." To which NEADS officer Jeremy Powell replied, "Is this real-world or exercise?" To which the FAA confirmed, "No. This is not an exercise. Not a test."[11]

Among other assets, NORAD has F-16 military aircraft at their disposal, which are capable of flying over 900 miles per hour at sea level. Despite this, NORAD failed to intercept even one of the four passenger planes, which are much slower. NORAD was not able to prevent the first passenger plane, American Airlines flight 11, which took off from Boston at 7:59 a.m., from crashing into the North Tower at 8:46 a.m. Apparently the warning time had been too short; NORAD was not informed of the hijacking until 8:38 a.m., the Kean report claims. But NORAD did not intercept United Airlines flight 175, which hit the South Tower fifteen minutes later, either. After that, another almost forty minutes passed before American Airlines flight 77 struck the Pentagon at 9:37 a.m. Once again, NORAD did not intercept the deviated aircraft. Finally, United

Airlines flight 93, which crashed near Shanksville, Pennsylvania, at 10:03 a.m., was not intercepted either. This constitutes a total failure of US air defense that day.[12]

How could this have happened? Which NORAD pilots were involved in the exercises? Which NORAD pilots had to defend the airspace? The investigation committee questioned General Ralph Eberhart, the commander of NORAD, on exactly this. On June 19, 2004, Congressman Timothy Roemer, who was a member of the 9/11 Investigative Committee, asked the Air Force general, "Who was responsible for coordinating the multiple war games running on the morning of September 11, 2001?" General Eberhart, however, refused to clarify this important question. His response was, "No comment."[13]

In addition to Exercise Vigilant Warrior, other exercises with different names were also ongoing, including Vigilant Guardian and Amalgam Virgo. Thomas Kean was not satisfied with the military's responses. Furthermore, he found the information provided by the various employees from the FAA to be untrustworthy. Time and again, both NORAD and the FAA changed their timelines on the hijackings, which created confusion. "The FAA and NORAD representatives presented a version of 9/11 that is untrue," Kean said. "We to this day don't know why NORAD told us what they told us . . . it was just so far from the truth."[14]

In Germany, Lieutenant Colonel Jochen Scholz was struck by the US Air Force's failure. "It is completely inconceivable that in a country like the United States, something can happen for almost two hours, without any intervention of their own air force," said Scholz, who served as a career officer in the German Air Force until 2000. His service included several years as a multinational NATO staff. NORAD has "every mouse on its radar screen." Even during military exercises, a part of the Air Force is still responsible for protecting the country, so the war games cannot possibly be the cause of the total aerial defense failure, Scholz said. Never do all pilots participate in an exercise—some of the pilots are always responsible for defending the country.

Four airplanes being hijacked over a period of two hours, without the Air Force intervening, that is "inconceivable, definitely inconceivable," Scholz stressed. After an air traffic controller loses contact with a passenger plane, for whatever reason, the Air Force is instantly informed. The pilots then immediately take to the air and make contact with the passenger aircraft. In 2001, this worked smoothly more than sixty times prior to the attacks, Scholz said, adding that it also worked again after 9/11, as it is routine procedure. Only on Tuesday, September 11, was there something wrong. "That can only be the case if someone interfered with this mechanism," Scholz concluded, adding that it could not have been Osama bin Laden.[15]

Millions in Profits with Put Options

In the days before September 11, 2001, unknown individuals amassed put options to bet on sharply falling stock prices of the affected airlines, banks, and reinsurers, thus earning millions. How did these unidentified people know that a terrorist attack would occur on September 11? These anonymous individuals had insider knowledge and they expected the prices of the stocks in question to plummet. When the American Airlines and the United Airlines planes hit the towers, the share price of these two carriers plummeted, resulting in a profit of about $9 million for the holders of the put options. The put options purchased on the shares of the financial institutions Bank of America, Merrill Lynch, Citigroup, and J.P. Morgan also paid off, because these banks had offices in the towers. After the terrorist attacks, their stock prices dropped and the owners of the put options realized a profit of $11 million. The insiders also speculated with put options on the European-based reinsurers Swiss Re and Munich Re, because they were the ones that would have to pay for the damage to the towers. This speculation also worked out and resulted in a profit of $11 million. All in all, the terrorist attacks were a multimillion-dollar bonanza for these insiders. They earned more than $30 million, while almost 3,000 people lost their lives.[16]

At least one member of the House of Representatives thought this was odd. "Those engaged in unusual stock trades immediately before September 11 knew enough to make millions of dollars from United and American airlines, and certain insurance and brokerage firms' stocks," said Representative Cynthia McKinney, criticizing these plots. "What did this administration know, and when did it know it about the events of

September 11?" The courageous Representative McKinney of Georgia, who has consistently championed the causes of the peace movement, said it was morally reprehensible that insiders had enriched themselves instead of warning people. "Who else knew and why did they not warn the innocent people of New York who were needlessly murdered?"[17]

What is a put option anyway? A put option is a legal financial product in which the buyer acquires the right, but not the obligation (hence "option"), to sell a share of, for example, American Airlines at a certain price on a certain day. Each put option has an expiration date, so it can only be exercised within a predetermined time frame. The holder must pay a price to buy the option, but does not have to buy the stock to which the option relates. If the stock collapses, the value of the put option increases because the holder of the option can then sell the stock above the current market price. If the stock does not fall, the option expires and the investor loses the money he spent on buying the option. With these put options, huge profits were realized, because the market price of these stocks really plummeted on September 11. It is important to know that nobody can buy put options anonymously. In order to make such a trade, one must be identified by name.

The terrorist attacks occurred before the stock markets in the USA had opened. Following the attacks on September 11, by orders of the US Securities and Exchange Commission (SEC), the stock exchanges in the US remained closed until September 17. In Europe, however, the stock exchanges were open when, shortly before 3:00 p.m. European time, news spread that a plane had hit the WTC in New York City. At first, some people thought it was an accident, but when the second plane crashed into the other tower at 3:06 p.m. European time, distress began to spread. All the retailers followed the events on television. Within minutes, share prices in the European stock markets plummeted. The shares of reinsurer Swiss Re suffered the biggest losses, dropping 14 percent, followed by Munich Re, which was down 12 percent. Once the dust had settled, some Europeans also took a closer look at the suspicious trading that had taken place with put options. Ernst Welteke, head of the German Bundesbank, spoke of "almost irrefutable proof of insider trading."[18]

Marc Chesney, a lecturer at the Institute for Banking and Finance at the University of Zurich, was able to prove these dubious transactions by conducting an elaborate analysis of stock market transactions during the time leading up to 9/11. He too was struck by the explosive increase in put option purchases right before September 11, 2001. "The statistical study clearly reveals extremely dubious trades that may have been made by insiders," explained Chesney, a financial expert who published his study in the *Journal of Empirical Finance*. For definite proof, the authorities in the US would need to demand that the SEC disclose the names and networks of those who bought the options. According to Chesney, there are more than enough suspicious facts to warrant a new and independent investigation into potential criminal activity. The insiders' profits amounted to over $30 million.[19]

How were these millions earned? Let's examine this by the example of the purchase of put options on American Airlines. Chesney found that on September 10, 2001—the day before the terrorist attacks—a record volume of 1,535 contracts were traded, each for 100 put options with a strike price of $30 and a maturity in October 2001. This trading volume was more than sixty times greater than the average of the total daily traded volume in the three weeks leading up to September 10. The put options each cost $2.15 and the American Airlines' stock price was at $29.70. As previously noted, the stock exchanges in the USA remained closed from September 11 to 17. Upon its reopening, those put options could be sold for $12—a return of 458 percent—while the share price dropped to $18. The options were all exercised by October 5, resulting in a cumulative profit of $1.18 million. United Airlines' share price behaved similarly, falling from $30 to $17.

Rather than identify the insiders who traded these put options by name, the Kean Commission tucked the sensitive issue into a small print footnote at the very back of the report, namely footnote 130 on page 499. "Some unusual trading did in fact occur, but each such trade proved to have an innocuous explanation," the Kean Commission asserted. "Yet, further investigation has revealed that the trading had no connection with 9/11," the commission said. "A single US-based institutional investor with no conceivable ties to al-Qaeda" bought most of the put options on American Airlines and United Airlines, it said. The names of the buyers should have been listed in the Kean report. This was not intelligence; it was a cover-up.[20]

The majority of the options had been purchased through the investment bank Alex Brown, *Hintergrund* magazine reported, pointing out that Alex Brown's longtime director, Buzzy Krongard, subsequently took a high position in the CIA. David Callahan, the managing editor of the US magazine *SmartCEO*, filed a request with the SEC under the Freedom of Information Act (FOIA), demanding that they release the information about who had bought the put options. The FOIA is intended to give the public broad access to government agency data collections, with the objective of promoting transparency in democracy. On December 23, 2009, however, the SEC told Callahan that it could not release this data, due to it having "been destroyed."[21]

The Blowing Up of WTC7

Most people, impressed by television, believe that only two towers collapsed in New York City on September 11, 2001. But that is not the case; there were actually three towers that collapsed. Namely, both of the well-known Twin Towers, WTC1 and WTC2, each 1,360 feet high, and WTC7, which was 610 feet high. Unlike the Twin Towers, however, WTC7 had not previously been hit by an airplane. Nevertheless, the massive structure with a solid steel skeleton collapsed at 5:20 p.m., in just seven seconds. It was puzzling. To this day, the collapse of WTC7 remains an unsolved mystery of the attacks, the *New York Times* stated a year after the attacks. Before 9/11, no skyscraper built of concrete and steel had ever collapsed due to fire in the United States. Is it a credible explanation to attribute the three towers collapsing to fire when this had never happened before? The collapse of WTC7 was sudden, with no apparent indication that it would happen, and the building collapsed entirely into its own foundation.[22]

At the time, reporter Jane Stanley of the BBC, who was reporting live from New York City on the day of the attacks, was the cause of a lot of confusion in England. On September 11, she reported on the collapse of WTC7 in the five o'clock news, with the building still standing and clearly visible behind her. Jane Stanley would later admit that reporting on WTC7's collapse twenty minutes too early "was a mistake." In 2008, BBC news director Richard Porter also apologized for the oversight. The BBC argued that it had received the news on WTC7's collapse from the Reuters news agency. But how did Reuters know about the building's collapse even before it happened?[23]

There are only two possible causes that the collapse of WTC7 can be attributed to. Either it was due to fire or it was due to controlled demolition. During the first two and a quarter seconds, the forty-seven-story tower came down at a free fall, without any resistance, at gravitational speed. "When a body begins to fall freely from a resting position, its velocity after one second is 35 km/h, and after two seconds, it is 70 km/h. WTC7 kept accelerating to well over 100 km/h, even after the initial free-fall phase," explains German physicist Ansgar Schneider, adding that "this is astounding, even for someone like David Copperfield." WTC7 came crashing down to the ground as fast as a skydiver would, if he jumped from the roof of the building without opening his parachute. How is that possible? WTC7 had a solid steel skeleton structure with a total of 81 massive vertical columns, 57 of which ran along the outer sides, while 24 columns formed the core. How can a solid steel frame suddenly collapse in free fall and, like a Porsche, accelerate to over 100 km/h?[24]

The answer to this important question was not found until eighteen years after the terrorist attacks. On September 3, 2019, US civil engineer Dr. Leroy Hulsey of the University of Alaska Fairbanks published a 114-page study of the collapse of WTC7. This in-depth examination was commissioned by a group called Architects & Engineers for 9/11 Truth and its president, Richard Gage. After four years of investigation, the Hulsey study came to a clear and unequivocal conclusion: "Fire did not cause the collapse of WTC . . . The collapse of WTC7 was a global failure involving the near-simultaneous failure of every column in the building." Although the term "controlled demolition" does not appear anywhere in the report, Hulsey's findings are unambiguous and convincing: WTC7 was blown up.[25]

This research finding is a sensation. The entire history of the terrorist attacks of September 11, 2001, and the subsequent wars of the United States, needs to be rewritten. As a historian, I have been interested in the collapse of WTC7 for many years. In 2006, I was working as a senior researcher in the Security Policy Research Center at the Swiss Federal

Institute of Technology (ETH) in Zurich when I discussed the collapse of WTC7 with other ETH lecturers in structural analysis and design. "In my opinion, WTC7 was most likely demolished professionally," Jörg Schneider, who is an ETH professor emeritus of structural analysis and design, explained to me at the time. Hugo Bachmann, also an ETH professor emeritus of structural analysis and design, concurred and told me that there was a high degree of probability that WTC7 was blown up. The Hulsey Report confirmed these statements in 2019.[26]

Physicist Ansgar Schneider has also justifiably classified the sudden and simultaneous yielding of all 81 steel columns as "extremely astonishing." Schneider goes on to explain that "WTC7 was an enormous building with a solid skeleton made of steel. It was a skyscraper, 186 meters high and 100 meters wide. That is gigantic! In Germany, there are only a handful of buildings that are taller, and they're all in Frankfurt, there is not a single other one." In Switzerland, WTC7 would be the tallest building, comparable to the Roche Tower in Basel on the Rhine. "Now, can you give me a scientific explanation of how isolated, localized fires allow for the steel columns at the eastern end to collude with those 100 meters to the west and then all give way at the same time?" asked Schneider in an interview published by *Rubikon*. Only a coordinated and controlled blast could explain this.[27]

For a few years, the claim was that WTC7 had collapsed because of fire. To this day, the Wikipedia page on WTC7 still explains that fire was the cause of the collapse, even though that is not true. The claim that fire had caused the building to collapse was made prominent by a report published on August 21, 2008, by the National Institute of Standards and Technology (NIST), a US government agency. At the time, NIST investigator Shyam Sunder claimed that when the North Tower, WTC1, collapsed at 10:28 a.m., debris fell onto WTC7—which was located over 350 feet away—and ignited office fires. There were indeed several smaller fires in WTC7, but Sunder's claim that due to these fires, the A2001 horizontal steel beam expanded and dislocated from its support on Column 79, is not true.[28]

After years of investigation, the Hulsey Report convincingly shows that steel beam A2001 could never have disconnected from Column 79; that would not have been possible. The girder was bolted down tightly, and even fires could not release it from its mount. This, in turn, means that Column 79 was never free-standing, as NIST had claimed as recently as 2008. Hulsey, the civil engineer, was able to prove through extensive testing that Columns 80 and 81 were also not disrupted by fire. "Columns 79, 80, and 81 did not fail at the lower floors of the building, as asserted by NIST," Hulsey explains. With this, the cause for the collapse of the entire building presented by NIST is eliminated. Fire could not have been the cause of the collapse of the high-rise building. WTC7 was blown up.[29]

US American architect Richard Gage also recognized that fire could not explain the collapse of WTC7. "We are a group of 2,200 architects and engineers, a nonprofit organization dedicated to finding out what really happened at the World Trade Center with the destruction of all three towers on that day," Gage said in an interview with C-SPAN. "[WTC7] drops like a rock . . . Free-fall acceleration, straight down, uniformly, symmetrically . . . A building with 40,000 tons of structural steel cannot fall straight down . . . due to normal office fires, the official reason given us by NIST . . . without all eighty columns on each floor being removed simultaneously." The fires in WTC7 were small. There had been much hotter and larger fires that had burned longer in other high-rise buildings in other cities, yet those buildings did not collapse, Gage correctly explained.[30]

US mathematician Peter Michael Ketcham, who worked at NIST from 1997 to 2011 but had not been involved in the WTC7 investigation, did not start reading the NIST reports until August 2016. "I quickly became furious. First, I was furious with myself. How could I have worked at NIST all those years and not have noticed this before? Second, I was furious with NIST," recalls Ketcham. "The more I investigated, the more apparent it became that NIST had reached a predetermined conclusion by ignoring, dismissing, and denying the evidence." The Hulsey Report has now clarified the NIST cover-up, making an extremely important contribution to elucidating the terrorist attacks of September 11, 2001.[31]

To support its fire thesis, NIST published a computer model of the collapse of WTC7 in which the outer walls of the building were severely deformed. In the actual collapse of the building, however, this was not the case. When citizens asked NIST for the computer simulation's input data, NIST refused. If scientists do not make the data they use publicly available, then it is not science. NIST argued that it could not release the data because it would jeopardize national security, but that is not credible. "There were many contributors to the NIST WTC investigation: Why not let them openly answer questions in their own voice with the depth of knowledge and level of detail that follows from the nuts and bolts of their research?" suggested former NIST employee Ketcham. It is quite important for the US to get down to the truth about 9/11 because "in truth is where our healing lies," Ketcham wisely declared.[32]

Explosives Are Found in the Dust of the Twin Towers

Designed by US architect Minoru Yamasaki, the Twin Towers opened their doors in 1973 and dominated the New York skyline for nearly thirty years. As the study conducted by Leroy Hulsey scientifically proves the demolition of WTC7, the collapse of the Twin Towers, WTC1 and WTC2, is now being debated again. Were the Twin Towers also brought down by controlled demolition? Or did they collapse because of the fires? This is unclear and everyone must form their own opinion on the subject to the best of their knowledge. The Hulsey Report, published in 2019, only focuses on WTC7 and does not address the Twin Towers.

In Denmark, chemist Niels Harrit, who was a lecturer at the University of Copenhagen, and US physicist Steven Jones, who taught at Brigham Young University in Utah, worked together to investigate the dust that settled over Manhattan after the collapse of the three towers. "We have discovered distinctive red/gray chips in significant numbers in dust associated with the World Trade Center destruction," Niels Harrit told Danish television in 2009. Nanothermite is a military-developed, highly energetic pyrotechnic or explosive material. "It has taken 18 months to prepare [this] scientific article," said Harrit, a chemist who published his research results in the *Open Chemical Physics Journal.* What were the explosives used for?[33]

The Towers Were Loaded with Asbestos

In the construction of the WTC, heat-resistant spray-on asbestos was used for fireproofing. "The WTC buildings contained hundreds of tons of asbestos," said US journalist Michael Bowker, who has written a book on asbestos and its victims. "Fireproofing spray foam was used on at least forty floors within the North Tower." He added that, despite this, the Environmental Protection Agency "intentionally used outdated measurement technology" in the hours and days after the terrorist attacks and failed to warn firefighters and police officers who were first responders at the scene about airborne asbestos. This was "shocking and inexplicable," Bowker stated.[34]

New York billionaire Larry Silverstein, who already owned the WTC7 building, signed a ninety-nine-year lease for the entire WTC complex six weeks before 9/11. The Twin Towers would have had to be renovated because of their asbestos contamination. Due to the terrorist attacks, however, these renovations were canceled, and because his insurance policy explicitly covered terrorist attacks, Silverstein received \$4.5 billion after the attack. These funds came from seven different insurers, including Swiss reinsurer Swiss Re. With this money, the real estate broker built a new WTC7 and, as a replacement for the Twin Towers, the 1,776-foot-high One World Trade Center, which was the tallest building in the US when it opened in 2014.[35]

When blasting or fire releases asbestos into the air, its microscopic fibers can lodge into the lungs. "More than 5,000 New Yorkers who breathed in the asbestos-laced dust that was settling over Manhattan after the collapse of the World Trade Center towers" developed cancer as a result, *Zeit Online* reported. Many firefighters and police officers have died as a result. According to *Zeit Online*, the North Tower alone contained 400 tons of carcinogenic asbestos. But because the health issues caused by asbestos don't appear until much later, it was not talked about for a long time. "What asbestos does only becomes apparent after decades," explains German occupational physician Hans-Joachim Woitowitz.[36]

CHAPTER 13

THE SO-CALLED WAR ON TERROR

After the terrorist attacks of September 11, 2001, the United States went on to wage wars against Afghanistan, Pakistan, Iraq, Libya, and Syria, among other countries. Under the UN's ban on the use of force, however, wars of aggression are strictly prohibited. Yet leading US media brands such as the *New York Times*, *Washington Post*, *Fox News*, CNN, and *USA Today* virtually never mention the UN ban on violence. Instead, they joined the president and Congress in declaring the so-called "war on terror" and supported the US's attacks on Afghanistan and Iraq, even though both wars clearly violated the UN's ban. Of course, it would also have been illegal for Iraq or Afghanistan to send their troops to attack the US. But since 2001, the so-called "War on Terror" has been the new narrative of the USA. It is the new frame, in which the well-known imperial wars are being portrayed in a different way in order to sell them to the US population and to the world. Therefore, the peace movement must reject the so-called "war on terror."

2001: The Attack on Afghanistan

President George W. Bush, Vice President Dick Cheney, and the leading media outlets immediately blamed Saudi Osama bin Laden and the Muslim terrorist network al-Qaeda for the attacks of 9/11. The fact that bin Laden told CNN that he had nothing to do with the September 11 attacks was of no interest to anyone in Washington. "I would like to assure the world that I did not plan the recent attacks," bin Laden affirmed in Afghanistan, adding that the attacks seemed "to have been planned by people for personal reasons." The US ignored this statement and on October 7, 2001, less than a month after 9/11, it launched an illegal war of aggression against Afghanistan. For the first time in its history, NATO declared an alliance case under Article 5 of the North Atlantic Treaty. Germany, under Chancellor Gerhard Schröder, also sent Bundeswehr troops to Afghanistan, without having first determined the exact circumstances surrounding the terrorist attacks of September 11.[1]

"The Cold War is over," journalist Peter Scholl-Latour declared during a conference in Berlin in 2012, pointing out that there are no more problems with Russia. "Who has taken the Soviet Union's place as an enemy?—Islamic terrorism." But terrorism is not an enemy, "it cannot be defined," Scholl-Latour warned, as it is just a concept—a form of waging war. The formula "war on terror" lacks a clearly defined target. "That would be like waging war against the Blitzkrieg in World War II," warned Scholl-Latour. NATO had gotten into the "fatal situation" of waging wars against indefinable opponents in countries far away, "which was not intended at all," he said. "And we just end up with decisions like the one in Afghanistan, where under the impression of the tragedy of 9/11—that is, the blowing up of the World Trade Center—there was such a wave of pro-American sympathy, which led to the invocation of NATO's Article 5, which in this case did not even apply, because it requires a defined adversary, and terrorism is not an adversary." Moreover, Scholl-Latour stated that it turned out that those responsible for the terrorist attacks on 9/11 "were definitely not Afghans." Scholl-Latour, who has often traveled to Afghanistan, pointed out that the culprits were Saudis, a.k.a. the "favorite allies of the West and closest economic partners of the United States."[2]

According to the US Constitution, Congress alone has the right to declare war; the president does not have that right. Shocked by the terrorist attacks, Congress overwhelmingly passed a new law on September 14, 2001. With this "Authorization for Use of Military Force" (AUMF) against terrorists, the president was granted permission to use all "necessary and appropriate force" against anyone who, in his judgment, "planned, authorized, committed, or aided" the attacks of 9/11, or harbored such organizations or persons. This law essentially gave the president a blank check to wage endless wars in various countries. Nearly twenty years later, Republican congressman Mac Thornberry stated that at the time, he never imagined that this law would be used for so many wars in so many different countries.[3]

The new law of the AUMF was waved through the Senate by a unanimous vote of 98–0. In the House of Representatives, 420 representatives voted in favor of the new law. Only one courageous woman, Representative Barbara Lee of California, refused to issue a permit for endless wars and voted "no." As a result, she was called a "communist" and a "traitor" and even received death threats. "Our nation is grieving, we're all mourning, we're angry," Lee said, justifying her rejection. "I believe fully and firmly that the Congress of the United States is the only legislative body that can say, 'Let's pause for a moment . . . and let's look at using some restraint before we rush to action.' Because military action can lead to an escalation and spiral out of control," she wisely cautioned. "I am convinced that military action alone will not prevent further terrorist attacks," she clarified, warning against giving too much power to the executive branch. "We must be vigilant right now, because under the cloak of national security, many of our civil liberties could be just wiped off the floor," Lee wisely warned, but she did not find a majority.[4]

Empowered by this new authority, the Bush administration declared the entire world a battlefield. US Special Forces, commanded by the Joint Special Operations Command, were given a multibillion dollar budget and they expanded to become the "paramilitary arm of the administration," as US journalist Jeremy Scahill said. Many covert operations formerly conducted by the CIA's Directorate of Operations were taken over by the US military and its special forces. Covert operations in which people were captured, tortured, or killed took place outside of declared war zones and the US population did not learn about any of them. Every use of force was sold as a counterterrorism operation. Scahill revealed that the US Special Forces operated not only in Afghanistan, Pakistan, and Iraq, but also in Somalia, Algeria, the Philippines, Indonesia, Thailand, Mali, Yemen,

Colombia, Peru, and other countries. In doing so, the empire disregarded the sovereignty of the affected states and the UN ban on violence.[5]

Bob Barr, who sat in the House of Representatives for Georgia from 1995 to 2003, had voted in favor of the AUMF and later regretted it. Presidents Bush, Obama, and Trump would cite the law to authorize actions "ranging from warrantless surveillance against American citizens, to cruise missile attacks on Syrian government air bases, and actions against ISIS throughout the Middle East region," Barr said. With this law, he said, Congress has "largely abdicated any responsibility" to help determine foreign policy and has ceded too much power to the White House. Of course, Congress can repeal the AUMF law, but so far there has been no majority in favor of doing so. "Power once ceded by the Congress to the president is not easily recaptured, if ever," Barr warned pensively in 2019.[6]

Combat Drones Revolutionize Warfare

The war on Afghanistan, which began in October 2001, marked the beginning of global drone warfare. It was the first time that the Special Operations Command deployed massive numbers of unmanned, remote-controlled drones of the Predator and Reaper types. Equipped with Hellfire missiles, these drones can surveil an area from very high altitudes, using visual cameras during the day and thermal imaging cameras at night. At the beginning of 2001, the United States owned no more than 50 combat drones worldwide; by 2013, it had more than 7,000 of them. "The US military now trains far more drone pilots than it does conventional fighter pilots," reports journalist Emran Feroz, who warns that other countries will soon follow suit and imitate the USA. The drone pilots only see their victims on their screens and do not physically enter the country that they are attacking. "Just like in a video game, at the push of a button they kill people who are many kilometers away," Feroz says. Afghans could not defend themselves against the high-flying drones. US American linguist Noam Chomsky, who has been involved in the peace movement for many years, condemned the use of drones and called it "the most massive terror campaign going on by a long shot."[7]

With each drone victim, a part of the rule of law dies, because in a democratic system, it is actually strictly forbidden to execute people without a fair trial and access to a defense attorney. However, within the new framing narrative of the "war on terror," suddenly everything was different. US soldier Brandon Bryant served as a drone pilot, operating the remotely powered aircraft from a windowless bunker in the Nevada desert. Because the US government and the leading mainstream media labeled the Afghans as terrorists, they were excluded from the human family. "They're bad people and we'd do well to get rid of them," Bryant, who at that point had never heard of the principle of the human family, also used to believe. While on the job, the drone pilots are in "zombie mode," Bryant explained, with no empathy for the victims. After six years of serving as a drone pilot, Bryant resigned. As a parting gift, he received a certificate that showed his accomplishments: 6,000 flight hours and 1,626 enemies killed in combat. That equates to more than half the death toll of the 9/11 terrorist attacks. "The number made me sick to my stomach," Bryant recalled.[8]

In drone warfare, the US has executed people in foreign countries without fair trial after the US president had deemed them criminals. The Pentagon trivializes the fact that innocent people were repeatedly murdered in the process, calling the killings "collateral damage." This development is a fundamental betrayal of the human family. Imagine the outrage if Germany or China used high-altitude drones to shoot people in the US after the German chancellor or Chinese president classified them as criminals. "To say that the president has the right to have citizens killed without due process is nothing less than tearing the Constitution into tiny pieces, setting it on fire, and ultimately trampling on it," protested US journalist Glenn Greenwald.[9]

The drone war was started by President George W. Bush and continued by his successor, President Barack Obama, and then his successor, President Donald Trump. By establishing death lists and expanding drone strikes to other countries, Obama had broken his promise of bringing counterterrorism policy in line with the US Constitution, criticizes Michael Boyle, a lecturer at La Salle University in Philadelphia. "The president has routinized and normalized extrajudicial killing from the Oval Office, taking advantage of America's temporary advantage in drone technology to wage a series of shadow wars in Afghanistan, Pakistan, Yemen, and Somalia.

Without the scrutiny of the legislature and the courts, and outside the public eye, Obama is authorizing murder on a weekly basis, with a discussion of the guilt or innocence of candidates for the 'kill list' being resolved in secret on 'Terror Tuesday' teleconferences with administration officials and intelligence officials."[10]

Most notably, the assassination of Iranian General Qasem Soleimani in Baghdad by US Reaper drones on January 3, 2020, led to worldwide criticism. Iran condemned the murder and called it an "act of international terror." President Donald Trump, however, publicly took responsibility for the murder and justified it as "fighting terror."

The American drones are controlled from the US air base in Ramstein. Germany also participated in the war against Afghanistan, after being pressured by the US to send German soldiers to the Hindu Kush. Some German officers and soldiers, however, have begun to think critically about the US empire. Among them is Jürgen Rose, a Bundeswehr officer with the rank of lieutenant colonel. In 2007, after listening to his conscience, he refused to participate in the Tornado mission in Afghanistan. Rose has studied the behavior of the US empire. He points out the drone assassinations, the death penalty, indefinite incarceration without charge in prison camps like Guantanamo, and concludes that "the US has degenerated into a ferocious empire of barbarism that defies description."[11]

The brutal wars against Afghanistan and Pakistan, which were triggered by 9/11, have taken a heavy toll on local populations. A study conducted by the Physicians for Social Responsibility in 2015 concluded that the war had killed 220,000 people in Afghanistan and 80,000 people in Pakistan. If, in the context of an arithmetic of horror, these 300,000 deaths were compared to the 3,000 deaths resulting from the terrorist attacks of September 11, 2001, then the US and its allies have killed 100 Afghans or Pakistanis for every American that was killed. And this is despite the fact that the Afghans and Pakistanis that were killed had nothing to do with the blowing up of WTC7, nor had they ever been to the United States.[12]

"One of the effects of nationalist thinking is a loss of a sense of proportion," explained US historian Howard Zinn after the attack on Afghanistan. "The killing of 2,300 people at Pearl Harbor becomes the justification for killing 240,000 in Hiroshima and Nagasaki. The killing of 3,000 people on September 11 becomes the justification for killing tens of thousands of people in Afghanistan and Iraq." This is wrong, said Zinn, whose analyses have repeatedly strengthened the peace movement. US soldiers are undoubtedly brutal, he said. "Yet they are victims, too, of our government's lies." The ongoing US wars are wrong, he said. "We need to refute the idea that our nation is different from, morally superior to, the other imperial powers of world history. We need to assert our allegiance to the human race, and not to any one nation," Zinn wisely urged, but was not heard.[13]

2003: The Illegal Attack on Iraq

The leading mainstream media is able to direct our thinking and feeling, at least when we are unconscious. As soon as we become aware, it is no longer possible to do so. Manipulation happens by means of combining texts, pictures, and videos in a way that nudges our thinking in a certain direction and triggers corresponding feelings. Prior to every war, leading media outlets in the US and in other NATO countries generated feelings of fear and hatred toward the country that the US was attacking. This was the case in World War I, when hatred and fear toward the Germans was stirred up. This was the case in World War II, when hatred and fear toward the Japanese was stirred up after Pearl Harbor. This was the case in 1964, with the illegal attack on Vietnam, when hatred and fear toward the Vietnamese was stirred up, and it was the case in 1999, before the illegal attack on Serbia, when the mainstream media spread stories that generated hatred and anger toward the Serbs. It has always worked. The mainstream media can direct the anger and hatred of the US population toward any country in the world.

The mainstream media determines both the selection of topics and the way people think about various issues. In the USA, the statements of the president and his staff dominate public discussion. Not all, but many US citizens still assume that their president tells the truth. This is despite the fact that historians can prove that US presidents have lied repeatedly. Even after the terrorist attacks of September 11, 2001, most US citizens blindly trusted the president and the mass media. The president misused this trust and attacked Iraq by claiming that Iraqi president Saddam Hussein had something to do with 9/11, which turned out to be a lie. By the second meeting of the National Security Council, Defense Secretary Donald Rumsfeld had already set his sights on Iraq and said, "What we should be thinking about is how to get rid of Saddam Hussein."[14]

The war against Iraq was planned long before 9/11 and had nothing to do with "fighting terrorism." Paul O'Neill, who was the treasury secretary in the Bush administration, confirmed that already in the first meeting of the NSC at the White House in January 2001, the overthrow of Saddam Hussein was the central issue. O'Neill said that "as early as February, the logistical implementation" of the Iraq campaign "was no longer about why, it was about how and how quickly." This means that the Iraq war was planned long before the September 11 terrorist attacks and the blowing up of WTC7. It also means that the so-called "war on terror" is just war propaganda, meant to confuse people.[15]

Before the Iraq war, thousands of peace activists in New York, London, Rome, Paris, Berlin, and Bern protested against the war. President George W. Bush and British prime minister Tony Blair, however, were not impressed. They led their countries into war on the basis of bold lies. Not only did they claim that Saddam Hussein had links to the terrorist attacks of September 11, they also claimed that Iraq possessed biological and chemical weapons of mass destruction. Both of these statements were blatant lies. Blair literally said, "Iraq has chemical and biological weapons . . . which could be activated within forty-five minutes." Such lies were spread by the leading media, generating fear and hatred.[16]

American soldiers were also confused by war propaganda. If a claim is repeated over and over throughout all of the leading media brands like the *New York Times*, *Washington Post*, *Fox News*, CNN and *USA Today*, people start to believe it after a while, regardless of whether it is true or not. What matters is that it is constantly repeated and that the claim appears on as many channels as possible. A poll conducted in 2006 revealed that 85 percent of US soldiers in Iraq said their "primary mission" was to "punish Saddam for his role in the terrorist attacks of 9/11." But Saddam Hussein had absolutely nothing to do with the terrorist attacks in New York and Washington. The soldiers had been deceived.[17]

For the people of Iraq, the war was a devastating disaster. Children were torn apart by cluster bombs, women were raped and killed, old people were shot. Many lost their homes and all of their belongings. US soldiers tortured Iraqis by attaching electrical wires to their hands and penises, as the Abu Ghraib torture scandal revealed in 2004. In 2015, the organization known as the International Physicians for the Prevention of Nuclear War (IPPNW) conducted a detailed investigation into the war in their study "Body Count," which concluded that since 2003, the war had killed one million Iraqis. Because "the invasion of Iraq was clearly an act of aggression and a violation of international law, the US and its allies are also responsible for the consequences thereof," the study concluded.[18]

After the outbreak of the war in Iraq, courageous journalists raised their voices against the war. Among those is Australian editor Julian Assange. In 2006, he founded WikiLeaks, a disclosure platform that anonymously publishes documents that are otherwise inaccessible to the public. In 2010, WikiLeaks published "Collateral Murder," a video documenting the offensive of US Apache attack helicopters on Baghdad on July 12, 2007. It shows US soldiers shooting eleven people, the majority of them civilians, from the helicopter with their on-board cannons. Because Assange so dramatically exposed the crimes of the US empire, the latter wanted to arrest him. To avoid this, he spent nearly seven years in the Ecuadorian embassy in London, until 2019, when Ecuador no longer wanted to protect him and he was imprisoned in London. "Today it is Julian Assange, tomorrow it can be any other journalist who has published truthful information in the public interest that runs counter to the narrative of the US government," warned Heike Hänsel, a member of the Bundestag from the Die Linke (The Left) party, who joined many committed people of the peace movement in calling for Assange's release.[19]

The suffering that has been generated by the Iraq war is enormous. Not only Iraqis—US soldiers are suffering too, and many veterans are finding it difficult to live independent, self-reliant lives after returning to the USA. Some have been disabled, have lost their legs or an eye, for example. Others suffer from post-traumatic stress disorders. War affects everyone: not only the person being shot, but also the person who fires the shot. Everything is interconnected and there are no isolated acts. Traumatized

US soldiers try to cope with it by resorting to alcohol or a daily cocktail of various pills. When they can't carry on, they commit suicide. In 2017, the US Department of Veterans Affairs estimated that every day, twenty veterans were killing themselves. That equates to 7,300 a year, more than twice as many lives as the terror attacks of 9/11 claimed.[20]

How the Leading Media Spreads War Propaganda

What would the reaction of the Western community of values have been if Russia, Nigeria, or China had attacked Afghanistan, Pakistan, and Iraq? Wouldn't our leading media immediately—and rightly—have criticized the flagrant violation of the UN's ban on the use of force? Wouldn't they have immediately referred to the right of the affected peoples to self-determination and declared that other countries must not interfere? Why was no one in the US upset about the fact that more than a million Iraqis were killed during the Iraq war? Why was no one bothered by the 300,000 dead in Afghanistan and Pakistan?

Very efficient US war propaganda prevented such basic questions, and if they ever did arise, the media ridiculed them and dismissed them as unimportant. Of course, there are well-intentioned and capable journalists in the US, in Europe, in many other places, but it is striking to see how many journalists have obediently followed the proclamations of US presidents and defense secretaries and just continued to spread the narrative of the "war on terror" without ever really checking whether that narrative is a reality. The leading mainstream media has repeatedly drummed for wars while diverting attention away from the many victims of US imperialism. The mass media reported on the terrorist attacks of September 11, 2001, in a very unbalanced and biased manner. Unanswered questions were concealed and President George W. Bush's story was blindly passed on to the masses without further examining the facts, including the blowing up of WTC7, which was not just ignored—it was deliberately covered up.

Leading media outlets like the *New York Times* also failed in their duty to report objectively before the attack on Iraq, as they helped spread the lie of weapons of mass destruction. "Here's what happened at the time," explained Ray McGovern, who worked at the CIA's International Analysis Division from 1963 to 1990 and then joined the US peace movement after retiring from the CIA. "In early September 2002, the White House handed Michael Gordon, a journalist at the *New York Times*, a report that stated aluminum tubes, which could only be used for the manufacture of uranium, were on their way to Iraq and that this was a sure indication that Saddam Hussein was working on the development of nuclear weapons—it was clear though, that they were artillery tubes. Two days later, the story appeared on the front page of the *New York Times*. That same day, Security Advisor Condoleezza Rice appeared on several television talk shows and on every one of them she was asked about the *New York Times* article. In her response she then explained that the administration had also received this information, that the developments were very, very dangerous, and that they wanted to avoid the proof of the Iraqi nuclear weapons program coming about one day in the form of a mushroom cloud. So, in a nutshell, the White House gave a report to Michael Gordon, who then printed it in the *New York Times*, and then the White House said that they could confirm the report published in the *New York Times*."[21]

Such deceptive tricks were a means to spread fear among the US population and prepare it for the war that President Bush would launch in March 2003. Of course, later it turned out that there were no weapons of mass destruction in Iraq. All the talk about WMD and about the alleged connection of Saddam Hussein to 9/11 was nothing but lies. At least US Secretary of State Colin Powell later apologized for the war propaganda he had helped spread in his address to the UN in New York before the war. In 2005 he said that he felt "terrible" that he had lied to the whole world at the time. That speech, Powell told ABC, was a "blot" on his record, "painful" to think about when reflecting upon his political career.[22]

The USA Produces the Greatest Show in the World

Harold Pinter was a British playwright who knew the techniques of mass communication very well. In 2005 he received the Nobel Prize for Literature. During his acceptance speech, he called US war propaganda and the invasion of Iraq a "bandit act." He went on to say, "Hundreds of thousands of deaths took place throughout these countries. Did they take place? And are they in all cases attributable to US foreign policy?" Pinter's select audience was surprised and irritated by the laureate's clear and direct words. "The answer is yes, they did take place and they are attributable to American foreign policy. But you wouldn't know it. It never happened. Nothing ever happened. Even while it was happening it wasn't happening. It didn't matter. It was of no interest." In the post-1945 period, no other country in the world has managed to conceal its crimes as masterfully as the United States. "The crimes of the United States have been systematic, constant, vicious, remorseless, but very few people have actually talked about them," Pinter said. "You have to hand it to America. It has exercised a quite clinical manipulation of power worldwide while masquerading as a force for universal good . . . It's a brilliant, even witty, highly successful act of hypnosis. I put to you that the United States is without doubt the greatest show on the road. Brutal, indifferent, scornful and ruthless it may be but it is also very clever."[23]

While many people are still unaware of this reality, and believe the show, more and more people are beginning to wake up and become aware of the facts. They are beginning to look behind the scenes of power politics and no longer blindly trust all the talk about the good nature of US foreign policy and that the wars of the West are all so well-intentioned and selfless. "The history of the West is a history of brutal violence and great hypocrisy," says the courageous German journalist Jürgen Todenhöfer, who has visited many war theaters and spoken with the people who are affected by them. "Nowhere in the world does the West fight for the values of civilization. It fights exclusively for its own short-sighted interests of power, markets and money, often by means of terroristic methods. The sufferings of other peoples and cultures are of no interest to it."[24]

According to psychologist Rainer Mausfeld, who taught at the University of Kiel, opinion management relies on fragmentation, decontextualization, and constant repetition of core messages. In this process, facts are broken down into tiny fragments so that the observer can no longer put their meaning and significance into context. This leads to facts being dissolved or even made entirely invisible. In decontextualization, information is torn out of its context, for example by concealing what had happened prior to the situation or occurrence being described. In addition to that, facts may be recontextualized. In other words, they are placed in a new context, which can lead to wars suddenly no longer being considered heinous and cruel, but a necessary sacrifice to fight evil. According to official figures and estimates, since World War II, the United States has been "responsible for the deaths of 20 to 30 million people, which they caused by attacking other countries," Mausfeld says. Hardly anyone knows about these numbers, though, Mausfeld points out. "It takes considerable fragmentation and radical recontextualization for the media to portray these crimes as a 'fight for democracy and human rights.' Doing so has allowed crimes of this magnitude to continue throughout history and remain virtually invisible to the public. Even though all of this is extensively documented, these crimes are almost completely absent from public perception," Mausfeld explains.[25]

Every day, people in North America and in Europe are overloaded with news, sports, advertising, and a flood of often useless information, which makes many of them feel that they are informed about everything that is important. "Citizens who read the *Süddeutsche Zeitung* at breakfast, visit *Spiegel Online* at noon, and watch the news in the evening are so complacent in their feeling of being well informed that they can no longer recognize the disease which they are suffering from," Mausfeld explains. This disease is the illusion of being comprehensively informed, and it is caused by constant and uncritical media consumption.[26]

The Alternative Media Strengthens the Peace Movement

Fortunately, this disease is curable. Everyone can decide to consume less media, and those who decide to go on a media diet also consume less war propaganda. Especially when feeling depressed and sad, a media diet can help. Combine this with good nutrition, conversations with friends, and spending time in nature. It is also advisable to read books instead of the news. Because news is very fragmented, it is hard for people to remember the news they read or heard even just a week before. Comprehensive nonfiction books, on the other hand, provide context and different examples on the same topic, which means that the information is stored in the brain much more effectively.

Of course there are courageous and independent journalists in the mainstream media, who are committed to truth and enlightenment and who stay true to their values, even in the face of opposition. Among them is Seymour Hersh, who exposed the My Lai massacre during the Vietnam War. Oftentimes, though, journalists are careful not to jeopardize their employment and therefore they do not want to violate the narrow boundaries of the predefined spectrum of opinion. Well-known leading media brands like Fox News, CNN, BBC, *Washington Post*, *New York Times*, *Economist*, MSNBC, *New York Post*, *ABC News*, *USA Today*, and the *Wall Street Journal* rarely report critically on the wars of the United States. The term "US imperialism" virtually never appears in these mainstream media outlets. Thus, television viewers and newspaper readers never really think about US imperialism and its consequences.

Only a few media brands that report in English are critical of US imperialism. They are less well known than the mainstream media, and their portrayal of international politics is therefore less read or seen by the majority of the population. They also have fewer financial resources. These alternative media outlets include *Democracy Now*, *The Nation*, *Global Research*, *The Empire Files*, *Truthdig*, *offGuardian*, *Zero Hedge*, *The Corbett Report*, *Russia Today*, *Information Clearing House*, *Veterans Today*, and others. It is the job of historians like myself, as well as critical eyewitnesses in general, to challenge both leading media outlets like the *New York Times* and the BBC as well as alternative media like *Democracy Now* and *Global Research*. Those who do so will quickly discover that *Democracy Now* reports on the Syrian war quite differently than *Fox News* does, and *Global Research* publishes completely different texts on 9/11 than the *New York Times* does. "Our supposedly leading and quality media gives the impression that the opinion of those in power is the prevailing opinion," explains political scientist Ulrich Teusch, who taught at the University of Trier. "In the fight against war, in the fight for peace, you cannot rely on the media of the rulers," he warns.[27]

Those who read in German have about eighty different media brands to choose from. Swiss Policy Research provides a useful overview of the various media brands. Anyone who wants to improve their media literacy can download the media navigator from the Swiss Policy Research website (www.swprs.org) free of charge. It is a useful tool that can be used when reading a text or watching a video, as it shows how the media brand that published the information is geostrategically oriented. As a historian, when focusing on a story and comparing reports of the leading media with those of the alternative media, it immediately becomes apparent that *Der Spiegel*, for example, reports on the terrorist attacks of September 11 exactly as dictated by the US president, not allowing for any critical questions. KenFM, by contrast, points out to its readers that WTC7 was blown up and dismisses the so-called "war on terror" as a deception. Personally, I appreciate the work of courageous journalists in the leading media as well as in the alternative media, as long as they know that they are committed to peace and are willing to leave the predefined corridor of opinion in order to do so.[28]

CHAPTER 14

THE DIGITAL EMPIRE

We are all living in the age of information, and we leave digital traces behind us every day. It was not too long ago that Steve Jobs, the CEO of Apple at the time, presented the first iPhone to the world in San Francisco. That was in 2007. Today, almost everyone carries a smartphone around with them. This has led to our movements being recorded every day. At the end of the year, it is possible to see all the places that a given person has been to by reviewing their movements on Google Maps. Never in the history of mankind has this been the case. When we pay with a credit card instead of cash, our purchase is registered, which is why proponents of total surveillance want to abolish physical currency—a.k.a. cash—worldwide. In subways or in soccer stadiums, cameras capture our faces. Each and every website visit is recorded. When we book a vacation home in Italy online, we will receive advertisements for vacation homes for weeks afterward. If we search for a table in a furniture store on our smartphone, we will receive furniture ads soon thereafter. If we watch videos on YouTube about vegan nutrition, we will receive further suggestions on the same topic.

Algorithms, or computer programs, record almost every step we take. They can beat us at chess or recommend a suitable dating partner in online dating applications. Every time we "like" something on Facebook, every time we watch a movie on Netflix, it is registered. Even the contacts on our smartphone can be tapped. All this data has created a digital file on each and every one of us. We ourselves, however, have no access to this digital file, which means we have no insight into the data and information that has been collected on us. We don't even know who all keeps such a digital file on us or who has access to one, and it is also not possible for us to delete our own digital file.

1990: The Fiche Scandal in Switzerland

Every country in the world collects data on its citizens and keeps government databases with at least a resident register. Oftentimes, however, much more data is collected. One example of such a case took place in Switzerland during the Cold War. The federal police created 900,000 files, so-called "fiches," on politically active people. The files were printed on cardboard, neatly sorted, and stored in archive cabinets at the Office of the Attorney General in Bern. About one in twenty Swiss citizens and every third foreigner had such a file, but knew nothing about it. Above all, the federal police recorded socialists, trade unionists, anarchists, members of the peace movement, writers, and people who had publicly demonstrated against nuclear power plants or against the dictator Augusto Pinochet, as well as foreigners. The file contained the person's name, date of birth, place of residence, occupation, nationality, and marital status, followed by a description of their political activity. The authorities' goal was to protect Switzerland from subversion by intelligence services from abroad and from radical political movements.[1]

When a Parliamentary Investigation Commission (PUK) under National Councillor Moritz Leuenberger from the Social Democratic Party of Switzerland (SP) revealed the existence of these secret registration cards in 1990, it triggered a political earthquake in Switzerland. There were public protests against the surveillance state, which was criticized as being a "snooping state." Some sued for violation of their privacy rights and the courts ruled in their favor. More than 300,000 Swiss people demanded that the federal police hand over their personal files, upon which they were allowed to view their fiche. "When I was able to read my fiche, I didn't know whether to laugh or cry—it was unbelievable," recalled journalist Jean-Michel Berthoud, who was a member of the Revolutionary Marxist League. "I was subletting from architects, and we had open conversations.

They told the police everything about me." And the latter wrote it into the file, without Berthoud knowing about it.[2]

The Surveillance of Citizens in China

Paper files, as in the case in the Fiche Scandal, are no longer in keeping with the times. Nowadays, the files are digital and they are stored on countless servers around the world. China also relies on digital files. They are combined with automatic facial recognition and the surveillance is no longer secret. In 2013, the Chinese city of Rongcheng, which has a population of one million, introduced a "social credit system for exemplary behavior." After the initial test phase, this social credit system is to be extended to the whole of China. In setting up the infrastructure for this system, major squares and streets were equipped with cameras for facial recognition. To begin the testing phase, all the residents of Rongcheng received a credit of 1,000 points each. Anyone who left trash on the street would forfeit three points. "That's why the buses and sidewalks are extremely clean; you won't see a single cigarette butt or any empty drink cans lying around anywhere," Amnesty International reports on the city on the Yellow Sea. Numerous surveillance cameras replace patrols by the police. Every day, the local television channel broadcasts a popular summary of all the missteps recorded by the surveillance cameras during the twenty-four hours preceding the broadcast. Anyone who cuts a neighbor's fruit trees, pulls a car out of a ditch, or accompanies an elderly person to the hospital is credited with points. By contrast, anyone who lets their chickens roam free loses ten points. For spraying graffiti that is critical of the government, fifty points are deducted. This monitoring system and the digital files not only keep the streets clean, which is welcomed by many, but also eliminate any governmental criticism, because expressing it would cost too many points.[3]

In order to shield the Chinese internet from topics, issues, conversations, and statements that the Chinese government deems unfit for the public, China has also built a digital wall around the entire country, blocking online services that are widely used in the US and in Europe. Websites that are controlled by the US empire, such as Google, YouTube, Facebook, Twitter, and Wikipedia, cannot be accessed in China. As a substitute,

Beijing offers its own Chinese services, which are controlled by the all-powerful Communist Party; WeChat replaces WhatsApp, and instead of Twitter there is Weibo. When Weibo was first launched in 2009, citizens discovered their power. Millions of Chinese people used Weibo to engage in animated discussions about food scandals, air pollution, police violence, and political corruption. After a short while, however, the Chinese government deleted the Weibo accounts of well-known posters who were critical of the government, such as artist Ai Weiwei and writer Murong Xuecun. "Deplatforming" is what social networks call turning off the microphone for selected individuals. This is happening not only in China, but also in the United States. After deplatforming, Murong Xuecun lost contact with millions of Chinese who had enjoyed reading his writing on Weibo. "The truth is that we are not allowed to speak the truth," Xuecun protested in the *New York Times*. "We are not allowed to criticize the system or discuss the reality in which we are living."[4]

This digital wall impacts the flow of information in China. For example, if you type "Tiananmen" into the search bar of Google, which is a US search engine, the first search result you get is Wikipedia's—which is also a US American company—entry on the "Tiananmen Massacre." It is followed by pictures of the man who stood in front of the Chinese tanks wearing a white shirt during the 1989 massacre. In China, however, Google does not exist. The Chinese version of Google is called Baidu and it is controlled by the Chinese Communist Party. If you enter "Tiananmen" into the search bar of Baidu, you will get beautiful tourist photos and reviews of the famous Tiananmen Square, which lies in the heart of Beijing. The picture of the man who stood in front of the tanks does not appear on Baidu. This example illustrates how search engines like Google and Baidu can in fact control the flow of information.[5]

Surveillance of Citizens in the USA

In the United States, politicians and the military also monitor the population, and because the US is currently the world's empire, they are even working on creating digital files on every world citizen. Information is power. By intercepting and decrypting Japanese military communications, US naval intelligence was able to foresee the attack on Pearl Harbor in

1941. At the time, the White House was in the know, while the US soldiers stationed in Hawai'i were not. The two parties did not have the same level of information, and the soldiers paid for it with their lives. By sacrificing its own soldiers, the White House was able to thrust the US population into turmoil, which was only possible because the people did not know that the White House could read the Japanese radio transmissions. Influential politicians, business leaders, and the military know how valuable information is today. "The world's most valuable resource is no longer oil, but data," *The Economist* asserted in 2017.[6]

The US National Security Agency (NSA) and powerful US technology companies such as Google, Facebook, Amazon, Apple, and Microsoft collect as much data as possible on millions of people around the world. The NSA was founded in 1952 and is headquartered at the Fort Meade military base in Maryland, also known as Crypto City. The NSA is a part of the US military and works in close cooperation with the British intelligence service called the Government Communications Headquarters (GCHQ). The NSA and the GCHQ monitor electronic communications across the world and evaluate the intercepted data. The NSA has used the terrorist attacks of September 11, 2001, as a justification to monitor and create a digital file on anyone and everyone around the globe.

"They want information on everything. That's really a totalitarian approach that so far has only been seen with dictators," said mathematician William Binney in a speech to the Bundestag in Berlin. Binney is an insider; he had worked for the NSA for thirty years before leaving the intelligence agency at the end of 2001, in protest against the data collection frenzy. "After September 11, everything changed," Binney explained. In the past, he said, they primarily monitored foreign militaries, but now the NSA aims to "collect data on all seven billion people on our planet," in other words, all of humanity. The NSA stores the data forever, he said. "They don't throw anything away. Once they've got something, they keep it."[7]

The activities of the NSA only became known to the general public in June 2013, after the courageous US American Edward Snowden described in detail the surveillance state that the NSA has built and in which we live today. Snowden has since been forced to live in exile in Moscow, because

Germany, Switzerland, France, and other countries refused to grant him asylum. The NSA and GCHQ are running "the largest surveillance program in the history of mankind," Snowden, the world's best-known critic of this surveillance state, revealed. "I don't want to live in a world where there's no privacy and therefore no room for intellectual exploration and creativity," he told the *Guardian*. Snowden is an insider; before becoming a whistleblower, he worked in an NSA office in Hawai'i as a computer specialist for the consulting firm Booz Allen Hamilton, where he had access to many classified NSA documents.[8]

President Barack Obama was not pleased with whistleblower Snowden and would have arrested him if Snowden had not fled to Vladimir Putin in Russia. Obama supported the expansion of the surveillance state. In Germany, where critics call the surveillance state the Stasi 2.0, the journal *Spiegel* revealed that the NSA intercepts about half a billion emails, text messages, and telephone calls every month. On peak days, it would be up to 60 million telephone connections. The NSA watches the Germans very closely. "Eavesdropping on friends, that is totally unacceptable," government spokesman Steffen Seibert warned in July 2013, but that did not faze the NSA. Following the Snowden revelations, German Justice Minister Sabine Leutheusser-Schnarrenberger also denounced the "storage craze" and spoke of a "catastrophe" and a "nightmare" because the NSA monitors every citizen in Germany without any grounds for suspicion. It must be assumed that there is a digital file on each and every one of us. If you read this book as an e-book, the NSA can even monitor which page you are currently on. Amazon also exactly evaluates how end users read e-books and when they put a book down.[9]

The NSA uses the latest technology and can basically monitor anyone. "America has tapped the chancellor's cell phone," the *Frankfurter Allgemeine Zeitung* indignantly revealed on October 23, 2013. German Chancellor Angela Merkel, who succeeded Gerhard Schröder and had moved into the chancellor's office in 2005, was embarrassed. In a telephone conversation with Obama, Merkel stated that she "unequivocally disapproves of such practices, should the indications be proven true, and considers them completely unacceptable." Politicians from all parties expressed outrage. "This insolence by the US must finally be stopped," demanded Gregor Gysi of the leftist party Die Linke. Member of parliament Hans-Peter Uhl of the Christian Social Union (CSU) party added, "Of course the chancellor must be able to communicate in a tap-proof manner." The politicians, however, did not know how to do that. Before Pearl Harbor, the Japanese had already tried to communicate in a tap-proof manner, and they did not succeed. The NSA can't crack every code, but it has a lot of experience in gaining access to data that is supposed to remain secret.[10]

Documents published by Edward Snowden revealed that the NSA does not just observe and collect, it also attacks. The NSA's director is also the head of the so-called Cyber Command of the US Armed Forces. Some of the NSA's 45,000 employees are cyber warriors who are responsible for destructive network attacks. This includes those who work on the third floor of the NSA headquarters building in the so-called "Remote Operations Center" (ROC) at Fort Meade. These NSA hackers can break into other people's computers and smartphones undetected and without leaving any traces. The end user doesn't even know that the NSA has broken into their device. ROC employees continually disregard other people's privacy and follow the motto: "Your data is our data, your equipment is our equipment."[11]

Time and again, courageous US citizens have protested the NSA's real-world surveillance state. It is not easy for whistleblowers, though. "When I contacted a reporter in 2006, the FBI stormed my house shortly thereafter," recalled Thomas Drake, who had worked at the NSA since 2001. "The Justice Department charged me, and I was supposed to go to prison for thirty-five years." Drake lost his job, his livelihood, and his circle of friends and was sentenced to one year of probation. But the US Department of Justice could not prove that Drake illegally betrayed any national secrets. As a whistleblower, he had only objected to the fact that mass surveillance had become a reality in the USA after September 11, 2001, and that data was being collected on Americans without reason or cause and without a court order. "Only a few agents knew the extent of the surveillance," explained the NSA insider. "But many of those on the inside were bellyaching about the illegal practices and the waste of money." None of the military personnel wanted to put their lives on the line, however. "No one wanted to take the fall—they saw what was happening to me. And that's exactly the warning my indictment was supposed to send: If you spill the beans, we will break you."[12]

As the NSA wants to create a comprehensive digital file on every single person in the world, it needs a lot of storage space, which it has in the state of Utah. In 2013, the NSA opened its data center in Bluffdale. This data center can "store at least 100 years of global communications," explained former NSA employee Binney. "This place should definitely terrify us. The NSA wants everything, at all times." The size of this storage is almost inconceivable. Binney, a mathematician, explained that the Utah Data Center can store twenty terabytes every minute. To put this in perspective, twenty terabytes is the equivalent of the entire Library of Congress in Washington, which is the largest library in the world. The Utah Data Center stores texts, images, and videos that people carelessly share on social media. "People don't pay attention to this until it's too late," warns US journalist James Bamford, who has published a standard work on the NSA. Those who want to delete their digital files, or those of their children, will not succeed. Nor does the NSA grant access to one's files. After the Snowden revelations, people protested in front of the data center in Bluffdale, but the NSA will not let anyone get too close. Yellow signs posted on the walls indicate that this is a military facility and that unauthorized people are not permitted inside. Cameras, dogs, and policemen guard the military data center and every protester is digitally recorded.[13]

The extent of global surveillance and data exploitation is enormous, criticizes Werner Meixner, who teaches at the Institute of Computer Science at the Technical University of Munich. The US's objective is to secure its global supremacy by means of digital surveillance, with American IT corporations providing "the foundations of US economic and military hegemony." Out of sheer convenience, the citizens who are being monitored do not care about their digital file. Most importantly, though, many are under the mistaken belief that resistance to the NSA, Facebook, and Google is not possible. This is not the case. "Invasion of privacy is a criminal act under general human law," Meixner explains, calling for resistance. "What prevents us from calling the destruction of our privacy a crime?" In order for proper resistance to be possible, individuals must recognize that the loss of their privacy is a problem.[14]

1994: The Internet Revolutionizes the World

"The Internet is new territory for all of us," German Chancellor Angela Merkel said in 2013 at a press conference with President Obama in Berlin. Merkel was thus rejecting criticism of the NSA's surveillance program PRISM, under which Facebook and Google share their data with the NSA. Merkel's observation was not entirely wrong. The history of the internet is, in fact, still very young, especially for historians like myself. We do not know yet where the journey will take us in the twenty-first century. The military can use the internet for total surveillance of all citizens, which is the dark side of a vision. On the other hand, in a brighter vision, the peace movement can use the internet to share information about war lies, organize peaceful protests, and initiate a change in consciousness, which is what I advocate for. I also have accounts on Facebook and on Twitter, as well as my own YouTube channel, and I use the internet to strengthen the peace movement.

I first came into contact with this new technology as a student. It was 1996, I was a twenty-four-year-old history student, and I was studying at the University of Amsterdam for a year. A fellow student, a pretty girl from Cyprus who was living in the same dormitory, asked me: "Daniele, do you want to join me in going on the internet?" My answer was, "What's that?" I had no idea what she was talking about. To which her explanation was, "I don't know either. But I think it's exciting. They opened a new internet room today." I was intrigued, so we went to this internet room together, where we found about a hundred computers, all connected to the internet. Many students surfed the internet for the first time in their lives that day. It was very exciting. Everyone immediately got an email address, because it was free. We were not thinking about the NSA, the surveillance state, or our digital file at the time—we were just having fun.[15]

People love to share information, and the internet makes this much easier. The internet was invented in the USA. In 1968, under the name Arpanet, a network of computers was built on behalf of the US Air Force to connect US universities that were doing research for the Pentagon. At the time, the Vietnam War was raging and students from Harvard and the Massachusetts Institute of Technology (MIT) protested against Arpanet, reports journalist Yasha Levine. They had learned from an MIT professor that this network was also being used by government agencies to collect as much data as possible on politically active students and war opponents.[16]

But these early protests could not stop the expansion of the internet. In 1990, the first website, "info.cern.ch," went online at the European nuclear research center CERN in Switzerland. It was programmed by the British computer scientist Tim Berners-Lee, the inventor of the World Wide Web. But hardly anyone took notice. It was not until 1994, two years before I used the internet for the first time in my life, that the Netscape Navigator web browser was launched in the US, soon to be supplanted by Microsoft's Internet Explorer. With Netscape Navigator, surfing became easier, and for the first time, the internet became interesting for millions of people. It is therefore not wrong to date the beginning of the internet to 1994. Today, people born in 1980 or later, who have grown up in a digital world, are referred to as "digital natives." Both of my kids belong to this group. They only know a world in which the internet, smartphones, Google, and YouTube have always existed. People born before 1980, however, including myself, are "digital immigrants" because they still remember a time when there was no internet. Digital immigrants like me will eventually become extinct.[17]

2018: Google Earned $30 Billion

The internet has changed many things, some for the better, some for the worse. One driver of this change is the US corporation Google, whose internet search engine is the most visited website in the world. Google's search engine has been online since 1997 and was developed by Larry Page and Sergey Brin at Stanford University in California. Google's influence is so great that the new verb "to google" was created, which means "to research something, to look something up." The search engine usually displays ten search results per page, and because most people choose from the top suggestions offered by Google, it can use algorithms to determine which information is read the most. Google mixes advertising into the search results and makes a lot of money from it. In 2018, the technology giant realized a net profit of over $30 billion on revenues of over $136 billion.[18]

In addition to the search engine, in 2005 Google also launched Google Maps, which is gradually displacing maps printed on paper. Google Maps processes satellite images and overlays them with geodata, allowing users to display the local map of any given city in the world via their smartphone, provided they have enough battery power and access to the internet. Google Maps also shows traffic jams in real time, by registering all smartphones with Google's Android operating system. Due to a great many people having their smartphones with them in their cars, the traffic jam information is very accurate, because when the smartphones jam, the cars jam. Google can even tell where we are going and where we are coming from. "One of the things that eventually happens . . . is that we don't need you to type at all," Google CEO Eric Schmidt confidently declared in 2010. "Because we know where you are. We know where you've been. We can more or less guess what you're thinking about."[19]

Google also owns YouTube, the video portal that was founded in 2005. On it, users can watch videos, rate them, comment on them, and upload their own videos. I myself have a YouTube channel where more than thirty of my lectures can be viewed free of charge. I try to strengthen the peace movement with my lectures. Google has another interest: they put commercials in front of my lectures and earn money in doing so. Google knows what we are interested in. Algorithms register what we watch on which devices and make suggestions that fit our interests. Google wants our attention and is building ever more powerful computers, so-called quantum computers, capable of even faster calculations.

Google's products, including YouTube, the search engine, and Maps, only appear to be free. In reality, however, people do indeed pay for the services: not with their money, but with their data. Unless, of course, one purchases subscriptions, in which case they also pay with their money. The products offer added value and therefore magically attract our attention. Google sells this attention to advertisers, who can then target their messages very specifically. "Google, Apple and Facebook know when a woman visits an abortion clinic, even if she tells no one else: the GPS coordinates on the phone don't lie," explained journalist Yasha Levine. Google Maps is used to monitor citizens. "One-night stands and extramarital affairs are a cinch to figure out: two smartphones that never met before suddenly cross paths in a bar and then make their way to an apartment across town, stay together overnight, and part in the morning." The tech companies "know us intimately," Levine said. They even know "the things that we hide from those closest to us." Those who are fed up with this surveillance system can fight back. They can leave their smartphone off or at home as often as possible, even removing the battery. Applications like Facebook, Twitter, YouTube, Instagram, and other social media apps can be deleted, and payments can always be made with cash, but few people do that.[20]

Facebook Displaces Newspapers Printed on Paper

The "pervasive surveillance and constant, subtle manipulation" by thousands of algorithms is "unethical, cruel, dangerous and inhumane," protests US American computer scientist Jaron Lanier. Facebook has deliberately made its products addictive, he said. When someone on Facebook sees that their post has been liked, that social recognition generates a dopamine kick. When this process is repeated, it creates an addiction that leads to people looking at their social media accounts several times a day, he said—not to learn something new, but to get that dopamine kick. And because this process is unconscious, users are unaware of their addiction. "To free yourself, to be more authentic, to be less addicted, to be less manipulated, to be less paranoid . . . for all these marvelous reasons, delete your accounts," Jaron Lanier advises.[21]

Currently, Facebook has more than 2 billion users worldwide, which is about a quarter of the world's population. Headquartered in California, the company was founded in 2004 and sells targeted advertising. In 2018, Facebook made a profit of $22 billion, making it comparable to Google and the like. While the NSA collects data in secret, Facebook does so publicly and for everyone to see. On Facebook, everyone creates their own digital file, which can then easily be tapped by the NSA. Facebook also owns the popular chat service WhatsApp and the photo platform Instagram. Facebook founder Mark Zuckerberg is one of the superrich in the USA, who steer the empire. According to the US magazine *Forbes*, his fortune in 2018 was $61 billion.[22]

Facebook also acts as a news channel. More and more people get their news through social media applications and search engines, rather than from branded print newspapers or online outlets such as *Spiegel Online*. Although the news feed contains news from various newspapers, neither

Facebook nor its users want to pay for it. It is understandable that this annoys the journalists in the various newspaper editorial departments, because Facebook now threatens their existence. Young people hardly buy printed newspapers anymore, so they are slowly but surely dying out because the number of subscribers is declining and advertising money is migrating to Facebook and Google. No newspaper editorial office in the world can compete with the financial power of Facebook.

2016: Facebook and the Election of Donald Trump

In addition to selling cars and laundry detergent, Facebook advertising can be used to influence presidential elections. This is completely new in the history of the United States. Republican Donald Trump's victory over Democrat Hillary Clinton in the presidential election of November 8, 2016, was close. With 65 million votes, Clinton actually received 2 million more votes than Trump. However, the total number of votes does not determine the winner of the presidential election in the US; it is the electoral votes that determine the winner. The candidate who wins a state, even if only by a narrow margin, receives all the electoral votes of that state. On Election Day, graphs illustrate this race: If Republicans win a state, it is colored red; if Democrats win, the state turns blue. There is no third party with influence in the United States.

Swing states are those states where both Democrats and Republicans have a chance of winning. Therefore, each campaign team wants to win the electoral votes in the swing states. Clinton received 227 electoral votes, but Trump prevailed in the key swing states like Florida and Wisconsin, securing his victory with 304 electoral votes. Trump's team knew the voters very well because they had analyzed their Facebook profiles and likes without the voters taking notice of it. After doing so, very specific messages were sent to undecided voters in swing states via Facebook's messaging stream, calling Hillary Clinton a corrupt politician, thereby weakening her.[23]

During the campaign, observers had yet to pay much attention to Facebook's influence. It was not until March 2018 that Christopher Wylie, a twenty-eight-year-old computer expert in London, revealed that Facebook had contributed to Trump's election victory. Wylie told a stunned public that his employer had "created psychological profiles of

230 million Americans" by analyzing their Facebook data. Wylie had been an employee of a previously unknown English firm called Cambridge Analytica. This company had evaluated the data of US Facebook users without their knowledge and had misused it for political purposes. "Huge data abuse disgraces Facebook," was the headline of the *Neue Zürcher Zeitung*. Wylie was involved in this data abuse, but rejected Trump's policies. When he realized that his company had supported Trump's election victory, Wylie became a whistleblower.[24]

US citizens over the age of eighteen who reside in one of the fifty states, as well as US soldiers and diplomats living abroad, are eligible to vote in the presidential election, which is held every four years. That is a total of 230 million people, and Cambridge Analytica had created a digital file on each one. Such comprehensive monitoring of voters had never been seen in the history of the United States. On behalf of presidential candidate Donald Trump and backed by US billionaire Robert Mercer, Cambridge Analytica collected data on all voters, including their first name, last name, photo, age, residence, income, religion, gun ownership, party affiliation, property ownership, bonus cards, medical data, club memberships, and magazine subscriptions.

However, the most interesting data for Cambridge Analytica were the Facebook profiles. Why was this data so valuable? The "like" button allows Facebook users to express what they like or support. Psychologist Michal Kosinski of Stanford University in California believes that Facebook likes can be used to measure a person's personality. According to Kosinski, who advocates for as many people as possible to be on Facebook and share their views publicly, sixty-eight Facebook likes can predict the color of a user's skin, whether they are homosexual, or whether they are a Democrat or Republican. For example, men who like the cosmetics brand MAC are most likely to be gay. One of the best indicators of heterosexuality is liking the New York hip-hop group Wu-Tang Clan. Lady Gaga followers are very likely to be extroverts. Those who like philosophy are more likely to be introverts. Seventy likes would be enough to outdo a friend's knowledge of one's nature, 150 to outdo a parent's. With 300 likes, a computer can predict a person's behavior more clearly than their partner, or so Kosinski claims.[25]

It was not until almost every US citizen had created a Facebook account that such measurements of personality traits became possible. Of course, campaign teams in the US had always distinguished between men and women, or between Latinos, African Americans, and White people, and also targeted these groups in different ways. But Cambridge Analytica significantly refined the various communications, dividing voters into "fearful" or "open-minded." During the 2016 election campaign, Alexandre Nix, the CEO of Cambridge Analytica at the time, said in a talk in New York that demographic concepts, which have been used in election campaigns in the past, are "a ridiculous idea." He went on to say that "All women get the same message just because they have the same gender—or all African Americans, because of their race?" That doesn't make any sense, Nix said. You can and must measure people's personalities and then address them with precisely tailored messages; only that will lead to success.[26]

The Cambridge Analytica Scandal Is Exposed

To find out more about Cambridge Analytica's dirty tricks, journalists from the British Channel 4 posed as wealthy clients trying to win elections in Sri Lanka and met with Cambridge Analytica's Alexander Nix and Mark Turnbull in London. Unbeknownst to Nix and Turnbull, the conversation was recorded. Turnbull explained that their company had already rigged elections in many countries by microtargeting voters, including the USA, Kenya, Mexico, Malaysia, Brazil, Australia, and Eastern Europe. Elections are always about emotions, never about facts, Turnbull stressed during the confidential interview. It's all about fear. Nix added that the stories that are circulated do not necessarily have to be true, they just need to be credible. Moreover, one could weaken a political opponent by offering them bribes, secretly filming the conversation, and then posting it online so as to have "video evidence of corruption," explained Nix, who did not realize that he himself was being filmed. Another option was to "send beautiful girls from the Ukraine to the candidate's house," Nix suggested, adding that that worked very well. He said that Cambridge Analytica had used these techniques successfully in the past and that they had won elections for their clients in various countries.[27]

In the USA, Alexander Nix also made use of microtargeting. Messages were precisely tailored to the targeted person and then presented to the voter via Facebook, through paid advertising. Such practices were not possible prior to the founding of Facebook; it would never have been possible to print letters that were so precisely tailored to each individual reader and then drop them in every single voter's mailbox, as that would have been far too time-consuming. Newspapers and TV programs cannot target individuals either, but Facebook has made it possible. Cambridge Analytica paid Facebook around $5 million to run the ad campaigns. Clinton's team, on the other hand, invested far less money into Facebook ads, as the documentary *The Great Hack* revealed.[28]

By evaluating people's likes on Facebook, Cambridge Analytica found that a preference for cars made in the USA was the top indicator of a potential Trump voter. Trump's campaign team would use Facebook to encourage this group of people to be sure to vote. The group of "undecided Democrats," on the other hand, was kept away from the polling stations. In Miami's neighborhood of Little Haiti, Cambridge Analytica fed residents news about the Clinton Foundation's failure to respond after the earthquake in Haiti. This kept leftists who were still in doubt, African Americans, and young women in Florida, who normally vote Democratic, away from the ballot boxes. This method was very efficient because many people around the world view and interact with their Facebook accounts several times a day, just like addicts. "We are thrilled that our revolutionary approach to data-driven communication made such a fundamental contribution to the victory for Donald Trump," Alexander Nix boasted after Trump's election.[29]

Whether Cambridge Analytica's influence was indeed "fundamental" to Trump's election is unclear, but microtargeting via Facebook was certainly an element that contributed to Trump's victory. Earlier presidents, such as Kennedy or Reagan, did not have access to such techniques during their election campaigns. Only a few US Americans have bothered to look behind the scenes of power. Among them is David Carroll, a media studies lecturer in New York, who for months fought for the release of his digital file that Cambridge Analytica had compiled on him. When Carroll finally received his digital file, he was surprised to find that all the data was accurate. "I think if Americans knew what was going on here, and internationally as well, they would be outraged."[30]

Cambridge Analytica knew that the swing states of Florida, Michigan, Wisconsin, and Pennsylvania would have to be won by Trump in order to garner enough electoral votes. The experts calculated that 70,000 undecided voters in these four states could decide the presidential election. Therefore, anxious and worried people in these states were particularly singled out because they could easily be influenced. In the weeks leading up to the election, these worried voters were worked on intensively: "Did you know that Hillary Clinton wants to take away your firearm?" was one message that Cambridge Analytica sent to voters via Facebook to discourage them from voting for Hillary Clinton. "Defeat crooked Hillary" was another Cambridge Analytica message, in which the "oo" in "crooked" was depicted as handcuffs.[31]

Voters did not know who had sent them these messages, nor did they know why they had received them. British journalist Carole Cadwalladr, a features writer for *The Observer*, criticized this opaque election interference. "A political debate should be held in public so everyone can see each other's arguments," Cadwalladr said. "But secretly targeting people and sending them all sorts of stuff on their phones and computers is wrong." When a party prints campaign ads in newspapers or puts up posters, that content can be found in the archives many years later. This data forms the basis of source work for us historians. In the US presidential election of 2016, however, the situation with these sources had changed dramatically. As a historian, I don't have access to Facebook's archive and I cannot sift through the messages that were sent to concerned and anxious citizens. "They could have said all sorts of things that we'll never know about because it's all gone now," explains Cadwalladr. Made-up stories, or fake news, were probably also sent out. Interestingly enough, it's still on the Facebook servers, but they won't release it.[32]

After Cambridge Analytica's manipulations first became public knowledge in March 2018, thanks to whistleblower Christopher Wylie, a storm of outrage broke out. Customers turned away from the company and legal fees soared. Alexander Nix was fired. In May 2018, Cambridge Analytica filed for bankruptcy and ceased operations. The scandal destroyed

Cambridge Analytica, but Facebook survived the scandal without a problem. Few deleted their accounts, and Facebook continued to grow, realizing a record profit of $22 billion in 2018. Facebook CEO Mark Zuckerberg did have to publicly apologize for the misconduct and even testified in front of the Senate. "This was a huge breach of trust. I'm sorry that happened," Zuckerberg told CNN remorsefully. But on the merits, Facebook stood firm: the controversial ads that were sent to anxious voters during the 2016 presidential election were not published. Facebook has still not made them accessible to journalists or historians.[33]

2016: Cambridge Analytica and Brexit

Those who believe that digital political campaigns and microtargeting are limited to the US alone are greatly mistaken. These techniques have also been used in other countries and will continue to be an integral part of political campaigns in the future. In the United Kingdom's Brexit vote on June 23, 2016, a very slim majority of referendum participants, 51 percent, voted in favor of the United Kingdom leaving the European Union. British journalist Carole Cadwalladr found that again, Cambridge Analytica had used microtargeting to influence undecided voters. "The focus was on people who were considered easily influenced—initially these were young, White, working-class voters," Cadwalladr explains. Digital files containing the personality profiles of all voters were also created in the UK. "This allowed us to find the key audience that would respond to the immigration issue," Cadwalladr says. In the days leading up to the Brexit vote, they "opened up the floodgates" and these people got to see Facebook ads tailored to them en masse.[34]

In military contexts, influencing thoughts and feelings is called psychological warfare or psychological operations, "psyops" for short. The modern peace movement must see through psyops because almost every war has been built on lies. Well-known psyops include deceiving the public by means of war propaganda, such as the story about Saddam Hussein's WMDs before the US's attack on Iraq in 2003, the incubator lie before the war in Kuwait in 1991, or the made-up story about the incident in the Gulf of Tonkin in 1964, which led to the US's attack on Vietnam. Dropping leaflets over enemy territory also counts as psyops. In my lectures, I show examples of psyops and explain how we can ward off psychological warfare by learning to strengthen our mindfulness and by observing our own thoughts and feelings from a certain distance. We are not our thoughts, nor are we our feelings. Our true self is a clear and calm consciousness in which these thoughts and feelings arise and then subside again. Those who realize this can neutralize psyops.

Microtargeting Influences Voting in Switzerland

Microtargeting has also been used in Switzerland. On February 28, 2016, Swiss voters had to vote on whether a second road tunnel should be built through the world's longest railway and deepest traffic tunnel Gotthard, as the existing tunnel needed to be renovated. Enigma, a Swiss communications agency based in Bern, influenced voters. "Indeed, we make use of similar tools to analyze data, influence voters and steer political campaigns as Cambridge Analytica does," company CEO Martin Künzi confirmed. "We have understood that it's all about emotions and simple, political messages . . . If a voter hears a message eight to twelve times, they believe it." He said they created more than a hundred different combinations of visual and text messages, tailoring them to resonate with various voters. "Our goal was to ensure that the fashion designer from Zurich's district 4, as well as the pensioner from Airolo, receive individual messages on the topic," said Künzi. Microtargeting via Facebook is highly efficient, he said. In any case, it is definitely more effective than covering all of Switzerland from Glarus to Lausanne with the same posters. Künzi had no moral reservations. "What's wrong with that? Everyone is on Facebook voluntarily, right?" he asks. With 57 percent, the Swiss voted in favor of the second Gotthard tunnel.[35]

Microtargeting was also used when the Swiss people elected a new parliament on October 20, 2019. Every citizen who visited the websites of the Free Democratic Party (FDP), the Christian Democratic People's Party (CVP), or the Swiss People's Party (SVP) was automatically reported to Facebook as a potential voter, upon which they would receive advertising from the respective parties, also via Facebook. Once again, it was the company Enigma that installed the data spy "Facebook Pixel" on the homepage of the Swiss CVP. Facebook Pixel secretly establishes a connection to the Facebook server without the user taking notice of it. Advertising on Facebook is much more efficient and cheaper than distributing printed brochures to individuals' mailboxes. Not everyone in Switzerland is on Facebook, though. If the potential voter did not have a Facebook account, they could not be targeted after visiting the CVP website.[36]

The press criticized the parties for "betraying the citizens who visited their websites and selling them out to Facebook" without asking for their permission to share their data. Adrian Lobsiger, the Swiss Data Protection Commissioner, was also incensed. "This is an attempt to trick and deceive people by manipulating data," Lobsiger said. He said citizens were being sent political messages via social networks that supposedly came from their friends, while in reality, they were actually receiving paid advertising from political parties. "Voters have a right to know what informational means are being used to process their data and how they are being addressed with personalized messages," Lobsiger insisted. There is an urgent need for more transparency and more education, because many people are not aware yet of how these technologies are being used.[37]

2001: The Founding of Wikipedia

Along with Facebook and Google, Wikipedia is one of the most frequently visited websites. Founded in the USA in 2001 by Jimmy Wales, Wikipedia has rapidly risen to become a monopolist. While the online encyclopedia is banned in China, it has managed to displace all other encyclopedias in North America and in Europe. Among the victims of Wikipedia is the Brockhaus Encyclopedia, which had been printed on paper in Germany since 1808. Now Brockhaus has died; it has not been reprinted since 2014. The takeover by Wikipedia happened silently and without significant resistance, and now the US encyclopedia dominates the interpretation of the world.

Wikipedia's resounding success can be attributed to the fact that this encyclopedia is free and can be accessed from anywhere in the world (except China), through any smartphone or computer. Nothing like this has ever existed before in the history of mankind. The twenty-four volumes of the Brockhaus Encyclopedia weighed over a hundred pounds. Normally people kept their encyclopedias in their warm and cozy living rooms; no one would have thought of carrying the encyclopedia around with them, as it was simply too heavy. Furthermore, Wikipedia comes in various languages. The English version contains more than 6 million articles, while the German version contains over 2 million articles. That is far more than the thirty-two-volume edition of the Encyclopedia Britannica, which contained about 75,000 articles. Just like the Brockhaus Encyclopedia, however, the Encyclopedia Britannica is no longer being published either.

Wikipedia is often the first option for internet research. It is considered reputable by many users, and this is true for undisputed topics. In the field of natural sciences, for instance, there are many excellent articles on Wikipedia. Let's take biology as an example: What is photosynthesis? The Wikipedia page correctly explains it as "a process used by plants and other organisms to convert light energy into chemical energy that, through cellular respiration, can later be released to fuel the organism's activities." Answers to questions about geography are also indisputable. If you don't know the capital of Ecuador, Wikipedia has the correct answer: "Quito is the capital of Ecuador, the closest capital city to the equator, and at an elevation of 2,850 m (9,350 ft) above sea level." Sports results are also correctly documented. If you have forgotten who won the 2014 Soccer World Cup in Brazil, you can reliably find the answer on Wikipedia: "Germany defeated Argentina 1–0 after extra time to win the tournament and secure the country's fourth world title, the first after German reunification in 1990."

However, when it comes to money, geopolitics, and worldviews, Wikipedia is not always objective and reliable. US journalist Helen Buyniski found that CIA computers were used to edit the Wikipedia entries on the US's illegal attack on Iraq in 2003, as well as the article on CIA Director William Colby, who armed the contras in Nicaragua. FBI computers edited the article on Guantanamo. CIA computers were also used to evaluate the Wikipedia pages on President Nixon and President Reagan. According to Buyniski, Wikipedia is therefore "rotten to the core."[38]

In addition to US intelligence agencies, the public relations industry also works on editing the online encyclopedia every day. Since almost all Wikipedia authors write under aliases, it is usually impossible to determine who changed any given article. This anonymity is the main problem of Wikipedia, and it has repeatedly led to abuse. "Under inconspicuous pseudonyms, Daimler had their use of forced laborers during fascism deleted, as they did for their secondment of a temporary manager to the Federal Ministry of Transport when the contract for the truck toll was being negotiated," explains German journalist Werner Rügemer, who teaches at the University of Cologne. "Actors as diverse as BMW, Ebay, Dell, the CIA, and the Vatican have manipulated entries. Information about incidents at the Biblis nuclear power plant was played down from an IP address within the RWE Group. The German political parties CDU (Christian Democratic Union) and SPD (Social Democratic Party) embellished their entries, FDP (Free Democratic Party) blabbermouth Christian Lindner had his entry changed forty times via an IP address from within the Düsseldorf state parliament." None of this would have been possible with the printed Brockhaus or Brittanica.[39]

It is well known that the Pentagon has hired PR agencies. We do not know, however, what exactly it is that they do. "The US military has vastly expanded its propaganda department. No stone is left unturned to influence public opinion," the *Tages-Anzeiger* reported as early as 2009. According to Tom Curley, the head of the American news agency Associated Press (AP), the Pentagon has over 27,000 people who are exclusively responsible for public relations. These employees work on the flow of information in newspapers, on the radio, on television, and presumably also on Wikipedia. The military's PR machinery cost the US taxpayers more than $4 billion in 2009. "What exactly these funds are used for, remains mostly secret," the *Tages-Anzeiger* complained.[40]

Schoolchildren, students, teachers, and journalists alike use Wikipedia. Most people, however, do not realize that influential groups in Wikipedia ensure that the transatlantic view dominates geopolitical topics. For example, the war in Syria is under the wrong heading of "Syrian civil war," but it is not a civil war. It is a proxy war, instigated by foreign powers, with the CIA trying to overthrow the Syrian government. The article "September 11 attacks" also shows the transatlantic bias. Wikipedia completely and uncritically reproduces the story disseminated by former President George W. Bush The blowing up of WTC7 is classified as false thinking and is treated in the separate Wikipedia page titled "9/11 conspiracy theories."[41]

The fact that Wikipedia classifies former President Bush, of all people, as a credible source and vehemently defends his narrative on 9/11 is quite striking, to say the least. After all, Bush lied when he presented the made-up story about Hussein's weapons of mass destruction and then attacked Iraq, which was illegal under the UN's ban on violence. That being so, Wikipedia is citing a war criminal, presenting his narrative as the truth. But why? "9/11 is the great taboo of the twenty-first century," says the courageous German journalist Mathias Bröckers. "And the legend that nineteen students with carpet knives, who were directed from an Afghan cave, managed to ground the entire US air defense forces for two hours all by themselves and pulverized three towers, even though only two of them were hit, is the dogma of this great taboo. It must not be challenged." Therefore, 9/11 "remains the litmus test for true journalism and the principles of enlightenment."[42] As a consequence, of course Wikipedia's article on Bröckers shines a rather negative light on him.

Indeed, people who criticize US imperialism and question the official narrative of 9/11 are punished by having a derogatory Wikipedia page written about them. I know this firsthand, from personal experience. Until I was thirty-five years old, there was no article about me in the online encyclopedia and I was not a person of public interest. But then in 2008, when I was teaching in the history department of the University of Basel, a history student created a Wikipedia page about me because she found my research exciting. I had nothing against it. The article was factual and stated, "Daniele Ganser (born August 29, 1972, in Lugano) is a Swiss peace researcher and historian. According to his own statements, Ganser's main research interests are: International contemporary history since 1945, covert warfare and geostrategy, secret services and special forces, as well as resource wars, economic policy and human rights." That was fair and objective.

Now I am forty-seven years old and I have had a Wikipedia page about myself for more than ten years. I have noticed that my Wikipedia page began to deteriorate as I started to ask critical questions about the illegal wars of the USA and about the terrorist attacks of September 11, 2001, in my public lectures. Wikipedia authors unknown to me inserted the words "conspiracy theory" at the very beginning of my article without me being able to do anything about it. As a historian, I am aware that there have been multiple conspiracies throughout history, including the assassination of Julius Caesar more than 2,000 years ago. But anyone who investigates conspiracies is defamed. Psyops uses the words "conspiracy theory" to create an uncomfortable feeling in the reader. Suddenly the article about me read: "He takes up conspiracy theories, especially about September 11, 2001, and presents them as explanations yet to be tested by scientists." A few months later, this sentence was reworded to read, "He disseminates conspiracy theories on various topics, especially on the terrorist attacks of September 11, 2001."[43]

The Wikipedia page about me is not neutral because the words "conspiracy theories" are clearly defamatory. If the entry were fair, it would read, "He asks critical questions about the terrorist attacks of September 11, 2001, and holds the view that WTC7 was blown up." That's exactly what the Wikipedia entry read on November 2, 2019, after editor "Dee. lite" corrected it. But this fair version survived for only a few minutes, before another editor named "Jonaster" deleted it again on the same day and reinserted the old, defamatory formulation, "He spreads conspiracy theories on various topics, especially on the terrorist attacks of September 11, 2001." Various people from Germany, Austria, and Switzerland, who know and appreciate my books and lectures, tried to delete this derogatory sentence. In a free, online encyclopedia, where everyone is allowed to correct an error, this would surely be rectified soon, many mistakenly believed. So far, however, that is exactly what has not been possible. The hierarchically higher placed editors, administrators, and bureaucrats prevented the words "conspiracy theory" from being deleted from the first five sentences of my page, because it makes up the core of the defamation. When users tried to change my entry several times, their accounts were banned and they could no longer be able to make changes to any other pages on Wikipedia either. Currently, my Wikipedia page forms the grounds on which a so-called "editing war" is taking place. A battle for the sovereignty of interpretation. How my page will develop in the future remains to be seen.[44]

Wikipedia has a little-known but strict hierarchy. At the bottom are the unregistered users, who make up the vast majority of people who frequent the online encyclopedia. They can read Wikipedia articles for free, but never write anything on Wikipedia themselves. One level higher are the confirmed users. They enjoy the encyclopedia and write an article now and then or correct mistakes in already existing texts. One level higher on the English Wikipedia are 60,753 "extended confirmed users," who can release and undo texts of new users. The next level higher are 1,049 "administrators," who are elected for life and supervise the users, have permission to make texts invisible, and can block users. Above the administrators are currently twenty powerful bureaucrats, who form the top of the English Wikipedia and control the almost 6.5 million articles.[45]

How does one become an administrator or an extended user? The art promoter Gottfried Böhmer from the Society of Friends of the Arts in Düsseldorf tells the following story: An IT company from Wiesbaden offered him $10,000 a month in additional income if he would write for Wikipedia on a regular basis. The proposal was that Böhmer would work his way up step by step and, with his reputation, would eventually acquire administrator rights by being elected by the Wikipedia community. "Böhmer's interlocutor, who was so extremely generous, concluded by telling Böhmer that he already had a large network of journalists writing for Wikipedia, and that they would, in due time, suggest Böhmer as an administrator," the online journal *Tichys Einblick* reports. Böhmer, however, refused. He did not want to partake in such opaque games.[46]

Now here is the problem: due to the fact that extended users, administrators, and bureaucrats work under pseudonyms, their real names are unknown to the public. This is astonishing. In science, nobody can publish an article in a journal without disclosing his or her real name. Every book prints the author's name on the cover. After all, it is always a person who writes the texts, and each person looks at the world differently. Why doesn't this simple rule also apply to Wikipedia? A reform is urgently needed. In my opinion, all Wikipedia users should be required to openly and clearly disclose their names. Furthermore, the names of the administrators and bureaucrats should also be known to the public, because anonymity protects those groups of people who manipulate information on Wikipedia.

The Dark Side of Wikipedia

Filmmaker Markus Fiedler created an exciting documentary film titled *Die dunkle Seite der Wikipedia* (*The Dark Side of Wikipedia*), in which he illuminated the history of the Wikipedia page about me. Since 2015, the film can be viewed on YouTube free of charge. Personally, I learned a lot about Wikipedia from this documentary. The film proves that a special group of people, who have made it their business to discredit critics of US policy, operates behind the scenes of the German Wikipedia. "Using the example of the Wikipedia article on the person of Dr. Daniele Ganser, we prove that character assassination is being carried out in a targeted manner," Markus Fiedler explains. The methods used include negative source selection, admission of unobjective opinionated newspaper articles, and deliberate misinterpretation of Wikipedia rules.[47]

The bureaucrat monitoring my page acts under the username "Itti." Her real name remains unknown. Metaphorically speaking, Itti has put a fence around my page and, together with other extended users and administrators, prevents my page from being worded neutrally. The statistics on my page also show that above all "Kopilot," "Phi," and "Jonaster" control my entry and censure me digitally. Of course, it is annoying to be defamed on Wikipedia. But it is not about me personally, it is about how Wikipedia works. Who is behind these aliases? Filmmaker Markus Fiedler was able to unmask Phi and Kopilot and knows their real names. Phi is a Latin and history teacher from Hamburg. Kopilot is a piano teacher from outside of Osnabrück. The identity of Jonaster is still unknown.

I have never met either the history teacher Phi or the piano teacher Kopilot, but I find it wrong of them to blemish my page under the protection of anonymity. Fiedler revealed that Kopilot has written a total of 50,000 entries on Wikipedia over the course of five years. That is an average of thirty-nine entries per day. He wrote without interruption, even on Christmas and Easter, and because Kopilot left his alias in all of the articles that he edited, it can be empirically proven that Kopilot contributed to the following articles on Wikipedia, while always claiming to be an expert: Daniele Ganser, Jesus Christ, Martin Luther, Barack Obama, Osama bin Laden, Holocaust, air raids on Dresden, crimes of the Wehrmacht, left-wing fascism, national anarchism, pacifism, Zionism, world Jewry, terrorist attacks of September 11, 2001, occupation of Iraq since 2003, Gladio, Vietnam War, Hamas, conspiracy theories on the attack on Pearl Harbor, Fukushima nuclear power plant, Alternative for Germany, and many more.[48]

When it comes to scientific articles and soccer results, Wikipedia is reliable. But when it comes to money, geopolitics, and world views, that is not the case. “Numerous empirical evidence has been presented that Wikipedia not only lacks the necessary objectivity, but that interested editors use the digital encyclopedia as a weapon to discredit political opponents with supposedly factual statements,” explains Hermann Ploppa, who has published writings on the topic of transatlantic networks. They are helped by the immunity that they enjoy through anonymity: “No one in the Wikipedia hierarchy is required to subject themselves to being checked and criticized by mentioning their real name,” says Ploppa, explaining the core problem of the free encyclopedia. Moreover, as the Wikimedia Foundation, which is a legal entity, is based in the US, taking legal action against unbalanced or defamatory Wikipedia articles is “almost impossible for ordinary citizens.”[49]

CHAPTER 15

THE FIGHT FOR EURASIA

In geostrategy, "Eurasia" refers to the vast landmass of the two connecting continents of Europe and Asia that has more than four billion inhabitants. The United States, with a population of only 330 million, is separated from Eurasia by the Atlantic and Pacific Oceans. Since the first US soldiers landed on the shores of Eurasia during World War I, the US empire has repeatedly intervened in various wars in Eurasia. It is no secret in Washington that the powerful states of China and Russia oppose US global domination and do not allow US military bases on their soil. China, in particular, is seeking to expand its global influence with the Belt and Road Initiative, aka the Silk Road. Some observers believe that China will replace the USA as the global empire in the twenty-first century. Whether this is true, only the future will tell.

"Divide and Rule"

Imperialism of the modern times began in the early 1500s with the conquests of the Spanish and the Portuguese, followed by the imperialism of the British, French, Dutch, and Belgians. The German imperialists were late to the party and did not acquire their first colony in Africa until 1884, when they conquered Namibia. "Ever since the continents started interacting politically, some five hundred years ago, Eurasia has been the center of world power," US geostrategist Zbigniew Brzezinski correctly explains. It was only after World War I and World War II that the United States rose to become the "paramount world power" for the first time in history. According to Brzezinski, the global supremacy of the USA in the future depends on how the empire "copes with the complex Eurasian power relationships—and particularly whether it prevents the emergence of a dominant and antagonistic Eurasian power."[1]

The USA would never be able to occupy the whole of Eurasia with soldiers—the area is far too large and the US soldiers would always be outnumbered. Therefore, over the past hundred years, the US has always relied on the strategy of "divide and rule" (Latin: *divide et impera*) in Eurasia, which was already used by the British to secure their empire. Once again, the US has strengthened and emphasized what divides a country or a region and weakened and minimized what unites it. According to the principle "the enemy of my enemy is my friend," the US has armed different groups, thus splitting Eurasia into multiple subgroups that have differing interests, turning them against each other. This "divide and conquer" strategy caused the divided countries and groups to fight each other and thus weaken themselves, instead of standing united against the US empire.

In Afghanistan, for example, the United States armed the Soviet Union's opponents, the mujahideen, in 1979 and engaged both in a long war. Zbigniew Brzezinski served as President Jimmy Carter's national security advisor at the time and remembers the war in the Hindu Kush this way: "According to the official version of history, CIA aid to the Mujahideen began during 1980, that is to say, after the Soviet army invaded Afghanistan on December 24, 1979 . . . But the reality, closely guarded until now, is completely otherwise: Indeed, it was July 3, 1979 that President Carter signed the first directive for secret aid to the opponents of the pro-Soviet regime in Kabul. And that very day, I wrote a note to the president in which I explained to him that in my opinion this aid was going to induce a Soviet military intervention." The French newspaper *Observateur* then asked, "Do you regret supporting Islamist terrorists?" The question was a good one, because many people believed the US would never arm terrorists. But Brzezinski praised the principle of "divide and conquer" and replied, "Regret what? That secret operation was an excellent idea . . . What is more important in world history? The Taliban or the collapse of the Soviet empire? Some agitated Muslims or the liberation of Central Europe and the end of the Cold War?"[2]

It is important to understand that there was no reason for the US to go to war in Afghanistan in 1979. The country was located very far away and did not pose a threat to the United States. The only goal of this US operation was to weaken Russia, which the empire succeeded in doing. This proxy war, which only ended in 1988, shed a lot of blood and took a heavy toll; about a million people died in Afghanistan, including 15,000 Russians. There was no real friendship between the CIA and the mujahideen, those "agitated Muslims," as Brzezinski called them. Only for a very limited time were they brothers in arms. After the defeat of the Soviet Union, the empire switched fronts again and in 2001, US troops landed in Afghanistan to fight those same men that Washington had armed just twenty years earlier.

Anyone who takes the issue of division seriously can recognize its presence everywhere. In Germany, the political parties Die Linke (The Left) and the AfD (Alternative for Germany) are fighting each other instead of working together to demand the withdrawal of US soldiers from Germany. In Turkey, the Turks and the Kurds are fighting each other instead of jointly demanding the closure of the US military bases in Turkey. In Serbia, the US seceded the province of Kosovo and established the US military base Camp Bondsteel, after arming the Muslim paramilitary Kosovo Liberation Army and supporting them in their fight against the Christian Orthodox Serbs. The Muslims in Kosovo were only a means to implement the "divide and rule" strategy in Serbia. The same was true in Nicaragua, where the US armed the contras to overthrow the Sandinistas, but in this particular case they did not succeed.

The US has pursued the same strategy with Iraq and Iran. First, the CIA brought Saddam Hussein to power in Iraq in 1979. Just a year later, he attacked Iran and became embroiled in a long war. At the time, the US stood by Hussein, although in secret, they also supplied weapons to Iran, which was exposed during the Iran-Contra affair. The war weakened both countries, as US geostrategist George Friedman of the Stratfor think tank explained in a lecture in Chicago in 2015. "The United States cannot constantly be intervening throughout Eurasia," Friedman said. "The policy that I would recommend is the one that Ronald Reagan adopted toward Iran and Iraq: He funded both sides, so they would fight each other and not fight us. This was cynical, it was certainly not moral, [but] it worked. This is the point: The United States cannot occupy Eurasia. The moment the first boot sets to ground, demographic differential means we are totally outnumbered." Friedman, who showed little empathy for the suffering of the affected population, explicitly counseled setting hostile countries against each other. "We can support various contending powers," Friedman said. "Britain didn't occupy India. It took various Indian states and turned them against each other."[3]

The same strategy was used to weaken Germany and Russia. According to Friedman, it is essential for the US that Germany and Russia do not cooperate, but rather fight each other. "The primordial interest of the United States, over which for centuries we have fought wars—the First, Second, Cold War—has been the relationship between Germany and Russia. Because united, they are the only force that could threaten us. And to make sure that that [cooperation] doesn't happen." Because the US opened the Second Front late in World War II, Germans and Russians killed each other. Millions died, which weakened both countries, which was exactly in the interest of the United States.[4]

Rarely is the "divide and conquer" strategy openly discussed in public. Many do not even know that this strategy exists. In the Bundestag in Berlin, the smart parliamentarian Sahra Wagenknecht of the Die Linke party picked up on Friedman's statements and warned against a confrontation with Russia. "The head of Stratfor recently explained the US's specific interests in Europe with impressive frankness: 'The main interest of the US is to prevent an alliance between Germany and Russia,'" said Wagenknecht, who called for Germany to foster good relations with Russia. She is absolutely right to do so, as peace between Berlin and Moscow is important.[5]

The bottom line is that the "divide and conquer" strategy has proven very successful for the United States. Prior to World War I, the US did not have a single military base in Eurasia. After the Great War, the empire succeeded in establishing military bases in many Eurasian countries by engaging in a multitude of wars. Today, these bases are located in

Afghanistan, Bahrain, Belgium, Bulgaria, Cambodia, Georgia, Germany, Greece, Holland, Hungary, Iceland, Iraq, Italy, Japan, Kosovo, Kuwait, Norway, Oman, Pakistan, Portugal, Qatar, Romania, Singapore, South Korea, Spain, Syria, Turkey, the United Arab Emirates, and Diego Garcia in the Indian Ocean, just to name a few.

Russia Is Just a Regional Power

In terms of landmass, Russia is the largest country in the world. It encompasses eleven time zones and is twice the size of the United States and seventy times the size of Great Britain. However, Russia is not an empire, it is "a regional power," as former President Barack Obama once correctly said. While the USA has eleven aircraft carriers and thus dominates the world's oceans, Russia has only one aircraft carrier, the *Admiral Kuznetsov*. The only combat mission it has been engaged in so far was in 2016 during the Syrian war. Russia is a land power. Moscow lacks an ice-free port with direct access to the world's oceans. Its ports on the Arctic Ocean are frozen over for several months of the year. Even the Russian Pacific port of Vladivostok is blocked by ice for about four months of the year. The port of Sevastopol in Crimea, located on the Black Sea, flows into the Mediterranean Sea, which is controlled by NATO.[6]

The Western media continuously invokes the image of the "evil Russian," who is armed to the teeth and a dangerous aggressor. This depiction of Russians is heavily influenced by US propaganda, with the objective of dividing Eurasia, Germany, and Russia in particular. The 150 million people in Russia have never allowed the US to establish military bases on Russian soil. Just like Iran, Russia is therefore constantly defamed in NATO-friendly media. The facts, however, clearly show that it is not Russia, but the USA that is armed to the teeth. In 2018, Russian military spending was $61 billion, while that of the US was $649 billion. In 1979, the Soviet Union invaded Afghanistan. While this was undeniably illegal and a clear violation of the UN's ban on the use of force, Russia has invaded far fewer countries than the United States. Russia also has far fewer military bases in foreign countries close to its borders, namely in Georgia, Armenia, Belarus, Vietnam, Kazakhstan, Kyrgyzstan, Tajikistan, Syria, and Moldova.[7]

NATO's Eastward Expansion Angers Russia

Russia has been overrun by the West several times. Under Napoleon, the French attacked Russia in 1812; the Germans attacked Russia in both of the world wars. The North European Plain, which stretches from France to the Ural Mountains, is flat and difficult for Russia to defend. In response to the US's establishment of NATO (North Atlantic Treaty Organization) in 1949, the Soviet Union, together with most of the communist states in Eastern Europe, established the Warsaw Pact in 1955, pledging mutual assistance and military defense. Within the Warsaw Pact, Russia suppressed every democratic movement, including the Prague Spring of 1968 in Czechoslovakia, which it brutally crushed.

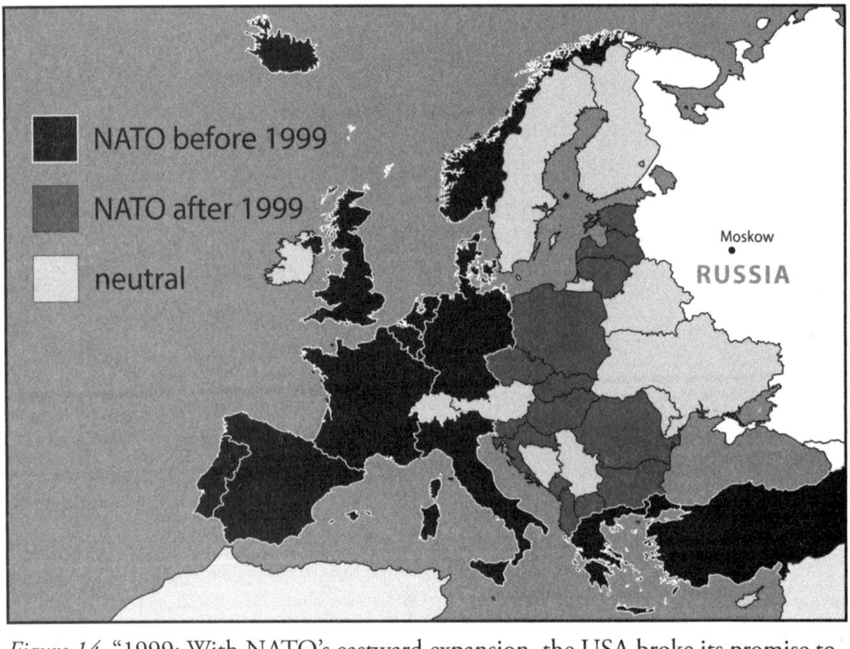

Figure 14. "1999: With NATO's eastward expansion, the USA broke its promise to Russia."

After the fall of the Berlin Wall and the collapse of the Soviet Union in 1991, the Warsaw Pact dissolved and the US empire took advantage of Moscow's weakness to extend its influence to Eastern Europe and to include the former Warsaw Pact member states in NATO. As a result, a large part of the Northern European Plain came under the sphere of influence of the United States, which stationed tanks and missiles throughout the region, even though they had promised the Russians that they would not do so. Poland, the Czech Republic, and Hungary became NATO members in 1999, on NATO's fiftieth anniversary, when the military alliance waged an illegal war of aggression against Serbia under President Bill Clinton. Bulgaria, Estonia, Latvia, Lithuania, Romania, Slovakia, and Slovenia joined NATO in 2004. Albania and Croatia were admitted to NATO in 2009, before Montenegro joined in 2017. The addition of North Macedonia in 2020 increased the number of NATO states to the thirty countries it includes today.

From the Russians' perspective, the expansion of NATO to the east was—and continues to be—a serious breach of promise and a provocation. After the fall of the Berlin Wall, German chancellor Helmut Kohl and his foreign minister Hans-Dietrich Genscher had succeeded in strengthening the friendly relations between Germany and Russia, which contributed to Soviet president Mikhail Gorbachev supporting the peaceful reunification of Germany. This also led to the German Democratic Republic (GDR) leaving the Warsaw Pact and becoming a member of NATO as part of newly reunified Germany. Moscow peacefully withdrew its 340,000 troops that were stationed in the GDR. Germany can be grateful to Russia for their peaceful withdrawal of Soviet troops because it was an important contribution to Germany's independence.

At the time, US Secretary of State James Baker had declared that the United States had nothing against Germany's reunification, so long as reunified Germany was to become a member of NATO. On February 9, 1990, Baker met with Gorbachev in the Catherine Hall of the Kremlin in Moscow and promised that NATO would not extend its sphere of influence further eastward. "Not one inch" were his exact words, as the original transcripts of the conversation that were made public by the National Security Archive in Washington show. This promise, however, has since been broken on many occasions. It was a deception reminiscent of the US's behavior toward the Indigenous peoples in the nineteenth century. Already then, Washington had promised various Native tribes that all they had to do was to retreat over the mountains and the US military would leave them alone. These promises were mere deceptions of war and they were always broken until the US military ultimately reached the Pacific coast and all of the Indigenous population had either been killed or driven out.[8]

The Russians cannot be driven out like the Native people of North America, and NATO's eastward expansion enraged the Russians. The United States, Germany, and other Western countries had promised that NATO would not move an inch eastward, Gorbachev said in 2009, when Albania and Croatia joined NATO. This repeated breach of promise led to the Russians no longer trusting the West and its promises. On March 18, 2014, during the crisis in the Ukraine, Russian president Vladimir Putin also said, "Our western partners, led by the United States of America . . . have lied to us many times, made decisions behind our backs, placed us before an accomplished fact . . . This happened with NATO's expansion to the east, as well as the deployment of military infrastructure at our borders."[9]

US defense contractors have profited from NATO's eastward expansion because they have been able to equip the new NATO member states with weapons, explains Colonel Lawrence Wilkerson, who served as a helicopter pilot in Vietnam. "Was Bill Clinton's expansion of NATO—after George H. W. Bush and [his Secretary of State] James Baker had assured Gorbachev and then Yeltsin that we wouldn't go an inch further east—was this for Lockheed Martin, and Raytheon, and Boeing, and others, to increase their network of potential weapon sales?" Wilkerson asked, and answered his own question by exclaiming, "You bet it was." As always, it is about money, power, and influence. "We dwarf the Russians or anyone else who sells weapons in the world," the retired army colonel continued. "We are the death merchant of the world."[10]

Up to the Urals, Russia is a part of Europe. With NATO's eastward expansion, the US has succeeded in dividing Europe and angering Russia. Europe is "America's essential geopolitical bridgehead on the Eurasian continent," declared Zbigniew Brzezinski. Europe is the US's "natural ally" because it is "the original homeland of a large majority of Americans," he said. "The Old World is of enormous geostrategic interest to the US" because without NATO, it would not be possible for the US to maintain military bases on the borders of Russia.[11]

2014: The USA's Coup d'État in Ukraine

At the NATO summit in the Romanian capital of Bucharest in April 2008, President George W. Bush decided to admit Ukraine and Georgia into NATO, which inflamed tensions between the Western military alliance and Russia. The Russians were enraged by the United States' actions. As early as August 2008, the US encouraged Georgia to attack the breakaway state of South Ossetia. Russia intervened and won the war in just five days. Swiss diplomat Heidi Tagliavini, who investigated the outbreak of the war on behalf of the European Union, concluded that Georgian president Mikheil Saakashvili had initiated the Georgian war on the night of August 7. Georgia was undoubtedly the aggressor, supported by the United States in the background, which had sent some of their military advisors to Georgia.[12]

In Ukraine, which directly borders Russia, the US empire also fueled tensions in accordance with the strategy of "divide and conquer" and overthrew the government in a secret coup d'état in 2014. President Vladimir Putin then occupied eastern Ukraine and secured the Crimean peninsula, which broke away from Ukraine after a referendum and now belongs to Russia. This time, the European Union did not form a commission of inquiry to investigate the coup more closely. *ARD*, *ZDF*, *Spiegel*, *Bild*, and *Süddeutsche Zeitung* were content with the accusations against Russia. This obscured the role of the US empire, which had triggered the war in Ukraine by instigating the coup d'état. "Imagine the outrage in Washington if China built an impressive military alliance and tried to include Canada and Mexico in it," US political scientist John Mearsheimer, who teaches at the University of Chicago, pointed out. Mearsheimer correctly recognized that President Barack Obama, not Russian president Vladimir Putin, had unleashed the conflict in Ukraine.[13]

The coup in Ukraine was triggered in Kyiv on February 20, 2014, when snipers shot both demonstrators and police alike, which plunged the country into chaos. President Viktor Yanukovych and Prime Minister Nikolai Azarov were forced to resign. The US installed Arseniy Yatsenyuk as the new prime minister and Petro Poroshenko as the new president. "It was a Western-sponsored coup. There's little doubt about that," declared the well-informed former CIA officer Ray McGovern. At the US State

Department, Victoria Nuland had been pulling the strings, along with Geoffrey Pyatt, the US ambassador to Ukraine. Phone conversations between Nuland and Ambassador Pyatt, in which they discussed the composition of the new government before the coup, were intercepted and caused uproar because Nuland had insulted the European Union by saying "Fuck the EU."[14]

The overthrown politicians in Ukraine understood that the US empire was responsible for the coup in Kyiv. "The Americans visibly forced this confrontational development," explained ousted prime minister Nikolai Azarov. The leaders of the demonstrations on the Maidan had been in and out of the US Embassy, from where they had been commanded. However, it was never really about Ukraine, Azarov explains—it was about the struggle for Eurasia. "Ukraine was only a wedge in the strategic operation of the Americans to prevent a Eurasian economic area, which would span from Western Europe to Vladivostok," Azarov says, thus alluding to and explaining the principle of "divide and rule."[15]

After the coup, Ukraine's Russian-speaking eastern districts of Donetsk and Lugansk declared that they did not recognize the new government that had overthrown Azarov in Kyiv. On April 12, 2014, as tensions between the government in Kyiv and the Russian-speaking population in eastern Ukraine continued to grow, CIA chief John Brennan flew to Kyiv on a secret mission and under a false name. In Kyiv, he met with Interior Minister Arsen Avakov and Oleksandr Turchynov, the former director of Ukraine's domestic intelligence agency, who served as Ukraine's interim president for four months after the coup d'état. What Brennan, Turchynov, and Avakov discussed is not exactly known, because the transcripts of their conversations are not yet available to historians. The US State Department only confirmed that Brennan was indeed in Kyiv, but claimed that it was just a routine visit. This is not very convincing. Presumably, Brennan was advising the coup government under Turchynov, which had been installed by the US, to launch a civil war against its own people in the east of the country.[16]

Upon Brennan's departure, Interior Minister Avakov immediately announced an anti-terrorist operation against its own people in eastern Ukraine to fight the resistance of the newly installed coup government. As early as April 15, 2014, the Ukrainian army began to deploy troops against its own people. However, some soldiers sided with the citizens of eastern Ukraine because they did not want to fire on their own people. Interim President Turchynov was not impressed by this and on May 2, 2014, the Ukrainian army attacked the city of Slovyansk in the Donbas region of eastern Ukraine with combat helicopters, whereupon the fighting escalated. The Ukrainian civil war lasted eight years and claimed 14,000 lives.

In the Western media there was little coverage of the obscure commencement of the Ukrainian civil war in April 2014 and the role of the CIA. Some journalists even tried to blame Russia for the coup and the civil war. But Sergei Nethayev, the Russian ambassador to Germany, categorically rejected these accusations. "The West's attempts to blame Russia for the devastating consequences of the unconstitutional coup in 2014 are counterproductive," the ambassador said. "The parties to the conflict are Kiev, Donetsk and Lugansk, and all that the latter are 'to blame' for is not supporting the coup and the anti-Russian slogans from the Maidan. That is why the new government in Kiev called them 'terrorists.' At the time, the West preferred to remain silent and to overlook the overthrow and the subsequent crimes of the nationalists."[17]

To fuel the civil war, the US supplied weapons to the government in Kyiv and the CIA sent advisors to the front lines in Ukraine. In addition to that, the CIA brought Ukrainian special forces from Ukraine to the United States, trained them there, and then flew them back into Ukraine. "The CIA is overseeing a secret intensive training program in the US for elite Ukrainian special operations forces and other intelligence personnel, according to five former intelligence and national security officials familiar with the initiative," the media reported. "The program, which started in 2015, is based at an undisclosed facility in the southern United States . . . The program has involved 'very specific training on skills that would enhance' the Ukrainians' 'ability to push back against the Russians,' said the former senior intelligence official. One person familiar with the program put it more bluntly. 'The United States is training an insurgency,' said a former CIA official, adding that the program has taught the Ukrainians how 'to kill Russians.'"[18]

On February 24, 2022, on the orders of Vladimir Putin, Russia attacked Ukraine with its own troops. This was a clear violation of the

UN ban on the use of force and a violation of Ukraine's sovereignty. The day after the attack, eleven out of fifteen countries on the UN Security Council condemned the illegal Russian invasion. One resolution called for a cessation of all hostilities. But as was expected, Russia's UN Ambassador Vasily Nebensya vetoed it, which left the Security Council deadlocked and unable to act. China, India, and the United Arab Emirates abstained.[19]

With Russia's invasion of Ukraine in February 2022, the conflict came to a dramatic head as the USA and Russia, both of which are nuclear powers, now faced off in a proxy war. The US and the European Union imposed comprehensive economic sanctions on Russia and sent weapons to Ukrainian president Volodymyr Zelenskyy. Prior to entering politics, Zelenskyy had been a successful actor and played Ukraine's president in the 2015 television series *Servant of the People*, in which he cleaned up corruption in the country by ousting oligarchs and led Ukraine to a prosperous future. The people were so moved by the series that they elected Zelenskyy president in May 2019 with 72 percent of the vote. Unlike on TV, however, Zelenskyy did not lead his country to a prosperous future, but continued the civil war against eastern Ukraine. This triggered the illegal Russian invasion and turned Ukraine into a theater of war in a geostrategic conflict between Moscow and Washington.

2014: The USA Bombs Syria

The US empire also intervened in Syria, but failed in their attempt to overthrow President Bashar al-Assad. At the time, the operation was conducted in secret, but now the relevant historical data is accessible. "State Department cables made public by WikiLeaks show that the Bush administration tried to destabilize Syria and that these efforts continued into the Obama years," US journalist Seymour Hersh revealed. In December 2006, more than five years before the outbreak of the war, William Roebuck, who worked in the US Embassy in Damascus, filed an analysis of the "vulnerabilities of the Assad government" in which he recommended stoking religious tensions. The US Embassy in Syria then went on to spend "$5 million financing dissidents," Hersh reported.[20]

The attack on Syria was no secret within well-informed circles in Washington. General Wesley Clark, who as Supreme Allied Commander

Europe (SACEUR) had commanded NATO forces in the US's illegal attack on Serbia in 1999, confirmed that the US wanted to overthrow President Bashar al-Assad. This, he said, was what Deputy Defense Secretary Paul Wolfowitz told him at the Pentagon as early as 1991, shortly after the Soviet Union collapsed. "One thing we did learn [from the Persian Gulf War] is that we can use our military in the region—in the Middle East—and the Soviets won't stop us," Wolfowitz had said back then. "And we've got about 5 or 10 years to clean up those old Soviet regimes—Syria, Iran, Iraq—before the next great superpower comes on to challenge us."[21]

The British also wanted the overthrow of President Assad, as former French foreign minister Roland Dumas disclosed to the French television station LCP. "I was in England two years before the violence in Syria on other business," Dumas recalled of 2009. "I met with top British officials, who confessed to me that they were preparing something in Syria," he said. As always, the British were working in secret and the British people had no idea of their government's preparations for war. But as Dumas confirms, "Britain was organizing an invasion of rebels into Syria. They even asked me, although I was no longer minister for foreign affairs, if I would like to participate."[22]

The war in Syria broke out in March 2011. In the city of Dara, near the border of Jordan, Syrian security forces stopped a truck that had come from Iraq and was carrying a large quantity of weapons and explosives. The Syrian government's news agency stated that the weapons were intended to "trigger actions in Syria that threaten Syria's internal security and to spread insurgency and chaos." While this truck was intercepted, other trucks reached their destinations, as it was impossible for Syria to systematically control all of its borders with Iraq and Jordan. A Facebook page called on the Syrian people to rise up against President Assad and demanded an end to corruption and oppression. The state responded to the demonstrations with water cannons and tear gas, and the first deaths occurred. Soon thereafter, Syria descended into chaos.[23]

President Barack Obama, who unjustly received the Nobel Peace Prize, was directly involved in the illegal attack on Syria. Once again, the "divide and conquer" strategy was employed. The CIA trained and armed President Assad's opponents, even though the UN ban on the use of force strictly prohibits arming militant groups in foreign countries. "We know they sent in the CIA to overthrow Assad," revealed US economist Jeffrey Sachs, who teaches at Columbia University. "It was Operation Timber Sycamore, people can look it up—the CIA operation." And this operation was authorized by Obama, but never discussed in public in the US. It was all done in secret. The bloody battles between the Syrian government and the rebels took a heavy toll of blood. "What we should do now is get out [of Syria]," Sachs insisted in 2018. "We have made a proxy war in Syria. It has killed 500,000 people [and] displaced ten million [others]."[24]

It is against international law to support rebels in another country who want to overthrow the government. "In the Nicaragua ruling, the International Court of Justice (ICJ) had recognized that arming and training paramilitary forces is a violation of the UN's ban on the use of force," the Scientific Service of the German Bundestag correctly explained. "This is also the case with the arming and training of Syrian rebel groups by the United States since 2012."[25]

The war against Syria was "one of the costliest covert action programs in the history of the CIA," the *New York Times* revealed. The CIA invested more than $1 billion in Operation Timber Sycamore, "one of the most expensive efforts to arm and train rebels since the agency's program arming the Mujahideen in Afghanistan during the 1980s." The US empire relied on the old familiar tactic of "divide and conquer" and also armed Muslim terrorists to topple Assad. "Al-Qaeda is on our side in Syria," Jake Sullivan, foreign policy advisor to US Secretary of State Hillary Clinton, famously wrote to his boss via email on February 12, 2012. The US public was unaware of this. In public, President Obama hypocritically emphasized that he was fighting terrorism, while at the same time the CIA was secretly arming terrorists.[26]

Due to the fact that the gangs in Syria, which had been armed by the CIA, were only moderately successful, Obama began bombing Syria on September 23, 2014. Again, this was a violation of the UN's ban on the use of force. Obama declared that this use of force was a necessity in fighting terrorism and called for the overthrow of Syrian president Assad. But Russia and Iran rushed to Syria's aid and on September 30, 2015, on President Putin's orders, the Russian air force commenced with the bombing of CIA-backed rebels in Syria, which also killed a lot of civilians. The Russian air force and the Syrian army were successful in forcing the rebels into retreat. In 2019, under President Donald Trump, the US withdrew most of its troops from Syria after the US had failed to topple Assad. "The world has done many things wrong in Syria," Günter Meyer, director of the Center for Research on the Arab World at the University of Mainz, summed up. "But we also have to state who did what wrong: And here, the main responsibility lies with the United States."[27]

1839: The Humiliation of China in the Opium War

In the twenty-first century, China is the biggest challenger of the US empire, not Russia. China also does not allow US American military bases on its soil. With 1.4 billion people, China is the country with the world's largest population. In its more than 4,000-year history, China has always been a land power and not a seafaring nation. That said, in the fifteenth century the Chinese did sail to Vietnam, India, Sri Lanka, and along the east coast of Africa as far as Mozambique with their so-called treasure fleet under Admiral Zheng He. They would bring giraffes to China, but the Chinese emperor never sought to sail his ships across the oceans to conquer foreign lands like the Europeans did. This was because the Chinese believed that their culture and economy were superior to all the others. And for a certain period of time, this was actually true. "China was far superior to the rest of the world during the late imperial period, which was roughly from the 11th to the 12th century," said sinologist Kai Vogelsang of the University of Hamburg. "China had cities of millions at a time when in Europe the largest cities had 20,000 to 30,000 inhabitants. China knew how to print, centuries before Europe. They had paper money long before there was ever any talk of it in Europe. China knew the compass and had gunpowder."[28]

Convinced of its own superiority, China sealed itself off from the "barbarians" and sank into self-imposed isolation behind the famous Great Wall, which is more than 13,000 miles long. The treasure fleet was destroyed, and the Chinese emperor forbade any further expeditions. "China was never particularly interested in conquering, occupying, and colonizing foreign states," explains sinologist Roderich Ptak of the University of Munich. It did not occur to them to conquer South America, North America, or Africa, which is why the European colonial powers never met any Chinese on their conquest expeditions.[29]

The Emperor of China also did not want to engage in any trade with the West. The "barbarians" and their "inferior products" were of no interest to him. Only through the port of Canton near Hong Kong did China allow for a limited amount of trade with the British, who mainly exported Chinese tea and silk to Britain. Conversely, however, the British had few goods to sell in China except for opium, which the British would import into China from India. Opium spread through Chinese society rapidly and it weakened the country, which was entirely in the interest of the British. "It was a very sophisticated crime," says Kai Vogelsang. "It was drug trafficking." Helplessly, the Chinese emperor tried to curb the opium trade, and even had it confiscated and publicly burned, but to no avail. The British then even criticized the destruction of their trade goods, and in 1839 the Opium War, which was instigated by the British, broke out.[30]

With that, it became clear that in terms of military technology, China was by no means the leading nation of the world. During the Opium War, the British crushed the weak Chinese navy and flooded the country with even more opium. "Where is your conscience?" asked Lin Zexu, the commissioner whom the Emperor of China had appointed as special envoy in the fight against opium smuggling. "Suppose there were people from another country who carried opium for sale to England and seduced your people into buying and smoking it; certainly your honorable ruler would deeply hate it and be bitterly aroused," Lin Zexu said in a letter to Britain's Queen Victoria. The Chinese demanded an immediate halt to drug imports. "We have heard heretofore that your honorable ruler is kind and benevolent. Naturally you would not wish to give unto others what you yourself do not want." But it didn't help. The British sent even more opium to China and forced the Chinese to open all their ports. Hong Kong was conquered by Britain, seceded from China, and in 1842, in the Treaty of Nanking, was ceded to London as a colony.[31]

The defeat in the Opium War and the loss of Hong Kong came as a shock to China, which had long considered itself the most advanced nation in the world. The Chinese were humiliated and knew that their military could not keep up with that of the British, whose cannons had a much longer range. "They can still hit us even when we cannot hit them," admitted Lin Zexu, who had unsuccessfully fought the drug trade on behalf of the emperor. The firepower of the British was superior to that of the Chinese. Every British soldier fired continuously, he said. "When they fire, it is like when a whole troop of our soldiers fire one after the other; [each of their soldiers can] fire continuously without stopping. When we fire one shot [our soldiers] need a lot of time hurrying around before another shot can be fired. This is the result of our unfamiliarity with these arts," Lin Zexu lamented. There were many Chinese officers and soldiers with military experience, but it was limited to close combat. Most had never experienced combat where "one has to fight without seeing the enemy's face," Lin commented in amazement.[32]

China Has the Largest Army in the World

More than 180 years have passed since the Opium War. In Europe and in the USA, this war is no longer a topic of conversation. But in China, this humiliation has never been forgotten. Beijing is arming itself and is in the process of building its own ocean-going navy. So far, China has only two aircraft carriers, while the US with its eleven aircraft carriers is currently still the leading power on the world's oceans. The Chinese aircraft carrier *Liaoning*, which has a launching ramp on its bow, began to operate in 2012. In 2018 it was followed by the Chinese's second aircraft carrier *Shandong*, which can carry fighter jets and helicopters. Never again will China bow to the US, the British, or any other colonial power. With two million troops, China has the largest army in the world. "Today, we are closer, more confident, and more capable than ever before of making the goal of national rejuvenation a reality," Chinese president Xi Jinping, who has led the country since 2013, declared.[33]

While the US empire has covered almost the entire world with military bases, so far China has only one military base in a foreign country, namely in Djibouti, Africa. However, China's arms spending is second only to that of the United States. In 2018, it reached $250 billion, compared to the United States' nearly $650 billion in the same year. The US views China's high defense spending very critically. "China is building a robust, lethal force," General Robert Ashley, the director of the US Defense Intelligence Agency, warned in a report in 2019. Future US presidents will face "a China insistent on having a greater voice in global interactions, which at times may be antithetical to US interests."[34]

Following Mao Zedong's establishment of the Communist People's Republic of China in 1949, China invaded Tibet on October 7, 1950. "At the time of the forcible incorporation of Tibet into the Chinese state federation, it had been an independent state," explains the Scientific Service of the German Federal Parliament. Therefore, the invasion of Tibet was—once again—illegal and a violation of the UN's ban on the use of force. On March 21, 1959, the Chinese brutally put down a popular uprising of the Tibetans. The Dalai Lama, who is the head of the Tibetan government, fled into exile in India that same year. For me personally, the Dalai Lama and Mahatma Gandhi are role models and figures of great inspiration for the peace movement. "As for me, I always emphasize the value of what I call inner disarmament," the Dalai Lama wisely explained. "It is done by reducing hatred and promoting compassion."[35]

China also laid claim to Taiwan. During the Chinese Civil War, the US had covertly intervened in China and supported Chiang Kai-shek, who then lost to Mao Zedong and had to retreat to the island of Taiwan off the coast of China with his followers, where he proclaimed the "Republic of China." To this day, the USA supports the island of Taiwan, which lies only 140 miles off the coast of China, diplomatically and militarily, thereby driving a wedge into Chinese society, following the principle of "divide and rule."

With the help of the USA, Taiwan was given a permanent seat on the UN Security Council in New York and only had to relinquish it to the People's Republic of China in 1971. The Chinese regard Taiwan as a renegade province and want to reunite the island with the mainland, by military force if necessary. The USA, which lies more than 6,000 miles away from the island, has armed the Taiwanese air force and their marine force with the latest US military equipment. Whether China will resort to military force against Taiwan is unclear. According to Alex Neill, who is a China expert at the London-based IISS Strategy Institute, it is rather unlikely that the United States could successfully prevent a Chinese invasion of Taiwan.[36]

China further lays claim to nearly all of the South China Sea and the raw materials that lie throughout the region. To underscore this claim, China has built up islands on reefs and atolls. That said, Malaysia, Taiwan, Vietnam, and the Philippines also assert their territorial claims in the South China Sea, and they are supported by the US Navy. Beijing calls the South China Sea islands an "inalienable part" of Chinese territory. "The Chinese nation has always loved peace," official Chinese military studies state. China will "not attack unless we are attacked first. But we will certainly retaliate if we are attacked."[37]

China has long recognized that the US military always takes the role of the good guys in Hollywood movies. Therefore, the Chinese now produce their own action movies. In 2017, *Wolf Warrior 2* managed to become the most successful Chinese film of all time. The plot, just like in Hollywood movies, is simple. At its core, it is pretty much identical to action movies from the USA, with the one crucial difference that now the Chinese, instead of the US Americans, are the good guys. The Chinese hero lands in Africa to avenge the murder of his beloved wife, but then he quickly finds himself having to rescue a group of Chinese compatriots from a murderous squad of White mercenaries. The final scene of the film shows an image of a Chinese passport with the following words projected on it: CITIZENS OF THE PEOPLE'S REPUBLIC OF CHINA! IF YOU ARE IN DANGER ABROAD, DO NOT BE AFRAID! A STRONG FATHERLAND STANDS BEHIND YOU.[38]

China Has the Second-Largest Economy in the World

The Chinese are proud of their country because it is a major global economic power and has lifted many Chinese out of poverty. The US and Europe are not used to the fact that with China, a non-Western power is making a global claim for the first time in 500 years. A hundred years ago, China was still a poor country in which simple farmers dominated the economy. After Mao Zedong founded the Communist People's Republic of China in 1949, material shortages were everywhere. "There were hardly any bicycles to be seen on the streets, let alone cars," recalled Geng Wenbing, who later represented China as its ambassador to Switzerland.

There was a shortage of everything. Grain, cloth, cooking oil, and meat were rationed and could only be obtained in exchange for stamps that were allocated by the communist government. "At that time, there was little difference between rich and poor, because everyone was equally poor," Wenbing said.[39]

It was only after the death of Mao Zedong in 1976 that Deng Xiaoping implemented profound reforms and opened the Chinese economy to foreign investors from the West. The income of the Chinese increased steadily thereafter, and the food supply became more diverse. Gross domestic product (GDP) grew by 10 percent year-over-year, taking China from the sixth-largest economy in terms of GDP to the second-largest in the world today, still behind the USA but ahead of Japan and Germany. China is a member of the World Trade Organization, and the Chinese currency, the yuan, also known as the renminbi, officially counts as the fifth world currency alongside the US dollar, the euro, the Japanese yen, and the British pound.

According to the German fund manager Dirk Müller, the official economic data from China and the balance sheet data of Chinese companies are manipulated and "often completely exaggerated." The rise of China over the last twenty-five years is without a doubt "the greatest economic miracle that has ever taken place," says Müller. If the US Federal Reserve were to raise interest rates, China's economy would collapse because investors would pull their money out. The US has "its finger on the trigger and can decide at what point it wants to pull the trigger all by itself," Müller believes.[40]

After the US, communist China is among the countries with the most billionaires in the world. In 2017, there were 250 billionaires in China, including Jack Ma, the founder of online retailer Alibaba, which makes more revenue and profit than Amazon and eBay combined. Some billionaires are at odds with the government of China. In New York, Chinese billionaire Guo Wengui lives in his $70 million apartment that overlooks Central Park. The real estate trader bought land in Beijing in 1999 for $15 per square meter. When China won the bid for the Olympic Games in 2001, the price of land increased a thousandfold. That's how he got rich. The Chinese politicians became jealous and the vice mayor demanded part of the money. When Wengui refused, he went to jail. "They tortured me every day," the billionaire told European TV channel Arte. "They wanted to kill me." As a result, he said, he fled to New York via Hong Kong and London, and now he uses social media to demand the overthrow of the Chinese government. "They kill people without a second thought and make them disappear," Wengui accuses. China demands his extradition, but the US refuses. Washington likes it when China's abusive practices are uncovered. Conversely, the US does not appreciate it when journalists like Julian Assange publicly document US crimes.[41]

In China, the Communist Party rules with an iron fist. The National People's Congress, the largest parliament in the world with about 3,000 members, meets for ten days in March every year. President Xi Jinping has been granted sweeping powers by parliament. In March 2018, the People's Congress decided to lift the presidential term limit, which had been stipulated in the Chinese constitution. Previously, a president was allowed to serve a maximum of two five-year terms. The decision was very clear: 2,958 voted in favor, only two voted against, and there were three abstentions. "Xi Jinping can thus remain president for the rest of his life," declared the *Süddeutsche Zeitung*.[42]

As party leader and commander in chief of the People's Liberation Army, President Xi is the most powerful man in China. But the notion that economic opening and growing prosperity would automatically bring about Chinese political liberalization and a multiparty system has not proven true yet. Press freedom in China is severely restricted, and criticism of President Xi or the Communist Party is not welcome. China has opened up to capitalism, but without subjecting the country to foreign companies. The Chinese Communist Party has studied the collapse of the Soviet Union closely and is doing everything possible to avoid a similar fate.

The economic rise of China has been rapid. Under Mao Zedong's rule, the Chinese still had to "eke out an existence in the Stone Age," explains Urs Schoettli, a Swiss expert on China. But then came economic growth, driven in part by US foreign direct investment. "Today, the Middle Kingdom impresses not only with glittering skylines, huge shopping malls, and gigantic industrial parks, but also with a world-class infrastructure," says Schoettli. China is dependent on export markets because domestic demand is still too weak to absorb all the goods and services produced in China. The US is aware of this and, under President Donald Trump, launched a trade war against China. Trump was bothered by the fact that the US imports far more from China than it sells there, and he tried to weaken China by means of punitive tariffs. The rivalry between the US and China is one of the great stories of the twenty-first century. Nobody today knows how this rivalry will look by the year 2050. The only certainty is that China is currently the biggest challenger to the US empire.[43]

2013: The New Silk Road

Chinese geostrategists know that the US empire dominates the world's oceans. Therefore, they are strengthening the Chinese fleet and investing massively in infrastructure on the landmass of Eurasia. In 2013, China's president Xi Jinping announced the "New Silk Road" mega-project, also known as the Belt and Road Initiative. With it, China has finally left behind its long period of self-imposed isolation. As part of the New Silk Road, a network of railroads, highways, deep-sea ports, and airports is currently being built in Eurasia, enabling ever more stable and faster trade links. China is thus trying to shape the international order in Eurasia according to Beijing's specifications and to push back the influence of the United States. This could also have many advantages for Europe. However, there is a great deal of mistrust. The New Silk Road represents "an attempt to establish a comprehensive system for shaping the world in China's interests," German Foreign Minister Sigmar Gabriel said, criticizing the developments at the Munich Security Conference in 2018.[44]

To gain access to the Indian Ocean and bypass the Malacca Strait that is controlled by the US Navy, China is working on building a deep-sea port in the city of Kyaukpyu in Myanmar as part of the New Silk Road, which will be connected to China via oil and gas pipelines and rail lines. The US is not amused about this. In 2017, riots broke out in Myanmar between the Muslim Rohingya minority, including many immigrants from Bangladesh, and Myanmar's Buddhist majority. The US immediately protested the oppression of the Rohingya, and Myanmar was also criticized in the European media. "Not many newspapers reported that there were bestial murders of Buddhist monks by Rohingya terrorists or that this Muslim minority was trying to force a secession of the territory that they inhabited from Myanmar, thus attempting to create a separate Islamic state," reports fund manager Dirk Müller. Saudi Arabia, which is closely allied with the US, has trained and financed the Rohingya terrorist arm in order to obstruct the construction of the Silk Road. The US knows that it can disrupt the construction of the Silk Road with unrest or even with war.[45]

The New Silk Road is reminiscent of the Baghdad Railway, which Germany wanted to build before the First World War. At the time, Germany knew that as a continental power it could not challenge the British Empire at sea. Therefore, the Germans sought the overland route to oil sources and planned to build a railroad from Berlin to Baghdad in Iraq. The Germans blasted tunnels into the rock, built bridges, and at the end of the nineteenth century successfully constructed an iron railroad line from Berlin to Istanbul and from there on to Konya in central Turkey. The British watched this development with great concern. Robert Laffan, the British military advisor in Serbia at the time, believed the Baghdad Railway threatened the British Empire. "If Berlin–Baghdad were completed," Laffan said, "a vast area where every conceivable economic wealth could be produced, but which would be unassailable to a naval power, would be under German control." The project, he said, must therefore be prevented at all costs. When World War I broke out in 1914, it marked the end of the Baghdad Railway.[46]

The Chinese do not want to suffer a similar fate as Germany did before them and therefore plan their steps very carefully. The New Silk Road is a gigantic international infrastructure project in which many countries in Europe are participating, including Greece, Poland, Hungary, and Italy. "Asia and the Silk Roads are rising, and that rise is happening fast—not in isolation from the West, not even in competition with it," British historian Peter Frankopan, who teaches at Oxford University, believes. The West must realize that the success of Asia is not at the expense of Europe, but that all of Eurasia can benefit from it. Along the Silk Road, he said, the trend is "toward reducing tensions and building alliances," and people are discussing solutions for mutual benefit. Frankopan believes that "the times when the West could still shape the world in its own image are long gone."[47]

CHAPTER 16

CONCLUSION

Throughout history, people have endlessly inflicted violence on each other in the cruelest ways, and they continue to do so to this day. As a result, some peace activists feel depressed and powerless. These feelings, however, do not help us. As human beings, we carry the responsibility for the violence, so we also hold the key to ending the drama, because war, terror, and torture are not natural forces like earthquakes or tornadoes to which we are helplessly exposed. Every use of force always involves at least one person; often it involves an entire group of people. More and more people are realizing that the destructive and disruptive level of consciousness we are on today has reached the end of its usefulness. "We have overcome slavery, the burning of witches, colonialism, racism and apartheid," Jürgen Todenhöfer emphasizes. "If we succeed in outlawing war as well, humanity will have taken another great step forward."[1]

The peace movement must trust that a world without war is possible. "Determination and confidence, as I know from my own experience, are the keys to success," the Dalai Lama wisely advises. Therefore, the first and most important step that is required is the will for peace. I am convinced that a fundamental exit from the spiral of violence is possible. The decisive factor is whether we really want inner and outer peace. If this will is strong enough, we can orient ourselves according to the following three principles: the human family, the UN ban on violence, and mindfulness. All of these principles can show us the way through the twenty-first century, like three brightly shining stars, to help us practically implement inner and outer peace.[2]

The principle of the human family is a central beacon for the peace movement. The examples of brutal European imperialism and ruthless US imperialism presented in this book demonstrate that the use of violence was made possible in each case by the imperialists' explicit exclusion of a group of people—Indigenous Americans, African Americans, Japanese, Germans, Vietnamese, Iraqis, Afghans, and many others—from the human family. Through wartime propaganda, all sympathy for the excluded group was erased. The Germans were referred to as "brutal and bloodthirsty Huns" and the Japanese were labeled "yellow apes." After that, the use of force, including the dropping of atomic bombs, was presented and accepted as a necessity. This madness shows how confused and unconscious we humans can be, again and again. When we remember the principle of the human family, we wake up from this unconscious state. Then we realize that by birth, everyone belongs to the human family, regardless of skin color, nationality, gender, education, religion, or wealth. As should be the simple rule in every family, people are allowed to hold different views, and they should not kill each other when these views do not completely align.

The principle of the UN ban on the use of force is another important beacon for the peace movement. In 1945, after the unspeakable sufferings brought about by World War II, people formulated a revolutionary new principle that strictly prohibits attacks by one country on another, as well as prohibiting covert arming of gangs to overthrow the government in another country. This was a major advance. The prohibition of violence, enshrined in the UN Charter in Article 2(4), is the international law in effect today, and it states that "all Members shall refrain in their international relations from the threat or use of force against the territorial integrity or political independence of any state, or in any other manner inconsistent with the Purposes of the United Nations." If each nation-state adheres to this ban on the use of force and does not send its soldiers abroad, but keeps them strictly within its own borders as a purely defensive army, this will facilitate peace. "The future of democracy depends on the people and their growing awareness of dignified treatment of all the people of the earth," US historian Howard Zinn aptly explains.[3]

The principle of mindfulness is the third shining star for the peace movement. We need a shift in consciousness and an increase in mindfulness in the twenty-first century. If we look inward with our eyes closed, we can see how various warmongers have purposefully confused our thoughts and feelings by means of war propaganda for decades, and they continue to do so today. The lie put forth by President Johnson about the Gulf of Tonkin incident in 1964 was devastating because it led to the Vietnam War. Likewise, the lie put forward by President George W. Bush about weapons of mass destruction caused great damage and triggered the illegal attack on Iraq in 2003. The blowing up of World Trade Center Building 7 on September 11, 2001, is also irritating. Those who wake up from their unconscious state will quickly realize that war and lies always go hand in hand. Israeli historian Yuval Noah Harari reports that he meditates for two hours every day, observing his breath with his eyes closed. "This is not an escape from reality," Harari explains. "On the contrary, it means getting in touch with reality."[4]

I myself also practice mindfulness, trying again and again to look inward and observe my own thoughts and feelings. In order to get out of the spiral of violence, we must leave all the lies of war behind us. Those who practice mindfulness can no longer be so easily deceived by psychological operations. Famous mindfulness teachers like Eckhart Tolle explain that we are mindful when we observe our thoughts and feelings from a certain distance, like clouds passing through the sky, and when we realize that we are not our thoughts and feelings, but the formless and clear consciousness in which they rise and then subside again. This formless consciousness lives in all members of the human family. Everyone can contribute to peace by practicing mindfulness and peaceful communication every day. Through mindfulness, inner peace is strengthened, and this is the basis for all peace in the outside world.[5]

CHRONOLOGY

Selected dates in the history of the USA

1492 The Italian navigator Christopher Columbus crosses the Atlantic on behalf of Spain and lands in the Bahamas.

1607 The English establish Jamestown as the first permanently inhabited English colony in North America.

1619 Dutch traders make the first shipment of twenty African slaves to the British colony of Virginia.

1646 Contact with the English ends in disaster for the Indigenous people of the Powhatan tribe. They are displaced and obligated to pay tribute taxes to Virginia in the form of furs.

1776 The Boston Tea Party "patriots" destroy English tea to demonstrate their opposition to the British colonial power.

1776 The thirteen British colonies in North America declare their secession from Great Britain and establish the new nation of the United States of America.

1783 After taking heavy losses, the British Empire is forced to release the thirteen colonies into independence in the Treaty of Paris.

1788 The Constitution of the United States comes into effect.

1789 George Washington is elected the first president of the United States of America.

1803 France sells its large colony of Louisiana to the USA for only $15 million, doubling the latter's national territory. The claims of the Indigenous peoples are ignored.

1823 The Monroe Doctrine forbids Europeans from intervening in America, while the USA promises not to do so in Europe either.

1831 In Virginia, Nat Turner's slave rebellion is put down.

1845 The USA conquers the Mexican province of Texas, thereby enlarging its national territory.

1846 The USA stages an incident on the Rio Grande and declares war on Mexico.

1848 In the Treaty of Peace of Guadalupe Hidalgo, Mexico is forced to cede half of its land, including California, to the USA. This completes the expansion of the USA to the Pacific.

1860 Abraham Lincoln is elected president.

1861 The slaveholding Southern states secede from the United States and form their own country, which they call the Confederate States of America. A bloody civil war ensues.

1865 The Civil War ends with the surrender of the Southern states. Slavery is banned in the USA. President Abraham Lincoln is assassinated.

1867 Russia sells Alaska to the USA for $7 million.

1870 Hiram Revels, an African American from Mississippi, becomes the first Black senator to enter Congress.

1890 The American Indian Wars end with the massacre at Wounded Knee. Of the original five million Indigenous peoples, only 250,000 remain. They are confined to reservations.

1893 In the Kingdom of Hawai'i, the US overthrows Queen Liliʻuokalani and takes over the government.

1895 In Cuba, the US supports the uprising of the local population against the colonial power of Spain.

1898 The warship USS *Maine* blows up in Havana Harbor. Despite Spain not being responsible for the incident, the USA declares war on Spain.

1898 In the Treaty of Paris, Spain is forced to cede Cuba, the Philippines, Puerto Rico, and Guam to the USA. The USA becomes an imperialist power.

1913 With the passage of the Federal Reserve Act by Congress and the signature of President Wilson, the US government delegates the power to create money privately to banks in the USA.

1914 In Europe, World War I breaks out after a murder in Sarajevo.

1915 President Wilson allows US banks to lend to European belligerents. After the war, Great Britain owes the USA more than $4 billion.

1915 A German submarine sinks the British passenger ship *Lusitania*, which was secretly transporting war materials from the USA to Britain, off the southern coast of Ireland.

1917 The USA declares war on Germany, lands troops in Europe for the first time, and helps Great Britain and France to victory in the First World War.

1919 In Versailles, Germany is made solely responsible for the First World War and is obligated to pay billions in reparations, which flow back to the USA via France and Great Britain.

1920 In the USA, women are granted the right to vote.

1921 France occupies Düsseldorf after Germany suspends reparations payments. Germany promises to continue the reparations payments.

1933 In Germany, after Adolf Hitler's Reichstag fire, the rights of freedom of expression, freedom of the press, and peaceful assembly are abolished.

1937 Japan attacks China, triggering the Second Japanese-Chinese War.

1939 Hitler's attack on Poland marks the beginning of World War II. The USA continues to supply Germany with oil.

1940 President Roosevelt successfully runs for a third presidential term.

1941 The USA, the largest oil-producing country, halts all oil exports to Japan in July.

1941 The Japanese attack on Pearl Harbor on December 7 comes as no surprise to President Roosevelt, but shocks the US population and leads to the USA's entry into World War II.

1944 The US opens the Second Front and lands soldiers in Normandy, France.

1945 President Truman drops atomic bombs over Hiroshima and Nagasaki.

1945 The UN ban on the use of force comes into effect and prohibits war worldwide.

1947 The US establishes the National Security Council and the CIA and endows the latter with broad covert warfare powers.

1948 The CIA manipulates the elections in Italy and prevents a victory of the Socialists and Communists.

1949 The USA and some European countries establish the NATO military alliance and assure that it is purely defensive in nature.

1953 In Iran, the CIA and the British secret service MI6 overthrow Prime Minister Mohammad Mossadegh in an illegal coup d'état.

1954 In Guatemala, the CIA overthrows President Jacobo Arbenz in an illegal coup d'état.

1959 Hawai'i becomes the fiftieth state to be incorporated into the United States of America.

1961 Outgoing president Eisenhower warns against the power of the military-industrial complex.

1961 In the Congo, the CIA has Prime Minister Patrice Lumumba, who led the country to independence, assassinated and installs dictator Joseph Mobutu.

1961 In the Dominican Republic, CIA-backed rebels assassinate dictator Rafael Trujillo.

1961 In Cuba, the CIA unsuccessfully attempts to overthrow President Fidel Castro through the illegal Bay of Pigs invasion.

1961 The CIA contracts the Mafia to assassinate Fidel Castro. They are unsuccessful.

1963 In Washington, Dr. Martin Luther King Jr. speaks about his dream of equality and peace in front of the Lincoln Memorial.

1963 In South Vietnam, the US supports a coup d'état against President Diem, who is overthrown and assassinated.

1963 President John F. Kennedy is assassinated in Texas, presumably at the behest of former CIA director Allen Dulles.

1964 The USA attacks Vietnam in an illegal war, after President Lyndon Johnson deceived his own population with a lie about an incident in the Gulf of Tonkin.

1965 In Indonesia, General Mohamed Suharto seizes power in a bloody coup d'état that is supported by the United States.

1967 In Bolivia, Che Guevara is arrested and shot by the Bolivian army on the orders of the CIA.

1968 In the USA, Dr. Martin Luther King Jr. is murdered in Memphis, Tennessee.

1969 The USA bombs Cambodia in an illegal war.

1970 In Chile, the CIA arms rebels who kidnap and kill General René Schneider.

1970 The National Guard kills four students during antiwar protests at Kent State University in Ohio.

1973 In Chile, General Augusto Pinochet overthrows President Salvador Allende in an illegal coup d'état supported by the CIA.

1980 In Thailand, the CIA arms and trains the communist Khmer Rouge, which had previously carried out genocide in Cambodia.

1981 In Nicaragua, the CIA supports the contra rebels and tries in vain to overthrow the government in an illegal war.

1987 In the USA, hearings on the Iran-Contra scandal are televised, which shake citizens' confidence in their government.

1989 President George H. W. Bush illegally invades Panama without a UN mandate.

1990 Iraqi dictator Saddam Hussein invades neighboring Kuwait in an illegal war of aggression after the US ambassador April Glaspie had assured him that he could resolve the conflict as he sees fit.

1991 President George H. W. Bush expels Saddam Hussein from Kuwait and establishes the first permanent US military base in the Gulf.

1994 In the USA, the web browser Netscape Navigator is launched. The age of the internet begins and revolutionizes the exchange of information.

2001 The terrorist attacks of September 11 spread fear and terror in New York and Washington. World Trade Center 7 is blown up.

2001 The USA declares the so-called "war on terror" and bombs Afghanistan and Pakistan in an illegal war of aggression without a UN mandate.

2003 President George W. Bush and British Prime Minister Tony Blair attack Iraq in an illegal war.

2008 Barack Obama is the first African American person to be elected president of the United States.

2011 President Obama bombs Libya in an illegal war of aggression.

2011 A war breaks out in Syria. The British and the US arm the rebels and attempt to topple President Bashar al-Assad without success.

2013 In China, President Xi Jinping launches the mega-project "New Silk Road," which is intended to revolutionize the transport of goods in Eurasia.

2013 Whistleblower Edward Snowden reveals the NSA's surveillance state and flees to Russia.

2013 In a global poll conducted by Gallup, the US is ranked as the greatest threat to world peace.

2014 In Ukraine, the CIA overthrows President Viktor Yanukovych and Prime Minister Nikolai Azarov, whereupon Russia occupies Crimea and, after a vote, integrates it into Russian territory.

2017 President Donald J. Trump moves into the White House.

2018 In China, the National People's Congress decides that Xi Jinping may remain president for the rest of his life.

2019 President Trump decides to withdraw US troops from Syria.

2020 President Trump has Iranian General Qasem Soleimani assassinated by drone in Baghdad.

2021 In the USA, President Joseph R. Biden Jr. moves into the White House.

2022 Russia illegally attacks Ukraine in February without a UN mandate.

NOTES

Acknowledgments

1. Noam Chomsky, *Was Onkel Sam wirklich will* [*What Uncle Sam Really Wants*] (Pendo Press, 1993), 142.

Introduction

1. Frans de Waal, "Ich glaube, dass wir Tiere sind." *NZZ am Sonntag*, April 10, 2011.
2. Torsten Krauel, "Die Folter-Bilder verfolgen die USA bis heute." *Die Welt*, May 1, 2014.
3. Mathias Bröckers, *JFK: Staatsstreich in Amerika* (Westend, 2013), 105.
4. Arun Gandhi, *Wut ist ein Geschenk. Das Vermächtnis meines Großvaters Mahatma Gandhi* (Dumont, 2017), 13 and 31.

Chapter 1

1. "Das ist das teuerste Kriegsschiff der Welt." *Spiegel Online*, July 22, 2017.
2. Paul Kennedy, *Aufstieg und Fall der großen Mächte. Ökonomischer Wandel und militärische Konflikte von 1500 bis 2000* [*The Rise and Fall of the Great Powers: Economic Change and Military Conflict from 1500 to 2000*] (Fischer, 1991), 794.
3. Paul Adams, "Happy New Year? The world's getting slowly more cheerful." BBC, December 30, 2013.
4. Fletcher Prouty, *JFK. Der CIA, der Vietnamkrieg und der Mord an John F. Kennedy* [*JFK: The CIA, Vietnam, and the Plot to Assassinate John F. Kennedy*] (Zsolnay, 1993), 278.
5. Dorothy Manevich und Hanyu Chwe, "Globally, more people see US power and influence as a major threat." Pew Research Center, August 1, 2017.

6. Simon Kaminski, "Was finden die Deutschen nur an Putin?" *Augsburger Allgemeine Zeitung*, April 21, 2018.
7. "Die Deutschen sehen die USA als größte Bedrohung für den Frieden." *Handelsblatt*, February 13, 2019.
8. *Sicherheitsreport 2019.* Centrum für Strategie und Höhere Führung, February 13, 2019; Vor Nordkorea und Russland, *Sicherheitsreport 2019: USA sind die größte Bedrohung für den Weltfrieden.* RTL, February 13, 2019.
9. Paul Craig Roberts, "A Government of Morons and War Criminals." Global Research, April 15, 2017.
10. Gabriel Kolko, *Century of War: Politics, Conflict, and Society since 1914* (The New Press, 1994), 412; Brett Wilkins, "Jimmy Carter: die USA sind die 'kriegerischste Nation der Weltgeschichte.'" *Telepolis*, April 21, 2019.
11. Helmut Scheben, "Das US-Rüstungsmonster ist 'too big to fail.'" *Infosperber*, December 15, 2017.
12. Hermann Ploppa, "Präsident Eisenhower warnte vor Militär-Industriellem Komplex." *Free21*, January 26, 2016.
13. Hartmut Wasser, *USA: Politik, Gesellschaft, Wirtschaft* (Springer, 1991), 144.
14. John F. Kennedy in front of the United Nations in New York, September 25, 1961. Cited in *Hamburger Abendblatt*, November 22, 2013.
15. Andrew Bacevich, *American Empire: The Realities and Consequences of US Diplomacy* (Harvard University Press, 2002), 30 and 127.
16. "Rumsfeld cuts Pentagon red tape." BBC, September 10, 2001.
17. Donald Rumsfeld speech. "Rumsfeld identifies his 'adversary,' the Pentagon bureaucracy. Mentions 2.3 trillion in missing receipts, talks about defense cuts." C-SPAN, September 10, 2001.
18. United States Department of Defense. "Fiscal Year 2016 Budget Request." January 20, 2015, 5.
19. "So setzen die USA ihr massives Militärbudget ein." *Tages-Anzeiger*, Februar 28, 2017.
20. Willy Brandt, *Der organisierte Wahnsinn. Wettrüsten und Welthunger* (Kiepenheuer, 1985), 10.
21. "Trends in World Military Expenditure 2018." Stockholm International Peace Research Institute, April 29, 2019.
22. "Trump unterzeichnet Verteidigungsetat über 716 Milliarden Dollar." *Frankfurter Allgemeine Zeitung*, August 14, 2018; Andre Damon, "Trump launches the most dangerous arms race in history." Defend Democracy Press, January 19, 2019.
23. David Stockman, "The Donald Undone: Tilting at the Swamp, Succumbing to the Empire." Information Clearing House, December 9, 2018.
24. "Waffenhandel. Weltweite Rüstungsproduktion steigt weiter—Russland holt auf." *Spiegel Online*, December 10, 2018.
25. Aude Fleurant, "The SIPRI top 100 arms-producing and military services companies, 2017." Stockholm International Peace Research Institute, December 10, 2018.

26. Reinhard Wolff, "Deutsche Panzer schwer im Kommen." *TAZ*, December 10, 2018.
27. Howard Zinn, *The Bomb* (City Lights Books, 2010), 23; James Rachels, *The Elements of Moral Philosophy* (McGraw Hill, 2015), 127.
28. "Vertrag über die Nichtverbreitung von Kernwaffen." *Auswärtiges Amt*, April 1, 2019.
29. Hans Kristensen, "Status of World Nuclear Forces." Federation of American Scientists, May 1, 2019.
30. Department of Defense, "Base Structure Report FY 2018 Baseline," 2 and 7.
31. Chalmers Johnson, *Nemesis: The Last Days of the American Republic* (Macmillan, 2007), 138 and 140.
32. George Friedman, presentation on the strategic objectives of the USA on February 4, 2015, upon invitation of the Chicago Council on Global Affairs. YouTube: "STRATFOR: The main objective of the US is to avoid a German-Russian alliance."
33. US soldiers including National Guard and reserves. Source: US Department of Defense, Office of the Secretary of Defense, "Defense Manpower Data Center: Military and Civilian Personnel by Service/Agency by State/ Country." September 2018.
34. Knut Mellenthin, "Angriffsbasen weltweit." *Junge Welt*, July 12, 2004.
35. Chalmers Johnson, *The Sorrows of Empire: Militarism, Secrecy, and the End of the Republic* (Henry Holt, 20004), 1.
36. Olaf Ihlau, "Ein militärischer Moloch." *Spiegel Online*, October 1, 2003.
37. Jürgen Heiser, "USA betrieben im 17. Jahr ihr illegales Gefangenenlager auf Marine- basis Guantanamo Bay in Kuba." *Junge Welt*, January 11, 2019; Manfred Berg, *Geschichte der USA* (Oldenburg Verlag, 2013), 68.
38. Sonja Blaschke, "Landaufschüttung für US-Basis erzürnt Japaner." *Die Welt*, December 27, 2013.
39. "Soll das US-Militär aus Deutschland abziehen? Loyal. " *Das Magazin für Sicherheits- politik*, Nr. 9, 2018.
40. Albrecht Müller, "Wir sind dem Feindbildaufbau und der Kriegsvorbereitung schutzlos ausgeliefert." *NachDenkSeiten*, September 22, 2018.
41. Elmar Thevessen, "Kosten für US-Streitkräfte. Die NATO vor der Zerreißprobe." ZDF, March 10, 2019.
42. "Mehrheit der Deutschen will vollständigen Abzug der US Truppen." RT Deutsch, July 12, 2018; YouTube, "Dr. Daniele Ganser: Stopp Air Base Ramstein (Kaiserslautern, September 8, 2017)."

Chapter 2

1. Noam Chomsky, *Requiem für den amerikanischen Traum. Die 10 Prinzipien der Konzentration von Reichtum und Macht* [*Requiem for the American Dream: The 10 Principles of Concentration of Wealth and Power*] (Ullstein, 2019), 10 and 162.

2. Jeffrey Winters and Benjamin Page, "Oligarchy in the United States?" *Perspectives on Politics*, 7 (04), December 2009, 738 and 741.
3. Stephen Kinzer, *Putsch! Zur Geschichte des amerikanischen Imperialismus* [*Overthrow*] (Verlag Eichhorn, 2007), 9.
4. Peter Phillips, *Giants: The Global Power Elite* (Seven Stories Press, 2018).
5. Peter Phillips, "Exposing the Giants: The Global Power Elite." Global Research, August 30, 2018.
6. Jürgen Todenhöfer, "Die Welt-Eroberer." *Rubikon*, March 14, 2019. See also: Jürgen Todenhöfer, *Die große Heuchelei. Wie Politik und Medien unsere Werte verraten* (Propyläen, 2019).
7. Winters and Page, "Oligarchy in the United States," 735 and 736.
8. Andreas von Bülow, *Im Namen des Staates. CIA, BND und die kriminellen Machenschaften der Geheimdienste* (Piper, 2003), 21.
9. Kim Bode, "Millionen sind in den USA auf Gratis-Essen angewiesen." *NZZ am Sonntag*, August 24, 2014; Thorsten Schröder, "Auf Kosten der Armen." *Zeit Online*, May 21, 2018.
10. Martin Greive, "Essensmarken. Trauriges Hunger-Schauspiel in US-Supermärkten." *Die Welt*, June 9, 2012.
11. Greive, "Essensmarken."
12. Angus Deaton, "The US Can No Longer Hide from Its Deep Poverty Problem." *New York Times*, January 24, 2018.
13. Board of Governors of the Federal Reserve System, "Report on the Economic Well-being of US Households in 2017," May 2018, 2 and 3.
14. Capgemini, "World Wealth Report 2018," June 2019, 11.
15. Wealth X, "World Ultra Wealth Report 2018," 16.
16. "2018 Forbes 400. The Definitive Ranking of the Wealthiest Americans," *Forbes*, October 3, 2018.
17. Kerstin Kohlenberg, "Geld stinkt nicht, es regiert." *Zeit Online*, June 7, 2017.
18. Chomsky, *Requiem*, 91.
19. Chris Hedges, "Der Wahnsinn der Milliardäre." *Rubikon*, November 10, 2018.
20. Chomsky, *Requiem*, 11.
21. Andreas Mink, "Am Ende aller Träume." *NZZ am Sonntag*, September 4, 2016.
22. Martin Gilens, *Affluence and Influence: Economic Inequality and Political Power in America* (Princeton University Press, 2014), Introduction.
23. Jimmy Carter on whether he could be president today: "Absolutely not." Oprah Winfrey Network (OWN), September 22, 2015; Eric Zuesse, "Jimmy Carter Is Correct That the US is No Longer a Democracy." *Huffpost*, August 3, 2015.
24. Lee Drutman, "How Corporate Lobbyists Conquered American Democracy." *The Atlantic*, April 20, 2015.
25. Carolin Wollschied, "Alexandria Ocasio-Cortez: 'Wir haben ein System, das grundlegend kaputt ist.'" *Frankfurter Allgemeine Zeitung*, February 8, 2019.

26. "Davos 2015: Nouriel Roubini says Income Inequality Creates US Plutocracy," YouTube, January 21, 2015.
27. "Study: US is an oligarchy, not a democracy." BBC News, April 17, 2014.
28. Martin Gilens and Benjamin Page, "Testing Theories of American Politics. Elites, Interest Groups, and Citizens." *Perspectives on Politics*, Volume 12, Issue 3, September 2014, 564–581. Particularly see pp. 575, 576 and 577. See also Gilens, *Affluence and Influence.*
29. Eric Zuesse, "The Contradictions of the American Electorate." *Counterpunch.* April 15, 2014.
30. Eckhart Tolle, *Eine neue Erde* [*A New Earth: Awakening to Your Life's Purpose*] (Arkana, 2005), 57.

Chapter 3

1. Chomsky, *Requiem*, 20.
2. Robert Fuson, *Das Logbuch des Christoph Kolumbus* [*The Log of Christopher Columbus*] (Gustav Lübbe Verlag, 1989).
3. Felipe Fernández-Armesto, *Amerigo: The Man Who Gave His Name to America* (Weidenfeld & Nicolson, 2006).
4. Figures from Bernd Stöver, *Geschichte der USA. Von der ersten Kolonie bis zur Gegenwart* (C. H. Beck, 2017), 57.
5. James Horn, "The Conquest of Eden. Possession and Dominion in Early Virginia." In Robert Appelbaum, *Envisioning an English Empire. Jamestown and the Making of the North Atlantic World* (University of Pennsylvania Press, 2005).
6. Stöver, *Geschichte der USA*, 36.
7. Stöver, *Geschichte der USA*, 95.
8. Vincent Wilson, *The Book of Great American Documents* (Donnelley & Sons, 1998), 15.
9. Berg, *Geschichte der USA*, 1.
10. Wilson, *Great American Documents*, 15.
11. Andreas Elter, *Die Kriegsverkäufer. Geschichte der US-Propaganda 1917–2005* (Suhrkamp, 2005), 15.
12. Jack Anderson and George Clifford, *The Anderson Papers* (Ballantine Books, 1974), 256.
13. Speech by Abraham Lincoln in the House of Representatives, January 12, 1848. Cited in Murray Polner and Thomas Woods, *We Who Dared to Say No to War: American Antiwar Writing from 1812 to Now* (Basic Books, 2008), 33.
14. Richard Bruce Winders, *Mr. Polk's Army: The American Military Experience in the Mexican War* (Texas University Press, 1997), 9.
15. Polner and Woods, *We Who Dared to Say No to War*, 40.
16. Mansur Khan, *Die geheime Geschichte der amerikanischen Kriege* (Grabert, 2003), 48.
17. Polner and Woods, *We Who Dared to Say No to War*, 28.

18. Christof Mauch, *Die Präsidenten der USA* (C. H. Beck, 2013), 162.
19. Alexis de Tocqueville, *Über die Demokratie in Amerika* (Zürich, 1987), 491.
20. Ben Kiernan, *Erde und Blut. Völkermord und Vernichtung von der Antike bis heute* [*Blood and Soil: A World History of Genocide and Extermination from Sparta to Darfur*] (DVA, 2009), 469. See also Stefan Korinth, "War es Völkermord?" *Rubikon*, December 12, 2017.
21. Benjamin Madley, *An American Genocide: The United States and the California Indian Catastrophe* (Yale University Press, 2016).
22. Aram Mattioli, *Verlorene Welten: Eine Geschichte der Indianer Nordamerikas 1700–1910* (Klett Cotta, 2017); Eric Frey, *Schwarzbuch USA* (Eichborn, 2004), 25.
23. Christof Münger, "Wie Amerika die Welt der Indianer zerstörte." *Tages-Anzeiger*, November 13, 2017.
24. *Sitting Bull: The Collected Speeches* (Coyote Books, 1998), 75.
25. Khan, *Die geheime Geschichte der amerikanischen Kriege*, 21.
26. Kiernan, *Blood and Soil.*
27. Korinth, "War es Völkermord?"
28. Joseph Epes Brown, *The Sacred Pipe: Black Elk's Account of the Seven Rites of the Oglala Sioux* (University of Oklahoma Press, 2012), 115.

Chapter 4

1. Jochen Meissner, *Schwarzes Amerika. Eine Geschichte der Sklaverei* (C. H. Beck, 2008), 9.
2. Jürgen Heideking and Christof Mauch, *Geschichte der USA* (UTB, 2008), 7.
3. Edmund S. Morgan, "Slavery and Freedom: The American Paradox." *The Journal of American History*, Vol. 59, No. 1, June 1972, 5–29.
4. Ira Berlin, *Generations of Captivity: A History of African American Slaves* (Harvard University Press, 2003), 3.
5. Kenneth Greenberg, *Nat Turner: A Slave Rebellion in History and Memory* (Oxford University, 2003).
6. Frey, *Schwarzbuch USA*, 43.
7. Polner and Woods, *We Who Dared to Say No to War*, 59.
8. Alan Dawley, *Working for Democracy: American Workers from the Revolution to the Present* (University of Illinois Press, 1985), 41.
9. Abraham Lincoln, "Second Inaugural Address 1865." Cited in Wilson, *Great American Documents*, 80.
10. Constitution of the United States of America of 1787. Thirteenth Amendment.
11. Eric Hansen, "Wann entschuldigt sich Europa für die Sklaverei?" *Zeit Online*, January 15, 2013.
12. Oliver Stone and Peter Kuznick, *Amerikas ungeschriebene Geschichte. Die Schatten-seiten der Weltmacht* [*The Untold History of the United States*] (Ullstein, 2016), 36.

13. Dr. Martin Luther King Jr., "I Have a Dream." Speech delivered during the March on Washington for Jobs and Freedom, August 28, 1963.
14. Dr. Martin Luther King Jr., "The Casualties of the War in Vietnam." Speech delivered in Los Angeles on February 25, 1967. Available online at www.thekingcenter.org.
15. Toni Morrison, *Die Herkunft der anderen* [*The Origin of Others*] (Rowohlt, 2018).

Chapter 5

1. Khan, *Die geheime Geschichte der amerikanischen Kriege*, 92.
2. Martin Löffelholz, *Krieg als Medienereignis* (Springer, 2013), 183.
3. Mira Beham, *Kriegstrommeln. Medien, Krieg und Politik* (dtv, 1996), 24.
4. Geoff Simons, *Cuba: From Conquistador to Castro* (Springer, 1996), 189.
5. Löffelholz, *Krieg als Medienereignis*, 183.
6. Upton Sinclair, *The Brass Check* (University of Illinois Press, 2002), 400.
7. Stone and Kuznick, *The Untold History*, 13.
8. Simons, *Cuba: From Conquistador to Castro*, 187.
9. Stone and Kuznick, *The Untold History*, 13.
10. Daniel Immerwahr, "How the US has hidden its empire." *The Guardian*, February 15, 2019.
11. Polner and Woods, *We Who Dared to Say No to War*, 93.
12. Polner and Woods, *We Who Dared to Say No to War*, 93.
13. David Hoggan, *Das blinde Jahrhundert: Erster Teil Amerika* (Grabert, 1992), 291.
14. Hyman George Rickover, *How the Battleship* Maine *was Destroyed* (Naval Institute Press, 1976).
15. James Bamford, *Body of Secrets: Anatomy of the Ultra-Secret National Security Agency* (Anchor, 2002), 91.
16. Bernd Steinle, "Paradise Lost." *Frankfurter Allgemeine Zeitung*, December 1, 2017.
17. Brian Landers, *Empires Apart: A History of American and Russian Imperialism* (Pegasus Books, 2011), 286.
18. Klaus Werner, *Das neue Schwarzbuch Markenfirmen. Die Machenschaften der Weltkonzerne* (Deuticke, 2004), 302.
19. Benjamin Beede, *The War of 1898 and US Interventions 1898–1934* (Taylor and Francis, 1994), 226.
20. Steinle, "Paradise Lost."
21. Stone and Kuznick, *The Untold History*, 14.
22. David Vine, "Most countries have given up their colonies. Why hasn't America?" *Washington Post*, September 28, 2017.
23. Polner and Woods, *We Who Dared to Say No to War*, 112.
24. Stone and Kuznick, *The Untold History*, 15.
25. Stone and Kuznick, *The Untold History*, 15.
26. Khan, *Die geheime Geschichte der amerikanischen Kriege*, 104.

27. Polner and Woods, *We Who Dared to Say No to War*, 103.
28. Bernard Weisberger, *The Life History of the United States, Vol. 8: 1890–1901* (Time, 1964), 138.
29. Hans Schmidt, *Maverick Marine: General Smedley D. Butler and the Contradictions of American Military History* (University Press of Kentucky, 1998).
30. Smedley Butler, *War is a Racket* (Feral House, 2003), 23.
31. Stone and Kuznick, *The Untold History*, 18.
32. Butler, *War is a Racket*, 40 and 41.

Chapter 6

1. Fritz Fischer, *Griff nach der Weltmacht. Die Kriegszielpolitik des kaiserlichen Deutschland 1914/18* (Droste, 1964), 97.
2. Christopher Clark, *Die Schlafwandler. Wie Europa in den Ersten Weltkrieg zog* [*The Sleepwalkers: How Europe Went to War in 1914*] (DVA, 2013), 716.
3. Gerry Docherty and Jim Macgregor, *Hidden History: The Secret Origins of the First World War* (Mainstream Publishing, 2013), Introduction.
4. Thorsten Giersch, "USA: Der große Profiteur des Weltkriegs." *Handelsblatt*, August 23, 2014.
5. Jörg Friedrich, *14/18: der Weg nach Versailles* (Propyläen, 2014), 677 and 682.
6. Stone and Kuznick, *The Untold History*, 22.
7. Andrew Glass, "Senator Nye assails 'Merchants of Death.'" *Politico*, September 3, 2016.
8. "Report of the Special Committee on Investigation of the Munitions Industry (The Nye Report)," US Congress, Senate, 74th Congress, 2nd session, February 24, 1936, 3–13.
9. Butler, *War is a Racket*, 27 and 28.
10. Wolfgang Effenberger and Willy Wimmer, *Wiederkehr der Hasardeure* (Verlag Zeitgeist, 2014); Wolfgang Effenberger, "Banker und Rüstungsindustrielle tricksten 1917 die, USA in den Krieg." *Neue Rheinische Zeitung*, April 24, 2019.
11. Walter Wittmann cited in "Auch die freie Marktwirtschaft hat Regeln." *Baselland-schaftliche Zeitung*, September 30, 2008; Nikolaus Piper, "Ron Paul: 'Schafft die Fed ab.'" *Süddeutsche Zeitung*, December 21, 2010.
12. Gerd Schultze-Rhonhof, *1939. Der Krieg, der viele Väter hatte* (Lau Verlag, 2018), 80.
13. Lusitania-Affäre, "Schmutziges Geschäft." *Der Spiegel*, October 30, 1972.
14. Khan, *Die geheime Geschichte der amerikanischen Kriege*, 126.
15. Lusitania-Affäre, "Schmutziges Geschäft."
16. *Who Sank the Lusitania?* Documentary by Nicholas Tomalin, BBC2, October 22, 1972; Schultze-Rhonhof, *1939. Der Krieg, der viele Väter hatte*, 81.
17. Eric Sauder, *RMS* Lusitania*; The Ship and Her Record* (Stout, 2009), 66.

18. Walter Millis, *Road to War: America 1914–1917* (Riverside Press, 1935), 187.
19. Rolf Steininger, *Der große Krieg 1914–1918 in 92 Kapiteln* (Lau Verlag, 2016).
20. Effenberger and Wimmer, *Wiederkehr der Hasardeure*, 304.
21. Steininger, *Der große Krieg 1914–1918 in 92 Kapiteln.*
22. Effenberger and Wimmer, *Wiederkehr der Hasardeure*, 342.
23. Elter, *Die Kriegsverkäufer*, 30.
24. Elter, *Die Kriegsverkäufer*, 39.
25. Steininger, *Der große Krieg 1914–1918 in 92 Kapiteln*, chapter 47.
26. Elter, *Die Kriegsverkäufer*, 51.
27. Alex Barnett, *Words That Changed America: Great Speeches That Inspired, Challenged, Healed, and Enlightened* (Rowman & Littlefield, 2006), 174.
28. Stone and Kuznick, *The Untold History*, 24.
29. Steininger, *Der große Krieg 1914–1918 in 92 Kapiteln*, chapter 48.
30. Stone and Kuznick, *The Untold History*, 25.
31. Stone and Kuznick, *The Untold History*, 31.
32. Schultze-Rhonhof, *1939. Der Krieg, der viele Väter hatte*, 658.
33. Eberhard Kolb, *Der Frieden von Versailles* (C. H. Beck, 2005), 91.
34. "Reparationen: Deutschland begleicht letzte Schulden aus Erstem Weltkrieg." *Die Zeit*, October 1, 2010; Kolb, *Der Frieden von Versailles*, 100.

Chapter 7

1. Figures from Rolf-Dieter Müller (Hrsg.), *Das Deutsche Reich und der Zweite Weltkrieg*, Volume 10. Appendix: *Die Menschenverluste im Zweiten Weltkrieg* (DVA, 2008).
2. Benjamin Carter Hett, *Der Reichstagsbrand. Wiederaufnahme eines Verfahrens* [*Burning the Reichstag: An Investigation into the Third Reich's Enduring Mystery*] (Rowohlt, 2016); Alexander Bahar and Wilfried Kugel, *Der Reichstagsbrand. Geschichte einer Provokation* (PapyRossa, 2013).
3. Lutz Hachmeister (Hrsg.), *Das Goebbels-Experiment. Propaganda und Politik* (DVA, 2005), 50.
4. Armin Fuhrer, "Historiker findet neue Belege: SA-Gruppe zündete 1933 den Reichstag an." *Focus Online*, September 8, 2016.
5. Leon Poliakov, *Das Dritte Reich und seine Denker* (Walter de Gruyter, 2015), 482.
6. Robert Goralski and Russell Freeburg, *Oil & War: How the Deadly Struggle for Fuel in WWII Meant Victory or Defeat* (William Morrow and Company, 1987), 24.
7. Rainer Karlsch and Raymond Stokes, *Faktor Öl. Die Mineralölwirtschaft in Deutschland 1859–1974* (C. H. Beck, 2003), 137; Goralski and Freeburg, *Oil & War*, 21 and 25.
8. Goralski and Freeburg, *Oil & War*, 26.
9. Goralski and Freeburg, *Oil & War*, 166.
10. Goralski and Freeburg, *Oil & War*, 26.

11. Ian Westwell, *Condor Legion: The Wehrmacht's Training Ground* (Ian Allan, 2004).
12. Antony Sutton, *Wall Street and the Rise of Hitler* (Clairview, 2010), 97; Gesche Sager, "Der Diktator von Detroit. Henry Ford und die Nazis." *Spiegel Online*, July 29, 2008.
13. Guido Preparata, "Die Siegermächte züchteten Hitler ganz bewusst heran." *Milieu*, September 15, 2019; Guido Preparata, *Wer Hitler mächtig machte: Wie britisch-amerikanische Finanzeliten dem Dritten Reich den Weg bereiteten* [*Conjuring Hitler: How Britain and America Made the Third Reich*] (Perseus, 2010); Edgar Dahl, *Das erste Opfer des Krieges ist die Wahrheit. Wie die USA den Zweiten Weltkrieg planten* (Alitheia Verlag, 2019).
14. George Morgenstern, *Pearl Harbor 1941. Eine amerikanische Katastrophe* (Herbig, 1998), 121.
15. Morgenstern, *Pearl Harbor 1941*, 316.
16. Antony Sutton, *Roosevelt und die internationale Hochfinanz* (Grabert, 1990), 15 and 142; Letter dated November 21, 1933, cited in Peter Appleseed, *Franklin Delano Roosevelt's Life and Times* (Civilogy Instituto Publishing House, 2014), 206.
17. Morgenstern, *Pearl Harbor 1941*, 90.
18. Wikipedia, "Angriff auf Pearl Harbor." Accessed on October 12, 2019; Berg, *Geschichte der USA*, 65; Beat Bumbacher, "Der Tag der Schande." *Neue Zürcher Zeitung*, December 7, 2016.
19. Elias Davidsson, "Die 9/11-Angst." *Rubikon*, November 8, 2018.
20. Robert Stinnett, *Pearl Harbor. Wie die amerikanische Regierung den Angriff provozierte und 2,476 ihrer Bürger sterben ließ* [*Day of Deceit: The Truth About FDR and Pearl Harbor*] (Zweitausendeins, 2003), 23.
21. Stinnett, *Pearl Harbor*, 29.
22. Stinnett, *Pearl Harbor*, 42.
23. Stinnett, *Pearl Harbor*, 41 and 64.
24. Daniele Ganser, *Europa im Erdölrausch. Die Folgen einer gefährlichen Abhängigkeit* (Orell Füssli, 2012), 79.
25. David Ray Griffin, *The American Trajectory: Divine or Demonic?* (Clarity Press, 2018), 306.
26. Stinnett, *Pearl Harbor*, 75.
27. Daniel Yergin, *Der Preis. Die Jagd nach Öl, Geld und Macht* [*The Prize: The Epic Quest for Oil, Money & Power*] (Fischer, 1991), 409.
28. Yergin, *The Prize*, 412; Morgenstern, *Pearl Harbor 1941*, 132.
29. Stinnett, *Pearl Harbor*, 197 and 323.
30. Morgenstern, *Pearl Harbor 1941*, 132
31. Yergin, *The Prize*, 413.
32. Stinnett, *Pearl Harbor*, 106.
33. Stinnett, *Pearl Harbor*, 252.
34. Stinnett, *Pearl Harbor*, 483.
35. Morgenstern, *Pearl Harbor 1941*, 44 and 294; Stinnett, *Pearl Harbor*, 410.

36. Stinnett, *Pearl Harbor*, 243.
37. Stinnett, *Pearl Harbor*, 82.
38. Morgenstern, *Pearl Harbor 1941*, 341.
39. Jean Edward Smith, *FDR* (Random House Publishing, 2007), 506.
40. Norma Smith, *Jeannette Rankin: America's Conscience* (Montana Historical Society Press, 2002), 184.
41. Smith, *Jeannette Rankin*, 185 and 189.
42. Morgenstern, *Pearl Harbor 1941*, 278.
43. Morgenstern, *Pearl Harbor 1941*, 285 and 293.
44. Morgenstern, *Pearl Harbor 1941*, 286.
45. Philip Shenon, "Senate Clears 2 Pearl Harbor 'Scapegoats.'" *New York Times*, May 26, 1999.
46. Stinnett, *Pearl Harbor*, 11.
47. Morgenstern, *Pearl Harbor 1941*, 44 and 361.
48. Daryl Borgquist, "Advance Warning? The Red Cross Connection." *Naval History Magazine*, Vol. 13, No. 3, June 1999.
49. Elter, *Die Kriegsverkäufer*, 72.
50. Dennis Bernstein, "Interview with legendary whistleblower Daniel Ellsberg." *Covert Action Magazine*, September 24, 2019; Matthias Heine, "McNamaras elf goldene Regeln: The Fog of War." *Die Welt*, September 30, 2004.
51. Elter, *Die Kriegsverkäufer*, 75.
52. Jane Claypool, *Hiroshima and Nagasaki* (Franklin Watts, 1984), 86.
53. Bryan Walsh, "The Morning We Learned How to Destroy the World." *Medium*, August 15, 2019.
54. Michael Beschloss, *The Conquerors: Roosevelt, Truman and the Destruction of Hitler's Germany 1941–1945* (Simon and Schuster, 2003), 229.
55. Valentin Falin, *Zweite Front. Die Interessenkonflikte in der Anti-Hitler-Koalition* (Droemer Knaur, 1995), 299.
56. Yergin, *The Prize*, 445.
57. Falin, *Zweite Front*, 322.
58. Falin, *Zweite Front*, 354.
59. Falin, *Zweite Front*, 495.
60. Falin, *Zweite Front*, 412.

Chapter 8

1. Eric Alterman, *When Presidents Lie. A History of Official Deception and its Consequences* (Viking, 2004), 1.
2. Stone and Kuznick, *The Untold History*, 244.
3. Christopher Andrew, *For the President's Eyes Only: Secret Intelligence and the American Presidency from Washington to Bush* (Harper Collins, 1995), 171.
4. John Prados, *Keepers of the Keys: A History of the National Security Council from Truman to Bush* (William Morrow, 1991), 27.

5. Ralph McGehee, *Deadly Deceits: My 25 Years in the CIA* (Ocean Press, 1983), Introduction.
6. William Corson, *The Armies of Ignorance: The Rise of the American Intelligence Empire* (Dial Press, 1977), 298.
7. Thomas Etzold und John Gaddis, *Containment: Documents on American Policy and Strategy 1945–1950* (Columbia University Press, 1978), 125.
8. "Profits not motive, says Mossadegh." Associated Press, October 22, 1951.
9. James Risen, "The CIA in Iran." *New York Times*, April 16, 2000; David Talbot, *Das Schachbrett des Teufels. Die CIA, Allen Dulles und der Aufstieg Amerikas heimlicher Regierung* [*The Devil's Chessboard: Allen Dulles, the CIA, and the Rise of America's Secret Government*] (Westend, 2016), 222.
10. Warren Hinckle and William Turner, *The Fish is Red: The Story of the Secret War Against Castro* (Harper & Row, 1981), 41.
11. William Blum, *Killing Hope: US Military and CIA Interventions since World War II* (Common Courage Press, 1995), 79.
12. Vor 45 Jahren, "Patrice Lumumba wird ermordet." WDR, January 17, 2006.
13. Werner Ruf, "Schlaglichter auf 50 Jahre Unabhängigkeit in Afrika." *AG Friedens-forschung*, August 25, 2010.
14. Talbot, *The Devil's Chessboard*, 345.
15. Scott Shane, "Lawrence R. Devlin, 86, CIA Officer Who Balked on a Congo Plot, Is Dead." *New York Times*, December 11, 2008. See also "Commission d'enquête parlementaire chargée de déterminer les circonstances exactes de l'assassinat de Patrice Lumumba et l'implication éventuelle des responsables politiques belges dans celui-ci." Brussels, November 16, 2001.
16. Christian Schmidt-Häuer, "Fluch der Karibik." *Zeit Online*, May 26, 2011.
17. United States Senate, *Alleged Assassination Plots Involving Foreign Leaders. An Interim Report of the Select Committee to study Governmental Operations with Respect to Intelligence Activities* (US Government Printing Office, 1975), 5.
18. Noam Chomsky, *Wer beherrscht die Welt?* [*Who Rules the World?*] (Ullstein, 2016), 266; Loch Johnson, "Senator Frank Church and the Intelligence Investigation in the United States in 1975." *Journal for Intelligence, Propaganda and Security Studies* (JIPSS), Vol. 12, No. 2/2018, 187.
19. United States Senate, *Alleged Assassination Plots*, 2 and 285.
20. United States Senate, *Alleged Assassination Plots*, 5.
21. US Department of Defense, "United States–Vietnam Relations, 1945–67. A Study Prepared by the Department of Defense. Part IV: The Overthrow of Ngo Dinh Diem May–November 1963, VIII"; Geoffrey Shaw, *The Lost Mandate of Heaven: The American Betrayals of Ngo Dinh Diem* (Ignatius Press, 2015), Conclusion.
22. United States Senate, *Alleged Assassination Plots*, 5.
23. Naomi Klein, *Die Schock-Strategie. Der Aufstieg des Katastrophen-Kapitalismus* [*The Shock Doctrine: The Rise of Disaster Capitalism*] (Fischer, 2007), 110 and 636.

24. Blum, *Killing Hope*, 214; Thomas Wagner, "Die Akte Allende ist geschlossen—endgültig?" *Zeit Online*, July 22, 2011.
25. Michael Greven, *Systemopposition: Kontingenz, Ideologie und Utopie im politischen Denken der 1960er Jahre* (Verlag Barbara Budrich, 2011), 106.
26. Peter Kornbluh, "The Death of Che Guevara: Declassified." National Security Archive Electronic Briefing Book No. 5: The White House. October 11, 1967; "Memorandum for the President. Subject: Death of 'Che' Guevara." See also Michael Ratner and Michael Steven Smith, *Who Killed Che? How the CIA Got Away with Murder* (OR Books, 2011), 67.
27. Talbot, *The Devil's Chessboard*, 426.
28. United States Senate, *Alleged Assassination Plots*, 74.
29. United States Senate, *Alleged Assassination Plots*, 77 and 80.
30. UN General Assembly, October 10, 1961.
31. United States Senate, *Alleged Assassination Plots*, 85 and 86.
32. Jim Garrison, *Wer erschoss John F. Kennedy? Auf der Spur der Mörder von Dallas* [*On the Trail of the Assassins: One Man's Quest to Solve the Murder of President Kennedy*] (Gustav Lübbe Verlag, 1992),100.
33. United States Senate, *Alleged Assassination Plots*, 92 and 95.
34. United States Senate, *Alleged Assassination Plots*, 92 and 95.
35. United States Senate, *Alleged Assassination Plots*, 95.
36. United States Senate, *Alleged Assassination Plots*, 109.
37. United States Senate, *Alleged Assassination Plots*, 117–120.
38. United States Senate, *Alleged Assassination Plots*, 7.
39. Bröckers, *JFK: Staatsstreich in Amerika*, 17.
40. Arthur Schlesinger, *A Thousand Days: John F. Kennedy in the White House* (Fawcett Publications, 1965), 215.
41. UN General Assembly, November 1, 1960.
42. Hinckle and Turner, *The Fish is Red*, 82.
43. Hinckle and Turner, *The Fish is Red*, 85.
44. Hinckle and Turner, *The Fish is Red*, 96.

Chapter 9

1. Charles Crenshaw, *JFK. Verschwörung des Schweigens* [*JFK: A Conspiracy of Silence*] (Heyne, 1992), 112, 119 and 136.
2. Judith Michel, *Willy Brandts Amerikabild und -politik 1933–1992* (V & R Unipress, 2010), 162.
3. Garrison, *On the Trail of the Assassins*, 38.
4. Garrison, *On the Trail of the Assassins*, 127.
5. Crenshaw, *JFK: A Conspiracy of Silence*, 72.
6. "Kein Meister traf den Kopf der Puppe." *Der Spiegel*, April 3, 1967.
7. Andrew Kiel, *J. Edgar Hoover, The Father of the Cold War* (University Press of America, 2000), 218.
8. *The Warren Commission Report: Report of President's Commission on the Assassination of President John F. Kennedy* (St. Martin's Press, 1964), 19.

9. United States Senate, *Final Report of the Select Committee to Study Governmental Operations with Respect to Intelligence Activities*, Book V, 1976, 5.
10. US House of Representatives, *Final Report of the Select Committee on Assassinations. Summary of Findings and Recommendations*, January 2, 1979, 3.
11. Garrison, *On the Trail of the Assassins*, 214.
12. Garrison, *On the Trail of the Assassins*, 256.
13. Garrison, *On the Trail of the Assassins*, 206.
14. Crenshaw, *JFK: A Conspiracy of Silence*, 17, 18, 135, 136 and 171.
15. Prouty, *JFK*, 30.
16. Garrison, *On the Trail of the Assassins*, 351.
17. McGehee, *Deadly Deceits*, Dedication.
18. CIA, "Countering Criticism of the Warren Report," January 4, 1967.
19. Bröckers, *JFK: Staatsstreich in Amerika*, 168.
20. Wikipedia, "Attentat auf John F. Kennedy." Accessed September 16, 2019.
21. Talbot, *The Devil's Chessboard*, 13, 44, 116, and 220.
22. Talbot, *The Devil's Chessboard*, 14.
23. Garrison, *On the Trail of the Assassins*, 236.
24. Talbot, *The Devil's Chessboard*, 517.
25. Talbot, *The Devil's Chessboard*, 17.
26. "Geheimakten über Kennedy-Attentat doch nur teilweise veröffentlicht." *Neue Zürcher Zeitung*, October 27, 2017.

Chapter 10

1. Prouty, *JFK*, 87.
2. Max Mittler, *Der Weg zum Ersten Weltkrieg: Wie neutral war die Schweiz? Kleinstaat und europäischer Imperialismus* (NZZ Verlag, 2003), 476.
3. Prouty, *JFK*, 60 and 92.
4. US Department of Defense, "United States—Vietnam Relations, 1945–67. A Study Prepared by the Department of Defense. Part II: US Involvement in the Franco-Viet Minh War 1950–1954," 2; Prouty, *JFK*, 255.
5. Edwin Reischauer, "What Choices Do We Have in Vietnam." *Look*, September 19, 1967.
6. Prouty, *JFK*, 109.
7. Prouty, *JFK*, 141.
8. Prouty, *JFK*, 211.
9. David Halberstam, *The Making of a Quagmire* (Random House, 1965), 211.
10. US Department of Defense, "United States—Vietnam Relations, 1945–67. A Study Prepared by the Department of Defense. Part IV. Evolution of the War. Phased Withdrawal of US Forces 1962–1964, Summary, I and IV."
11. Robert McNamara, *In Retrospect: The Tragedy and Lessons of Vietnam* (Vintage, 1995), 444; Prouty, *JFK*, 155
12. Stone and Kuznick, *The Untold History*, 222.

13. Lars Klein, *Die "Vietnam-Generation" der Kriegsberichterstatter* (Wallstein Verlag, 2012), 170.
14. Stone and Kuznick, *The Untold History*, 222.
15. Speech by President Lyndon B. Johnson on August 4, 1964. YouTube: "Lyndon Johnson—Report on the Gulf of Tonkin Incident."
16. UN Security Council, August 5, 1964.
17. Robert David Johnson, *Ernest Gruening and the American Dissenting Tradition* (Harvard University Press, 1998), 1.
18. Marvin Gettleman, *The Middle East and Islamic World Reader* (Open Road, 2012), Chapter 34.
19. Martin Kilia, "18 Leitersprossen bis zur Freiheit." *Tages-Anzeiger*, April 30, 2005.
20. Donald Schmidt, *The Folly of War: American Foreign Policy 1898–2005* (Algora Publishing, 2005), 264.
21. Bamford, *Body of Secrets*, 296.
22. John Prados, "Tonkin Gulf Intelligence 'Skewed' According to Official History and Intercepts." National Security Archive, Washington, December 1, 2005. See also Joachim Hoelzgen, "Der Torpedo-Angriff, den es nie gab." *Spiegel Online*, November 15, 2005.
23. Peter Lennon, "The attack that never was." *The Guardian*, April 17, 1999.
24. Sebastian Moll, "Die Lüge im Golf von Tonkin." *Frankfurter Rundschau*, August 1, 2014; Lennon, "The attack that never was."
25. Robert Neer, *Napalm: An American Biography* (Harvard University Press, 2013), 111.
26. Neer, *Napalm*, 111.
27. Kathy Sheridan, "Kim Phuc, the napalm girl: Love is more powerful than any weapon." *Irish Times*, May 28, 2016.
28. Neer, *Napalm*, 138.
29. Polner and Woods, *We Who Dared to Say No to War*, 246.
30. Polner and Woods, *We Who Dared to Say No to War*, 249 and 250.
31. Reymer Klüver, "Die gespaltene Nation." *GEO Epoche Vietnamkrieg*, July 22, 2016, 97.
32. Chrissie Hynde, *Reckless* (Ebury Press, 2015), 80.
33. Klüver, "Die gespaltene Nation," 101.
34. Elter, *Die Kriegsverkäufer*, 130.
35. Geoffrey Robinson, *The Killing Season: A History of the Indonesian Massacres 1965–66* (Princeton University Press, 2019), 113.
36. Blum, *Killing Hope*, 194.
37. Talbot, *The Devil's Chessboard*, 549.
38. Stone and Kuznick, *The Untold History*, 230.
39. Cordt Schnibben, "My Lai—die Karriere eines Kriegsverbrechens." *Die Zeit*, September 12, 1986.
40. Polner and Woods, *We Who Dared to Say No to War*, 251.
41. Chomsky, *What Uncle Sam Really Wants*, 48.

42. Jörg-Uwe Albig, "Das seltsame Leben der Gis in Indochina." *GEO Epoche: Der Vietnamkrieg*, July 22, 2016, p. 119.
43. Michael Steven Smith, "Inside the Organized Crime Syndicate known as the CIA: An Interview with Douglas Valentine." *Covert Action Magazine*, November 21, 2019.
44. Elter, *Die Kriegsverkäufer*, 149.
45. Johannes Strempel, "Kambodscha. Der rote Wahn." *GEO Epoche: Der Vietnamkrieg*, July 22, 2016, 148; John Pilger, "How Thatcher gave Pol Pot a hand." *New Statesman*, April 17, 2000.
46. Gregory Elich, "Who supported the Khmer Rouge?" *Counterpunch*, October 16, 2014.
47. Jack Colhoun, "On the side of Pol Pot. US supports Khmer Rouge." *Covert Action Quarterly*, Issue 34, Summer 1990.
48. Pilger, "How Thatcher gave Pol Pot a hand."
49. John Pilger, "Dance on Thatcher's grave, but remember there has been a coup in Britain." *New Statesman*, April 23, 2013.
50. Pilger, "How Thatcher gave Pol Pot a hand"; Tom Fawthrop and Helen Jarvis, *Getting Away with Genocide? Elusive Justice and the Khmer Rouge Tribunal* (University of New South Wales Press, 2005), 68.
51. Pilger, "How Thatcher gave Pol Pot a hand"; "Butcher of Cambodia set to expose Thatcher's role." *The Guardian*, January 9, 2000.
52. "Kerkermeister Duch bekommt lebenslänglich." *Spiegel Online*, February 3, 2012.

Chapter 11

1. Ulrich Schiller, "Bilanz der Iran-Contra-Affäre: Viele Fragen bleiben offen." *Die Zeit*, August 7, 1987.
2. Tim Weiner, *CIA. Die ganze Geschichte* [*Legacy of Ashes: The History of the CIA*](Fischer, 2009), 496.
3. Jürgen Bellers, *Handbuch der Außenpolitik: Von Afghanistan bis Zypern* (Walterde Gruyter, 2018), 439.
4. Peter Kornbluh and Malcolm Byrne, *The Iran-Contra Scandal: The Declassified History (A National Security Archive Documents Reader)* (New Press, 1993), 1.
5. UN General Assembly, "Definition of Aggression," December 14, 1974.
6. Investigative report commissioned by the Washington office on Latin America by Congressman James Jefferson (R-VT) and Peter Kostmayer (D-PA), February 1986.
7. Blum, *Killing Hope*, 293.
8. Blum, *Killing Hope*, 293.
9. Weiner, *Legacy of Ashes*, 503.
10. Weiner, *Legacy of Ashes*, 524.
11. Kornbluh and Byrne, *The Iran-Contra Scandal*, 3.

12. *Nicaragua v. United States of America*. Decision of the International Court of Justice, June 27, 1986, in The Hague. See also *The Times*, June 28, 1986.
13. Lee Hamilton (Chairman), "Report of the Congressional Committees Investigating the Iran-Contra-Affair." Washington DC Government Printing Office, November 13, 1987, 18.
14. Hamilton, "Iran-Contra-Affair," 4 and 15.
15. Hamilton, "Iran-Contra-Affair," 4 and 16.
16. Leslie Cockburn, *Guns, Drugs and the CIA*. Documentary, PBS *Frontline*, May 17, 1988. See also Leslie Cockburn, *Out of Control: The Story of the Reagan Administration's Secret War in Nicaragua, the Illegal Pipeline, and the Contra Drug Connection* (Atlantic Monthly Press, 1987).
17. Peter Dale Scott, *Cocaine Politics: Drugs, Armies, and the CIA in Central America* (University of California Press, 1998), 10.
18. Ein Star, "Oberstleutnant Oliver North hatte seinen großen Auftritt vor dem Untersuchungsausschuss des Kongresses." *Der Spiegel*, July 13, 1987.
19. Robert Kennedy, "Why the Arabs don't want us in Syria." *Politico*, February 23, 2016.
20. Ramsey Clark, *The Fire This Time: U.S. War Crimes in the Gulf* (Thunder's Mouth Press, 1992), 6.
21. Weiner, *Legacy of Ashes*, 556.
22. YouTube: "KenFM im Gespräch mit Dr. Udo Ulfkotte (1960–2017)," December 4, 2014.
23. Hamilton, "Iran-Contra-Affair," 7.
24. Weiner, *Legacy of Ashes*, 528.
25. Hamilton, "Iran-Contra-Affair," 22.
26. Alexander Cockburn, "Air Cocaine." *Counterpunch*, November 4, 2016.
27. Peter Philipp, "Die Iran-Contra-Affäre." *Deutsche Welle*, July 20, 2009.
28. Philipp, "Die Iran-Contra-Affäre."
29. Kornbluh and Byrne, *The Iran-Contra Scandal*, 408.
30. Kornbluh and Byrne, *The Iran-Contra Scandal*, 411. See also Lawrence Walsh, *Firewall: The Iran-Contra Conspiracy and Cover-Up* (Norton, 1998).
31. Larry Everest, *Oil, Power and Empire: Iraq and the US Global Agenda* (Common Courage Press, 2004), 125.
32. Clark, *The Fire This Time*, 3.
33. Blum, *Killing Hope*, 311.
34. Nicholas Cull, *Propaganda and Mass Persuasion: A Historical Encyclopedia, 1500 to the Present* (ABC-CLIO, 2003), 158.
35. Muhammad Faour, *The Arab World after Desert Storm* (US Institute of Peace Press, 1993), 16.

Chapter 12

1. Project for the New American Century, *Rebuilding America's Defenses* (Washington, DC: 2000), p. IV and 51.
2. Bob Woodward, *Bush at War* (Pocket Books, 2003), 37.

3. Thomas Kean (Chair) and Lee Hamilton (Vice Chair), *The 9/11 Commission Report. Final Report of the National Commission on Terrorist Attacks upon the United States* (Norton, 2004).
4. "The 9/11 Commission & Torture: How information gained through waterboarding & harsh interrogations form major part of 9/11 Commission Report." *Democracy Now*, February 7, 2008.
5. David Ray Griffin, *The 9/11 Commission Report: Omissions and Distortions* (Olive Branch Press, 2005), 28.
6. Eric Boehlert, "The president ought to be ashamed." *Salon*, November 22, 2003.
7. Evan Solomon interviews Lee Hamilton, "9/11: Truth, lies and conspiracy." CBC News, August 21, 2006; Thomas Kean und Lee Hamilton, *Without Precedent: The Inside Story of the 9/11 Commission* (Knopf Doubleday Publishing Group, 2006). See also Griffin, *The 9/11 Commission Report: Omissions and Distortions.*
8. Interview of Thomas Meyer with Catherine Austin Fitts, "Chartres, 9/11, Financial Fraud, and the Story of Gideon." *The Present Age*, December 2018, 13.
9. "Chartres, 9/11, Financial Fraud, and the Story of Gideon."
10. Richard Clarke, *Against all Enemies; Inside America's War on Terror* (Free Press, 2004), 5.
11. Kean and Hamilton, *The 9/11 Commission Report*, 20.
12. Timings from Kean and Hamilton, *The 9/11 Commission Report*, 32.
13. Michael Ruppert, *Crossing the Rubicon* (New Society Publishers, 2004), 394.
14. Kevin Barrett, *Truth Jihad: My Epic Struggle Against the 9/11 Big Lie* (Progressive Press, 2007), 20.
15. Oberstleutnant a.D. Jochen Scholz, "Das Versagen der Luftabwehr." *Nuoviso*, January 30, 2011.
16. Urs Gasche, "Erhärteter Verdacht auf Insider handel vor 9/11." *Infosperber*, November 21, 2016.
17. Cynthia McKinney, "Thoughts On Our War Against Terrorism," *Counterpunch*, April 13, 2002.
18. "Wichtige Ermittlungsakten zu verdächtigen Finanztransaktionen im Vorfeld des 11. Septembers von US-Behörden vernichtet." *Hintergrund*, 3. Quartal 2010, 21.
19. Gasche, "Erhärteter Verdacht auf Insider handel vor 9/11"; Marc Chesney, Remo Crameri, and Loriano Mancini, "Detecting abnormal trading activities in option markets." *Journal of Empirical Finance*, March 26, 2015.
20. Kean and Hamilton, *The 9/11 Commission Report*, 499.
21. Lars Schall, "Insider Trading on 9/11." *Global Research*, September 17, 2015; "Wichtige Ermittlungsakten zu verdächtigen Finanztransaktionen im Vorfeld des 11. Septembers von US-Behörden vernichtet."
22. James Glanz, "Burning Diesel Is Cited in Fall Of 3rd Tower." *New York Times*, March 2, 2002.

23. "The Conspiracy Files: 9/11—The Third Tower." BBC News, July 6, 2008.
24. Ansgar Schneider, *Stigmatisierung statt Aufklärung. Das Unwesen des Wortes "Verschwörungstheorie" und die unerwähnte Wissenschaft des 11. Septembers als Beispiel einer kontrafaktischen Debatte* (Peace Press, 2018), 42.
25. Leroy Hulsey, Zhili Quan, and Feng Xiao, "A Structural Reevaluation of the Collapse of World Trade Center 7." Draft. University of Alaska Fairbanks, September 3, 2019; Daniele Ganser, "Der dritte Turm." *Weltwoche*, September 18, 2019.
26. Daniele Ganser, "Der erbitterte Streit um den 11. September." *Tages-Anzeiger*, September 9, 2006.
27. Klaus-Dieter Kolenda, "Geplanter Zusammenbruch." *Rubikon*, May 10, 2019.
28. Eric Lipton, "Fire, Not Explosives, Felled 3rd Tower on 9/11, Report Says." *New York Times*, August 22, 2008; NIST, "Global Structural Analysis of the Response of World Trade Center Building 7 to Fires and Debris Impact Damage." US Department of Commerce, November 2008. See also Wikipedia, "World Trade Center 7." Accessed October 21, 2019.
29. Hulsey, Quan, and Xiao, "A Structural Reevaluation of the Collapse of World Trade Center 7."
30. Richard Gage in the *Washington Journal*, C-SPAN, August 1, 2014.
31. Peter Michael Ketcham, "Thoughts from a Former NIST Employee." *Europhysics News*, November 25, 2016.
32. Ketcham, "Thoughts from a Former NIST Employee."
33. Danish TV Channel TV2, April 6, 2009. YouTube: "Sprengstoff im Staub vom WTC erwiesen. Niels Harrit über Nanothermit"; Niels Harrit et al, "Active Thermitic Material Discovered in Dust from the 9/11 World Trade Center Catastrophe." *Open Chemical Physics Journal*, 2009.
34. Michael Bowker, *Fatal Deception: The Terrifying True Story of How Asbestos is Killing America* (Simon and Schuster, 2003), 278.
35. Heike Buchter, "Der Wolken-Kratzer." *Zeit Online*, August 31, 2006.
36. Lara Malberger, "Was Asbest anrichtet, zeigt sich erst nach Jahrzehnten." *Zeit Online*, September 10, 2016.

Chapter 13

1. "Bin Laden says he wasn't behind attacks." CNN, September 17, 2001.
2. Peter Scholl-Latour, "Der Kalte Krieg mit Russland, die heißen Kriege im Nahen Osten und die Rolle Deutschlands." Sovereignty Conference in Berlin, November 24, 2012. YouTube: "Der neue Kalte Krieg mit Russland—P. Scholl-Latour (November 2012)," minute 32.
3. Kathy Gilsinan, "How can Congress authorize war when it can't decide what war is?" *The Atlantic*, July 21, 2019.
4. Barbara Lee, "A Lone Voice of Dissent." *Counterpunch*, September 18, 2001.
5. Jeremy Scahill, *Schmutzige Kriege. Amerikas geheime Kommandoaktionen* [*Dirty Wars: The World Is a Battlefield*] (dtv, 2015), 230 and 232.

6. Bob Barr, "An 18-year-old congressional authorization shouldn't enable a new war." *Liberty Guard*, July 8, 2019.
7. Emran Feroz, *Tod per Knopfdruck. Das wahre Ausmaß des US-Drohen-Terrors oder wie Mord zum Alltag werden konnte* (Westend, 2017), 10; Emran Feroz, "Die mörderischste Terror-Kampagne der Gegenwart." *Telepolis*, July 6, 2015.
8. Ragnar Vogt, "Geständnis eines Drohnenpiloten. Es sah aus wie eine kleine menschliche Person." *Zeit Online*, October 27, 2013.
9. Scahill, *Dirty Wars*, 598.
10. Scahill, *Dirty Wars*, 594.
11. Jürgen Rose, "Wegtreten NATO. Die Entsorgung des transatlantischen Kriegsbünd-nisses ist überfällig." *Rubikon*, October 29, 2018.
12. Physicians for Social Responsibility and International Physicians for the Prevention of Nuclear War, "Body Count. Casualty Figures after 10 Years of the War on Terror. Iraq, Afghanistan, Pakistan." March 2015.
13. Howard Zinn, "Put Away the Flags." *Progressive*, July 4, 2006.
14. Scahill, *Dirty Wars*, 32.
15. Ron Suskind, *The Price of Loyalty* (Simon & Schuster, 2004), 96.
16. "Zwei Jahre danach, Bush's endloser Krieg gegen den Terror." *Der Spiegel*, September 18, 2003.
17. Martin Amis, "The real conspiracy behind 9/11." *The Times*, September 2, 2006.
18. IPPNW, "Body Count. Opferzahlen nach 10 Jahren." September 2015, 16, 17 and 33.
19. Heike Hänsel, "Verfolgung von Julian Assange schafft einen gefährlichen Präzedenz-fall." *Telepolis*, October 21, 2019.
20. Rita Schwarzer, "Jeden Tag nehmen sich 20 US-Kriegsveteranen das Leben." *Neue Zürcher Zeitung*, November 11, 2017.
21. Ray McGovern, "Wir haben keine freie Presse mehr." *Hintergrund*, September 9, 2014.
22. "Powell Calls His UN Speech a Lasting Blot on His Record." *New York Times*, September 9, 2005.
23. Harold Pinter, "Kunst, Wahrheit & Politik—Nobel lecture, December 7, 2005." *Free21*, February 14, 2018.
24. Jürgen und Frederic Todenhöfer, *Die Große Heuchelei. Wie Politik und Medien unsere Werte verraten* (Ullstein, 2019), 314.
25. Rainer Mausfeld, *Warum schweigen die Lämmer? Wie Elitendemokratie und Neoliberalismus unsere Gesellschaft und unsere Lebensgrundlagen zerstören* (Westend, 2018), 40 and 42.
26. Mausfeld, *Warum schweigen die Lämmer?* 33.
27. Ulrich Teusch, *Der Krieg vor dem Krieg. Wie Propaganda über Leben und Tod entscheidet* (Westend, 2019), Preface.
28. See Media Navigator at Swiss Propaganda Research: www.swprs.org.

Chapter 14

1. "Sie rückten unsere Tätigkeit in die Nähe der Stasi." *Tages-Anzeiger*, November 17, 2014.
2. Simon Bradley, "Fichenskandal kaum noch ein Thema—zu Unrecht?" *Swissinfo*, December 11, 2014.
3. René Raphael, "Der dressierte Mensch. Amnesty." *Magazin der Menschenrechte*, August 2019.
4. "Murong Xuecun's Acceptance Speech for the 2010 People's Literature Prize." *New York Times*, November 6, 2011.
5. *Chinas mediale Gegenwelt*. Documentary. *Arte*, May 31, 2019.
6. "The world's most valuable resource is no longer oil, but data." *Economist*, May 6, 2017.
7. "US-Informant vergleicht NSA mit einer Diktatur." *Spiegel Online*, July 3, 2014.
8. Johannes Kuhn, "Prism-Informant Snowden auf der Flucht. Obamas Jagd auf die Wachhunde." *Süddeutsche Zeitung*, June 10, 2013.
9. Tobias Brunner, "Dr. Merkels gesammeltes Schweigen. Regierungs-Reaktionen auf NSA-Skandal." *Spiegel Online*, July 19, 2013.
10. "Amerika hat das Handy der Kanzlerin abgehört." *Frankfurter Allgemeine Zeitung*, October 23, 2013. See also Jacob Appelbaum, "Merkel beschwert sich bei Obama." *Spiegel Online*, October 23, 2013.
11. Jacob Appelbaum, "Neue Snowden-Dokumente. Die NSA rüstet zum Cyber-Feldzug." *Spiegel Online*, January 18, 2015.
12. Steven Geyer, "Ex-NSA-Agent Thomas Drake: 'Auch Deutschland bräuchte einen Snowden.'" *Berliner Zeitung*, June 9, 2014.
13. Andre Meister, "NSA-Whistleblower William Binney: BND erhielt von NSA Quellcode des Abhör- und Analyseprogramms ThinThread." *Netzpolitik*, July 25, 2013; "Welcome to Utah, the NSA's desert home for eavesdropping on America." *The Guardian*, June 14, 2013.
14. Werner Meixner, "Der Digital-Imperialismus. Manifest gegen die digitale Diktatur und das Ende der Privatsphäre." *Rubikon*, October 13, 2018.
15. Patrick Beuth, "Prism: Die Kanzlerin von Neuland." *Zeit Online*, June 19, 2013.
16. Yasha Levine, *Surveillance Valley: The Secret Military History of the Internet* (Icon Books, 2018).
17. John Perry Barlow, "A Declaration of the Independence of Cyberspace." Electronic Frontier Foundation, February 8, 1996. See also Tim Berners-Lee, *Der Web-Report. Der Schöpfer des World Wide Webs über das grenzenlose Potential des Internets* [*Weaving the Web: The Original Design and Ultimate Destiny of the World Wide Web by its Inventor*] (Econ, 1999).
18. Daniel Sokolov, "Google-Mutter Alphabet erzielt 2018 über 30 Milliarden US-Dollar Reingewinn." *Heise Online*, February 5, 2019.
19. Yasha Levine, "Google's Earth: How the Tech Giant is Helping the State Spy on Us." Guardian, December 20, 2018.

20. Levine, "Google's Earth."
21. Jaron Lanier, *Zehn Gründe, warum du deine Social Media Accounts sofort löschen musst* [*Ten Arguments for Deleting Your Social Media Accounts Right Now*] (Hoffmann und Campe, 2018), 14 and 38.
22. "Umsatz und Nettoergebnis von Facebook weltweit bis 2018." *Statista*, August 9, 2019.
23. Federal Election Commission, "Official 2016 Presidential General Election Results." January 30, 2017.
24. "Riesiger Datenmissbrauch blamiert Facebook." *Neue Zürcher Zeitung*, March 18, 2018; Carole Cadwalladr, "The Cambridge Analytica Files. Meet the Data War Whistleblower." *Guardian*, March 18, 2018.
25. Hannes Grassegger und Mikael Krogerus, "Da ist eine Bombe. Brexit, Trump: Wie die britische Firma Cambridge Analytica die Politpropaganda auf den Kopf gestellt hat." *Das Magazin*, December 3, 2016.
26. Hannes Grassegger und Mikael Krogerus, "Da ist eine Bombe." *Das Magazin*, December 3, 2016.
27. Andy Davies, "Revealed: Trump's election consultants filmed saying they use bribes and sex workers to entrap politicians." Channel 4 News, March 19, 2018.
28. Karim Amer, *The Great Hack*. Netflix, July 2019.
29. "Diese Firma weiß, was Sie denken." *Tages-Anzeiger*, December 3, 2016.
30. TV documentary, *Thomas Huchon: Fake America Great Again. Wie Facebook und Co. die Demokratie gefährden*. *Arte*, October 25, 2018.
31. Karim Amer, *The Great Hack*.
32. *Thomas Huchon: Fake America Great Again. Wie Facebook und Co. die Demokratie gefährden*.
33. "Mark Zuckerberg räumt Fehler ein." *Neue Zürcher Zeitung*, March 22, 2018.
34. Harald Schumann, "Carole Cadwalladr zwang Facebook in die Knie, indem sie Verflechtungen zwischen dem Trump-Wahlkampf und Brexit-Kampagne bewies." *Tagesspiegel*, March 22, 2019.
35. David Torcasso, "Facebook-Krise. Für Schweizer Politkampagnen setzen wir Bots und AI ein." *Handelszeitung*, March 23, 2018.
36. Timo Grossenbacher, "Keine Chance auf Widerspruch. Wie uns Parteien ungefragt an Facebook verraten." *SRF*, June 27, 2019.
37. Iwan Santoro, "Bauernfängerei mit Daten. Parteien betreiben Datenmissbrauch." *SRF*, June 18, 2019.
38. Helen Buyniski, "Wikipedia: Rotten to the Core." *Medium*, October 26, 2018.
39. Werner Rügemer, "Wie Wikipedia die Wahrheitsfrage ausblendet." *Neue Rheinische Zeitung*, April 2, 2014.
40. Marc Brupbacher, "27,000 PR-Berater polieren Image der USA." *Tages-Anzeiger*, February 12, 2009.
41. Wikipedia, "Bürgerkrieg in Syrien seit 2011" and "Terroranschläge am 11. September 2001" and "Verschwörungstheorien zum 11. September 2001," accessed on October 18, 2019.

42. Mathias Bröckers, "Du Verschwörungstheoretiker! Kurze Geschichte eines psycho-logischen Kampfbegriffs." *Zeitpunkt*, September 1, 2018.
43. Wikipedia entry on Daniele Ganser. Accessed on September 3, 2019 and October 23, 2019.
44. "Medial vermittelte Feindbilder und die Anschläge vom 11. September 2001—Presentation by Daniele Ganser." YouTube. Published on February 3, 2015.
45. "Propaganda in der Wikipedia." *Swiss Propaganda Research*, October 1, 2018.
46. Alexander Wallasch, "Enttarnung eines Wiederholungstäters—Wikipedia: das kontaminierte Lexikon." *Tichys Einblick*, September 12, 2018.
47. Geschichten aus Wikihausen, "Documentary: Die dunkle Seite der Wikipedia." *KenFM*, October 21, 2015.
48. Ilona Pfeffer, "Wird Wikipedia von der Transatlantifa gesteuert?" *Sputnik*, May 29, 2018; Ulrike Sumfleth, "Wikipedia regulieren? Tja, wenn Sie betroffen wären." *NachDenkSeiten*, February 4, 2018.
49. Hermann Ploppa, "Wikipedia an der Propagandafront gegen Historiker." *Telepolis*, September 19, 2018.

Chapter 15

1. Zbigniew Brzezinski, *Die einzige Weltmacht. Amerikas Strategie der Vorherrschaft* [*The Grand Chessboard: American Primacy and Its Geostrategic Imperatives*] (Fischer, 1999) 15.
2. Vincent Javert, "The CIA's Intervention in Afghanistan." *Nouvel Observateur*, January 15, 1998.
3. George Friedman in Chicago in a presentation for the Chicago Council on Global Affairs, February 4, 2015. YouTube, "STRATFOR: US-Hauptziel seit einem Jahrhundert war, Bündnis Russland+Deutschland zu verhindern."
4. "STRATFOR: US-Hauptziel seit einem Jahrhundert war."
5. Plenary protocol of the German Bundestag, March 19, 2015.
6. Tim Marshall, *Die Macht der Geographie. Wie sich Weltpolitik anhand von 10 Karten erklären lässt* [*The Power of Geography: Ten Maps that Reveal the Future of Our World*] (dtv, 2017), 93.
7. "Russian Military Bases Abroad: Facts and Details." *Sputnik*, October 8, 2016.
8. "Record of conversation between Mikhail Gorbachev and James Baker in Moscow. February 9, 1990." National Security Archive, December 12, 2017.
9. Ralph Pöhner, "Gemeinsam zogen sie Gorbatschow über den Tisch." *Basler Zeitung*, December 30, 2017; Marie Katharina Wagner, "Das große Rätsel um Genschers angebliches Versprechen." *Frankfurter Allgemeine Zeitung*, April 19, 2014.
10. Ben Norton, "'We are the death merchant of the world': Ex-Bush official Lawrence Wilkerson condemns military-industrial complex." *Salon*, March 29, 2016.

11. Brzezinski, *The Grand Chessboard*, 91.
12. Reinhard Veser, "Georgien hat den Krieg begonnen." *Frankfurter Allgemeine Zeitung*, September 30, 2009.
13. John Mearsheimer, "Warum der Westen an der Ukraine-Krise schuld ist." *Foreign Affairs*, September 1, 2014.
14. Harald Neuber of weltnetz.tv in conversation with Ray McGovern on September 11, 2014, in Berlin. YouTube: "Ex-CIA-Offizier: Das sind die wahren Schuldigen am Ukraine Krieg." September 21, 2014.
15. Stefan Korinth, "An unseren Händen klebt kein Blut." *NachDenkSeiten*, October 22, 2015; Nikolai Asarow, *Ukraine: Die Wahrheit über den Staatsstreich. Aufzeichnungen des Ministerpräsidenten* (Das Neue, Berlin 2015).
16. Christoph Sydow, "Brennan in der Ukraine. Was machte der CIA-Chef in Kiew?" *Spiegel*, April 15, 2014.
17. "Die Deutschen werden gezwungen, auf vertrauensvolle Beziehungen mit Russland zu verzichten." *Deutsche Wirtschaftsnachrichten*. February 6, 2022.
18. Zach Dorfman, "CIA-trained Ukrainian paramilitaries may take central role if Russia invades." Yahoo News, January 13, 2022.
19. "Resolution gegen Russland scheitert." *ARD Tagesschau*, March 26, 2022.
20. Seymour Hersh, "Die Akte Assad" ["The Assad File"]. *Cicero*, April 28, 2016.
21. Speech by Wesley Clark on October 3, 2007 at the Commonwealth Club in San Francisco. Cited in Glenn Greenwald, "Wes Clark and the neocon dream." *Salon News*, November 26, 2011.
22. Christof Lehmann, "Dumas, 'Top British officials confessed to Syria war plans two years before Arab Spring,'" MSNBC, June 1, 2013. See also T. J. Coles, *Britain's Secret Wars: How and Why the United Kingdom Sponsors Conflict around the World* (Clairview, 2018), 14.
23. Tim Anderson, *The Dirty War on Syria: Washington, Regime Change and Resistance* (Liepsen Verlag, 2016), 57.
24. Professor Jeffrey Sachs, Columbia University, April 19, 2018, MSNBC. YouTube: "Professor Jeffrey Sachs lays down the truth about the Syrian War."
25. "Völkerrechtliche Bewertung der russischen, amerikanischen und israelischen Beteiligung am Syrienkonflikt." German Bundestag Berlin. Scientific Service, June 28, 2018.
26. Mark Mazzetti, "Behind the sudden death of a 1 billion dollar secret CIA war in Syria." *New York Times*, August 2, 2017; Max Blumenthal, *The Management of Savagery: How America's National Security State Fueled the Rise of Al Qaeda, ISIS and Donald Trump* (Verso, 2019), 1.
27. Syrien Krieg, "Hauptverantwortung liegt bei den USA." ZDF heute, December 22, 2016.
28. Stefan Brauburger, "Supermächte—Angst vor China?" ZDF, August 16, 2019.
29. Andreas Lorenz, "Unter roten Seidensegeln." *Der Spiegel*, August 29, 2005.

30. Brauburger, "Supermächte—Angst vor China?"
31. Berthold Seewald, "So stieg England zum weltgrößten Drogendealer auf." *Die Welt*, January 20, 2018.
32. Mao Haijian, *The Qing Empire and the Opium War: The Fall of the Heavenly Dynasty* (Cambridge University Press, 2016), 491.
33. Brauburger, "Supermächte—Angst vor China?"
34. "China: Military Power. Modernizing a Force to Fight and Win." Defense Intelligence Agency, 2019.
35. Dalai Lama, *In die Herzen ein Feuer* (Barth Verlag, 1996), 44; German Bundestag Berlin. Scientific Service, August 12, 1987.
36. Fredy Gsteiger, "Bei einer Invasion in Taiwan wären die USA machtlos." SRF, May 31, 2019.
37. Patrick Zoll, "Die USA gefährden den Weltfrieden—sagt China." *Neue Zürcher Zeitung*, July 25, 2019.
38. Kai Strittmatter, *Die Neuerfindung der Diktatur. Wie China den digitalen Überwachungsstaat aufbaut und uns damit herausfordert* (Piper, 2019), 57.
39. Geng Wenbing, "Mein Vaterland und ich." *Weltwoche*, September 18, 2019.
40. Dirk Müller, *Machtbeben. Die Welt vor der größten Wirtschaftskrise aller Zeiten* (Heyne, 2018), 184 and 203.
41. Sebastien Le Belzic, "China: Milliardäre verschwinden einfach." *Arte*, September 20,2019.
42. "Xi Jinping, Präsident auf Lebenszeit." *Süddeutsche Zeitung*, March 11, 2018.
43. Urs Schoettli, "Geopolitik als Treiber der Weltwirtschaft." *Notenstein Privatbank Fokus Asien*, June 2015.
44. Müller, *Machtbeben*, 221.
45. Müller, *Machtbeben*, 217.
46. Robert Laffan, *The Serbs: The Guardians of the Gate* (Dorset Press, 1989), 163.
47. Peter Frankopan, *Die neuen Seidenstraßen. Gegenwart und Zukunft unserer Welt* [*The Silk Roads: A New History of the World*] (Rowohlt, 2019), 52, 60, and 289.

Chapter 16

1. Jürgen Todenhöfer, *Du sollst nicht töten. Mein Traum vom Frieden* (Bertelsmann, 2015), 5.
2. Dalai Lama, *In die Herzen ein Feuer* (Barth Verlag, 1996), 44.
3. Howard Zinn, *A People's History of the United States* (Harper, 2015), 682; Daniele Ganser, *Illegale Kriege. Wie die NATO-Länder die UNO sabotieren. Eine Chronik von Kuba bis Syrien* (Orell Füssli, 2016).
4. Yuval Noah Harari, *21 Lektionen für das 21. Jahrhundert* [*21 Lessons for the 21st Century*] (C. H. Beck, 2019), 410.
5. Tolle, *A New Earth*.

LITERATURE

Recommended Books for Further Study

Blum, William, *Killing Hope: US Military and CIA Interventions since World War II* (Common Courage Press, 1995)

Brzezinski, Zbigniew, *The Grand Chessboard: American Primacy and its Geostrategic Imperatives* (Perseus Books, 2016)

Chomsky, Noam, *What Uncle Sam Really Wants* (Odonian Press, 1993)

Garrison, Jim, *On the Trail of the Assassins: One Man's Quest to Solve the Murder of President Kennedy* (Skyhorse Publishing, 2012)

Griffin, David Ray, *The American Trajectory: Divine or Demonic?* (Clarity Press, 2018)

Kennedy, Paul, *The Rise and Fall of Great Powers: Economic Change and Military Conflict from 1500 to 2000* (HarperCollins, 1988)

Polner, Murray and Woods, Thomas, *We Who Dared to Say No to War: American Antiwar Writing from 1812 to Now* (Basic Books, 2008)

Scahill, Jeremy, *Dirty Wars: The World Is a Battlefield* (Bold Type Books, 2014)

Stinnett, Robert, *Day of Deceit: The Truth About FDR and Pearl Harbor* (Free Press, 2001)

Stone, Oliver and Kuznick, Peter, *The Untold History of the United States* (Gallery Books, 2019)

Talbot, David, *The Devil's Chessboard: Allen Dulles, the CIA, and the Rise of America's Secret Government* (Harper, 2016)

Zinn, Howard, *A People's History of the United States* (Harper, 2015)

INDEX